Carving Out a Humanity

Carving Out a Humanity

RACE, RIGHTS, AND REDEMPTION

Edited by Janet Dewart Bell
and Vincent M. Southerland

THE
NEW
PRESS

NEW YORK
LONDON

See page 386 for additional permissions information.

Requests for permission to reproduce selections from this book should be
made through our website: https://thenewpress.com/contact.

Published in the United States by The New Press, New York, 2020
Distributed by Two Rivers Distribution

ISBN 978-1-62097-620-3 (hc)
ISBN 978-1-62097-621-0 (ebook)

CIP data is available

The New Press publishes books that promote and enrich public discussion and
understanding of the issues vital to our democracy and to a more equitable
world. These books are made possible by the enthusiasm of our readers; the
support of a committed group of donors, large and small; the collaboration
of our many partners in the independent media and the not-for-profit sector;
booksellers, who often hand-sell New Press books; librarians;
and above all by our authors.

www.thenewpress.com

Composition by Westchester Publishing Services
This book was set in Fairfield

Printed in the United States of America

2 4 6 8 10 9 7 5 3 1

Contents

A Brief History of the
Derrick Bell Lectures

Founded in 1995, the Derrick Bell Lectures were originally created as a birthday present from Janet Bell to her husband, and were designed to highlight not only Derrick Bell's legacy as the father of the Critical Race Theory (CRT) movement, but also to give that movement exposure in the academy and beyond. Janet Bell worked tirelessly to endow the series, which has continued after Derrick's death in 2011. Over the years, the series has featured an elite group of CRT scholars and offered them a distinguished platform at New York University Law School to talk about race in America. The series was originally set up under the auspices of then-dean John Sexton. In 2016, NYU Law School dean Trevor Morrison and NYU law professor Tony Thompson arranged to have the series formally incorporated into the law school's new Center on Race, Inequality, and the Law, whose executive director, Vincent Southerland, is an editor of this volume.

Because of Professor Bell's well-known love for gospel music, musical performances always played a part of the lecture, and the singing of Stevie Wonder's "Happy Birthday" was very much a part of the tradition.

While many of the lectures were recorded and could be transcribed for this volume, in the early years that was not the case. Where possible, the editors have reconstructed lectures from the lecturer's written notes. In a few cases, law review articles or book chapters based on unrecorded lectures were included in the lectures' stead. In 2006, University of North

Carolina School of Law professor John Calmore was scheduled to give the annual lecture. When he took ill, Professor Bell delivered his lecture from notes provided by Professor Calmore; the transcription provided is of Professor Bell's words. In 2000 a panel discussion took the place of an individual lecture. Unfortunately, the panel discussion was not recorded. Lani Guinier was one of the featured panelists, and her remarks on the panel informed her subsequent book *The Miner's Canary* (co-authored with Gerald Torres), a brief excerpt of which is included here.

The Derrick Bell Lecture continues to be one of the most cherished cultural and scholarly events at NYU School of Law.

intellectual and a fearless harbinger of change. He was a man who inspired many to advocate for civil rights, hiring equity, and judicial reform,
and his stories of individual protest will be a timeless call to action for all
who stand for justice. We continue to look to Professor Bell's legacy and
the outstanding quality of his life's work.

Derrick Albert Bell Jr. was born to Derrick Albert and Ada Elizabeth
Childress Bell on November 6, 1930, in Pittsburgh, Pennsylvania. He graduated from Schenley High School and became the first member of his
family to attend college, receiving his bachelor's degree in 1952 from
Duquesne University. In 1957, after serving as an Air Force officer for two
years, Professor Bell earned his law degree at the University of Pittsburgh
School of Law, where he was the only black student.

With the recommendation of U.S. Associate Attorney General William
Rogers, Professor Bell took a position with the Civil Rights Division of the
U.S. Department of Justice, where he was the only black staff member.
When, in 1959, the department asked him to relinquish his membership in the National Association for the Advancement of Colored People
(NAACP), Professor Bell resigned. This would be the first of several high-
profile resignations proffered in protest of racial injustice. He soon joined
the NAACP Legal Defense and Educational Fund, where he oversaw
more than three hundred school desegregation cases.

In the mid-1960s, Professor Bell served as faculty and executive director
of the University of California's Western Center on Law and Poverty. In
1969, partially as a result of black students' protests for a minority faculty
member, Professor Bell was recruited to teach at Harvard University—where
after two years he became the Ivy League school's first black tenured professor of law. He established new coursework and published law review articles
dedicated to civil rights law, became an invaluable mentor to students of
color, and called on the university to improve its minority hiring record. In
1972, he published *Race, Racism, and American Law*, a book that became a
staple in law schools and is now in its sixth edition.

In 1980 Professor Bell left Harvard to become one of the first African
American deans of a non–historically black law school, at the University

Introduction

CONGRESSWOMAN BARBARA LEE

As a student during the 1970s, I was also a community worker with the Black Panther Party in Oakland, California. There were very few academics who, for me, spoke about systemic and structural racism in an honest and forthright manner. Derrick Bell was one of the few professors who, in many ways, embodied the principles guiding the work of black, progressive, "revolutionary" organizations. Derrick's visionary work and clarity about racism, the laws that continue to perpetrate this system, and how to dismantle them and create a true system of justice, helped me formulate my political consciousness and work.

I remember that, while I was working for a great warrior for peace and justice—the late Congressman Ronald V. Dellums—I had the privilege to meet Derrick Bell, mainly at conferences and lectures, and thought he should run for public office. I told Ron that, and we concluded that Derrick was too valuable as a renowned attorney and scholar, whose work should undergird the agenda of black elected officials committed to transforming this country. Derrick Bell's brilliance was as important then as it is today—as we witness the movement for black lives throughout the country. We owe Derrick Bell a debt of gratitude for his brilliant legal mind as he addressed racism at its core. I am privileged to have been a student from afar of this great human being.

A bold legal scholar, educator, author, activist, veteran, husband, father, brother, mentor, and friend, Professor Derrick Bell was a preeminent of Oregon School of Law. However, he resigned five years later when the school did not offer a teaching position to an Asian American woman. After returning to Harvard in 1986, he led a five-day sit-in inside his office to protest the school's failure to grant tenure to two professors whose work involved Critical Race Theory. In 1990 he took an unpaid leave of absence, pledging not to return until Harvard Law School asked a woman of color to join tenured faculty for the first time. (Eight years later, Professor Lani Guinier achieved that milestone.)

By the time the school refused to extend his leave, Professor Bell was already teaching at New York University School of Law, where he continued to be a visiting professor until his passing. Professor Derrick Bell's long legacy as a pioneer of Critical Race Theory and as an unwavering upholder of principles earned him a comparison by Barack Obama, a Harvard law student at the time, as a civil rights hero akin to Rosa Parks.

Professor Bell dedicated his life to challenging academic paradigms and seeking justice for the systemically marginalized. His legacy will serve as a reminder that we must not be afraid to ask critical questions and to defend individual principles on behalf of future generations. The Derrick Bell lectures, established as a wonderful birthday tradition by Professor Bell's wife Janet, perpetuate that tradition, bringing some of the deepest and most creative legal minds of our lifetimes to bear on the questions that mattered most to Derrick Bell.

1

No Justice, No Peace

CHARLES OGLETREE

1995

Charles Ogletree is the Jesse Climenko Professor at Harvard Law School and Founding and Executive Director of the Charles Hamilton Houston Institute for Race and Justice. He is a recipient of the ABA Spirit of Excellence Award, the National Black Law Students Association's Lifetime Achievement Award, and the City of Boston's inaugural Rosa Parks Civil Rights Award, and he has also been recognized as one of Ebony *magazine's 100+ Most Influential Black Americans. He obtained his BA and MA from Stanford University, and his JD from Harvard Law School. His most recent publication is a book co-edited with Professor Austin Sarat of Amherst College* entitled Life Without Parole: America's New Death Penalty? *Other publications include* The Presumption of Guilt: The Arrest of Henry Louis Gates, Jr. *and* Race, Class, and Crime in America.

It is indeed an honor and a privilege to have the opportunity to give the first Derrick Bell Lecture on Race in American Society. If I ever had to pose a question to my students about Derrick Bell, this is the question that would be on the exam: is Derrick Bell brilliant or crazy or both? And I think if they had to answer that question, they would say that there is some brilliance in Derrick Bell that's indicated in his struggle as a lawyer, for he had to tolerate racist judges who would turn their backs on him when he argued for the government against segregation. There was something brilliant about his decision to think about progressive lawyering and start an institution in Southern California. There was something brilliant about his decision to resign from the government because they didn't like the fact that he joined the NAACP; they thought that was a conflict of interest, as you can imagine.

And yet, there is something that's also kind of crazy about Derrick Bell. The craziness is that he has such insight and foresight that it's unimaginable. When Derrick Bell left Harvard out of protest recently, it was not for the first time. This was not Derrick's first time leaving Harvard, and I'm not sure it's his last time. The first time he left because Harvard had not tenured other people of color and wanted him to carry the entire burden. Once he left, they did find some people they could tenure, and Derrick went on to Oregon, a small but progressive law school, where he was the dean. When that school chose not to tenure an Asian American woman, the crazy Derrick Bell resigned and left. He went to Stanford, California, to Stanford Law School, to teach constitutional law. But instead of talking about the Commerce Clause and separation of powers, and the rule against perpetuities, and things like that, he talked about slavery. Can you imagine someone associating slavery with constitutional law? His law students complained because they didn't think slavery had anything to do with constitutional law, and they wanted to study the Commerce Clause. And the brilliant and somewhat crazy Derrick Bell then agreed to be part of the student protest against his own class.

The brilliant-but-crazy Derrick Bell for some reason came back to Harvard, and when he came back, he set a tone as well. At Harvard Law School, the foreword to the *Harvard Law Review* is the most important part of the *Law Review* on an annual basis. It's been around for generations, and has offered up some very provocative and creative thought. In 1985, the *Harvard Law Review* had its second woman president, Carol Steiker. She asked Derrick to write about the Constitution. And in 1985, the brilliant Derrick

Bell had this crazy idea of writing about an African American woman who goes back to 1787, to the founding fathers, to try to explain to them what happened as a result of two hundred years of constitutional law. She first had to explain to them how in the hell a black woman could even be talking to them. And only the brilliant-but-crazy Derrick Bell was able to pull that off with the 1985 *Law Review*. And then the brilliant-but-crazy Derrick Bell came forward and offered us his first important book, *And We Are Not Saved*, which told us about the problems of racism in America and introduced us in a much more passionate way to Geneva Crenshaw. The brilliant-but-crazy Derrick Bell brought us *Faces at the Bottom of the Well* and set off a firestorm of talk about the permanence of racism in our society.

Today, in my imagination, the brilliant-but-crazy Derrick Bell, if you can imagine—you've read his allegories and his narratives—wakes up on his sixty-fifth birthday this morning at about five a.m., and, as he wakes up, he hears that voice again: it's Geneva Crenshaw. She says, "Derrick you fool, you finally got what you wanted."

Still trying to clear his head and wake up, Derrick says, "What are you talking about, Geneva? What do you mean?"

"Derrick, remember at one of those speeches at Harvard in 1990, you said that if Harvard Law School ever tenured a woman of color, you would agree to be a white man." She says, "Derrick, your wish has come true. Harvard has just tenured six African American women. They're teaching law and economics, the principles of market analysis, estate planning and insurance law."

Derrick says, "That's great, Geneva. But what does that have to do with me?"

"It means you have to keep your promise, and you will become a white man."

And, of course, Derrick says, "It will be a cold day in hell before that happens, Geneva."

She says, "Okay, fool. You wouldn't listen to me then, and now you're going to regret it."

Still a little bit hazy, Derrick stumbles to the bathroom and there he turns around and looks in the mirror. He is a white man. He has blond hair, crystal blue eyes, and a bad case of acne. He can't believe what is happening, and he shouts out, "Janet, Janet, come here!" And of course Janet comes to the bathroom, 5′ 9″, 110 pounds, with her bright red hair, green eyes, and crystal clear white face.

"Yes, Derrick, what's your problem?"

"Janet, what happened to you?"

"Nothing, Derrick, why do you say that?"

"Janet, you are white!"

"Derrick, I've been white as long as I've known you. Is there a problem?"

Derrick assumes he is losing his mind. He can't believe this, so he rushes and heads to NYU Law School. He goes into his office, and there on his wall, where he has all of that famous and expensive African art, are a number of prominent pictures. Right in the center of his desk is one of General Robert E. Lee. There's another picture of Derrick firmly shaking hands with former President Richard Nixon. And then the one that takes everyone's eye, a picture of Derrick Bell, a bright, energetic law clerk, sharing a smile and a laugh with Chief Justice Warren Burger. And the final picture, blown up out of proportion, is Derrick in his tennis shorts talking and enjoying a friendly game of tennis with Chief Justice William Rehnquist.

Overcome by this, Derrick runs to the Federal Courthouse and into the chambers of his dear friend and colleague and mentor, Robert Carter. As Derrick bursts into Judge Carter's chambers, before he can even speak, Judge Carter swings around, and he too is a white man. Derrick rushes from the judge's chambers and heads back to NYU, where a student rally is waiting for him. He says, this is where I'll have my moment. He runs to the student rally and he sees signs that say "White Students' Union," "End affirmative action," "No more immigrants," and "States' rights now." As Derrick is turning away, they say, "no, no, no, come on up, Derrick!" And there to introduce him as a speaker is none other than the Speaker of the House, Newt Gingrich. "I'm very proud to introduce my friend, my colleague and compatriot, Derrick Bell."

Derrick again, in complete shock, leaves and runs back to his home. In another conversation with Geneva he says, "What can I do? What can I do to change the situation?"

She says, "You better pray."

So Derrick gets on his knees and says, "Dear Lord, please forgive me, for I have sinned. I know I've spent a lifetime criticizing white folks, but I really didn't want to be like them. I wanted to enjoy being black, Lord, and I want my life back. If you give me just one more chance as a black man, I promise I'll never criticize white people again."

And the Lord says, "Derrick are you sure you want to keep this promise?"

Derrick looks up and says, "Well, never mind."

For Derrick's sake, that's simply a hypothetical. But it brings me to the topic of "No Justice, No Peace," which stems from a little-remembered quote from Frederick Douglass more than a century ago. Douglass said that the justice system is bound to treat people differently because of their race, and that a black man hauled into court will never have the rights of a white man. The topic moves forward with the eloquent words of W.E.B. Du Bois who told us clearly that the problem of the twentieth century was the problem of the color line. And then a stranger to this land came here in 1944: Gunnar Myrdal. And he looked at our system and told us that something was amazing in America. He recognized the subordinate position of negroes and saw it as the most glaring conflict in the American conscience and the greatest unsolved task for American democracy.

Unfortunately, what Mr. Myrdal observed more than fifty years ago has a striking resemblance to America for African Americans today. It has a striking resemblance because Myrdal talked about the egregious situation of African Americans in the Southern states in the 1930s and 1940s and forward, and alluded to the less egregious situation of African Americans in Northern states, where he found the situation stemming more from blacks being poor and uneducated than from the color of their skin. While he tried to make that connection, what we all learned was that one's race was largely determinative of whether justice could be found, particularly in the criminal justice system. What he noticed back in 1944 was that policemen stand not only for civic order by formal laws and regulations, but also for white supremacy and a whole set of social customs.

In both the North and the South, blacks were treated more harshly by police than whites. Blacks were more likely to be arrested under suspicious circumstances. Once in custody, the third degree was common, with brutal beatings to try to force confessions. Myrdal talked about police having a philosophy that made sure that blacks were kept subordinate: blacks should be punished, and punishment was the only device to keep blacks in their place. He cited cities where the rates of blacks being murdered by police were shockingly high. He also noted that more than half of all African Americans killed by whites at that time were killed by the police. He talked about the unequal distribution of justice throughout the system: Prosecutors preferred to target the disenfranchised African American population. They could run for office and continue to get re-elected as long as they continued to lock up blacks. He noticed the fact that many blacks did not have any kind of a representative or advocate on their side. They simply depended on the justice system to save them. He also noticed the fact that many of them had inexperienced lawyers to represent them in perfunctory ways in the system. Moreover, it was clear that there was greater reliance on any white man's testimony in the case of an African American. He wrote that when the defendant was black, there was an astonishing atmosphere of informality and lack of dignity in the courtroom, and speed more than justice was the ultimate goal. He also talked about the disparities in punishments between blacks and whites.

Since Gunnar Myrdal's findings in 1944, we've had major changes in the law, from the revolution of *Gideon v. Wainwright* to *Miranda v. Arizona*, and other progressive cases. But the black man's burden is still the criminal justice system. We find in 1995, as we talk about the justice system and extreme punishment, that it is no longer South Africa, which has abolished the death penalty, or the Soviet Union, which has been destabilized, that are the leading perpetrators of the ultimate injustice. It is the United State that is now the leading advocate and proponent of capital punishment and that continues to warehouse hundreds and hundreds of African American men and women facing the ultimate penalty, many without competent counsel or resources to defend themselves.

We find in 1995 that one in three African American males between the ages of twenty and twenty-nine is in prison or jail, awaiting trial, on probation or parole, and the number will only get worse by the end of this century. We find that so many African American males who are in prison, seem to see it as a step up in society, because they have rent-free lodging, twenty-four-hour medical service, free heat, and room and board. It is an irony that prison has become the preferred abode of so many African American males. We find in 1995 that there are over 800,000 African American men in prison, and that this country spends over six billion dollars annually to house and incarcerate them. We find as well that they represent over 50 percent of those incarcerated in our jails, while they represent less than 12 percent of the nation's population. And even as we talk about disparity and differences and discrimination, our most revered leaders play into this racial narrative.

It started long ago, when President Reagan very effectively talked about welfare mothers, and never once mentioned that the vast majority of people on welfare are white. We found President Bush, when he ran for office, bringing out the Willie Horton argument that blacks are going to rape and injure and kill white women, effectively destabilizing the candidacy of Mike Dukakis. We found Jesse Helms telling North Carolinians that if they voted for Harvey Gantt, they were voting for affirmative action and preferences for blacks. We found in Boston a white man, Charles Stuart, telling the police that the person who took his wife and stillborn child's lives was a black man—when in fact it was Stuart himself; black men were beaten and brutalized in Boston as a result. We found a white woman, Susan Smith, using as her defense in the tragic death of her children in South Carolina, the powerful claim that a black man had driven away with her two sons, and the nation stood in shock wondering whether or not it was true, when in fact Smith herself had drowned her own children. As much as we think we've made progress from the time of Gunnar Myrdal's days, we are still in a mire when it comes to the criminal justice system.

And now it's time for somebody to stand up and say something about what's going on in this system. In the O.J. Simpson case, we have a jury comprised of some of the most conscientious and remarkable citizens, listening to the evidence, weighing the evidence, and coming back and saying, whether you like it or not, the government did not prove Simpson's guilt, and reasonable doubt matters. The same people who condemned this jury were the people who talked about four white police officers being acquitted in the Rodney King beating and said, "Well, the system works." The same people laughed and grinned when an all-white jury would not deliver a conviction for Medgar Evers's killer; they still said the system worked. The same people thought it was okay for Emmett Till's murder to go unanswered. And now they are outraged and talking about justice in the O.J. Simpson case. We still find today a dual system of justice, one black and one white.

The dichotomy extends beyond the criminal justice system. We also find it in our country's selected leader for black America and our rejected leader for black America. The "great military man," the "brilliant strategist," the "man who went into the Gulf and turned it around in an incredibly short period of time," is now deemed to be black America's choice for president. In Colin Powell, the country has found an acceptable black man. Isn't that amazing? Colin Powell. The country found Colin Powell because what was effective about him is that he's "articulate." Hmm, what does that mean? The country found Colin Powell, but what they haven't found is that in every major poll taken, black people don't know who he is. Many wouldn't recognize him if they saw him, and they certainly don't see him as the savior of the day. And yet, he is the selected black leader of America in 1995.

And then there's the rejected leader. Louis Farrakhan has said so many "awful" and "ugly" and "unforgiveable" things, dominating the press while people ignore the African American public's scream for leadership, for direction, for hope. We find Farrakhan being condemned and people saying you can't separate the messenger from the message. And yet, a lot of people on the mall for the Million Man March came away saying, "I'm going to go back home, and I'm going to stop being an abuser." I was there, and Derrick was there, and you didn't see anybody who wasn't sober, you didn't see anybody selling or using drugs. The phrase of the day was "Brother, where are you from?" A term of endearment, not a threat. I stepped on more brothers' feet that day than I've ever done before, and all anyone said was, "It's alright, Brother. Everything's alright." The black men there were joined together in an incredible bond, with a sense of pride and respect and dignity, but also responsibility. It wasn't enough to march, that was only the beginning. It was time to go back home and do something. And that's what we must do.

The men at the March noted the great ironies in the criminal justice system, and realized that the responsibility to change them does not belong to anyone else but us. Just one example of the irony of our system is the drug courier profile. According to law enforcement, you can tell a drug courier when they're traveling through the airport, not because they're African American, but because when they buy their tickets they always use cash . . . or a check . . . or a credit card. And when they buy their ticket, they're always traveling alone . . . or with another person . . . or with several people so they won't be detected. And as they travel on the plane, it's not that they're black, but that they're always carrying no luggage . . . or a small amount of luggage . . . or a lot of luggage, so you won't notice them. But most important, you can always tell the drug courier profile because they're always the first off the plane . . . or the last . . . or somewhere in the middle, so they won't be detected. You can always tell the drug courier profile not by the color of their skin, but because they're always flying from a city where drugs are sold . . . or to a city where drugs are sold . . . or over a city where drugs are sold. The drug courier profile is just one small example of the great irony of our criminal justice system.

So, when Derrick Bell told us the horror harvest has come, the summer has ended, and we're not saved, that has currency today. When he told us

to "look at the face at the bottom of the well, and you will see the permanence of racism," he was not talking about 1787, 1863 with Frederick
Douglass, the 1900s with W.E.B. Du Bois, 1944 with Gunnar Myrdal, or
even 1995. He was talking about what appears to be the permanence of
racism in its ugliest form, presented to us every single day in the criminal
justice system.

Justice William Brennan had the unfortunate task of writing a dissent
in *McCleskey v. Kemp*, a death penalty case in 1987. He told Warren
McCleskey that one day McCleskey was going to ask his lawyer, "Why am
I dying? Why am I as a black man, of all the people charged with homi-
cides, going to get the death penalty?" And Justice Brennan said, a truth-
ful answer from the lawyer would have to be, "It's not because of the
charge or your past record, or where the offense was committed. It's
because of race." He would have to say that, if your victim is white, that's
almost a guarantee that you will be given the death penalty. And if, as a
defendant, you are black, that only increases the possibilities. But the
court, in responding to Justice Brennan, said, "racial disparities in our
criminal justice system are *inevitable*."

This takes us back to my friend and mentor's words that "racism in our
system is inevitable." But it's not forever, I hope. And I hope that when we
see black men going through the revolving door of our justice system, someone will stand up and say it's wrong. I hope when we see these drive-by
shootings of blacks shooting blacks for target practice, that someone will
stand up and say it's wrong. I hope when we see police like those who beat
Rodney King and police like the racist Mark Fuhrman in the O.J. Simpson
case, who injured all of us, somebody will stand up and say it's wrong. I
hope when we see people like Malice Green being beaten to death in Detroit that somebody will stand up and say it's wrong. I hope when we see
black police officers in New York City working the subway undercover,
and white police officers shooting them not once, not twice, not five, not
sixteen times, but nineteen times, that somebody will stand up and say it's
wrong.

What makes me have a sense of hope and inspiration is that one person has already stood up to say it's wrong and has given me the sense that we can overcome these injustices, and that is my dear friend, colleague, and mentor, Derrick Bell. Justice may be blind, but we cannot be blind to injustice. And if we are going to make a change in this society, we have to listen to Derrick and not think he's crazy, but recognize his brilliance and recognize that if we are going to survive in the twenty-first century, we had better start now in erasing the problems of racial prejudice in our society.

2

Each Other's Harvest

CHARLES LAWRENCE

Spring 1998

Charles Lawrence is a professor at the William S. Richardson School of Law and University Centennial Professor, Emeritus, at the University of Hawai'i, Manoa. He began his teaching career at the University of San Francisco in 1974, and has been a tenured professor at Stanford and George-town. Professor Lawrence obtained his BA from Haverford College and his JD from Yale Law School, and he is best known for his prolific work in an-tidiscrimination law, equal protection, and Critical Race Theory. He received the University of San Francisco School of Law's Most Distinguished Professor Award, Stanford Law School's John Bingham Hurlburt Award for Excellence in Teaching, and the Society of American Law Teacher's national teaching award. His most recent book, We Won't Go Back: Making the Case for Affirmative Action, *was co-authored by Professor Mari Matsuda.*

The title of my talk tonight, "Each Other's Harvest," comes from a poem by an individual with much greater talent and skill than mine at poetry, Gwendolyn Brooks. But I can't do a lecture in Derrick Bell's name with-out reading a poem that I wrote for him, quite a long time ago, when Derrick Bell first received the Society of American Law Teachers teaching award. The poem is titled "Derrick Bell Superstar." And the subtitle of the poem is "And He Looked Good Doing It, Too."

DERRICK BELL SUPERSTAR
They called it affirmative action.
"If you want to play in the big leagues," they said,
"you've got to prove you're qualified."
And he knew the "you're" meant us as well as him.

You've got to dance in the classroom, though we seldom do.
"To be a podium Fred Astaire," they said,
"you've got to prove you're qualified."
And he showed them the James Brown and the Michael Jackson too.

"You've got to write a deathless prose, and lots of it too
To be Stravinsky of the printed page," they said.
"You've got to prove you're qualified."
And he introduced them, to Duke Ellington and Stevie Wonder.

"You've got to make a contribution to the law school
To be our conscience and our spokesman too.
You've got to prove you're qualified."
And he took the loaves and fishes of his 24-hour day and fed the multitudes.

"You've got to walk on water," they said.
And when he did, and looked good doing it too
They said, "By God, we think you're qualified."
And Derrick cried because he knew the "you're" meant him not us.

But we rejoiced as our man took it to the hoop.
We said, "Right on, blood." And slapped high-fives.
And each of us took careful notes.
We knew we'd have to walk on water too.

A recent Doonesbury cartoon depicts Joanie Caucus returning to the Berkeley Law School for alumni weekend.

"Here's your reunion packet," an earnest young man from the Development Office, says to Joanie. "Welcome back to Berkeley."

"Thanks very much," says Joanie.

"Is this your first visit since graduation?" the young man asks Joanie.

"Yes. I guess it is," she says.

"Well, I think you'll find Boalt Hall is the same fine place you remember in every respect, practically."

"Practically?" Joanie asks.

"Well, we no longer admit black people, but other than that."

Trudeau's genius is the truth his characters speak. The earnest young man's face exudes liberal angst. But rather than the expected excuses and euphemisms, he simply says, "We no longer admit black people."

In fact, the law school at Berkeley admitted fourteen African American students last year, seventy-five fewer than had been admitted the year before. All of them wisely, I think, decided to attend law school elsewhere. Leaving as the lone black person in this year's entering class a young man who had deferred his admission from the previous year. At UCLA, only twenty-one black students had been admitted, an 80 percent drop from the year before, and the lowest number of African Americans offered admission since 1970. The decline among Latino students at each law school was similar. At the University of Texas at Austin law school, there are three black students in the first-year class, and only fifteen African American students overall—this at a school that had almost 150 African American students in its most recent graduating class.

The stark reality is that, unless something is done to reverse this trend, these will soon be segregated institutions, in fact if not in law. If you do not believe that the re-segregation of these state flagship law schools is significant and even tragic, consider that the University of Texas has 650 African American alumni. That's since the very recent case of *Sweatt v. Painter*. The University of Texas has 1,350 Mexican American alumni. Berkeley and UCLA have, together, graduated more than 600 black lawyers and more than 800 Mexican American lawyers in just the past ten years. Take a look around NYU and think about the colleagues who would not be here but for a door pushed open by affirmative action.

There were four black students in my class at Yale Law School. When I first met Derrick Bell, in 1969, the minority professors at the Association of American Law Schools Conference could all sit down at one not-very-large table. I began my law teaching career at the University of San Francisco in 1974. I was one of four new professors hired by USF that year. Three of us—Stephanie Wildman, David Garcia, and I—did not look like what our students expected to see when they walked into their classes. USF had never had a Chicano law professor before. And, while a black woman had taught there two years previously, her stay was short-lived. Stephanie and I were, respectively, the only woman and the only African American on the faculty. We were the law school's first diversity hires. We were pioneers integrating a segregated institution. And we were proud to be the beneficiaries of affirmative action.

The student body was as white as the faculty. There was one black student in my first constitutional law class. Later, I learned that after my first class, a small delegation of white students had gone to the dean to complain that they had been assigned to my con law section. They felt short-changed that they were being taught by the affirmative action hire. I remember feeling a mixture of pain and anger at hearing this. I was certain that they had not bothered to find out who I was, to discover that, even by traditional criteria, I was easily as well qualified as my colleagues. However, I was not surprised. The ideological attack on affirmative action had already begun in earnest, and the legal attack would soon follow.

Even at this early stage in the integration of these institutions, when the number of people of color teaching and studying at law schools was minuscule, white students were familiar with the rhetoric of reverse discrimination and preferential treatment, and fearful that our presence would somehow mean less room for them. In later years, when I welcomed first-year minority students who'd been admitted under USF's fledgling affirmative action program, I would tell them the story of my first days as a law teacher. I wanted them to know that their black professor, who by then had won the Law School's teaching award and begun to build a reputation as an up-and-coming young scholar, understood what they were about to experience.

They would be asked what they had scored on the LSAT, as if that score defined their whole being. Their classmates would tell them about a white college roommate with better scores whose place they had taken. They would be accused of lowering the standards of the entire school and told that they were responsible for the declining bar pass rate. The message would not always be explicit. It might take the form of lowered expectations or surprise at demonstrated excellence. But they would hear the message: you do not belong here. And their first lesson was to know that this message was false. I wanted them to understand that these were words spoken in defense of privilege disguised as merit. They were as bright as any of their classmates. If separate and unequal educational systems had deprived them of skills given to their white classmates, these were skills that could be learned and mastered.

They could match their peers at every task that was put before them. But I wanted them to remember that they were not there simply to play the game as it had always been played, to add a soupçon of colorful pigment and exotic culture to the world of the privileged. They were there to help change the law school, and when they graduated, the institutions where they would work: the firms, the boards, the prosecutors' and public defenders' offices, the judiciary, the boards of supervisors, and state legislatures. They had been admitted because, in addition to their intellect and academic skills, they brought with them special gifts of experience, understanding, insight, anger, compassion, and even love that are the legacy of the struggle against oppression.

When they graduated, they would take these gifts back home again to their families and communities, enhanced by new skills and an increased understanding of the politics of power that is law. Just as important, these were gifts to be shared with white classmates, teachers, and colleagues, and with friends and allies from other communities of color. These were the gifts most necessary to the achievement of our collective liberation from the disease of racism. Several years ago, I was invited to speak at the induction ceremony of a former student, Maria-Elena James, who had just been appointed United States Magistrate in the U.S. District Court of the Northern District of California.

Maria had been one of my students at USF. She was admitted under our affirmative action program and graduated with distinction. She had, during ten years as a public defender and family court judge, become a highly regarded and much-valued member of the San Francisco bar. The auditorium at the Federal Court building in Oakland was filled to overflowing with Maria's large and loving family, and with people from every walk of life whose lives had been touched by this gifted and generous woman. It was a multicultural gathering that embodied what is best about this country. When the dignitaries in the audience were introduced, I could not help but swell with pride. Among them were two superior court judges, Martin Jenkins and Peggy Hora, and the U.S. attorney, Mike Yamaguchi; all had been my students, as had many others in the room.

On the stage with the other federal judges sat Saundra Brown Armstrong. Saundra had received one of the two highest grades in my evening constitutional law class. I smiled as I remembered the day Saundra came to talk with me in my office. As she rummaged through her handbag to find a pen, she pulled out a rather large gun and placed it on my desk. "Oh, you didn't know I was a police officer?" she said when she saw the shocked look on my face. Saundra had earned straight As in the evening division while working days as an Oakland police officer. She had come to see me that day to seek my counsel. She had interviewed at several prestigious downtown San Francisco law firms, and, despite her outstanding record, none had made her an offer.

These individuals, and many others like them, who have changed the face of California and the nation's bar, were part of a generation of minority and women students who came to law school in the early years of affirmative action. They ignored the many messages that told them they did not belong and became valued members of these law school communities.

They founded the Black American Law Students Association (BALSA), La Raza, the Asian-Pacific American Law Students Association (APALSA) and the Women's Law Association. They made life-long friends of all races.

When Allan Bakke filed his reverse discrimination suit and the first full-scale assault was launched against affirmative action, these students were in the front lines of resistance against that assault. They marched and held rallies and teach-ins. They signed petitions and helped draft amicus briefs. An understanding of what would be lost if the doors of these institutions were once again shut to folks of their communities, and a deep commitment to racial justice, were their gifts to their teachers and classmates. The struggle itself was a critical part of the education that makes them what they are today.

On October 12, 1977, the United States Supreme Court heard oral arguments in the *Bakke* case. Across the street from the Court and in cities from New York to Berkeley, multiracial crowds of young people raised placards and shouted, "We won't go back," putting the Court and the world on notice: Whatever the outcome of the proceedings inside the velvet-curtained courtroom, the struggle would continue in the streets. The protestors would not accept the return to the days when they and their communities were excluded from institutions of power and privilege.

When the Court announced its decision it was sharply divided. Four justices voted to strike down the medical school affirmative action program and order Bakke's admission. They avoided the constitutional issue of whether a race-conscious affirmative action program violated the Equal Protection Clause and concluded that Bakke had been treated unlawfully, in violation of Title VI of the 1964 Civil Rights Act. Another four justices voted to uphold the University of California, Davis, admissions program. They found it violated neither the Civil Rights Act nor the Equal Protection Clause.

Justice Lewis F. Powell cast the deciding vote in an opinion that straddled the two camps in the Court and struck a compromise between the forces for and against affirmative action. He agreed with four of his colleagues that Bakke had been wronged. But he agreed with the other four that it was legitimate to use race as a factor in selecting applicants. Powell's opinion said that all racial classifications are suspect and can be justified only if necessary to achieve a compelling state interest. Remedying past societal discrimination was not such a compelling interest, he said. Societal discrimination was "too amorphous," but a court, a legislature, or a government agency could consider race in order to remedy specifically identified past discriminatory acts that were in violation of the law.

Furthermore, a university could consider race in admissions if it was essential to the creation of a diverse student body. A university faculty, he argued, had a compelling interest in exercising its First Amendment right to academic freedom, and the freedom to select a student body of its choosing was part of that right. If a university faculty believed that a racially diverse student body was important to its students' education, and it could achieve such a student body only if it considered the race of its applicants, then it was constitutional to consider the race of an applicant as one of many factors in the admissions process. By way of example, Powell referred to the admissions program at Harvard, where he said race or other ethnic background was deemed a plus on a particular applicant's file without insulating that individual from comparison with other candidates.

Almost twenty years after the Supreme Court announced its decision in *Bakke*, we are in the midst of another assault on affirmative action. In California, a bare majority of voters amended the California constitution to outlaw race- and gender-based affirmative action in all public agencies. And anti–affirmative action activists are launching similar measures in eighteen different states. In Texas, a Fifth Circuit Court of Appeals panel invalidated the admissions program at the state's flagship university law school and once again the op-ed pages and the talk shows are filled with the familiar tropes of racial preference, anti-merit, quota, stigma. And reverse discrimination.

What is the future of affirmative action in higher education and in our schools? Many people believe the answer to that question lies in the *Bakke* decision's meaning and in its fate. Did the *Bakke* court set out a justification for affirmative action in higher education that can be distinguished from the Court's decisions invalidating contracting set-asides in *Croson* and in *Adarand*? If so, is that justification still viable given the current composition of the Supreme Court? Opponents of affirmative action contend that *Bakke* is dead. They argue that *Croson* and *Adarand* make clear that the only compelling interest that justifies race-conscious affirmative action is the remedy of the continuing effects of specifically identified past discrimination and that such programs must be narrowly tailored to that remedial purpose.

Thus in *Hopwood,* the Fifth Circuit opined that the purpose of achieving a diverse student body is not a compelling interest. The court noted that Supreme Court decisions subsequent to *Bakke* state that nonremedial state interests will never justify racial classifications, and insisted that classifications of persons on the basis of race for the purpose of diversity frustrate rather than facilitate the goals of equal protection.

By contrast, affirmative action supporters have looked to Powell's *Bakke* decision for the salvation of affirmative action in higher education. They have argued that *Croson* and *Adarand* have not overruled *Bakke,* and that Powell's diversity reasoning is uniquely applicable to the educational setting where pedagogic purposes of affirmative action and the flexible processes of admission and faculty hiring distinguish it from the contracting set-aside cases.

As an advocate of affirmative action, I have argued not just for the maintenance of affirmative action but for its expansion. I stand in solidarity with my colleagues in the academy and in the public interest bar who pursue what they no doubt see as the most pragmatic strategy for saving affirmative action in higher education: to separate the fight for the integration of the university from the apparently doctrinally undermined fight for the integration of the workplace, and to distinguish the diversity rationale from the remedial rationale. But I believe that this distinction is misconceived. The diversity rationale is inseparable from and interdependent with the purpose of remedying our society's racism.

More importantly, I believe that this seemingly pragmatic approach is a misguided strategy. In the end, the fight for affirmative action in our universities and our workplaces is a political struggle. To rely upon the formalism of legal doctrine to save university affirmative action will only further entrench existing regimes of race, gender, and class privilege.

Diversity cannot be an end itself. It is substanceless. It has no inherent meaning and cannot be a compelling interest unless we ask the prior question: diversity to what purpose? The answer to this question is that we seek racial diversity in our student bodies and faculties because a central mission of the university must be the eradication of America's racism. We cannot pursue that mission without the collaboration of a significant number of those who have experienced, and continue to experience, racial subordination. This freedom-fighting purpose may be only one of several reasons for seeking racial diversity in the academy, but it should be the primary one. Once articulated, it makes apparent the necessary connection between affirmative action's backward-looking purpose, remedying the effects of our nation's history of slavery and racial apartheid, and its forward-looking purpose of preparing students for the work of fighting the disease of racism and creating a better world.

Two aspects of Justice Powell's opinion contribute to a shallow and ultimately retrogressive understanding of diversity. The first is Powell's division of the state's justificatory interest into backward-looking and forward-looking affirmative action. The second is his argument that the university's interest in racial diversity is grounded in its faculty's First Amendment rights to free speech.

Powell saw the university's interest in race-conscious admission as consisting of two distinct kinds: (1) remedial interests where affirmative action is intended to provide redress for or correct the effects of past harms, and (2) institutional interest, where affirmative action's purpose is the achievement of the university's pedagogical goals of transmitting certain information, ideas, and mores. Powell believed remedial affirmative action was appropriate only when fault is established, and a blame-worthy perpetrator identified. Affirmative action in pursuit of the university's academic interest in diversity is more easily justified and survives strict scrutiny so long as quotas are not employed. By decoupling these two interests, and treating them differently, Powell failed to recognize that they are two sides of the same coin. For Powell, the remedial or backward-looking affirmative action was permissible only when it was designed to correct identified instances of past discrimination. Societal discrimination was too amorphous, he said. Today's white applicants should not be held responsible for the sins of the distant past. We are a nation of minorities, Powell argued, most of whom have been discriminated against at some point in our history. Justice O'Connor embraced this position in her majority opinions in *Croson* and *Adarand*, and it is the view of the majority of the Court today.

Law professor Alan Freeman called this view of anti-discrimination law "the perpetrator perspective." It is a model of equal protection that was firmly established by the discriminatory intent requirement in *Washington v. Davis*. No matter how extensive the tangible evidence of the continuing effects of past racism, there is no legally cognizable harm unless a blame-worthy perpetrator is identified and shown to have caused the injury. And for constitutional purposes, this perpetrator must also be a state actor.

By this judicial sleight of hand, the injuries of past and contemporary discrimination are transformed into no injury at all. I call this perspective "the big lie." The Court tells us in these cases that our nation has overcome its racism. To believe this, we must accept a formal and extremely narrow definition of racism under which only self-professed bigots are racist and none of us is held responsible for perpetuating the white supremacy of even the very recent past. The big lie is seductive because most Americans want to believe it.

Powell's restriction on backward-looking affirmative action incorporates the big lie into affirmative action doctrine. The recent Fifth Circuit decision in *Hopwood* is an example of Powell's restriction on remedial affirmative action taken to its logical extreme. In *Hopwood*, a federal district court held that a revised version of the law school admissions program at the University of Texas that considered race a plus was constitutional because it was necessary to remedy continuing effects of a history of official discrimination in primary, secondary, and higher education in Texas. This discrimination was well documented in history books, in case law, and in the record of the trial, said the district court. And it was not a relic of the past. In 1994, desegregation lawsuits remained pending in over forty different Texas school districts.

Although the public-school population was approximately half white and half minority, the vast majority of both white and minority students attended schools that were segregated in fact if not by law. The high school graduation rate for whites was 81.5 percent compared to 66.1 percent for blacks and 44.6 percent for Hispanics. At the university level, a United States Department of Education Office of Civil Rights investigation conducted between 1978 and 1980 found that Texas had failed to eliminate vestiges of its former de jure racially dual system, which segregated blacks and whites, and that there were strong indications of discrimination against Latinos. In 1994, the OCR had still not determined that Texas had eliminated its segregated system of public higher education.

The opening sentences of the Fifth Circuit opinion reversing the District Court were typical of the upside-down rhetoric of reverse discrimination. "In order to increase the enrollment of certain favored classes of minority students, the University of Texas law school discriminates in favor of those applicants by giving them substantial racial preferences in its admissions programs," said the court. "The beneficiaries of this system are blacks and Mexican Americans, to the detriment of whites and other non-preferred minorities."

In fact, the University of Texas had instituted affirmative action precisely because these minority groups were disfavored by traditional university admissions practices, and by historical and contemporary racial discrimination in the Texas educational system. Texas is a state with an active Ku Klux Klan and regularly reported hate crimes against people of color—a state that admitted blacks to its law school only when it was forced to do so by the United States Supreme Court in 1950. As recently as 1960, the University of Texas segregated Mexican American students in campus housing—that's 1960!—and assigned them to a dormitory known as the barracks. And until the mid-1960s, a Texas Board of Regents policy prohibited

blacks from living in or visiting white dorms. All of this was erased by the
Fifth Circuit Court's willful disregard of the district court's detailed findings of fact. Adopting Powell's reasoning, they noted that the state did not
have a compelling interest in remedying the present effects of societal
discrimination and went on to hold that the district court had erred in ex-
panding the remedial justification to reach all public education within the
state, because that too was a vague and amorphous injury.

The second troublesome feature of Powell's *Bakke* opinion is his argument that the attainment of a diverse student body is compelling because
it furthers the academy's First Amendment right of academic freedom.
Because the faculty's free speech rights give it the right to determine what
will be taught, they must also be free to choose those students who will
best contribute to the achievement of those pedagogic goals. This argument is troublesome because it constitutionalizes the power of a privileged
educational establishment to determine what learning shall be valued and
who shall be taught.

A racially diverse student body is a compelling interest for only as long
as those who run the school think it so. Powell's reasoning could as easily
justify an all-white school as one that is racially diverse. Of course, in the
context of *Bakke*, the faculty's goal of achieving a racially diverse student
body was in pursuit of the pedagogical goal of teaching students about the
world and about each other, and the implication is that what is often eu-
phemistically called "race relations" is what must be learned.

But while Powell's opinion rejects the purpose of remedying societal discrimination as too amorphous, surely what we teach and learn about "race
relations" is in pursuit of that amorphous goal. How does one explain this
contradiction? Powell could not admit that racism in America was still concrete and real, without abandoning the court's commitment to legal formalism and the big lie. Nonetheless, he had heard Archibald Cox's prophetic
warning, at oral argument, that if the Court forbade any consideration of race,
our universities would again be virtually all white. He believed Cox, and he
believed the young people who had shouted loud and clear that they knew
they belonged inside the university's gates, and they would not go back.

So Justice Powell, in his Solomon-like wisdom, gave half the baby to the unreality of legal formalism, and half to the political pragmatism of legal realism. But dividing the baby in two is never a just solution. And when the argument for racial diversity is grounded in the speech rights of faculties, affirmative action is divorced from its true purpose, anti-racism, and we risk losing sight of that important goal.

When racial diversity's purpose is identified as anti-racism, or more inclusively, anti-subordination, its defense is clear and straightforward. Solving what Du Bois called the problem of the twentieth century is still among our most pressing and perilous concerns as we enter the twenty-first. Certainly, a university is justified, and I would argue morally and constitutionally obligated, in making the disestablishment of white supremacist structures and ideologies central to its pedagogy and research. Once we acknowledge the continuing existence of racism, and commit ourselves to its disestablishment, it is evident that the applicant who has been identified and treated by society as a subordinated racial minority will bring to that enterprise a life experience that makes her peculiarly qualified for the task.

This is not to say that she will have the same qualifications as every other person who shares her racial identity. Certainly, it does not mean that she will have the same point of view, as the *Hopwood* court suggested. What she does share with all of her brothers and sisters of color is a lifetime of experience as a colored person in a racist society. No white person has this qualification.

In addition to the qualification of experience, the minority applicant will have the qualifications of motivation and commitment to the fight against racism. While all of us are harmed by the damage that racism does to the social fabric and our souls, the injury that racism does to racial minorities is concrete, immediate, personal, and unceasing. When Asian American students in my class read the most recent figures on the alarming increase in hate crimes against Asians, they saw more than statistics. They were suddenly conscious of their own vulnerability and of their fears for their family's safety.

African American students know firsthand the look that crosses the face of the interviewer from the downtown law firm—a look that tells them there will be no callback, no matter how bright and charming and non-threatening they might seem. The white colleague who compliments the Latina Stanford Law School graduate on her facility with English may be unaware that his words are a reflection of America's racism, but she will feel the presence of the color line that separates them. Black, Asian, Latino, and Native American students have no choice but to do the work of fighting racism, because not to fight is to deny oneself.

One of my white colleagues, as a part of his criminal justice class, shows a video of an actual police interrogation and confession. At the end of the tape, he asked the class for a show of hands indicating whether or not they thought the confession was coerced. He was shocked, although you may not be, to find that the vote was divided strictly along racial lines. Not one white student thought the confession was coerced. Not one student of color thought it voluntary. My colleague says, "You could cut the tension in that room with a knife." But for a skillful teacher, and my colleague is one, this was a learning moment. It was a moment that would never take place in segregated classrooms.

In noting that minorities are uniquely qualified to pursue the goal of fighting racism, I am not arguing that white students, faculty, lawyers, or judges may not also bring talents, skills, and values that are essential to the project of our common liberation. The fight against racism must in the end be an interracial collaboration.

Mari Matsuda, my wife, colleague, and sometime co-author, and I are in the midst of co-authoring two small children, and we do not often get out to the movies. But last year we were fortunate to catch the film *Rosewood*, John Singleton's powerful depiction of the story of a small black town in Florida attacked by a white mob. Beginning on New Year's Day in 1923, and for six days thereafter, a vigilante mob set fire to the houses of the town's thirty black families and shot or hung every black person they could find. The orgy of racial violence and lynching was sparked by a young white woman's disputed story that she had been assaulted and beaten by a black intruder while her husband was away at work.

It is a stunning and tragic story, but more than the horror and violence itself, I was struck by how intimately connected were the assailants and the assaulted. Connected by their humanity, by their destiny to live in a world ruled by the hateful ideology of white supremacy.

I thought about how the legacy of a history ravaged by thousands of lynchings and burnings ties all of us to each other. How we are connected by the everyday violence of poverty, injustice, and the very color line that divides us. If we are ever to heal ourselves, if we are ever to find reconciliation, we must confront this history and know how it lives with us today. It is no solution to deny it by calling it amorphous. It will not do to apologize only for the past misdeeds of others, as if racism is a relic of the past. It is imperative that we resist the attack on affirmative action and the re-segregation of our law schools and our profession.

The only way to fashion a just world out of an unjust past is to learn the truth from one another about our shared history, and its legacy. And we cannot have that conversation unless all of us are here.

3

The Archetypes That Haunt Us

PATRICIA J. WILLIAMS

Fall 1998

Patricia J. Williams is the James L. Dohr Professor of Law, Emerita, at Columbia Law School. She earned her JD from Harvard Law School and her BA from Wellesley College. She has served on the faculties of the University of Wisconsin School of Law, City University of New York Law School, and Golden Gate University School of Law. Williams practiced as deputy city attorney for the Office of the Los Angeles City Attorney and as staff lawyer for the Western Center on Law and Poverty. She is published widely in the areas of race, gender, and law, and on other issues of legal theory and legal writing. She writes the "Diary of a Mad Law Professor" column for The Nation, *and her books include* The Alchemy of Race and Rights, The Rooster's Egg, *and* Seeing a Color-Blind Future: The Paradox of Race. *Williams was a MacArthur fellow, and served on the board of trustees at Wellesley College.*

When I was growing up in the 1950s and 1960s, the only black women in the national eye were Marian Anderson and Butterfly McQueen, and they, in their very polarity, symbolized the rock and the hard place of African American womanhood: the martyr and the mammy; the hyperarticulated

classicist and the folksy frump; the chin held high and the ample encompassing bosom. These were the most visible models, and there were also random sightings of jezebels and sapphires, exotic women in skirts of bananas, insurrectionary half-white witches whose gift of half a white brain was always undone by the curse of a really bad black attitude.

Now, suppressed but haunting us too were the archetypes of pansy and prissy. They were the silly trollops in *Gone with the Wind*, the ones with the squeaky voices who knew nothin' about birthing babies, who made terrible servants but very fine comics. And white people of that era would wink and laugh, in the parlance of that time, about certain little black girls having grown like Topsy when they mysteriously turned up pregnant, and the babies would always be light-skinned and fatherless. "The night has no eyes," my grandmother would sigh.

Today we live in a great memory-gobbling global marketplace, and our sense of racial history has expanded and contracted in marvelously complicated ways. "Growing like Topsy," I read in the *New York Times* recently in an article authored by William Safire, means nothing to people beyond Harriet Beecher Stowe's original reference, in *Uncle Tom's Cabin*, to a young slave untutored in religion. The array of black women in the national imagination now ranges from Toni Morrison to Vanessa Williams, from Rosa Parks to Lani Guinier, from Erykah Badu to Carol Moseley Braun. And while almost all of the aforementioned women have been the objects of attack, of struggle, of controversy, I guess none of us really expected this to come easily.

I say all this as a prelude to what's happening in the news today. My phone has been ringing off the hook; because there has been nothing but slack-jawed amazement greeting the news that Thomas Jefferson really did father one of Sally Hemings's children. What kind of mass hypnosis allows so many to claim they hadn't a clue? I got a call just saying the *New York Times* is doing a series of front-page stories about this. By most estimates, at least four-fifths of African Americans have some slave master mixed up in them. And that has nothing at all to do with the recently growing, but still minuscule, rates of intermarriage. You have to remember

that 80 to 90 percent of blacks lived in the rural South until the great migrations of the 1960s. Anti-miscegenation statutes were not struck down until 1967.

This has nothing at all to do with the now-hailed revolution in intermarriage. I think it's fine to celebrate, but not unduly, in the sense that the rate of interracial marriage has risen from about 1.2 percent to 1.9 percent. You would think that somehow we've had this enormous change. And again, compare that to Great Britain, where the intermarriage rates are 40 percent.

So the pervasiveness of this history is as plain as the faces all around us. Yet most journalists are scurrying back and forth between revisionist explanations that evoke Romeo and Juliet on the one hand and lustful sagas in which Jefferson is depicted as some sort of originative, patristic Mandingo.

What I find most disturbing is that so many commentators seem not to understand the actual and historical meaning of slavery as a system of human ownership. Television anchors repeatedly refer to the relationship as illicit or illegitimate. But those words mean unlawful, not permitted. A master's breeding his slaves was not only permissible but widespread. After all, the system of what was called chattel slavery meant precisely that: you got to treat your slaves like livestock. Yes, some slaves were treated better than others, and some dearly loved by their masters, some put out to pasture to make their way freely on their own. But then, so were a lot of horses, cows, and sheep.

Notes on the State of Virginia, Jefferson's clinical delineations of how to improve the "stock of one's slaves," are a subset of his views on animal husbandry. Far from being an aberration, his views evince a gentlemanly familiarity with the dominant theories of race science at that time: "Are not the fine mixtures of red and white the expressions of every passion by greater or less suffusions of color in the one, preferable to that eternal monotony, which reigns in the countenances, that immovable veil of black, which covers all the emotions of the other race? Add to these, flowing hair, a more elegant symmetry of form, their own judgment in favor of the whites

declared by their preference of them, as uniformly as is the Orangutan for the black women over those of his own species."

But if this added mixture of so-called white blood into black was deemed an improvement to erstwhile dusky-hued unfortunates, the mixing of black blood into white was a calamity to be avoided at all costs. Jefferson warned emphatically of the sullied sensibilities and lowered faculties thus engendered, concluding that "among the Romans emancipation required but one effort. The slave, when made free, might mix without staining the blood of his master. But with us, a second is necessary, unknown to history. When freed, he is to be removed beyond the reach of mixture."

Now, some historians have found Jefferson's stance on this contradictory. But Jefferson's bias against race mixing was not really aimed at preventing male slave owners from bedding their slaves in the pursuit of more progeny as property, and let us not forget that a lighter-skinned slave in this unfortunate economy was often higher priced. Rather, Jefferson, in line with the general anti-miscegenist sentiments of the day, was more concerned with ensuring a system of regulating marriage and of primogeniture, based on presumed purity of white bloodlines.

Such a system of privilege required an obsessive monitoring of the socially constructed boundaries of blood and race at the same time that it actively disabled white women and people of color, including Native Americans, from assuming agency in the creation of families of their own. Indeed, one of the most powerful ways that the logic box of slavery operated was by suspending the vocabulary of a familial, or a filial, relation and supplanting it with a discourse of commerce. Substituting words like *master* and *owner* for other words, like *father* and *brother*, made invisible both the ties of family and the taboos, including incest. We struggle to this day with the gaps engendered by those institutionalized denials.

Consider, for example, William Safire's recent observation in the *New York Times* that Jefferson's "wife's father was also the father of the slave Sally." Or the *Washington Post*'s description of Hemings as Jefferson's wife's illegitimate half sister. Now, such tortured designations hide the fact that in today's world we would simply call such a person a sister-in-law, and a fourteen-year-old sister-in-law at that when it began. But there was little in law that recognized Hemings's humanity, to say nothing of a sisterly bond.

Moreover, since slaves did not have the legal capacity to contract, they could not be formally married. Thus, the concepts of adultery, of illegitimacy or bastardy, so called, were legally inapplicable to slaves. And in a system where paternity functioned chiefly to regulate the passage of property rights and citizenship, the notion of slaves as progenitors of their own families was judicially beside the point.

Given all of this, is it nonetheless possible that Jefferson and Hemings were a star-crossed set of hearts, as were the Capulets and Montagues? A very confident Orlando Patterson, also in the *New York Times*, asserts, "It is not possible that he could have had a relationship with an African American that likely lasted more than three decades and deny the very human reality in the presence of her being, her progeny, and the people with whom she was identified."

Similarly, Brent Staples writing in the same newspaper, because people were in such a state of shock that there were three editorials on one day, makes note of slave owners' penchant for, quote, "slave lovers." But let us remember that *lover* was almost never the term used to describe such relationships at the time. A more common word, and one used in an article specifically about Hemings, in 1802 in the *Richmond Recorder*, was *concubine*, which means, literally, to lie together with hips joined.

But aside from his denials of any relationship, rumors of which he denounced as scurrilous, embarrassing, and shameless, Jefferson himself provided perhaps the best clues as to the nature of his affection for Hemings. Again in *Notes on the State of Virginia*, he opines that "love seems with them to be more an eager desire than a tender delicate mixture of sentiment and sensation. Their love is ardent, but it kindles the senses only, not the imagination."

Now, who knows? I certainly do not. It may well be that Jefferson loved Hemings. It may well be that Hemings loved Jefferson. But since slavery was a system premised on the practiced constraint of slave choice, and on absolute control, I wonder at the rush to embrace love as the overarching feature of their bond. With the exception of Nazi Germany, our system of slavery authorized perhaps the most complex and sustained-over-time legal assault on psychic and corporal integrity in modern history. I talked to a friend of mine who's a political scientist and historian, a German who's been studying the Holocaust and was trying to think of other examples that measured up to it. She came up with slavery. She's researching Mayan slavery, because that involved a great deal of ritualized human sacrifice, but there are very few examples really in human history—certainly in modern history—that equal slavery's sustained limitations on integrity.

Let us remember that Thomas Jefferson owned Sally Hemings. He owned Hemings's children, whether they were biologically related to him or not. He had the power always to sell any one of them at any time to a stranger. If he fell into poverty, they would be auctioned off as his property along with the horses, cows, sheep, and bed stands. And this was a power over them that he affirmed as a right, weaving it into the very structure of the nation he helped found.

It is very high time we acknowledge the great genetic stew of a family circle that our history hides, and that our DNA relentlessly reveals. But let us not project modern notions of romance upon those unions born of trauma, of dependence, of constraint. Let us not use easy claims of love as a further deflection from confronting the infinitely more painful emotional hierarchies with which our peculiar institution has left us flailing still.

What would or could Sally Hemings have done but love Thomas Jefferson? I've written before about an 1835 case in Louisiana. Kate, a slave, had run away repeatedly, and she was eventually brought by her master into court in order to have her returned to the man who had sold her to him. The claim that the purchaser made of the vendor was based upon the assertion of a so-called retributory vice, an old type of civil claim. The claim was for the return of the price paid. And the vice alleged was that Kate was, in the words of the court, crazy. I did not make this up. They said she was crazy, to use the precise language of the court. The vendor's defense was that, and again I am quoting, "she was not crazy but only stupid."

Now, the amount of money at issue, legally speaking, would have been based on the market valuations of the buyer and the seller on their agreement, on their expectations, on their speculation. Kate's value would have been fixed by their mutually negotiated imagination of her worth as measured against the fair average of a reasonably stupid, but not crazy, fertile female slave. This they encapsulated in the price, which, as a contracts professor, I know is aptly enough called the consideration. Kate's worth was measured, in other words, by the consideration, the literal consideration of owners in the past, present, and future. Her alienation and acquisition depended upon their shared regard, the marriage of expectations, whose vector fixed her worth, their will be done, amen.

Kate was deemed useless by this judicial decree, and her purchaser was allowed to return her. And what I find interesting is the tension imposed by the structure of alternatives. On the one hand, the finding of craziness amounted to a holding that she was uncontrollable, unpredictable, worthless. As a subcategory of property, few expectations could ever have been formed about her. She would perpetually subvert their best desire, and such a finding presupposed that she was never what she seemed, so it would be hard, even impossible, to speculate about her.

Like a mad dog or a wild horse, she wouldn't make good property in the system that envisioned property as the extension of the will, and we call consideration "will theory," an extension of the will of the owner. Stupidity, on the other hand, didn't interfere with her as good property, because stupidity in slaves was foreseeable, part of the assumed risk of purchasing slaves, a built-in expectation of reasonable slave traders.

Another way to look at Kate is that she was neither stupid nor crazy, but very, very smart. The facts showed that she had burned up her master's bed, and then run away. It doesn't take too much, I think, to read between those lines. Thus, she seems quite rational to me. Now, Kate's so-called crazy behavior may seem rational to many of us from today's historical perspective, standing as we are, somewhat beyond the particular social arrangements of that time. Yet perhaps it requires assuming the perspective of the owner of human property to understand how lack of control of the owner could be deemed the stupidity of the slave, an intrinsic defect of the property, an inherent biological difference, or how the exercise of slave will, the willfulness of property, could be defined as crazy or vice.

For all of what I deem to be her abundantly apparent sanity and good sense, there is a certain symmetry of thought—dare I say logic—that at that time and in that place, in the paradigm of his contract for her sale, Kate could not have been seen as smart and sane. It would have risked throwing the whole property/slave system and contract system into disorder. It would have risked leaving her vendor and her purchaser out of control.

I retell the story of Kate because I think many aspects of this dynamic live on subtly but very powerfully today. When we romanticize the relationship between Sally Hemings and Thomas Jefferson, we attribute to her a sanity as well as a devotion, as opposed to Kate, the crazy woman who runs away. The degree to which certain passionate social proclamations of rational order might disguise more sinister investment and pure, self-serving rationalization is a phenomenon that we as a society must track very vigilantly indeed.

Is there, I wonder, a way in which the traces of a social logic rooted in white supremacy survive in the shiftiness of labels like crazy, stupid, willful? What I'm suggesting is that, in the context of racial politics, rationality reserves for itself not merely the right of choice, but the protective cloak of infinite will, of an expressive willfulness for which there is no perceived necessity for sanction and no apparent limit.

Hypothetically, then, a white, rational actor would mean not merely one who acts rationally, but one who, like Kate's owner, acts and thereby is rationalized. And perhaps there is a perceptual category handed down over time for those in Kate's inherited position, irrational actors being not merely those whose actions are irrational, but those who by acting are inherently irrational.

Is it status, rather than choice, to paraphrase Henry Main's way of putting it, that determines who may own their actions and who is to be acted upon? Indeed, perhaps contemporary human property is identifiable not as slave but as a social being in whom both irrationality and willfulness are said to coexist, in whom willfulness, per se, is thought to be a subcategory of the irrational.

So what does it mean in today's world, for example, when whole communities are effectively dismissed as crazy, with the employ of such terms as "culture of pathology"? What does it signal when Bernhard Goetz, the subway shooter who apparently is thinking of running for mayor of New York, is widely perceived to be a generally upstanding model of the new age of civic virtue for gunning down four black youths—Goetz, who was acquitted of all but a gun possession charge based on the defense of "reasonable racial fear."

And perhaps it is the mere characterization of somebody like Rodney King as somebody who acted at all that produced the extremeness of the beating he endured for drunk driving. Perhaps it was the signature success of what I've called "spirit murder," soul control, the impersonal overkill of breaking in a proper property relationship. In any event, I don't have to resolve Kate's ambiguous status here, nor my own. I'm convinced that most of the things that make you stupid are also the things that drive you crazy. And that sometimes the craziest people survive only because they are very, very smart. But I am interested in how the conjunctives, or disjunctives, the *and*s or the *or*s—the places between words like *crazy, stupid, smart, sane*—vary with time and the vestments of power, as with Kate the crazy slave, and Sally Hemings, the "attractive help," as William Safire praised her.

These categories addressed, moreover, what the full power and violence of legal sanction of life and death, of the magical power of secrets, suppressed. I heard about a lawsuit recently. It is a lawsuit about magic. You might have heard about it. It's brought by the International Brotherhood of Magicians against the Fox Network. Fox has been broadcasting the secrets behind the best tricks of famous magicians, and Fox claims that magic tricks are in the realm of what is called the public domain. The magicians claim that Fox has occasioned the loss of illusion in a profession where amazement and wonder is the product being sold, where magic is art, but also an investment of much time and money. And the magicians claim that Fox's revelation of how magic is done reduces their acts to secrets, rather than art. I think that slavery is still our society's most tenaciously guarded secret. The keepers of that secret of intimate and uncontrolled rape and boundary-smashing have been all of us, but most especially blacks, and most especially black women. The secrets of our Topsy-driven wombs, the secrets kept to allow the illusions to sustain themselves, the front maintained in a world that does not love, or desire, or romanticize you. You do not trust. You do not put out. And so, you maintain an edited self, a well-groomed self, a commercial, compressed, and well-oiled self prepared for presentation, the strain of providing only certain parts of oneself in a world that invents you, projects you, mixes you up, makes cyborgs with your parts. You rationalize it as artful, rather than keeping secrets. It is a matter of choice rather than difference, comportment rather than disguise.

Oprah Winfrey posed on the cover of *Vogue* recently, and I was interested because just a couple of weeks ago NBC's movie critic Gene Shalit reviewed the new movie version of *Beloved*. And in that review, he failed to mention that *Beloved* was a ghost story about history's power to hurt. Instead, he described it as a long and "unceasingly mournful story of a resolute ex-slave who is visited by a strange girl named Beloved." And, oh boy, is she strange. And I was really intrigued by the sinistrality of his omission. For without mentioning that Beloved is the ghost of Sethe's baby daughter, whom she killed to prevent her being taken by slave catchers, all the rich allusiveness, the layers of metaphors of the story are lost. Without a sense of history the deeply traumatic vibrations that haunt and disorder the entire community are reduced at random to the unfathomable craziness of an old black man screaming on a street corner.

As Shalit's review masked the psychic and social tensions at the heart of *Beloved*, so I think that most commentary has left secret the relationship between Toni Morrison's *Beloved*, as a work of fiction, and the actual historical event upon which Morrison based her novel. If Shalit thinks that *Beloved* is unceasingly mournful, he should be aware that it is the emotional equivalent of something uplifting next to the real story. The real Margaret Garner—the real Sethe—was a slave who escaped the cruelty of her master by fleeing from Kentucky to the free state of Ohio. She took with her four children, at least some of whom were apparently sired by her master, a Mr. Archibald Gaines, and their recapture became the most famous prosecution under the Fugitive Slave Act of the time, even though it is not terribly well known today.

The slave-breeding aspect of the case was so common a practice as to be relatively ignored at the time, although perhaps less ritualistically denied than in today's world. Knowing about it lends a certain dimension to Mr. Gaines's tracking her down and successfully invoking the Fugitive Slave Act to insist upon the return of what the courts called his property. Knowing this, however, lends dimension to Margaret Garner's frenzied acts of infanticide. Knowing it makes all the more chilling Mr. Gaines's insistence upon the return, unlike in the movie, in which she cries and walks away. In real life, Mr. Gaines insisted upon the return of the bodies, both living and dead, so as to be able to recommit the living to slavery, and so as to bury the dead in soil, as he described it, consecrated to slavery.

So while some commentators complain that the film Beloved is too grim, or that it exaggerates the travails of slavery, we need to keep in mind that it ends on an infinitely more hopeful note than did the reality. After all, the ghost of the dead child, Beloved, is exorcized after only one generation, and the movie ends with Sethe's daughter Denver walking off into the sunset dreaming of going to Oberlin College.

Now, I don't mean to imply that this ending, though fictional, is altogether unrealistic. That ending was one of the founding premises of Oberlin College. And my mother's grandmother, also the progeny of her master, was among those lucky few to emerge from slavery unscathed enough to take advantage of what few educational opportunities existed at that time. My ghosts are small indeed, given our history, my relative equilibrium, the product of several generations of terribly hard work and tremendous good luck. But this statistically small cluster of those blacks, or whites—I want to underscore "or whites," because this is our mutual history—who emerged from the plantation experience with their heads on straight should not be used to blind us to the ugly pervasiveness of a system that sanctioned and underwrote Archibald Gaines's legal, social, and, yes, family violence. However, the slave system disguised the true nature of the tortured family relation between owners and their chattel, between fathers and their utterly disowned children; it implicates us all.

I don't want to end on a pessimistic note, for the magic of reinvention can go both ways. I was at the deCordova museum in Lincoln, Massachusetts, this summer, and on display were various works by an artist named Vico Fabbris from his series called "The Botanical Unknown." These were lively illuminations imitating medieval depictions of plants that he had imagined, which he called invented extinct plants, plants that he said might have been. And this became an evocative compendium of pharmacological fantasy, of long-lost alchemical ingredients of horticultural hotdish surprise. Their form is innocent as nature. Their biology is improbable as a peacock. Their beauty is so inexplicable. Their function is mysterious. It made me think of the way in which art always invents what is already extinct, gives life by thinking of it, and therefore it is. Thenceforth, it exists. Art as resurrection as much as invention.

Imagining is a form of memory. Memory is an act so wildly beyond the pale of the banal that ultimately it must become us all.

4

Derrick Bell's Toolkit—Fit to Dismantle That Famous House?

RICHARD DELGADO

1999

Richard Delgado is the John J. Sparkman Chair of Law at the University of Alabama School of Law. He received his AB from the University of Washington and his JD from the University of California, Berkeley. He has also taught at the University of Pittsburgh, Colorado, and UCLA; his teaching and writing focus on race, the legal profession, and social change. Delgado's books, including Race and Races *and* The Rodrigo Chronicles: Conversations About America and Race, *have won eight national book prizes, including six Gustavus Myers awards for outstanding books on human rights in North America, the American Library Association's Outstanding Academic Book Award, and a Pulitzer Prize nomination.*

In the world of literature and music, *Bluebeard's Castle* is both a French fairy tale and an opera by Béla Bartók. Both tell the story of a nobleman who marries a series of women and spirits them away to his castle, where they remain hidden for the rest of their lives. In Bartók's version, the principal character, Judith, Bluebeard's fourth wife, is attracted to the "strange and awe-inspiring" noble whose heart she hopes to touch with the humanizing power of her love. Despite her family's warnings and the evidence of her senses, she allows herself to become entranced with Bluebeard and takes increasing risks as their relationship develops. When Judith visits Bluebeard's castle, she finds a forbidding, windowless fortress, so damp and sunless that, in a signature aria, she sings that the very stones must be weeping.

Walking along a central hallway, Judith spies a series of seven locked doors. Hoping to find a ray of light to relieve the castle's gloom, Judith asks Bluebeard to throw them open. He refuses, asking her to accept him on faith. But she persists, certain that the rooms will contain what her hopes tell her must be there—some sign that life with Bluebeard will contain more than the all-pervading dreariness that envelops his castle. When she finally persuades Bluebeard to open the doors and peers inside, she discovers a series of vistas, each more horrifying than the last—instruments of torture and hoards of wealth, all stained by blood. Undaunted, Judith insists on admission to the final room. Over Bluebeard's objections she enters, fearing the worst—that she will find the murdered corpses of Bluebeard's three previous wives. Instead, the door opens to reveal that Bluebeard has not murdered them. They are quite alive, pale and bedecked in jewels, crowns, and splendid dresses. As they advance, Bluebeard seizes the wide-eyed Judith, who pleads for mercy. But to no avail: Bluebeard drapes her with shining raiment, crown, and jewels, and she slowly, inevitably, takes her place with the others behind the closed doors.

For Derrick Bell, Judith's fate is an allegory for blacks' hopes and fears and a metaphor for American racial progress. The six locked rooms of the castle correspond to major developments in civil rights history, such as *Brown v. Board of Education* and 1960s-era civil rights laws. Judith's hope as she opens each door mirrors the black community's celebrations following each milestone; her disappointment, that of African Americans as each advance inevitably is cut back by narrow judicial interpretation, foot dragging, and delay. Bell takes issue with his illustrious predecessor, Martin Luther King Jr., who wrote that "the line of progress [may] never

[be] straight," but that a traveler who perseveres will nevertheless "see the city again, closer by." Instead, just as Bluebeard shuts Judith away when she opens the final door, so America will always shrink from the light so that, "[d]isappointed, resigned to our fate, we will watch as the betrayal of our dreams is retired to some somber chamber while the stage grows dark and the curtain falls."

Why did Bell choose a French fairy tale to illustrate a point about African American history and experience? Perhaps to illustrate a universal truth about empowered groups' cynical use of hope to keep the peasantry in line. Perhaps, too, Bell was drawn to the story of Bluebeard because he saw himself in Judith, whose transformation from besotted idealist to disillusioned bride mirrors, in some respects, Bell's own path. As the opera opens, Judith entertains a vision of an ideal life with Bluebeard and, despite warnings, takes risks to achieve it. When finally allowed access to the castle, she recognizes it for what it is—just as Bell, despite his early hopes, now recognizes the reality of a persistently racist country. The castle may also represent, on one level or another, Harvard Law School, whose hallways resisted, to the end, Bell's efforts to bring humanism and light. Despite her growing horrific realization, Judith clings to the faith that her marriage will succeed, just as civil rights activists once clung to the hope of a better world.

As Bell recounts it, the force of Bluebeard's story lies in its use of repetition, the seven doors standing in for milestones in black history, but also serving to highlight the maddening similarity of each step, with its repeat cycle of curiosity, hope, revelation, and disappointment. Similarly, the eerie image of the imprisoned brides, coma-like in their consciousness, is driven home through repetition. Three, now four, seemingly identical, pale, imprisoned women forcefully remind us of the fate of a people who fail to grasp their situation or who listen to dreamers who tell them that salvation lies just around the corner.

In Bell's allegory, Judith could have avoided her predicament by staying home and tending her garden, just as Bell, the sometime cultural nationalist, has encouraged his fellow African Americans to foreswear integration and settle instead for building strong black communities. As I will argue later, she need not abjure love entirely but should instead seek it with a different, more steadfast suitor.

We might begin by taking a closer look at the architecture of that castle, its arrangement of rooms, and the relationships they set up among Bluebeard's four wives. Like an Eastern potentate with a harem, Bluebeard may be playing them off against each other, maintaining everything nicely under his control. Recall how at the very time *Brown v. Board of Education* announced a ringing breakthrough for black schoolchildren, U.S. Attorney General Herbert Brownell was ordering Operation Wetback, a massive roundup of Mexicans, many of them U.S. citizens, for deportation to Mexico, and how just a few years earlier, a presidential decree had ordered all Japanese Americans living on the West Coast to wartime detention centers, many losing farms and businesses in the process.

By the same token, during Reconstruction southern planters refused to hire the newly freed blacks, instead bringing in Mexicans and Asians to carry out the work the slaves previously performed. In similar fashion, Texas school authorities in the wake of *Brown* certified certain schools desegregated after cynically arranging pupil assignment so that the schools were 50 percent black, 50 percent Mexican American.

Ignoring how society racializes one group at the expense of another, then, is risky business. To understand when one is being manipulated or used to suppress someone else, each minority group must attend to the broader scale. Castle doors may be opening and shutting in a more complex sequence than we will realize if we focus only on the fortunes of one occupant.

When Bell carries out this larger exploration, the desperate urgency that he illustrated through the Bluebeard metaphor will gain even more force. He will be able to show that what minorities saw as social and legal advances actually moved us closer to the forfeiture of our dreams, and how the dominant society arranged it so. Like Judith, then, we will learn to be skeptical because "neither love nor life can be sustained on unearned trust."

This is even more so because the tyrannical Bluebeard, like some of today's conservatives, rationalizes that he did his bedecked, bejeweled, but still imprisoned wives a favor.

Judith's entrancement with Bluebeard may stand as a metaphor for the dichotomous quality that afflicts much racial thought today. As scholars such as Juan Perea have pointed out, traditional civil rights thinking deems a single group paradigmatic, with the experiences and concerns of other groups receiving attention only insofar as they may be analogized to those of this group. Binary thinking often accompanies what is called "exceptionalism," the belief that one's group is, in fact, so unusual as to justify special treatment, as well as nationalism, the belief that the primary business of a minority group should be to look after its own interests.

Consider, now, the many ways that binary thinking—like Judith's initial refusal to consider the fates of Bluebeard's three previous wives—can end up harming even the group whose fortunes one is inclined to place at the center. The history of minority groups in America reveals that while one group is gaining ground, another is often losing it. From 1846 to 1848, the United States waged a bloodthirsty and imperialist war against Mexico in which it seized roughly one-third of Mexico's territory (and later colluded with crafty lawyers and land-hungry Anglos to cheat the Mexicans who chose to remain in the United States of their lands guaranteed under the Treaty of Guadalupe Hidalgo). Yet only a few years later, the North fought an equally bloody war against the South, ostensibly to free the slaves. During Reconstruction (1865 to 1877), slavery was disbanded, the Equal Protection Clause was ratified, and black suffrage was written into law. Yet this generosity did not extend to Native Americans: in 1871, Congress passed the Indian Appropriations Act, providing that no Indian nation would be recognized as independent and capable of entering into a treaty with the United States. A few years later, the Dawes Act broke up land held jointly by tribes, resulting in the loss of nearly two-thirds of Indian lands. In 1879, Article XIX of the California constitution made it a crime for any corporation to employ Chinese workers. And in 1882 Congress passed the Chinese Exclusion Laws that were soon upheld in *Chae Chan*

Ping v. United States. Goodwill toward one group, then, does not necessarily translate into the same for others.

In 1913, the California Alien Land Law made it illegal for aliens ineligible for naturalization to lease land for more than three years, a measure that proved devastating for the Japanese population, many of whom derived their livelihood from agriculture. A few years later, Congress *eased* immigration quotas for Mexicans because they were needed by large farm owners. Go figure.

During the first half of this century, Indian boarding schools sought to erase Indian history and culture, while California segregated black and Chinese schoolchildren to preserve the purity of young Anglo girls. Yet, in 1944, *Lopez v. Seccombe* found segregation of Mexicans from public parks to violate the Equal Protection Clause, and a short time later a federal court declared California's practice of requiring Mexican American children to attend separate schools unconstitutional. And, in a horrific twist, in the 1940s, the United States softened its stance toward domestic minorities, who were needed in the war industries and as cannon fodder on the front, but turned its back on Jews fleeing the Holocaust.

Shortly after the war, at a time when vistas were beginning to open up for returning black servicemen, Congress reversed its policy of giving U.S. citizenship to Filipino World War II veterans. Even today, the patchwork of progress for one group coming with retrenchment for another continues. For example, at a time when Indian litigators are winning striking breakthroughs for tribes, California has been passing a series of anti-Latino measures, including English-Only, Proposition 187, and restrictions on bilingual education.

Not only does binary thinking conceal the checkerboard of racial progress and retrenchment, it can hide the way dominant society often casts minority groups against one another, to the detriment of both. For example, in colonial America, white servants had been treated poorly. In 1705, however, when the slave population was growing, Virginia gave white servants more rights than they had enjoyed before, to keep them from joining forces with slaves. In the same era, plantation owners treated house slaves (frequently lighter skinned than their outdoor counterparts) slightly better than those in the fields, recruited some of them to spy on their brothers and sisters in the field, and rewarded them for turning in dissidents.

In the years immediately following the Civil War, southern plantation owners urged replacing their former slaves, whom they were loath to hire for wages, with Chinese labor. They succeeded: in 1868, Congress approved the Burlingame Treaty with China, under which larger numbers of Chinese were permitted to travel to the United States. Immediately following the Civil War, the Army recruited newly freed slaves to serve as Buffalo Soldiers putting down Indian rebellions in the West.

In *People v. Hall*, the California Supreme Court used legal restrictions on blacks and Native Americans to justify banning Chinese from testifying against whites in criminal trials. The court wrote: "It can hardly be supposed that any Legislature would attempt . . . excluding domestic negroes and Indians, who not unfrequently have correct notions of their obligations to society, and turning loose upon the community the more degraded tribes of the same species, who have nothing in common with us, in language, country or laws."

Similarly, Justice Harlan's dissent in *Plessy v. Ferguson* staunchly rebuked segregation for blacks, but supported his point by disparaging the Chinese, who had the right to ride with whites. And, in 1912, when the House of Representatives debated the question of American citizenship for Puerto Ricans, politicians used the supposed failure of other minority groups to justify withholding rights from the newly colonized.

During California's Proposition 187 campaign, proponents curried black votes by portraying Mexican immigrants as competitors for black jobs. Earlier, even the sainted George Sánchez exhorted his fellow Mexican Americans to oppose further immigration from Mexico, on the ground that it would hurt Mexican Americans already here.

Sometimes the pitting of one minority group against another, inherent in binary approaches to race, takes the form of exaggerated identification with whites at the expense of other groups. For example, early in Mississippi's history, Asians sought to be declared white so that they could attend schools for whites. Early litigators followed a similar "other white" policy on behalf of Mexican Americans, arguing that segregation of Mexican Americans was illegal because only the variety directed against blacks or Asians was expressly countenanced by law.

Chinese on the West Coast responded indignantly to *People v. Hall*, the Chinese testimony case, on the grounds that it treated them the same as supposedly inferior Negroes and Indians. Later, Asian immigrants sought to acquire U.S. citizenship but learned that a naturalization statute that had stood on the books for 150 years, beginning in 1790, denied citizenship to anyone other than whites. In a series of cases, some of which reached the United States Supreme Court, Asians from China, Japan, and India sought to prove that they were white.

Anglocentric norms of beauty divide the Latino and black communities, enabling those who most closely conform to white standards to gain jobs and social acceptance, and sometimes to look down on their darker-skinned brothers and sisters. Box-checking also enables those of white or near-white appearance to benefit from affirmative action without suffering the worst forms of social stigma and exclusion.

Binary thinking can also impair moral insight and reasoning for whites. Justice John Harlan, author of the famous dissent in *Plessy v. Ferguson*, wrote a shockingly disparaging opinion on the Chinese just a few years earlier in the Chinese Exclusion case, *Chae Chan Ping*. Recently, Asian American scholars have pointed out how the great Justice turns out to have suffered a blind spot that besmirches his reputation. Similarly, others have pointed out how Earl Warren, who enjoys towering fame as a liberal Justice who supported civil rights for blacks and, as governor of California, put an end to school segregation for Asian and Mexican American schoolchildren, was a prime mover in the effort to remove Japanese Americans to concentration camps in the beginning months of World War II. Until recently, most historians and biographers embraced the official version in which Warren played at most a minor role. It seems quite likely that binary, monocular thinking made possible the selective empathy that enabled these two famous figures to misstep as they did.

Binary thinking can easily allow one to believe that America made only one historical mistake—for example, slavery. If so, the prime order of business is to redress that mistake by making its victims whole; the concerns of other groups would come into play only insofar as they resemble, in kind and seriousness, that one great mistake. But simplifications of that form are always debatable, never necessary, and rarely wise. As a leading Native American scholar put it: "To the Indian people it has seemed quite unfair that churches and government agencies concentrated their efforts primarily on the blacks. By defining the problem as one of race and making race refer solely to black, Indians were systematically excluded from consideration." The truth is that all the groups are exceptional; each has been racialized in different ways; none is the paradigm or template for the others.

Blacks were enslaved. Indians were massacred and then removed to the West. Japanese Americans were relocated in the other direction. African Americans are stereotyped as bestial or happy-go-lucky, depending on society's shifting needs; Asians, as crafty, derivative copycats or soulless drones; Mexicans as hot-tempered, romantic, or close to the earth. Blacks are racialized by reason of their color; Latinos, Indians, and Asians on that basis but also by reason of their accent, national origin, and, sometimes, religion as well. All these groups were sought as sources of labor; Indians and Mexicans, as sources of land. Puerto Ricans, Indians, and Mexicans are racialized by reason of conquest. Latinos, Indians, and Asians are pressured to assimilate; blacks to do the opposite. The matrix of race and racialization thus is constantly shifting, sometimes overlapping, for the four main groups.

This differential racialization renders binary thinking deeply problematic. Consider the recent trial of Ronald Ebens for the murder of Vincent Chin, whom he beat to death for being a "Jap" supposedly responsible for the loss of jobs in the automobile industry. After Ebens's first trial in Detroit, which resulted in a twenty-five-year jail sentence, was overturned for technical reasons, his attorney moved for a change of venue on the ground that Ebens could not be tried fairly in that city. The motion was successful, and the second trial was held in Cincinnati, where Ebens was acquitted. A United States Commission on Civil Rights report speculated that the acquittal resulted from the limitations of the black/white paradigm of race, which may have misled the Cincinnati jury, sitting in a city where Asian Americans are few, into disbelieving that racism against Asians played a part in the crime: "The ultimate failure of the American justice system to convict Ebens of civil rights charges, perhaps partly because of the Cincinnati jury's difficulty in believing in the existence of anti-Asian hatred, also implies that many Americans view racial hatred purely as a black-white problem and are unaware that Asian Americans are also frequently targets of hate crimes."

Black/white or any other kind of binary thinking can also warp minorities' views of themselves and their relation to whites. As social scientists know, Caucasians occasionally select a particular minority group as a favorite, usually a small, nonthreatening one, and make that group overseers of the others or tokens to rebut any inference that the dominant group is racist. Minorities may also identify with whites in hopes of gaining status or benefits under specific statutes, such as the naturalization statute, that limit benefits to whites. The siren song of specialness may also predispose a minority group to believe that it is uniquely victimized and entitled to special consideration from iniquitous whites. Latino exceptionalists, for example, sometimes point out (if only privately) that Latinos have the worst rates of poverty and school dropout; are soon to be the largest group of color in the United States; fought bravely in many foreign wars and earned numerous medals and commendations; and are racialized in perhaps the greatest variety of ways of any group, including language, accent, immigration status, perceived foreignness, conquered status, and certain particularly virulent stereotypes. Needless to say, specialness lies entirely in the eye of the beholder and can be maintained only by presenting a particular interpretation of history as the only true one.

Binary thinking and exceptionalism also impair the ability to learn from history; they doom one to reinvent the wheel. For example, when recent scholars put forward the theory of interest convergence to account for the ebb and flow of black fortunes, the theory came as a genuine breakthrough, enabling readers to understand a vital facet of blacks' experience. Yet the long train of Indian treaty violations, as well as Mexicans' treatment in the wake of the Treaty of Guadalupe Hidalgo, might have led commentators to arrive at that insight earlier and to mold it into a broader, more powerful form. By the same token, the treatment of Asians, with one group first favored, then disfavored when conditions change, might have inspired a similar, more nuanced theory. And in Mexican American jurisprudence, *Mendez v. Westminster School District*, decided seven years before *Brown v. Board of Education*, marked the first time a major court expressly departed from the rule of *Plessy v. Ferguson* in a challenge to de jure segregation. Had it not been for a single alert litigator on the staff of the NAACP Legal Defense Fund who recognized the case's importance and insisted that the organization participate in *Mendez* as amicus, *Mendez* would have been lost to African Americans and the road to *Brown* would have been harder and longer. Finally, when Mexican Americans were demanding their rights, George Sánchez, anticipating one of the arguments that the NAACP used to great effect in *Brown*—namely, that continued discrimination against blacks endangered the United States' moral leadership in the uncommitted world—argued that mistreatment of Latinos in the United States could end up injuring the country's relations with Latin America. Earlier, the Japanese in California had effectively deployed a similar argument when San Francisco enacted a host of demeaning rules.

Writings by Derrick Bell and Gerald Rosenberg pointing out the limitations of legal reform for minorities are foreshadowed in the experience of American Indians when the state of Georgia refused to abide by the Supreme Court's ruling in *Worcester v. Georgia* and President Andrew Jackson did nothing to enforce it. After Bell wrote his signature chronicle of the Space Traders, Michael Olivas observed that Latino and Cherokee populations had experienced literal removal several times in history.

Finally, dichotomous thought impairs groups' ability to forge useful coalitions. For example, neither the NAACP nor any other predominantly African American organization filed an amicus brief challenging Japanese internment in *Korematsu v. United States,* or in any of the other cases contesting that practice. Earlier, the League of United Latin American Citizens (LULAC), a politically moderate litigation organization for Latinos, distanced itself from other minority groups and even from darker-skinned Latinos by pursuing the "other white" strategy. And in Northern California, Asians, Mexican Americans, and blacks recently have been at loggerheads over admission to Lowell High School and UC-Berkeley.

Sometimes, minority groups do put aside differences and work together successfully. For example, Chinese- and Spanish-speaking parents successfully challenged monolingual instruction in San Francisco in *Lau v. Nichols.* Jews and blacks marched hand in hand in the 1960s. A coalition of California Latinos and Asians collaborated in litigation striking down Proposition 187, which denied social services and public education to undocumented immigrants. And another coalition of minority groups has been working to change the nearly all-white lineup on current television programs.

The school desegregation case *Mendez v. Westminster School District,* that rare exception to the inability of minority groups to generalize from other groups' experiences, is worth recounting in some detail as an example of minority groups working together successfully. By the 1920s, Mexican immigration had made Mexican Americans the largest minority group in California. Although state law did not require school districts to segregate Mexican American schoolchildren, pressure from parents led most school boards to do so on the pretext that the Mexican children's language difficulties made this in their best educational interest. On March 2, 1945, a small group of Mexican American parents filed suit in federal district court to enjoin that practice. The court ruled, nearly a year later, that because California lacked a segregation statute, the doctrine of "separate but equal" did not apply. Moreover, it found that sound educational reasons did not support separation of the Mexican children, that separation stigmatized them, and ruled the practice unconstitutional.

The school districts appealed to the Ninth Circuit Court of Appeals, at which point the case came to the attention of the American Jewish Congress and the NAACP Legal Defense Fund. The NAACP's amicus brief,

prepared by Robert Carter, advanced many of the same arguments the attorneys for the Mexican plaintiffs had put forward in the trial court, but
added a new one based not on legal doctrine or precedent, but on social
science. Relying heavily on data collected by Ambrose Caliver, an African
American researcher employed by the U.S. Department of Education, Carter argued that racial segregation would inevitably lead to inferior schools
for minorities because few school districts could afford the cost of a dual
system and would inevitably cut corners with the schools for Mexicans and
blacks. Citing the work of Gunnar Myrdal and others, Carter also argued
that racial segregation demoralized and produced poor citizenship among
minority individuals and thus contravened public policy.

The NAACP's brief was cautious and incremental in arguing that segregation invariably led to spending differentials. At the same time, its social science was rudimentary, relying as it did on studies of the adverse
effects of segregation in general, rather than on studies showing that segregated education harmed minority schoolchildren. A second brief authored
by a group of social scientists and submitted by lawyer and historian Carey
McWilliams supplied many of the links missing from the NAACP's brief.
The social scientists marshaled studies showing that young children were
especially vulnerable to the crippling effects of forced racial separation and
were quick to absorb the lesson of their own inferiority. Segregation became a psychologically damaging "badge of inferiority" that could not be
squared with the Fourteenth Amendment. This more narrowly targeted argument was the very one the NAACP would adopt, years later, in *Brown v.
Board of Education*.

Although the Ninth Circuit affirmed the trial court opinion, it did so on
the narrow ground that California law lacked any provision for the segregation of the Mexican schoolchildren. Two months later, Governor Earl
Warren eliminated that loophole by signing a bill repealing all of California's statutes requiring racial segregation. Thus, official segregation in California came to an end.

While the appeal was pending, the NAACP sent their brief to William
Hastie, one of the principal figures in the campaign against segregated

schooling. Appreciating its significance, Hastie wrote to Thurgood Marshall, encouraging him to develop the argument contained in the social scientists' brief, "with as little delay as possible." Marshall agreed, and assigned Annette H. Peyser, a young staff member with a background in social science, to do so. She did, and other social scientists, learning of the NAACP's interest, pursued their own studies of the intrinsic harm of forced racial separation, many of which found their way into the graduate school litigation cases, and ultimately into *Brown* itself.

The *Mendez* case demonstrates that narrow nationalism not only deprives one of the opportunity to join with other groups, it also closes one off from the experiences and lessons of others. It can conceal how the American caste system, in a complex dance, disadvantages one group at one time and advantages it at another. It can disguise the way American society often affirmatively pits groups against one another, using them as agents of each other's subordination, or uses mistreatment of one group as a template for discrimination against another. Because almost all racial binaries consist of a non-white group paired with whites, they predispose outgroups to focus excessively on whites, patterning themselves after and trying to gain concessions from them, or aiming to assimilate into white society.

Minority groups in the United States should consider abandoning all binaries, narrow nationalisms, and strategies that focus on cutting the most favorable possible deal with whites, and instead set up a secondary market in which they negotiate selectively with each other. For example, instead of approaching the establishment supplicatingly, in hopes of a more favorable admission formula at an elite school or university system, Asians might approach African Americans with the offer of a bargain. That bargain might be an agreement on the part of the latter group to support Asians with respect to an issue important to them—for example, easing immigration restrictions or supporting bilingual education in public schools—in return for their own promise not to pursue quite so intently rollbacks in affirmative action or set-asides for black contractors. The idea would be for minority groups to assess their own preferences and make trade-offs that will, optimistically, bring gains for all concerned. Some controversies may turn out to be polycentric, presenting win-win possibilities so that negotiation can advance goals important to both sides without compromising anything either group deems vital. Like a small community that sets up an informal system of barter, exchanging jobs and services moneylessly, thus reducing sales and income taxes, this approach would reduce the number of times minorities approach whites hat in hand. Some gains may be achievable by means of collective action alone. When it *is* necessary to approach whites for something, a nonbinary framework allows that approach to be made in full force. It also deprives vested interests of the opportunity to profit from flattery, false compliments, and mock sympathy ("Oh, your terrible history. Your group is so special. Why don't we . . .").

Ignoring the siren song of binaries opens up new possibilities for coalitions based on level-headed assessment of the chances for mutual gain. It liberates one from dependence on a system that has advanced minority interests at best sporadically and unpredictably. It takes interest convergence to a new dimension.

Bluebeard's Castle could just as easily have served as an allegory about gender imbalance and the social construction of marriage between unequals. Although Bell does not draw this lesson from it, it is certainly as implicit in the French fairy tale as the lesson Bell extracts about black progress. Seen through this other lens, a straightforward solution, one that Judith apparently never contemplated, would have been to engage in collaborative action with Bluebeard's three previous wives against their common oppressor, the gloomy noble bent on subjugating them all—in short, an injection of feminist solidarity. Persisting in an unsuccessful strategy, waging it with more and more energy, can prove a counsel of despair. Sometimes, as with the black/white binary, one needs to turn a thought structure on its side, look at it from a different angle, and gain some needed distance from it before the path to liberation becomes clear.

5

Enlisting Race, Resisting Power, Transforming Democracy

LANI GUINIER

2000

Lani Guinier is the Bennett Boskey Professor of Law, Emerita, at Harvard Law School, where she became the first woman of color appointed to a tenured professorship. She received her BA from Radcliffe College, Harvard University, and her JD from Yale Law School. She was previously tenured at the University of Pennsylvania Law School, worked in the Civil Rights Division at the U.S. Department of Justice, and headed the voting rights project at the NAACP Legal Defense Fund. She has been honored with the Champion of Democracy Award from the National Women's Political Caucus; the Margaret Brent Women Lawyers of Achievement Award from the American Bar Association's Commission on Women in the Profession; and the Rosa Parks Award from the American Association of Affirmative Action. She is the author of The Tyranny of the Meritocracy *and co-author, with Gerald Torres, of* The Miner's Canary.

In 2000 a panel discussion took the place of an individual lecture. Unfortunately, the panel discussion was not recorded. Lani Guinier was one of the featured panelists, and her remarks on the panel informed her subsequent book *The Miner's Canary,* a brief excerpt of which is included here.

Race, for us, is like the miner's canary. Miners often carried a canary into the mine alongside them. The canary's more fragile respiratory system would cause it to collapse from noxious gases long before humans were affected, thus alerting the miners to danger. The canary's distress signaled that it was time to get out of the mine because the air was becoming too poisonous to breathe.

Those who are racially marginalized are like the miner's canary: their distress is the first sign of a danger that threatens us all. It is easy enough to think that when we sacrifice this canary, the only harm is to communities of color. Yet others ignore problems that converge around racial minorities at their own peril, for these problems are symptoms warning us that we are all at risk.

Achieving racial justice and ensuring a healthy democratic process are independently knotty problems; at points where the two problems intersect, they have seemed intractable. Yet we believe progress can be made. Our goal is to explore how racialized identities may be put in service to achieve social change through democratic renewal. We also seek to revive a cross-racial project of social change. Toward these ends, we link the metaphor of the canary with a conceptual project we call "political race," and in so doing we propose a new, twenty-first-century way of talking about this distinctly American challenge.

The metaphor of the miner's canary captures the association between those who are left out and social justice deficiencies in the larger community. The concept of political race captures the association between those raced black—and thus often left out—and a democratic social movement aimed at bringing about constructive change within the larger community. One might say that the canary is diagnostic, signaling the need for more systemic critique. Political race, on the other hand, is not only diagnostic; it is also aspirational and activist, signaling the need to rebuild a movement for social change informed by the canary's critique. Political race seeks to construct a new language to discuss race, in order to rebuild a progressive democratic movement led by people of color but joined by others.

The political dimension of the political race project seeks to reconnect in-dividual experiences to democratic faith, to social critique, and to mean-ingful action that improves the lives of the canary and the miners by ameliorating the air quality in the mines.

The miner's canary metaphor helps us understand why and how race continues to be salient. Racialized communities signal problems with the ways we have structured power and privilege. These pathologies are not located in the canary. Indeed, we reject the incrementalist approach that locates complex social and political problems in the individual. Such an approach would solve the problems of the mines by outfitting the canary with a tiny gas mask to withstand the toxic atmosphere.

Political race as a concept encompasses the view that race still matters because racialized communities provide the early warning signs of poison in the social atmosphere. And then it encourages us to do something dif-ferent from what has been done in the past with that understanding. Po-litical race tells us that we need to change the air in the mines. If you care to look, you can see the canary alerting us to both danger and promise. The project of political race challenges both those on the right who say race is not real and those on the left who say it is real but we cannot talk about it. Political race illustrates how the lived experience of race in America continues to serve an important function in the construction of individual selves as well as in the construction of social policy.

Political race is therefore a motivational project. Rebuilding a movement for change can happen only if we reclaim our democratic imagination. . . .

At its genesis, we referred to this concept as "political blackness." Our effort to develop a terminology arose in reaction to the neoliberal and neo-conservative attempts to reduce race to its biological and thus scientifi-cally irrational and morally reprehensible origins—that is, to eliminate race as a meaningful or useful concept. But it was also a reaction to the civil rights advocates' inadequate response, which tended to embrace race as skin color and thus to limit the radical political dynamism of the Civil Rights Movement to persons "of color." In the view of the neoconservatives, race is merely skin color and is thus meaningless and ignorable. In the view of the civil rights advocates, race is skin color plus a legacy of slavery and Jim Crow that is now realized through stigma, discrimination, or prejudice. But to those outside this subtle debate, it often appears that both sides see race primarily as being about skin color. They differ simply on whether such a definition of race is meaningless and thus should be abandoned, or is meaningful and thus should be at least temporarily acknowledged. The word *political* in the term *political blackness* was an attempt to dislodge race from this color-of-one's-skin terminology and to extend its social meaning from a moral calculus that assesses blame as a precondition for action to a political framework that cultivates and inspires action directly. It was also an attempt to dislodge race from simple identity politics; it was a reaction to the cultural or race nationalists for whom one's personal identity constitutes one's political project.

We sought a phrase that would name the association between race and power that is lost in the current debate. But in responding to inquiries about the meaning of political blackness, we found ourselves bombarded by boundary questions: Who is inside and who is outside the category? For example, one graduate student persisted in seeing political blackness as a membership category. "Is a black woman lesbian middle manager inside the political blackness idea?" she asked. We responded that the term covers three elements: it has a diagnostic function, it embraces an aspirational goal, and it hopes to jumpstart an activist project. We then insisted that it was up to each person to determine whether she was part of this project. Action and commitment, not predetermined descriptors, would be the guide: we were not gatekeepers.

Meanwhile, we also discovered that many black Americans were offended by the substitution of "political blackness" for "race" because, by opening up the category "black" to anyone who wished to enter, this semantic move discounted the material reality black Americans faced every day and misappropriated the cultural community they experienced. In our view, these were all substantial reasons to find another term. Thus we substituted the term *political race project*. This terminology is also subject to ambiguity, but it seemed to minimize these specific confusions and liabilities. And while we moved to the more inclusive nomenclature of political race, blackness—and the experience of black people—is nevertheless at the heart of our argument.

6

Accountability for Private Life

ANITA ALLEN

2001

Anita Allen is the Henry R. Silverman Professor of Law, Professor of Philosophy, and Vice Provost for Faculty at the University of Pennsylvania Law School, and Chair of the Provost's Advisory Council on Arts, Culture and the Humanities. She received her BA from New College, her MA and PhD from the University of Michigan, and her JD from Harvard Law School. She served on President Obama's Presidential Commission for the Study of Bioethical Issues and is an expert on privacy law and ethics, recognized for contributions to legal philosophy, women's rights, and diversity in higher education. She has been given a Lifetime Achievement Award by the Electronic Privacy Information Center and was elected to the National Academy of Medicine. She is the author of books including The New Ethic, Why Privacy Isn't Everything, Accountability, Unpopular Privacy, *and* Privacy Law and Society.

We are accountable not just for how we run our businesses and our governments and our schools, but also for how we run our personal lives. Earlier this year, acknowledging his accountability publicly, the Reverend Jesse Jackson apologized for an extramarital affair and an out-of-wedlock daughter. He said, "This is no time for evasions, denials, or alibis. I accept responsibility and I am truly sorry for my actions." But why did Jesse Jackson have to account to us? To call a realm or activity private is to imply that we are unanswerable to any earthly being for conduct within that realm.

Accountability for private life thus has the ring of an oxymoron. We imagine ourselves as citizens of a free society, each entitled to enjoy a private life for which we are not answerable to others, but it's simply not true and we need to acknowledge it. One of the greatest literary depictions of accountability for private life is found in Hawthorne's *The Scarlet Letter.* Poor Hester, we think. Oh, the injustice of society in which you have to be perpetually accountable. You must disclose your intimate conduct to fellow citizens. You must wear the scarlet letter on your bosom. We Americans tend to hate accountability for private life. So we love the liberal romanticism of John Stuart Mill.

In 1859, Mill published his famous essay "On Liberty." In the fifth and final chapter of that essay, he asserted two maxims about accountability. The first maxim was this: The individual is not accountable to society for his actions insofar as these concern the interests of no person but himself.

Second maxim: For actions that are prejudicial to the interests of others, the individual is accountable and may be subjected either to social or to legal punishment. The word *privacy* does not appear in "On Liberty," but many theorists have interpreted Mill as a great defender of the idea of a private life—that is, a life free from societal or governmental interference.

According to Mill, when it comes to actions that concern the interest of no persons but ourselves, we ought not to face accountability. Accountability for private life, though, is a cultural fact. Accountability for private life is the rule, not the exception. In our society, certain areas of conduct get labeled private, even though they are not walled off.

Practices and policies, some legal, some moral, some customary, that scrutinize what goes on in personal, intimate areas, flourish. We ignore a stark feature of our moral lives if we allow shared liberal ideals and aspirations to obscure the diverse ways in which we are constantly called upon to explain, to justify, to rationalize, and to suffer the choices we make about our own lives.

We may be liberal in theory—I certainly am—and to that extent presumptively opposed to collective interference with individuals' personal affairs and self-regarding choices. But in practice, we are not at all that liberal. Many of us and many of our laws recognize reasons to hold other people accountable for their private life. For example, because they are a public official.

And many of us and many of our laws recognize respects in which so-called personal and self-regarding acts are also social and other-regarding. For example, narcotic drug use. Although accountability for conduct should not be and cannot be total, a degree of accountability is essential for social order.

We are all accountable to our families, our friends, our ethno-racial groups, our employers, and the general public. We are accountable for sexuality, intimacy, health, and finances. Although privacy is important, accountability is important too. One's entitled to say "none of your business" in some contexts, in response to some requests for information, explanation, and answers, but not in others.

"None of your business" is sometimes the decidedly wrong, incorrect, irresponsible, immoral response to others who scrutinize our private lives. Thurgood Marshall knew this. Marshall's first wife died in 1955. She was African American. The very same year that she died, Marshall wanted to get married again. He wanted to marry a woman who was of Filipino ancestry, not African American. Set on this interracial marriage, Thurgood Marshall had to account for himself. Even though he was the most powerful black lawyer in the world, and even though he was one of the best-known men in America who had the ears of the president, this man had to explain himself to the public.

Why are you not marrying a black woman? He was persuaded by his friends at the NAACP to hold a press conference. How many of you have held a press conference before you got married? I didn't, but the purpose of the press conference was to get the public to accept his marriage by making a dignified introduction of his wife, and also to reassure the public that he was not going to abandon the cause. He was not going to stop working on behalf of Black America because of his new wife. But how strange, how quintessentially American, to have to account for your private life.

Accountability is real and it's normal, but it can also be a bad thing sometimes. It can be unjust and oppressive and humiliating. It can rob people of their basic dignity and their basic freedom. And there are some things about which people should not have to be accountable, like their fantasies and their thoughts.

There are also those more controversial things people should not have to be accountable for. I think that policymakers, judges, legislators, and corporate executives should pay attention to norms of accountability that are fostered by what they do, what they propose, what they practice, what they decide, because these things matter greatly.

Many of the traditional privacy claims we assert that go back to intimacy and sexuality and health are very plausible and very legitimate. People should neither give up nor be deprived of their privacy casually, but it's important to understand why some privacy claims simply are illegitimate, even some that are very common.

We must not demand more privacy than the just and vigilant society can afford to give us, a problem or thought that we are very much focused on right now in the context of Homeland Security. We must be private and enjoy our privacy. We must also sacrifice a little bit of it in order to be a more vigilant society.

Now, philosophers commonly recognized three different kinds of accountability, or three senses of accountability. There's accountability in the sense of simply giving people information about yourself. Secondly, there is accountability in the sense of providing an explanation, a narrative justification for why you do what you do. And then, finally, there's accountability in the sense of being morally or legal answerable about private life, including being open to punishment.

A couple of examples will help to better clarify what these various forms of accountability are like in ordinary life. A few years ago, a man who was a manager at the Coca-Cola company was discovered by his firm to have posted nude photos of himself on the internet. He did so after hours. Was he accountable to his employer, to his company, for his behavior?

Around the same time a policewoman was fired because she posed nude for *Playboy*. Was she accountable to her city for the choice she made? She lost her job over that one. In 1999, a Japanese woman named Ayumi Karata was forced to leave her job as a popular TV talk show host in Japan because she had had a divorce, and the public learned that she'd had that divorce without telling them. A common, but by no means universal, sentiment in Japan is that professional women are accountable to the public for their private lives—moreover, that the public has a right to know that the family life of a woman who's become a public figure has changed.

It seems pretty clear that Vice President Dick Cheney was accountable to us, the public, for his life-threatening heart troubles. But what about the Israeli entertainer Ofra Haza? In March 2000 in Israel, the private truth that she had died of AIDS was finally reported to the newspapers. Out of respect for Ofra's medical privacy, at first the papers didn't mention why she died, a young woman. But the week after she died, rumors began to circulate, gossip, whispering, and the newspaper *Haaretz* decided that it was time to quell the rumors and to speak truth, and it reported that she had indeed died of complications of AIDS.

If the Coca-Cola Company manager and the police officer were deemed to have a duty to tell their employer about their provocative activities, they'd be accountable in the first sense, just being informationally accountable. "Yes. I did this, end of story." But if they had to explain why, they'd be accountable in a stronger sense—the justification, explanation sense. "Tell me why you did this." And you could imagine an employer would want to know not just that their employee had posed nude for *Playboy*, but why would you, a police officer, do such a thing? If they lost their jobs, they'd be accountable in the last sense of punishment. They would have been sanctioned for your conduct.

Accountability for sex takes many forms in the United States. Homosexuals in the military face peculiar demands of privacy and accountability. On the one hand, they're told to keep information about their sexual orientation a secret. Don't ask, don't tell. Yet, if they are discovered to be homosexual, then they're required to explain themselves, and then they'll be punished with discharge from the military. They are accountable in a very negative sense of the word.

Many people agree that the government and public officials and public employees and large institutions ought to be accountable to the general public, with some exceptions. But people are a little bit more ambivalent about the extent to which the rest of us, those of us who don't have the kind of power that big corporations or the government have, ought to be accountable as well.

But we are accountable, and we know it. The topic of accountability of public officials was a topic of great interest in our country, and I guess it still is. The Iran war has somewhat turned our mind away from the likes of congressional conduct and Bill Clinton, but we still remember. Just a few months ago we were obsessed with whether or not there was an affair between Representative Gary Condit and Chandra Levy, and if so, to what extent that affair may have been co-mingled with his professional duties.

How much did he have to tell the press? How much did he have to tell the authorities? And when? These are questions about accountability for private life. As a practical matter, high public officials rarely enjoy the physical informational privacy that other people enjoy, but they should, I think, have some privacy. My own rule of thumb is that if the official co-mingles—I like that word—the discharge of their duties with their personal affairs, then they should expect the public will have an interest, a justifiable one, in knowing about that affair. So in my view, if you're in the White House and you're sitting in the Oval Office and you have a telephone in one hand and an intern on your lap, you're co-mingling and you're accountable.

But if you go out to Arkansas, some cabin in the woods, and an old girlfriend from twenty years ago shows up, then maybe you're not accountable for the tryst. We do today, though, place officials suspected of illicit sex, sexual harassment, drug use, pornography, offensive speech, and medical problems under the microscope. Journalists and lawyers use the concept of the public's right to know to justify investigation and reporting about the personal conduct of public officials. You've heard the arguments that people in the limelight waive their right to privacy by accepting fame and responsibility for public duties. But it's not just famous people who are subject to accountability. It's the rest of us, too, in our ordinary marriages and in our ordinary parent-child relationships. We worry that teenagers and tweenagers who are not held strictly accountable will fall prey to drugs and sex and violence, but we also worry that kids, children, teenagers will have to submit unfairly to their parents' corporal punishment, to random drug tests in their own homes, and to eavesdropping by their nosy mom and dad.

The husband-wife and parent-child relationships are not the only kinds of kinship ties that generate expectations of accountability. Along with expectations of mutual aid and support come obligations of accountability. A man with a drug addiction, for example, who asks his sister for money should not be surprised if she wants to know about his cocaine dependency in detail, and she rejects "none of your business" as a response, because, after all, he's asking her to give up her money and her time to help him, so he's accountable to her in response.

An important kind of accountability, the kind that Derrick Bell and I talked about ten years ago, is accountability to one's racial group, one's ethnic group, one's religious community. A case down in Georgia recently underscored the importance of thinking carefully about the parameters of this kind of accountability. A church, House of Prayer in Atlanta, run by a minister named the Reverend Arthur Allen, had a practice of beating children whose parents told the church congregation that they misbehaved.

So, if Mom and Dad told the church that Johnny, age eight or nine, had, say, stolen a cassette tape or had come home late from a party or had sassed, the ministry might well say to the congregation, "Hold him down and let us all join hands and beat the child, to live out that Biblical mandate, spare the rod and spoil the child." Well, this went on for years. And in fact in 2002, Reverend Allen was actually put in prison for thirty days because he had a fifteen-year-old girl beaten in this way because she had had sex, contrary to the church doctrine's teachings. This past winter, the reverend was again arrested, this time because a little boy told his schoolteacher he'd been beaten by the church, and he had welts and broken skin. A judge in Atlanta did the right thing, in my view. The judge actually had the children of the congregation who had been beaten removed from their homes and placed in foster care for a year to communicate to parents that one may not, in the name of religion, beat one's children. Well, what did the Reverend Allen say to the world about this event? Tragic by any standard. He said, "We," meaning the black congregation of his church, "We're getting persecuted. They," the white people and the blacks who were in cahoots with them, "want to dominate us with their way of life."

Now, there is a strong privacy interest, right? And being able to exclude the rest of the world from your religion, from your practice, and to see the world as us and them is normal and natural. But I don't think that that gives the church—any church, black or white or any color church—the entitlement to expect non-accountability from the legal system, from the child welfare authorities.

Parents are right to want their children to be accountable to them for their conduct. But the parents are not justified in asking the children to also be accountable in the form of punishment, beatings, whippings, from an entire congregation of adult men and women.

In the Native American community, there's accountability, and if a Native American woman wants to place her child for adoption, she must first clear it with her tribe. The American federal law, the Indian Child Welfare Act, requires that the priority go to an Indian family over any non-Indian family the mother might prefer for her child. Native American women who want to place their children for adoption are accountable to their tribe in a way that the rest of us are not accountable to our groups, by federal statute.

The past several years, new levels of concern about threats to employee privacy have forced us to ask hard questions about worker accountability. Although employers once exercised nearly complete dominion over their employees, in the middle of the last century, most workers could conceive of having personal lives beyond the scrutiny of employers. Many, though, could not.

Even today, if you're in the army or the navy or the marines, or you're a migrant farmworker, you've still got to be accountable to your employer for your life in a very extreme way. Officers in our army still face punishment for marital infidelity. Gay and lesbian service members, again, are accountable for their sexual orientation.

I want to shift here slightly for just a moment and talk about the question of who can we blame, if anyone, for our recent obsession with accountability, with wanting to hear from people who have committed acts of sexual misconduct—what they did and why they did it. It's important to understand that feminism cannot be blamed for the current accountability obsession, because accountability is nothing new and certainly predates feminism.

I recently read a book that some of you may have read, about a court case, *Rhinelander v. Rhinelander*, that took place eighty years ago. A wealthy white man sought to have his marriage to a black woman annulled on the grounds that she had deceived him as to her race. He asserted that he married her not knowing she was black. The legal proceedings and journalistic frenzy that followed their divorce filing was an amazing display of pure interest in people's private lives. In the courtroom drama that ensued, the young white man, Kip Rhinelander, was forced to endure having to explain and detail each and every time he had sex before marriage with his fiancée.

Where did you do it? What did you do? All their love letters became evidence. They were read in court. They were so explicit that they had to actually excuse the ladies in order to have the men hear the evidence of sexual fantasies about masturbation, and oral sex and other forbidden pleasures. This is eighty years ago, in open court. It was quite amazing. In order for this poor guy to get his divorce, he had to lay himself bare to the public. And of course, in doing so, humiliate himself and also his disappointed bride.

And what about the bride? Her own lawyer devised a very clever defense: "Well, if you take off your clothes in open court, then the court can see that you're really black. Right?" So, her own lawyer had her bare her "dusky naked breasts and legs" to the jury to prove that her lover turned husband had to have known that she was colored when he married her.

Wasn't it Flip Wilson who said, "What you see is what you get"? Well, the point here is that he saw her, maybe her face was under a hat, and was fair, but when she took off her clothes, he could see that she was colored. That was the theory. Therefore, the divorce should not be granted. Therefore, she's entitled to the full benefits of being the wife, the black wife of a wealthy white man.

The plaintiff wife won her case. Equally bizarre in this case, though, was that apparently Alice Rhinelander mentioned in a letter to her fiancé that she had met someone named Al Jolson at work, and that this Al Jolson had winked at her, flirted with her in some very innocuous way. So, the court called in the real Al Jolson to explain the nature of his relationship with this woman.

Al Jolson had to stand up and be accounted for! That is an amazing example of how comfortable American society has been, pre-feminism, with the idea of people having to account for their private life not only in unofficial senses, but also in official senses—in the courtroom—in this very extreme way. That's accountability in America.

Although the phenomenon of accountability for private life clearly preceded contemporary feminism, feminism is blamed for some of the current controversies surrounding public accountability for sex and domestic conflict. It's charged with having been too successful at making the personal political. It's not really clear to me, though, as an academic theorist anyway, exactly what role feminism has had in fostering public accountability for sexual conduct. It's not even clear to me as an academic what kind of theory of accountability would follow from basic feminist principles.

So, I began to wonder, what would a theory of accountability look like if it were advanced by a feminist? Well, of course it would be one that had a basic assumption of gender equality, that men and women were to be accountable in just the same way. Back in the 1950s, a man might be able to stay out a little bit later at night and not exactly explain where he was, but the woman had an expectation that she would tell all. Well, that's no longer the case. But the point here is that one thing you'd expect in a feminist theory of accountability is that men and women have a similar obligation.

A feminist account of accountability would probably be very significantly anti-formalist and very significantly anti-libertarian. And I think my own intuitions about accountability are consistent with these features. As an anti-formalist, one wants to see a theory of accountability that does not take categories as conclusive. Just saying "this is private," "this is family," "this is sexual," "this is religious" is not in the discussion about whether it ought to be private and free from accountability norms. On the contrary, they're just words and we can look closer at whether or not, in this situation, the personal, the familial, the sexual, the private, the religious turns out to be something for which there is no accountability.

Accountability then requires that we not treat those kinds of privacy terms as unamenable to revision and reassessment. Accountability norms are I think, in practice, quite contextual. For example, spouses are usually accountable to one another for their sexual conduct. But they might not be in certain situations. For example, if you are estranged, then you are not accountable in the same way.

Mills's enthusiastic embrace of the idea of self-regarding conduct would not be very attractive to a thoroughgoing feminist, even a feminist who was in a liberal camp. But I think that feminists doubt the existence of purely self-regarding conduct. I discovered this the hard way in my own life. My sister, at the age of about thirty-five, a middle-class government worker and civil servant with a top secret security clearance, became a crack addict. And suddenly our whole family was involved in her problems and in her child's problems, rescuing her repeatedly from her own addiction. So I learned it's not about your own body alone. You are part of a network of people who care about you, in most instances, and they, too, have a role in what happens to you. What you do to your own body can also impact other people.

Purely self-regarding conduct is clearly something of a myth. Our lives are, as many feminists have said, interconnected and interdependent. If I use cocaine and I neglect my children, if I drive a gas guzzling, flip-over-prone SUV, my choice affects other people.

People who purport to live by themselves in a realm apart from others are generally profoundly mistaken. There are externalities, there are consequences of their own conduct. Those people who sit in their comfortable suburban homes up there in Mount Kisco or Pleasantville and have a little cocaine party are accountable for being complicit in the drug trade. Little children, little boys and girls—thirteen, fourteen, fifteen—are getting killed in Upper Manhattan, while they sit in their comfortable homes, enjoying a little sniff, a little snort.

We're connected.

I think that's what being sensitive to the limitations of the libertarian view about accountability means. Being sensitive to the demands of anti-formalism means being sensitive to gender equity; it means a theory of accountability that is thoroughly contextual. It may seem at times arbitrary. What are the rules of accountability? Are there bright-line rules? Well, I think that there aren't many bright-line rules in this area. But I do think that it's important to recognize that some kinds of privacy are very, very vital to self-fulfillment and self-determination. Our friendships, our gardens, our diaries, our poems, our spirituality—these things deserve to be protected by rituals of privacy. At the same time, the quest for such goods does not make us immune from the scrutiny of our fellows.

What do I think of what we should say to Jesse Jackson and to Reverend Allen? I will conclude with those words:

Reverent Jackson, you are a black hero. But you are accountable to us. Not to the *New York Times*, by the way, but to us: the black community, the Rainbow Coalition, the people who support you—your family and your friends. You're accountable to all of us for what you've done.

We don't have to know in a Ken Starr–esque style exactly what you and she did. I think one of the abuses of accountability has been that recently we want to know the details, the nitty gritty. We don't want to know that, Jesse. But as someone who has asked us to join you in a life of spirituality, that includes a certain dedication to family and community, a certain kind of honesty and integrity, you should tell us that you did it. We have a right to the information that you did it. The honest truth and then some explanation of why you did it. Of how you reconcile your personal conduct with your belief; the belief that you share with us. We don't require a psychological explanation that goes deep in your psyche. Just an explanation of how, on a very general level, you can reconcile your faith and your beliefs with your actions. That's what you owe us. We're not going to send you to jail, Reverend. We're not going to punish you in that sense, but we may well condemn you if we don't like your explanation for what you now tell us you have done.

And to Reverend Allen: You should not hold those little black boys and girls accountable to you and your entire congregation for their youthful errors. It's wrong to beat them. It's especially wrong for so many people to beat them. For you, as a child abuser, the state rightfully asked you to account. You're held accountable with justice, to welfare authorities, to the courts. Don't hide behind family privacy. It's not an excuse for your conduct. Don't hide behind the religion excuse. Be kind to those babies. The judge who took those kids from their parents did the right thing in the interest of child welfare, painful as it was. I think those kinds of messages are the kinds of messages that are demanded of us.

I think we have to face the fact that we are indeed accountable and give up the myth of unaccountability. We must try very hard to respect privacy while recognizing the ties that bind.

7

Somebody Else's Child

MARI MATSUDA

2002

Mari Matsuda is an American lawyer, activist, and law professor at the William S. Richardson School of Law at the University of Hawai'i. She was the first tenured female Asian American law professor in the United States, at the University of California, Los Angeles School of Law in 1998, and one of the leading voices in Critical Race Theory since its inception. She has won an AALDEF Justice in Action Award and a Regents Medal for Excellence in Teaching. Matsuda obtained her BA from Arizona State University, her JD from the University of Hawai'i, and her LLM from Harvard University, and she specializes in the fields of torts, constitutional law, legal history, feminist theory, Critical Race Theory, and civil rights law. She is the co-author of Words That Wound: Critical Race Theory, Assaultive Speech, and the First Amendment *along with Charles Lawrence, Richard Delgado, and Kimberlé Crenshaw.*

I recently heard Studs Terkel on a radio call-in show. An elder from Florida asked him for his views on the proposed war against Iraq. Mr. Terkel answered in the shorthand, parable-ized style of hard-earned elder wisdom: "During the Vietnam war, we were haunted by the picture of a little girl running away from a bombing. She is running down the road, naked, crying.

Until we can see that little Vietnamese child, that little Iraqi child, as our child, we are all going to continue to suffer violence in our lives."

I will remember the picture Studs Terkel refers to all my life. When I first saw it, I was the same age as that child; skinny and Asian like her; scared, as all children are, of pain and of separation from parents; aware, as all children are, of our dependency on the powers of adults who can choose to make wars, to control schools, to decide everything for us. The necessity that adults make benign decisions combined with the inability of children to require that they do so was encapsulated in that picture of someone who looked like me running terrified—naked and without adult protection—through the streets. I believed then that it could happen to me and I still do. With that image, I began a quest to see every child as Our Child, as Ourselves.

Much of what I read and hear these days is information exhorting parents to make sure to obtain the very best for their very own child. A recent article in *Washingtonian* magazine reports without one whit of irony that if one wants to gain admission for one's child into one of the ten DC-area schools that range in rank from 13 to 279 on the list of schools that send the highest percentage of graduates to Princeton, Yale, and Harvard, "parents can't afford mistakes that contribute to rejection." With Sidwell Friends (ranked at 28, with 9% of its graduates going to the top three Ivies) accepting "only 15%" of "non-Priority" applicants, "competition has grown fierce." The article went on to describe the availability of consultants that parents hire when their children are as young as three years old, at $2,000 for a package consultation or $400 an hour for the à la carte rate. Many of these consultants are former admissions staffers at the preparatory schools, all the better to ensure the inside track.

Meanwhile, in just one week in the DC public schools, the superintendent was in the paper twice, once because of a shooting at one of our high schools, luckily only involving "outsiders" (i.e., dropouts) rather than "our students," even though it happened on school grounds while school was in session. Across town, in a rare fit of public outrage, the superintendent suspended a principal and a cafeteria manager after decaying rat carcasses were found in the food preparation area. I smiled to myself, seeing it as a pathetic sign of health that finally something that happened in my city's public schools was serious enough to provoke outrage. I have observed the process of losing outrage. How quickly it happens.

When I first showed up as a new parent at my local DC public school, I was outraged that there was no soap in the bathroom and no doors on several bathroom stalls. A *Washington Post* reporter happened to show up at a PTA meeting, and I dragged him back to the bathroom to show him. "I've seen worse," he said, simply. "Don't tell me you're upset about a missing door when schools 'east of the river' have raw sewage backups." On another day, I happened to ask a teacher if there was anything she wanted to add to the PTA's list of needed maintenance and repairs. "Well, there are the mice," she said, and when pressed showed me the cupboards and corners where rodent feces lay amid the art supplies. I promptly swept the droppings into a baggie and carried them to the next PTA meeting at which the school district representative showed us a chart with the available budget for repairs overlaid against the needed repairs at all schools. The end result was that our repairs, deemed less urgent than the collapsing walls at other schools, put us at a priority level under which our repairs would be addressed at about the same time our children graduate from high school.

I rose with my little bag of rodent poop to make my protest. My law professor voice of authority was lost to me and I had only the voice of the stepped on and forgotten. "You can't do this to our children." The next day a private exterminator showed up mysteriously at our school, but this year the mice are back and a teacher has asked me not to make a fuss again or they will send back the same incompetent rodent eradication people who will throw poison around the school supplies.

On some days I can still remember that the privilege of law training means I have to speak up when others cannot. I have dragged a city council member into the school bathroom to see the stopped-up sink. I have had my paint roller confiscated by polite security guards at the city council hearing room where I went to protest budget cuts. I have held meetings at my home urging my neighbors to send their children to the local public school. "I can't," said one neighbor. "I took one look at the bathrooms. I only have one child. I can't fight that fight." What could I say to this woman who is already leading the fight against the drug sellers on the corner, when she tells me she cannot take on the bathrooms, too? To tell you the truth I have stopped complaining about the bathrooms. Last week there was no soap and no toilet paper. When I complained, loudly, at home, to my resident school board member, he asked whether I had complained to the principal. Regretfully, I confessed, "No."

There is a socialization process under which one learns to accept the unacceptable, to give up the bathroom complaints as petty. One begins to lose that middle-class outrage and sense of entitlement. "Pick your fights," the experienced warriors say. This quickly devolves into losing the fight altogether. The new pre-kindergarten parents come in and say, "Have you seen the bathroom?" and the sixth-grade parents smile wryly, "Oh, yes, we have." Welcome to the colonized District of Columbia.

This is the view from the ground, alongside a view of heartbreaking beauty: of teachers who start each school year believing every child will learn and who make it happen in spite of the mouse poop and the late book delivery and the broken furnace and the stopped-up bathroom sink. The physical plant might send a message that these children are not worth the effort, but I have seen teachers stomp out that message through the power of their belief and practice.

I have seen children who came to school without the privilege of educated parents and overflowing bookshelves, the ones from troubled circumstances who are supposedly preordained to failure, treated as learners and winners from whom academic excellence is expected, and I have seen those children rise to their teachers' expectations. I am on my knees with admiration for the teachers who do this. To the second-grade teacher who in the wake of 9/11 taught my daughter's class to recognize the artistry of illuminated manuscripts of the Koran, to the pre-kindergarten teacher who had my son's class singing phonics to their own added Afrocentric backbeat, over the melody of hokey, scratchy old phonograph records salvaged from a back closet somewhere. I have seen the alchemy of teaching from nothing, opening the door of reading and lifelong learning. I bow down to these teachers. We ought to carve monuments to them, or at the very least pay them what we pay our dear law students in their summer jobs downtown.

Because I have seen this miracle of learning, because I value the amazing mix of families and perspectives that only public education can provide my children, and because no preparatory school teacher starts the year with the presumption that the best learner in the class is going to be a child of color, I choose to keep my children in a deeply distressed urban public school system. This is seen as a private and personal choice; one that my friends might question behind my back but that will rarely surface in conversation, just as my critique of the parents who hire consultants to help them get into the right feeder preschool is generalized, and not couched as a challenge to my many friends, including the majority of my professional peers, my neighbors, and my best friends from childhood, who are sending their children to the best schools their money can buy. Choice is the watchword—the most personal and challenging choice of how we make a good life for our offspring—seen as untouchable and separate from any structural problem, such as the collapse of urban public education.

This separation feeds right into the current right-wing strategy to solidify the privatization of education and to harden the current divide between have and have-not all in the name of equal access. They call it choice.

School choice is debated as a public policy reform. Vouchers, standards, back-to-basics education, and charter schools are presented as educational reforms of which we should consider the pros and cons. The debate then proceeds as an empirical debate: Will these reforms produce better results than the current system?

There is significant evidence that the answer is no, but then, the debate continues: If the current system is also a known failure, why shouldn't we experiment with these new systems without the empirical proof that they work?

I could spend a lot of time proving to you that vouchers and standardized testing will not work, but that would concede too much to the debate.

It would concede its legitimacy. It would concede that George W. Bush's support of vouchers stems from his concern for the education of poor urban children of color and from his belief that he has a better way. I will not concede that ground.

We know what works to educate children. I would like to say that again. We know what works to educate children. It is a complete lie that this question is up for grabs. The empirical proof abounds. Think tanks and foundations right here in this city have in their archives irrefutable and replicated proof of what works: early intervention, small classes, well-paid, highly trained, and committed teachers who believe children can learn work. Head Start works. The earlier the intervention, the more intense, the more coordinated the family support mechanisms, the better the results.

I started my career as a social critic as a Head Start volunteer. I was twelve years old. I saw one small corner of what was envisioned as the Great Society: parents were trained as teachers. They learned to read to their children, and if they could not read they were themselves given a tutor. Children were guaranteed nutritious meals. They ate with gusto and never once complained, "I don't eat that." I learned what hungry children look like and how they eat. Teachers taught colors and concepts—opposites, feelings, sequences—that in my middle-class world were taken as obvious. I was taught to ask a child, "Will you tell me about your drawing?" Never, "What is it?" We went to ordinary places like supermarkets and restaurants and the children collected nouns. What is that? An artichoke. The children did not consider this work. They wanted to collect nouns, just as children want to collect superhero trading cards.

Head Start teaching was designed to feed the natural craving that children have to know their world. I was a child myself and I learned then much of what I know about education. Children want to learn, and if you meet them halfway, they will soar. Some children come from circumstances impoverished in school preparation experiences. They are not dumb or lazy or permanently impaired. They just need the toolkit that children of well-educated parents receive automatically. They need to see people reading, to collect a bigger list of nouns, to hear conceptual speech, to talk to people who have the time and energy to take their speech seriously, to learn colors and numbers and letters and crayons and glue and scissors so that on the first day of kindergarten they are not outsiders to the world of schoolwork.

It was obvious to me then, in 1968, that Head Start was absolutely a benefit to these children. Forty years of longitudinal research, matched controlled studies, and trained anthropological observation offers scientific proof for those who require it. Poor children who get quality early-childhood education are more likely to stay in school, become employed, go to college, stay out of the criminal justice system, avoid drug addiction, stay off public assistance, and pass on benefits of their education to their own children. There is hardly a social problem you could name that we could not impact through high-quality early-childhood education.

It works and we do not do it. Instead, the president's men offer vouchers. The "good" private schools in DC, the ones for children whose parents hire consultants to negotiate the admissions process, cost well over $20,000 a year. This is the kind of school George Bush himself went to. The vouchers that Bush and others are talking about are not going to pay that kind of tuition. At best they offer a couple of thousand dollars to use at predominantly religious schools that do not have the huge endowments and hand-picked student bodies and stunning physical plant of the preparatory schools. So far, we have spent more on television advertisements touting vouchers as the considered choice of concerned Black parents than we have spent training teachers to meet the challenge of urban education.

I focus on choice and privatization in education not only because they are the smokescreen covering the actual choice to abandon the dream of decent public education for all, but because they are part of a deep ideological shift from a democratic theory of the public good to a theory of individual self-maximization as the only public good. This ideological shift characterizes the transition from my parents' generation to my children's generation. We were once a nation in which no one needed to make the case for public education. From Jefferson to Dewey, the link between a free, democratic society and free, high-quality public education gained common acceptance. You see it in our state constitutions, our land grant colleges, and even the recent phenomenon of "find your classmates on the internet." The public school was our commons, where the classes and the masses with their wide distribution of talents meet.

Jefferson, our founding scientist, believed that talents were randomly and equally distributed among the classes. If we did not educate the masses, we would fail to find the budding Jeffersons among the yeoman farmers. This new nation, built on ability, not caste, would ferret out every last bit of genius by providing basic education for all, and thus it would triumph over the moldy old dynasties that allowed inheritance to stand for more than talent. Jefferson himself was aware of the massive contradiction of slavery in light of his theories, and he left that legacy to haunt us to this day, but he also supported a complete estate tax. Each generation should build personal wealth anew, so that no lazy bum could benefit from having a rich parent. Have you noticed which modern presidents oppose Jefferson's view on estate taxes?

This new matched set of vouchers and cutting the estate tax is no accident. Instead of education for all and an equal starting line, we are offered tax cuts for the rich, and public school budget cuts in exchange for the market. You get what education you can scramble for in this marketplace of choices, and if you end up a loser, it is the result of your own poor choices.

How did this happen? How did we go from a nation of the New Deal, of the G.I. Bill, of deep-seated commitments to quality, free, government-provided education for all, to a nation in which turning elementary education over to for-profit corporations is seriously discussed; in which it is not a mark of shame to push your child to the head of the private school admissions line with high-priced consultants?

It is a story both simple and complicated. One of the complicating facts is that we have not given up on public education. Most Americans will still tell the pollsters that they support public education and that they will even pay higher taxes if it would mean better schools. In the most privileged suburbs, there are excellent public schools to which connoisseur parents flock. At my neighborhood urban public school, they run out of the trucked-in premade pizzas and the last kids in line eat leftover cold cereal from the free breakfast program. At public schools in Palo Alto, the children choose between sushi, mesclun mix salad, and fresh-baked pizza. My friends and relatives in the less privileged heartland, in places like Green River, Wyoming, and Cedar Rapids, Iowa, still expect that they and everyone they know will send their children to public schools and these public schools will prepare their children for a college education. It is not just Silicon Valley moguls who hold on to this sense of entitlement to a quality public education. In many parts of the United States, it is still the mainstream expectation.

We are selective about the places in which public education is endangered. The proposals for privatization, for giving up on the notion that local school boards and professional administrators, and teachers unions and PTAs, could work together for the good of children, are coming from our urban areas, riding the wake left by the exodus called white flight. Broken cities equal broken schools. That is what happened to public education. I asked one experienced civic leader in Newark what we could do to reform public education, and he said, "Close all the schools, fire all the teachers, and start from scratch." I understand this view. I have seen examples of both incompetence and disregard of children in the public schools I have known, including the ones I attended as a child. I understand why, when the worst is allowed to become the norm, good people refuse to stand by and watch, and cast a death wish over the whole enterprise of warehousing children and preordaining their failure. I, too, have shared the impulse. Let's just close them down and start from zero.

This legitimate anger is hijacked by the choice rhetoric. We are told to let the market ordain which schools will survive. Choice means the lousy schools will fade away because no one will go there. With a $2,000 voucher or a roving pass to choose among public and charter schools, parents will find what is best for their children.

A lot is presumed here: that the better schools will in fact step forward to accept these children, that parents will have the information and wherewithal to shop among them, that a system of transportation exists for the thousands of children crisscrossing the city in every direction choice leads them, and that parents and children will consider a change of school a cost-free move. This last one is the deal-breaker for many who know the actual life of children. They do not like change of any kind. They hold a physical sense of belonging to place much deeper in their hearts than adults do, and a change of school is a threat to the sense of well-being and mastery that it is one of the tasks of childhood to achieve.

This is not to say that parents would not change schools in a heartbeat. If the better school across town did materialize, many would find the way to go there. Choice, however, does not guarantee that the better schools will appear.

Many private schools succeed because of selective admissions. The elite handpick the students guaranteed to succeed, and the less elite carefully weed out the unmotivated, the behavioral troublemakers, the children other parents see as a threat to their own. In fact, this is what many of these schools openly market. Some voucher programs are designed to require schools to take all comers, but this requirement takes away the major lever many private schools have used to deliver better results.

It is not my intent here to make the full case against privatization. That is a strong case, well made elsewhere. Suffice to say that no right-wing education proposal offers poor children a voucher sufficient to send them to George Bush's high school, nor does any require that elite schools accept, as a condition of continuing tax exempt status, a number of poor and disabled children that will put them on parity with public schools.

What I do want to do is acknowledge the enticement of the choice model. If only poor parents could do what wealthy parents do, opt out of schools with decaying infrastructure and burnt-out teachers. We do not have the time to wait for the utopian city on the hill in which there are no high-poverty failing schools because there is no poverty.

In the meantime, what do we tell desperate parents?

One of the reasons we never carried out the full promise of Head Start was that in its best incarnation, it was a community change agent. While it taught poor children numbers and opposites, it taught parents budgets and strategies of empowerment. The opposite of a rat-infested cold-water flat is getting together with ten thousand other mothers on welfare and registering to vote. My mother was a Head Start training officer, and she believed that to teach a child, you teach the whole family, and to teach a whole family, you start from the premise of their worth and their power as social and political agents. When people who thought this way became the rear guard of the war on poverty, the powers that be declared the war over.

A vague myth covers up this story of the real reason we gave up on the Great Society. The myth, which many young people I talk to have internalized, is that we tried to help the poor through social programs, which generated inefficient bureaucracies and perpetuated a culture of dependency, which keeps people poor. This is a lie. We abandoned the war on poverty because of fear that it would work. That the poor would see that their poverty is not inevitable and that they would demand, as elites in this country have feared they would since the very beginning, that the state work actively to eradicate wealth inequality.

I would tell desperate parents this: if your child cannot get a decent education in your public school, find other parents like you and know that you have the power to require redress, whether it is school reassignment or school transformation—which good school superintendents know how to do—or firing a bad teacher. Human-made systems respond to social and political pressure and they decay in the absence of the same. That is how it goes. It is called politics and we have forgotten how to work it.

Here is where the public loops back to the private. Public schools are something we have created and something we own, socially and politically, as a human mutual aid society constitutive of our collective life chances. Allowing the private opting out by the privileged disregards this common good.

A hip, liberal couple moves into the city, refurbishing a neglected Victorian in what the realtors call a transition neighborhood. The galleries and the coffee bars follow them and they enjoy the life of urban pioneers. Then they have a baby and the drug sellers on the corner go from prop indicative of edgy lifestyle to sinister threat. The urban pioneers have heard enough about the lousy local school. They skip the open house and start looking for a place in the suburbs when their baby turns four years old.

Across town, a Black mother on the gold coast reads the literature on Black male academic underachievement. Gathering up the fierce spirit of her enslaved foremothers, she determines that her son is nobody's statistic. Her white hippie neighbors might conduct socially conscious experiments by sending their children to the local public school, but she cannot take that risk with her son. In her experience, Black children don't get second chances, much less a third and a fourth. She has one shot to get the best education she can for her child, now. She gets a friend of a friend who knows the admissions director at the fanciest private school in town to write a letter, and she takes out a second mortgage to cover the first three years' tuition.

When I told the realtor I did not want a house in an all-white neighborhood, she said, "I can't steer, it's against the law." Realtors regularly and eagerly steer by school district. One number in a zip code, or one side of the street versus another, dictates wild fluctuations in price depending on whether the address provides access to the good school. We assume parents will school shop. It is our charge—we guardians of those little tyrants who want everything from us and can provide next to nothing for themselves— to make decisions that will bring them a good life. Thus, the educated, mostly white, and exclusively well-off parents cross to the better side of the street where the houses cost several hundred thousand dollars more, and their children fulfill the realtor's promise by performing well on standardized tests, because, of course, their parents did before them. Each of us acts for our own children and none dares call it segregation.

How can I judge? I, while confessing nothing, feel intimate connection with the one who started a fetal health maximization regime before conception, who researched adoption strategies through transcontinental phone calls, who starts and ends each day not with a prayer, but a strategy session for child betterment. How can I do best for them, best by them, keep them safe in an unsafe world, keep them free from anxiety when my own is mounting, appreciate each moment in their precious lives while I feel the crushing fatigue of working and parenting bearing down like a boulder, and was the homework checked, and what is on the agenda for tomorrow and the next day in their lives of enrichment, regular physical exercise, and learning?

Good parents, particularly those with education and enough leisure to contemplate child betterment as a discrete task of life, spend a good deal of time talking about their children, planning for their children, thinking about what is best for their children. Our culture supports this at every turn: read the magazines on the rack at the gynecologist's office, the notes sent home from school, the advice columnists in the newspaper. During the sniper attacks in DC, I received a letter from the school advising me to be honest with my children about my fears while avoiding transmission of anxiety and reassuring them about their safety. This is the Zen kōan that is modern American childrearing advice, and parents sit there with legs crossed considering how to answer the unanswerable, how to do the impossible, all for the good of the children.

Those children who do not have a full-time child advocate, child development researcher, kōan contemplator, school district boundary watcher, and school information radar receiver known as the educated and involved parent at their disposal, will, of course, not have the ideal outcome. Why are we all working so hard unless we know this is true?

No criticism is intended of the age-old, evolutionarily determined predilection of each of us to seek out the best food for our offspring. The criticism is of the false corollary that the consequences of our aggressive foraging, the children we leave behind, are not also ours.

I went to a doctor who went to my public high school. Like many of my classmates, he sends his children to a private school. Public school was good enough for us, I prodded. Look, you're a doctor. I'm a lawyer. We did okay. "It's not the same today, you don't understand," he said. "Look, he said, my nephew is in public school. There are thirty kids in his class. The teacher spends most of her time on three kids who have behavior problems. How is my nephew going to learn anything? The good kids get shortchanged. I'm not going to let that happen to my kids."

I didn't say the next line, which would be a terrible breach of etiquette: "But you will let it happen to someone else's child."

So, you can find a corner of this troubled world in which your child can learn unfettered by interference from what used to be called the slow kids. But you cannot make all those you leave behind go away. They still live with your children, in the same city, and if they do not learn, if they do not become the best citizen they can become, will there be no cost to your own precious ones in the world you bequeath to them?

This is not a rhetorical question; it is so real I can hardly bear to ask it. How do we keep our children safe and warm in a nation in which there is no ethos of responsibility for the other? The prayers of protection my mother-in-law sends out, I wrap like a blanket around my loved ones in spite of my disbelief that prayer could shelter them from the harm of human free will run amok in this world of somebody else's child. The carjacker, the sniper, the mugger at the ATM, the prisons bursting at the seams, the guns that angry men have seemingly endless access to, the jobless, the undocumented, the forgotten people with AIDS, the collapse of the health care system, the disappearing pensions, the bitterness growing in pockets of my dear city where rage burns as prelude to larger burning. I have seen cities of have and have-not in other countries, where rolls of razor wire line the high walls of the nice houses. Your good zip code will not protect you when it all blows at the seams.

Then there is the simple cost of each life diminished by the absence of quality education. The books left unread, the potential left unreached. Thomas Jefferson had a master plan of a good basic education for all and a classical education beyond that for the most talented. He founded a university as part of that plan. He imagined and predicted the good Abe Lincoln, the child of humble origins who, given a basic education, could rise with no limits. After Lincoln, the dream took hold in a brief and shining moment of reconstruction for the Freedmen. W.E.B. Du Bois described the heady rush to learning. Have you learned to read yet? Crowds gathered on corners as the one literate, emancipated person held forth for the eager others. Grabbing education on the street, hungry for it, determined to hold its liberating power.

A man aptly named Moses carries the dream, still, that poor Black children will find liberation through algebra. He has a system he has proven works, involving trips on subway trains: one stop forward, three stops backward, learning through the physicality of movement in space the concept of numbers going forward and backward, positive and negative, responsive to your manipulation just as you can choose to get off or get on the train. If children are not learning, Moses says, it is because we do not want them to. Here is the way:

I believe many trains lead to education. Although I sing the praises of Bob Moses's algebra project, the method is less important than the belief that all children can learn, and the provision of active, engaged, well-educated, and intelligent teachers who have not yet given up, not yet been acculturated into accepting the failure of even one child.

That is what "no child left behind" would really look like. Not a battery of tests, but a commitment to treat teachers as professionals so we can demand professionalism from them. Pay them what we pay lawyers. Their job is more important. Fire the bad ones and give the good ones raises.

What has happened under the larger privatization model is that the parents with the political clout to re-envision public education have retreated to better school districts, where they can extract a passable if unimaginative education for their children. Not a lot different, in the unimaginative department, from your fancy prep schools, I might add.

We are left with failing schools in poor neighborhoods, and here is another secret: it is supposed to be that way. It serves ideological interests that run deep. Jefferson believed a talented few reside in every class, but he also believed there were very few. The vast majority is ordinary and uninspired in their talents, and they end up with mediocre lives and status because that is their just place in the stasis.

I live in Walt Whitman's America, not Jefferson's. Langston Hughes's America, not Booker T.'s. I see an endless pool of human talent, glory, and intelligence still tightly bound up by the old order, still unfree. The problem of the twenty-first century is the education line. We see education as a good for sale in a market, divided in market segments, bad, okay, better, best, whatever you can bargain for. This presumes a majority of citizens left behind in the education game, a presumption under which we all lose.

Somos el barco. We are all in this together. When the *Washington Post* editorial page supports cuts to the DC public school budget, one has to ask how the elites in this city, whose fate is tied to public education by the strings of their purses, can oppose improving education. They own the property languishing as speculation parking lots, waiting for the boom that will come only when people start moving into the city instead of out. Why don't they want the good schools that are a prerequisite to bringing the big money back into the city? Why would they act against apparent self-interest? What about Derrick Bell's famous formula: when white self-interest coincides with Black liberation, then Black liberation, in this case saving DC public schools, ought to win.

Someone needs to see urban public schools fail. These schools are now, typically, Black schools: Black students, with Black teachers, Black school administrators, Black mayors, Black school board members presiding over the burnt-out, defunded, strip-mined wreck that comprises urban public schools. The demographics may not match up as perfectly Black, although in DC it comes pretty close. I am speaking of Black as a reading of urban, encompassing brown and yellow as it does in California, as the code by which urban becomes "not us," and becomes constitutive of us as superior. Someone needs to believe Black schools will fail in order to maintain a belief system that means more to them than their money. I have now said three taboo things.

Here, Derrick Bell's interest convergence theory meets Charles Lawrence's unconscious racism. Nobody thinks they want public schools to fail, nobody acknowledges that when they say urban they see Black, or that Black does not equal educated, competent, and in charge. It is all happening at a level of consciousness inaccessible even to the players themselves.

Look for the racial code in statements like "We can't just throw money at this problem" and "The problem is waste, not lack of funds." Who is running the schools accused of waste and inefficiency? Warrior-scholars like Charles Lawrence and Roger Wilkins sit on the DC school board. They see schools as today's civil rights movement. They are not about wasting a single dime that could go to buy a book for a child. Neither is the technocrat mayor with a soft spot for children, Anthony Williams. Neither is the hard-working and nationally recognized superintendent of schools, Paul Vance. These are Black men, picking up the pieces of something that was deliberately broken, trying to put it back with prayer and Band-Aids and working around the clock, with half the budget they need to do it right. The presumption that they will fail, and the *Washington Post*'s support of school funding cuts that seal that presumption of failure, is racist. Not in the way of Jim Crow, but in the way of individual choice. The barriers to advancement are gone, and those who do not make it are the ones we always knew were inferior. Too bad; we never wanted it to turn out that way.

Go look at these schools. See the slime growing in what was once a swimming pool, the painted-over windows, the children studying in parkas and mittens on the days the furnace won't turn up, the children yawning and sweating until their clothes are soaked on the days the furnace won't turn down. Take a picture of the rat carcass in the cafeteria. If you live in a city, go and be a witness, and holler outrage because someone else who sees it every day has given up hollering. A $2,000 voucher and an army of nuns could not solve this problem, and George Bush is either lying or immensely ignorant if he tells you otherwise.

We need a New Deal for schools: rebuild the decaying buildings. The old ones are quite beautiful, neoclassical buildings constructed in a time when we believed learners were the royalty of the public sphere. Send our best and brightest in as teachers and inculcate them in the spirit of W.E.B. Du Bois: to know that a hunger for learning has always burned among the outcast.

In classes on various forms of subordination I have asked students what their utopian vision is. They do not believe this is a sincere question. They have spent most of their learning time thinking about what is wrong and have little practice in imagining the ideal. Eleven years ago, a student suggested a modest thing that has stayed with me. "I'd like teachers to live in the neighborhood where they teach," he said.

I try to teach the stretch. "Yes," I said, "and let's buy the house for the teacher so it will happen, and have the teachers send their children to the school where they teach." The students caught on to the exercise and added a house for the police officer and the social workers and the letter carriers and all the people that make up Mr. Rogers's neighborhood. Let their children go to the neighborhood school. That is how accountability and community are forged. Let's have mental health services in the schools, someplace to go for children or adults who are sad, angry, anxious, unable to cope, and doctors and lawyers. Why not? Sports teams and music and dance, for adults and children, so the schools become a center of community life, where all are welcome and all feel ownership. Let the whole community celebrate the accomplishments of students. Fly a big flag saying Takisha counted to one thousand! Put it on a marquee: Ms. Crockett's class read one hundred books this month! Bring in every generation to help with tutoring and nurturing of children. Have them eat lunch at circular tables. And so on and so forth.

Any group of people who have lived through schooling can think of better ways to do it. There are smart, perceptive teachers and teachers of teachers who have devoted their lives to assessing what works to educate children. Prototypes exist for the community school model my students began to imagine. These are not unknowns. They are fruit we have chosen not to pick.

The last taboo thing is to call it evil. The deliberate choice to let the urban schools fail, and the offering up of the bogus solution of shuffling voucher-bearing students around like peas in a shell game, all the while refusing to bring serious money to the table for education, is child abuse. It is an unnatural wrong of the highest order, one that makes us barely human to the extent we tolerate it. There are a hundred ways to try to make it on your own. We have become unknowing survivalists when it comes to education. Families who would not try to render their own tallow or card their own wool are taking education on as a personal problem with individual solutions. Bless them to the extent they succeed for their children, but call them back to the table for the job yet undone, for their own children's sake.

Dewey said no democracy can flourish if the people are not educated enough to exercise self-governance. He would have an erudite and wordy way of saying, "I told you so," if he could see current voter turnout rates.

October 2002 in DC was marked by the biggest anti-war demonstrations since the Vietnam era. I stood with my fellow citizens and read their signs: Money for Schools Not for Bombs; Not in My Name; and Where's My Pension are a few I remember and note here to help counteract the peace information blackout of the *New York Times*. I also recall these signs to make the connection between peace and social justice issues, including education. We live in a world at war, a world in which human agency is used to rip apart bodies. A professor in Israel sent a polite email of concern to me in DC at the height of our sniper crisis, and I did not even have time to form the words to respond with the humility I felt before the news flashed of another bombing on the road leading into his city. Dewey's basic law, which he laid down as a logic problem rather than a moral imperative, is that people must learn to think, to evaluate information, to question their leaders, to demand good results, if good results are what we want.

The result I want is a peaceful world for all children. I want to promise my own that no boogeyman, whether war, or terrorism, or economic collapse, will get them. It is a promise we parents cannot keep until we declare, believe, and act as though every child is our own. Human beings are linked, and they can impose terrible harm upon one another. Teach every child, feed every child, shelter every child, embrace every child in the love human beings are entitled to, and then will come peace at last.

8

From the West to the Rest: Interest Convergence in California Racial Politics

CHERYL I. HARRIS

2003

Cheryl I. Harris is the Rosalinde and Arthur Gilbert Foundation Chair in Civil Rights and Civil Liberties at UCLA School of Law. She is a graduate of Wellesley College and Northwestern University Pritzker School of Law. Since joining the UCLA law faculty in 1998, Professor Harris has continued to produce groundbreaking scholarship in the field of Critical Race Theory, particularly engaging the issue of how racial frames shape our understanding and interpretation of significant events. Professor Harris has served as a consultant to the MacArthur Foundation and has been on the board of leading academic societies, including the American Studies Association.

This year—2003—saw the declaration of war and the purported opening of another front in the war on terrorism. The particular target this year—although at least by the current administration's lights there is a never-ending list—is Iraq. This war is being fought by an army whose foot soldiers are disproportionately black and brown, under the leadership of a command team that is at least photogenically diverse.

President Bush, chosen by the Supreme Court after a highly racially polarized election, has now appointed two blacks, Condoleezza Rice and
Colin Powell, to positions of power in his administration; equal opportunity has now come to the White House. Condoleezza has become the leading cheerleader for a failing occupation in Iraq, and Colin has been given
the unenviable task of trying to sell this agenda to and/or buy support from
an increasingly skeptical international community that seems less and less
willing to underwrite this administration's call for endless war.

Meanwhile, the Republican Party exhorts the recalcitrant black masses
to abandon their faith in Democrats and come and join the trickle-down
party. Out front, Republicans deploy Spanish-speaking operatives at every
available opportunity to demonstrate racial inclusivity. By and large, Democrats are trying to locate their voice and reclaim a working-class (read:
white) constituency.

The year has also brought the issue of affirmative action directly back
into the national spotlight. While affirmative action has been a wellspring
of contention for several decades, the most significant cases concerning the
appropriate use of race in the admissions process, *Grutter* and *Gratz* against
the University of Michigan, came before the Supreme Court this year and
were resolved in a way that preserved the possibility of race-conscious affirmative action, albeit through a split decision.

In California, Proposition 54, the so-called Racial Privacy Initiative,
sought to ban state government from "classifying any individual by race,
ethnicity, color, or national origin in the operation of public education,
contracting, or public employment." This initiative was the brainchild of
Ward Connerly, the (black) face of Proposition 209, which, in 1996,
amended the California state constitution to "ban any preference based on
race or gender in the award of contracts and hiring or in admissions decisions." After essentially wrecking the admissions policies at all the state's
major universities and throwing the situation back into something approx-
imating the early 1950s, with one or two blacks enrolling in classes at the
state's most selective graduate schools, Ward decided there was more work
to do. So, he argued, since the California constitution now forbids state

government from "discriminating against or granting preferential treatment to any citizen on the basis of race," the government has no reason to classify persons by race. Why should it even ask us for this data? According to Connerly's website, "like religion, marital status, or sexual orientation, race should become a private matter that is no business of the government's. Think of how refreshing it would be to throw out the entire system of checking little boxes." Essentially his position is "Let's eliminate racism by eliminating the idea of race."

Initially, polls showed that the measure enjoyed considerable support, with approximately 50 percent of the electorate in California in favor. Yet two months later, at the October special election, it was resoundingly defeated. Some good news.

Meanwhile, some eight months after the reelection of Democrat Gray Davis as governor of the state of California, the campaign to recall him began. Initially funded by a conservative and somewhat obscure politician named Darrell Issa, the drive for the recall took off, and 135 people, including the actor Gary Coleman, filed to run for the governor's office. I'm not making this up.

The end result was that, less than a year after Davis took office, he was removed in a special recall election and Arnold Schwarzenegger was elected as governor of the state. It's hard for me to even say that. I'm practicing, I'm recovering, I'm going through the step program here.

In September, prior to his defeat, Davis signed a state law allowing undocumented immigrants to obtain state driver's licenses. Now, barely a month after the recall election, there is a drive to repeal that bill.

How have we come to this pass, and what does this all mean? What does the recall of Davis and the election of the Terminator mean? What explains the resounding defeat of Proposition 54 after its initial strong showing and its claim to implement color blindness, a pitch that had won over the voters once before? What is the meaning of the controversy over the awarding of driver's licenses to undocumented immigrants? What does this have to do with affirmative action and the decisions in the *Grutter* and *Gratz*

cases? How and in what ways are any of these far-flung and somewhat diz-
zying events connected?

In trying to gain some purchase on the current situation, I begin, as always,
with Derrick Bell. Even as many of us who study race have found Derrick's
work provocative, lucid, dead-on right, or sometimes worrisome, maddening,
or contradictory, it is always foundational. My article "Whiteness as Property"
began when I was trying to teach constitutional law and read the entire opinion in *Plessy v. Ferguson* for the first time—not just that segment that they put
in the case book—and found out that Homer Plessy had advanced another
argument besides the equal protection claim. Plessy was phenotypically a
white man, which is to say in common parlance, he "looked white." His lawyer
made the claim that by allowing the train conductor to assign Plessy to the car
reserved for blacks, the railroad company arbitrarily denied his property interest in being regarded as white. I used that argument as the basis of a presentation that I made at a 1991 Conference on Constitution-Making in South
Africa to try to explain the very vexed nature of affirmative action jurisprudence in the United States. As I further researched *Plessy*, I came to learn
that Derrick Bell, as always, had lighted the way, and in a previous article had
specifically talked about this property interest in whiteness.

I now want to offer a particular reading of Bell that I hope will shed some
light on what may seem to be these wide-ranging events and perhaps even
wildly variant set of outcomes connecting Gray Davis's recall to the Supreme Court's decision in *Grutter*, the driver's license bill to affirmative
action in higher education, the election of Schwarzenegger (God help us)
to *Gratz*. I want to suggest that one way to process and understand these
seemingly far-flung events is through the lens of interest convergence. I
want to consider interest convergence as both an explanatory and a pre-
scriptive model—an analytic framework for unpacking the complex racial
politics of our times, and, on a provisional reading, a kind of political com-
pass for navigating this terrain.

The basic thesis of interest convergence is that racial justice occurs only
when the interests of racially oppressed groups converge with the interests

of whites. In his classic essay, "*Brown vs. Board of Education* and the Interest Convergence Dilemma," Bell contends that, while *Brown* is legitimately seen as a case of major import, it was not simply a result of a change in the U.S. racial gestalt. Bell argues that *Brown* is better understood as a story in which the demands for racial equality were accommodated because they converged with the interest of dominant white elites. Ending de jure segregation had become such an interest because the country's racial policies had become a liability in the foreign policy arena where there was fierce competition between the United States and the Soviet Union for influence in the emerging nations of Africa and Asia.

In addition, returning black servicemen, confronted by racist violence and discrimination, were a potentially incendiary social force that had to be both confronted and, in some ways, accommodated. Having fought for the nation, these black veterans found the long-standing pattern of de jure segregation to be an unacceptable denial of the basic rights for which many black soldiers had lost their lives.

The economic imperative was also salient. Industrialization and development of the American South was undermined by de jure segregation even under conditions where separate was anything but equal. Thus Bell argued, "translated from judicial activity in cases both before and after Brown, this principle of 'interest convergence' provides: The interest of blacks in achieving racial equality will be accommodated only when it converges with the interest of whites. . . . Racial remedies may instead be the outward manifestation of unspoken and perhaps subconscious judicial conclusions that the remedies, if granted, will secure, advance, or at least not harm societal interests deemed important by middle- and upper-class whites. Racial justice—or at least its appearance—may from time to time, be counted among the interests deemed important by the courts and by society's policymakers." According to Bell, once these interests cease to be compelling, in the absence of new convergences, the impetus needed to sustain effective change wanes. *Brown's* rejection of de jure segregation provided legal impetus for a major shift in U.S. race relations and for the emergence of transformative social movements. Yet we are now faced with the near irrelevance of *Brown* and the post–de jure landscape in which most primary and secondary schools are as segregated as before. Some data even suggest that patterns of segregation in the South may be more stark than prior to *Brown*. Interest convergence explains why gains such as *Brown* are often partial, transitory, and difficult to sustain. Victory and defeat are often played out in the context of shifting perceptions of interest. As an explanatory model, interest convergence locates the constraints of racial power in shaping the terrain within which the contestations for racial justice occur.

At another level, Bell's model can be read prescriptively, pointing toward the critical role of mobilizing whites' self-interest as a necessary predicate for meaningful racial justice. At the same time, however, interest convergence points to how perceptions of interest will themselves be highly racialized. The deeply embedded structure of white privilege results in material differences in how different racial groups will perceive and define their self-interest. This insight resounds with the classic notion of the "wages of whiteness" described by W.E.B. Du Bois, in *Black Reconstruction*, as the way that "even when whites received a low wage, [they were] compensated by a sort of public and psychological wage." Thus the perception of and mobilization of racially subordinated groups and whites around common interests have to confront the difference that race makes in terms of assessing interests.

Let me offer a provisional reading of today's racial geography as mapped by interest convergence. I begin with what I consider to be the more obvious case of the decisions in *Grutter* and *Gratz*. In a split decision, the Court held that the narrowly tailored use of race in admissions to further a compelling governmental interest in securing the educational benefits that flow from diversity is not prohibited by the Equal Protection Clause. The admissions policy at the University of Michigan Law School passed this test as a permissible consideration of race as a plus, while the university's undergraduate admissions program, which extended consideration of race, as well as a range of other factors, by assigning points for each criteria—including economic disadvantage, child of alumni, Advanced Placement credits, and so forth—was struck down. If the distinction between these two policies seems to be obscure, that's because it is.

Nonetheless, I think the distinction that the Court attempts to draw between what is permissible under *Grutter* and what is not permissible under *Gratz* marks a significant constraint—a way in which, even as remediation is allowed, it is limited—a central insight of interest convergence. At one level, even the split decision represents a remarkable victory, given the context out of which the case arose. But below the surface, I want to apply an interest convergence lens to *Grutter*, beginning with situating the case historically and politically.

I think that *Grutter* can actually be seen as part of an ongoing conservative assault on affirmative action that began thirty years ago, nearly simultaneous with the implementation of affirmation action. From the outset, the claim has been that, even though affirmation action was only a partial remedy for the centuries-old system of racial subordination, it imposed untenable burdens on innocent white victims. In inverting the trajectory of harm and claiming racial injuries, the initial plaintiffs in the early so-called reverse discrimination suits were white men like Allan Bakke. Bakke's age—thirty-seven at the time he applied to medical school—and his solid but not outstanding record marked him as a less-than-overwhelming candidate at ten schools that had rejected him. But because UC-Davis as a state school implemented a limited form of affirmative action, setting aside sixteen out of one hundred seats for disadvantaged students, Bakke argued that race—specifically his race, white—was the reason for his rejection.

In essence, Bakke's assertion that because his MCAT scores and undergrad GPAs exceeded the average scores of sixteen students admitted through the program, he had been denied equal protection of the law and invited the Court to constitutionalize a mathematical representation of merit. The Court, in a highly splintered decision, 4-1-4, largely agreed; it concluded that Bakke should be admitted, and that he had in fact suffered a constitutional injury, this despite the fact that he never proved—and indeed it is likely that he could not have proven—that race was the reason for his exclusion. As a recent article by Goodwin Liu, "Causation Fallacy:

Bakke and the Basic Arithmetic of Selective Admissions," explains, lawsuits like *Bakke* rest on an illogical premise. Simply because some students of color were admitted with lower test scores and GPAs does not mean that Bakke would have been admitted had there been no affirmative action plan. Indeed, there were whites with lower test scores and GPAs who were admitted while Allan Bakke was not. That does not mean that Bakke was more white than the whites who were admitted. It simply points to the fact that test scores and grades, while highly significant, are not always outcome-determinative.

As it turns out, the *Bakke* case did not simply reveal the splits and contradictions between the judges; it also disclosed splits and contradictions within the reasoning of each individual opinion itself. Principal among these was the opinion of Justice Powell, the swing vote. Justice Powell's opinion rejected all rationales to justify affirmative action. He rejected the idea that affirmative action could be justified on the grounds of remediating societal discrimination. He rejected it on the grounds that it could be designed to reduce the deficit of minority doctors. He rejected it on the grounds that it would increase the number of doctors who would serve communities that were currently underserved. The only interest that he accepted was the university's First Amendment right to promote a robust exchange of ideas through the creation of a diverse class. Race could then be considered, said Powell, but only as one of several "diversity factors." In this sense, race could function as a plus, like coming from a rural environment or playing the cello. I didn't make that up either; that's in the opinion.

Normatively and doctrinally, however, Powell's opinion marked out the ideological landscape for the next several decades, asserting that because the notion of a "dominant white majority"—and in Powell's opinion he does put that phrase in scare quotes—was illusory, the same doctrinal analysis should be applied to efforts to ameliorate racial inequality as was applied to efforts to instantiate it. Powell's articulation of the justification for this nineteenth-century-inspired racial formalism was as influential as his argument justifying diversity (if not more so). So at the same time that Powell affirmed diversity as an interest, he also laid the groundwork for applying strict scrutiny to all forms of race-conscious remediation as though it were de jure segregation.

Indeed, Powell's critique of affirmative action and his tentative justification for it became the schizophrenic space that framed the dominant understanding of affirmative action. Major universities and corporations came to inhabit and naturalize this tension between, on the one hand, a regime of strict scrutiny, treating race as conceptually aberrant, exceptional, and a potentially poisonous albeit irrelevant trait, and on the other hand, treating race as a legitimate aspect of culture and experience such that it could, in certain limited circumstances, be treated as a plus. We sort of lived with that contradiction under Powell's opinion in *Bakke* and tried to make the best of it.

The image of Bakke as the wronged white male was certainly emblematic of this transitional period in which gains in addressing racial inequality were translated as the direct and immediate threat to the welfare of whites, and in particular the white working class, in a relentless zero-sum game. In the wake of *Bakke* and the modest compromise that it struck, increasing numbers of students of color were admitted into higher education and to elite institutions in particular, at the same time other indicia of racial inequality increased. In one sense, one might say that, with respect to communities of color, this dichotomy of increasing progress and increasing inequality reflected the tension in *Bakke* itself. To the extent that race is seen as irrelevant, so too is extant inequality, which is neither seen nor addressed; to the extent that race is seen as salient, some modest gains can then be achieved.

The plaintiffs in most of the high-profile cases challenging affirmative action echoed Bakke's indictment that the policies elevated race over merit. While the Supreme Court did not specifically consider a case involving undergraduate or graduate admissions after *Bakke* up until *Grutter*, sufficient signals came from the Court to indicate that it was inclined to agree with Bakke's view. The most important indications came in the case of *Croson v. City of Richmond* (1989) and *Adarand v. Peña* (1995), both of which consolidated the analytical framework under which affirmative action could be eliminated. While Powell's had been the single opinion in *Bakke* applying strict scrutiny, by the time we got to *Croson* a majority of the Court affirms that strict scrutiny is the appropriate standard to review a remedy for racial inequality.

Adarand v. Peña continued the trend, confirming that, notwithstanding the many denials that strict scrutiny review was "strict in theory and fatal in fact," the standard consistently operated to defeat affirmative action. No interest, not even the federal government's constitutional mandate under the Fourteenth Amendment to enact legislation carrying out the promise of equal protection, could override the Court's solicitous concern for the rights of innocent whites. In *Adarand* the Court invoked notions of "consistency" and "congruence" (a kind of weird alliteration) to argue that because affirmative action, like de jure segregation, considered race, both should be subjected to the same constitutional standard—strict scrutiny. The Court argued basically what's good for the goose is good for the gander, and declared the federal government's affirmative action requirements in contracting unconstitutional. This amounted to the imposition of a fictive symmetry, what Justice Stevens in his dissent announced as a false equivalence between a "no trespassing sign and a welcome mat."

In the early 1990s, the face of a white victim took a gendered turn. Reflecting a more sophisticated strategy, the legal arm of the organized right, including the Center for Individual Rights, launched a series of assaults on affirmative action in which white women were enlisted as plaintiffs. Ironically, this strategy occurred after the Supreme Court had adopted a different and more lenient standard to review gender-based affirmative action, and in fact approved such programs. So, just as the Court said gender-based affirmative action is to be measured under a different standard, and it's okay, now we have this recruitment of white women to become plaintiffs in lawsuits against race-conscious affirmative action. These lawsuits also occurred after more than twenty years of affirmative action in higher education had reaped particularly significant gains for women.

Nonetheless, Cheryl Hopwood, a white female applicant to the University of Texas law school, became the new face in the pantheon of white victims of affirmative action. Exploiting the ambivalence with which significant numbers of white women viewed affirmative action, the right saw that the way forward in its assault was to obfuscate and divide the question of race from gender. Affirmative action was then cast as a set of racialized preferences that harmed not only white men but white women, particularly single, working-class mothers who, like Cheryl Hopwood, were prevented from attaining what they had earned by unfair racial preferences.

Hopwood did not represent an isolated instance of the realignment of white women with regard to affirmative action. The rapid gains attained by white women under affirmative action programs that included race and gender obscured the importance and relevance of affirmative action policies to subsequent generations of white women who took their increased representation as a given, natural development in which gender barriers just fell away. Moreover, because in public discourse, affirmative action and merit were positioned as contradictory, the impulse among many of the beneficiaries of affirmative action to disidentify with it was heightened.

Consider the campaign to defeat Proposition 200, an anti–affirmative action provision that mimicked Proposition 209 in California and was passed in Washington State. In a wonderfully insightful article entitled "Understanding White Women's Ambivalence to Affirmative Action," Professor Sumi Cho examines the Washington campaign as reflective of an aspect of the relationship between race and gender that has been under-examined. She notes that leaders of the campaign to defeat Proposition 200 in Washington had studied the failures of the pro–affirmative action camp in California, as well as the successful strategies employed by advocates of affirmative action in Houston, where a similar city initiative to end affirmative action was defeated. The kind of truth-in-labeling strategy deployed in Houston, based on educating the electorate that the seemingly innocuous language of the ordinance was designed to eliminate affirmative action, had worked in part because Houston is a city with a majority of people of color. Since people of color form such a small part of the

CHERYL I. HARRIS103

electorate in Washington State, it was clear that a similar strategy would not work. Early on, the pro–affirmative action coalition in Washington State identified white women as a key constituency and turned its focus to stressing the ways in which the elimination of affirmative action would harm not only people of color, but the economic well-being of white women.

The campaign had a lot of money and the backing of major Washington-based corporations and yet, despite appearing to do everything right, Proposition 200 passed and affirmative action was eliminated in the state with 51 percent of white women voting to end it. This was consistent with the voting patterns in the earlier passage of Proposition 209 in California, where 58 percent of white women voted in favor of the measure and against affirmative action. Professor Cho suggests that a large part of the explanation of white women's voting patterns against affirmative action lies in the perception by white women that affirmative action that benefited people of color would injure the material interests of their own families. Anecdotal evidence in exit interviews confirmed the sense among white women that their white male relatives either had been harmed or would potentially be harmed by affirmative action. Here, the ethic of care takes on a racial dimension in the context of the white family, which is continually reproduced as white. (Notwithstanding representations of interracial marriage, it still remains the case that the vast majority of whites marry other whites.)

According to Cho, "a majority of white women voting in Washington rejected the presumed unit of analysis—the white woman as the individual in the workplace—and substituted instead the white woman in the economy and larger society." In short, the political analysts underestimated the role that race, racism, and material whiteness would play in redefining white women's individual interests through the narrative of the family. Anthropologist Karen Brodkin calls this "kinship-mediated racial loyalty."

The careful selection of Barbara Grutter and Jennifer Gratz by the well-funded legal think tanks that backed these white women's lawsuits reflects a strategy that was designed to invoke identity, here especially gender identity, against the notion of racial justice, by repositioning white women as victims rather than as beneficiaries of affirmative action and thus further undercutting the possibility of any potential alignment between white women and people of color.

Given the overall trajectory in which affirmative action had taken a beating, both in the electoral arena in California and Washington, and in the courts, despite the extraordinary investment made in defending Michigan's policies, and the tremendous mobilization, the likelihood of a favorable outcome in the *Grutter* and *Gratz* cases had appeared slim. What emerged from the decisions is a decidedly mixed bag, both far from the defeats sought by the right and far from the clear endorsement of race-based remediation sought by the defenders of Michigan's policies. On the one hand, *Grutter* determined that the law school's admissions policy was permissible; on the other hand, the school's undergraduate policy was struck down, with Justice O'Connor providing the swing vote. What the Court said specifically was that the law school's program "awards no mechanical predetermined diversity bonuses based on race or ethnicity," thus suggesting that the sin of the undergraduate admissions program was that it was being specific about the way in which race matters.

The effect of this "yes, but" outcome is that it provides a relatively narrow basis on which to protect considerations of race in admissions; it has the effect of endorsing the principle of affirmative action while permitting only the most oblique consideration of race. This reluctance to engage and confront the meaning of race that has been part and parcel of the Court's racial jurisprudence over the past decade was thus sustained in *Grutter* and *Gratz*. That being said, however, the question might be reframed not as "What didn't we get from *Grutter* and *Gratz*?" but "What explains why the Court didn't strike down the admissions policy in *Grutter* as well?" In other words, why didn't the law school's admissions policy fall by the wayside as the undergrad policy did in *Gratz*?

If, as Bell suggests, the interests of dominant whites must be implicated in order for even limited racial justice to occur, what was at stake here that tipped the balance in favor of *Grutter*? In some ways, I think that the evidence of interest convergence is lying right on the surface of the case. Indeed, it's almost a textbook case of interest convergence, reflecting how dominant interests can temporarily, at least, converge with the interest in eliminating racial injustice and produce a partial victory.

In what has to be a case of the most propitious timing, the case was argued before the Supreme Court on April 1. When I first heard that, I thought surely this can't be right, they can't actually be doing this, but yes, indeed, they did. The significance of this date is not that it celebrates the fool, but that it marks the eve of the invasion of Baghdad. Why is this significant? An important voice in the debates before the Court was that of the American military. In an amicus brief—one among the record number filed in the case—top military leaders, including General Stormin' Norman Schwarzkopf, Wesley Clark, and other high-ranking leaders in all of the branches of the armed forces argued, "a highly qualified racially diverse Officer Corps, educated and trained to command the nation's racially diverse enlisted ranks, is essential to the military's ability to fulfill its principal mission to provide national security." The brief is strikingly candid, asserting that in an army that is almost 40 percent people of color, 21 percent black, and almost 10 percent Latino/Latina, having an overwhelmingly white officer corps compromises the military mission and is a danger to national security. In the absence of using affirmative action to recruit and educate minority officers into the ROTC and the military academies, the brief argued, the military would not be able to attain a racially diverse officer corps.

Now, why does the military conclude that a racially diverse officer corps is essential to carrying out its mission and protecting national security? In a word: Vietnam. The brief states as follows:

The military learned the importance of racial diversity in its leadership the hard way. After President Truman integrated the military in 1948, the military became one of America's most integrated institutions. But through the 1960s and 1970s, minorities' presence was almost entirely in the enlisted ranks; the officer corps remained almost exclusively

white. . . . In the context of the Vietnam conflict, a nearly all-white officer corps leading enlisted ranks heavily comprised of minorities
proved to be a recipe for intense racial strife; hundreds of racial incidents and race-based violence erupted throughout the military. . . . By
the 1970s, racial tensions in the military ran so high that they actually
caused the Armed Forces to teeter "on the verge of self-destruction." . . .
Years later, the U.S. Department of Justice reported to the President in
its review of federal affirmative action programs that "[r]acial conflict
within the military during the Vietnam era was a blaring wakeup call
to the fact that equal opportunity is absolutely indispensable to unit
cohesion, and therefore critical to military effectiveness and our national security."

Now, here you have the military making this argument just as the army
is getting ready to go into Baghdad. During oral argument, it became apparent that this issue of the relationship between racial diversity and national security was of particular interest to several of the justices, including
O'Connor, who included the military's argument in the opinion she authored in *Grutter*. The interest in national security was clearly an important factor in the decision and was one that was brought home by the timing
of the case. This war, not unlike the Cold War in *Brown*, was brought to
bear in advancing limited progress toward racial justice. In one sense, then,
shoring up affirmative action has become part of a legitimation project for
the military industrial complex. Both the military and American business
are asserting that the nation's security, both economic and military, can
be compromised if the racial gap is too great. As O'Connor asserted in
Grutter, the question is one of perceived legitimacy: "In order to cultivate
a set of leaders with legitimacy in the eyes of the citizenry, it is necessary
that the path to leadership be visibly open to talented and qualified individuals of every race and ethnicity."

Of course, there's a lot that gets left out from this perspective. While
racial diversity is upheld as a value and defended on the grounds of its benefits to the security interests of the United States, other substantive bases

for the policy of affirmative action are ignored. Remedying past and present forms of discrimination and correcting the ways in which current admissions practices and forms of assessment function to reinforce inequality and limit educational opportunity are simply ruled out as part of the discussion. What *Grutter* and *Gratz* leave untouched is the presumption that current admissions practices are race neutral, when there is much evidence to suggest that they are not, either in form or effect. Indeed, in the absence of policies that consider race as an offset to exclusionary institutional practices, like standardized tests, these institutions will resegregate with respect to black and Latino students, returning to the days when Heman Sweatt, the plaintiff in the landmark case *Sweatt v. Painter*, was the one black student in the entire class.

This is not a matter of hypothetical supposition. At the UCLA law school in 1994, out of 458 black applicants to the law school, 117 were admitted, and 46 enrolled in the class. Of 653 Latino applicants, 113 were admitted, and 57 enrolled. Asian/Pacific Islander students constituted approximately 21 percent of the class, and whites 46.9 percent. This effectively meant that in that year, in 1994, no one group constituted a racial majority. There was a plurality but no majority. This was reflected in the first class that I taught at the school in 1995, where out of a class of forty students, there was no racial majority. Contrast this with the class of 1999, admitted three years after the adoption of Proposition 209. That was also the year that the school enacted an admissions policy in which economic disadvantage was explicitly taken into account. There were 234 black applicants, 19 admitted, and 2 enrolled—2 out of a class of 300. There were 437 Latino applicants, 58 admitted, and 18 enrolled. Thus, in the class there were 2 black students and 18 Latino students out of a class of 300 in the most racially diverse state, in the most populated part of that state, at a publicly funded institution, in the year 1999.

I had the unique experience in the spring of 2000 of teaching *Brown v. Board of Education* to a constitutional law class that had no black students. None. I've experienced few things more disheartening or surreal in my lifetime. In the four years since, there has been a modest and hard-fought-for improvement, with the last couple of years seeing black enrollment at around twelve or thirteen in a class, and Latino enrollment at around thirty-five or so per class. But I want to stress that staying within the constraints of Proposition 209, as well as the self-imposed constraints of LSAT medians and *U.S. News & World Report*'s ratings of law schools that relies in part on LSAT scores, has made achievement beyond this modest recovery all but impossible. As the student interveners in *Grutter* argued, what is missing in the discussion about affirmative action is the fact that desegregation is a compelling governmental interest, and, in the absence of affirmative action, what you get is the effective resegregation of higher education.

Interest convergence suggests why the Supreme Court decision both affirmed and constrained affirmative action, and why this victory is partial and is likely to be transitory and difficult to sustain. What, then, does interest convergence suggest about the politics of race and Governor Davis's recall, and the defeat of Proposition 54 (the "Racial Privacy Initiative")?

Under California law, voters get to enact law by direct vote if a sufficient percentage of the voters sign petitions to do so. In 1993 an initiative entitled Proposition 187 was placed on the ballot, calling for the exclusion of undocumented residents from medical services, from public education, and from other public services. Proposition 187 was promoted by then Republican governor Pete Wilson, and had the backing of a number of Republican celebrities, including Schwarzenegger. The campaign leading up to the vote was highly racially charged, with ads showing footage of Mexicans running across the southern border near San Diego and a voiceover that invoked tropes of invasion and siege.

Although Proposition 187 was approved, its implementation was stayed by a federal court, which ruled in part that the state could not regulate the question of immigration, as that was a matter of national policy under the control of Congress. While the law did not ever take effect, a number of lawmakers, eager to demonstrate their affinity with its sentiments, enacted measures designed to combat illegal immigration, and the legislature for the first time required proof of legal status before an applicant could obtain a California driver's license.

The whole political atmosphere in the wake of Proposition 187 remained highly charged, as anti-immigrant groups argued that the state was at risk of being overrun by Mexicans, and that it was in fact a plot by Mexicans to reclaim the ancestral Aztec homeland of Aztlán; Mexico was going to win now what it had lost in 1848. Right-wing talk show hosts such as Roger Hedgecock of San Diego, a defrocked mayor indicted for perjury and conspiracy in the 1970s—maybe that's a prerequisite for getting a radio talk show—argued that immigrants were swamping the welfare system and causing violent crime. In 1990, Hedgecock became the leading advocate for a kind of vigilantism on these issues of patrolling the borders through promoting a "light up the border" initiative in which hundreds of citizens drove to the border and pointed headlights on those immigrants seeking to cross illegally. In point of fact, the issue for many was not the issue of so-called illegal immigration, although it is estimated that there are approximately 2.3 million undocumented workers in the state. The issue that some of the more vocal groups asserted is the fear that the state is becoming non-white.

Two-thirds of adult Latinos in Los Angeles County are foreign-born, and the white population of the state is hovering just under 50 percent for the first time. Some have called this "fear of a brown planet." As one leader of a group called Voices of Citizens Together argued, "because so many of the immigrants are Spanish speakers, in order to get a job here you'd have to be bilingual. Most Americans are not. So that in order to live in their own country, you would have to learn Spanish." In his view, his argument continued, a Latino L.A. would be inherently poor, uneducated, and crime ridden.

Following on the heels of Proposition 187, the politics of race continued to foment with Ward Connerly and Proposition 209, the so-called California civil rights initiative, which passed in 1996, with its devastating effects on admissions to higher education. In 1998, California faced another initiative banning bilingual education. That was followed by Proposition 54, which seemed in some ways a logical extension of Proposition 209: if color blindness is now a matter of state policy, the state has no reason to collect data based on race; racial identity is a matter of only private concern. Proposition 54 was on the same ballot as the Governor Davis recall vote. Early indicators showed significant support for the proposition: two months before the recall election in October, 50 percent of the electorate supported it and 29 percent were opposed. Moreover, despite the changing racial demographics of the state, although whites make up a bare majority of the state's population, they make up 72 percent of those who voted in the November 2002 election. I've not evaluated the numbers for the recall completely, but suffice it to say that with 2.1 million absentee ballots turned in in the recall election, it's a fair supposition that the voter participation rates of whites remain significantly higher than all other groups, because we can pretty much guess who the absentee voters were.

Indeed, if the rates don't change, some estimate that whites will continue to make up over half of the state's voters in 2040, even though they will then account for only 30 percent of the population. This dynamic is also driven by the number of Latinos and Asians who remain unable to vote because they are either undocumented or legal permanent residents without voting rights. Proposition 54 was designed to appeal to the white electorate, and it all seemed to be going really well for them. But a week before the recall election, a *Los Angeles Times* poll revealed a significant shift, showing that 54 percent were now opposed to Proposition 54, in contrast to the earlier polls showing that it had a comfortable margin of support. In fact, according to the final tally of the vote taken, Proposition 54 was defeated by a huge margin: 63.9 percent against 36.1 percent of the vote. What happened?

One part of the explanation offers a lesson in successful coalition building: nearly $9 million was raised from Democrats, labor unions, and health care organizations, including $4.6 million from the lieutenant governor, Cruz Bustamante, who had in turn received that donation from several California Indian tribes engaged in the gaming industry. Focus groups revealed that the argument against Proposition 54 that got traction was that it would compromise health care. It would have prevented doctors from tracking how disease affects different racial and ethnic groups.

Once the focus groups identified the public health argument as the most attractive, it poured its energy into making that case, and it was able to reach the electorate with the slogan "Prop. 54: it's bad medicine; it's bad for your health." C. Everett Koop, the former surgeon general and a Republican, was enlisted for a set of highly effective TV ads in which he said, "on October 7th you get to make a life and death decision affecting every Californian. Prop. 54 would block information that can help save lives, and it would end prevention efforts directed at those at risk for cancer, diabetes, and other diseases. To save lives, vote no on 54." Simple; to the point.

Exit polls showed that having a moderate, conservative, white endorsement of the "no" vote apparently worked, as 58 percent of whites voted against the proposition, including 69 percent of those sixty-five and older. Why did that issue gain traction even among whites who arguably had not seen that much at stake in poorer health care for minorities? After all, County USC hospital in L.A. teeters on the brink of insolvency every year, and there is no groundswell of support to demand funding for it. Moreover, the argument about denying health care to undocumented immigrants didn't seem to matter in the debate about Proposition 187, which passed despite the concerns of the health care community in 1993.

Interest convergence suggests that dominant interests were seen to be at stake in this fight over Proposition 54. And what was that dominant interest? The control of contamination. As the *San Francisco Chronicle* argued, "the most compelling arguments came from public health officials fearing uncontrollable epidemics." They said it would have blunted their ability to identify and stomp out sources of contagious and potentially deadly diseases. Indeed, one of the prime examples cited involved a tuberculosis outbreak in Santa Clara County among Mexican and Filipino communities. Public health care officials argued that, without information about where the disease was concentrated and a targeted campaign to those communities, it would have spread. Racial justice as reflected in the defeat of Proposition 54 then became tied to the dominant interest of controlling contamination and the risk of spreading disease to whites. Of course, the reality is that Proposition 187 posed the same risk, as denying health care to undocumented immigrants raised the possibility that diseases like tuberculosis would start in certain communities and easily spread throughout the population. But because denying health care to immigrants looked like "their" problem not "ours," the election result went the other way. The fact that the campaign to oppose Proposition 54 was successful and the campaign to oppose Proposition 187 was not implicates an insight from interest convergence: while mobilizing white self-interest is a necessary predicate for attaining racial justice, perceptions of self-interest broadly defined—for example, as national security, economic security, or health security—can all work on different and sometimes contradictory trajectories.

To take the point further, consider the outcome of the recall election. Here, the vote in favor of the recall was 55.4 to 44.6—a decisive margin. Schwarzenegger was elected as the replacement candidate with 48 percent of the vote, over a Democrat with 31 percent and a conservative white Republican with 13.4 percent. Exit polls showed that Schwarzenegger's margin was white voters: 52 percent of whites voted for Schwarzenegger, as compared with 17 percent of blacks and 31 percent of Latinos. When the vote is examined by race and gender, the results are even more interesting: 55 percent of white male voters voted for the Terminator, as did 48 percent of white women. It turns out that the gender gap, to the extent that there was one, was with women of color: only 28 percent voted for Schwarzenegger. One thing is fairly clear from this preliminary data: while white supporters saw their interests converge with those of racial minorities on the issue of Proposition 54, their interests with those same communities diverged when it came to the question of recall and the election of Schwarzenegger.

While it should perhaps come as little surprise that white voters by and large supported the white candidate, there was some reason to think that Schwarzenegger would have had some trouble winning, and indeed winning by such a significant margin. In recent times, California has been a decidedly Democratic state. Indeed, the Republican Party had been unable to take a single statewide office in recent years. Bush wasn't even going to bother to visit. While it's true that party labels have less salience in an ostensibly nonpartisan election like the recall, Schwarzenegger was clearly identified as Republican, albeit some would argue a moderate one given his stand on certain social issues like abortion.

The second reason one might have expected that there would be some trouble with Schwarzenegger was that the policies most directly blamed for triggering the state's fiscal crisis, in particular the energy crisis, were the product of Republican regimes in both DC and California. Most significant among them was the decision to deregulate the utilities industry, which, along with Republican big money capital and organizations such as Enron, reaped the profits from the energy crisis two summers ago. Somehow, even though Schwarzenegger was reported to have been present in an off-record meeting where deals were cut triggering the spiraling cost of energy in the state, the blame fell on Gray Davis. Go figure.

And of course there was the little matter of sexual harassment; days before the election, the *Los Angeles Times* broke a meticulously documented story showing that over the years Schwarzenegger had groped, exposed himself to, and humiliated as many as fifteen women. He never denied it outright. He declared it to be an example of bad behavior for which he was apologizing, but for which he should not be pilloried.

Hundreds of readers were outraged . . . at the *Los Angeles Times*! They canceled their subscriptions—not because the facts were false, but because it was "unfair to the candidate." Why was Schwarzenegger able to overcome all of this and win by such a decisive margin? In part, I contend, it's because the implicit racial text of the campaign was clear: "This one's for you."

The first shot across the bow came when Schwarzenegger announced he would seek the repeal of the bill permitting undocumented immigrants to secure driver's licenses. The bill had only recently been signed by Davis in the heat of the recall campaign. Supporters of the bill pointed out that it was a public safety issue, as it's nearly impossible to get around in California without a car, so a lot of people were driving anyway and had no insurance. Even though other states had similar licensing laws, Schwarzenegger took the argument against the driver's license bill in a distinct direction when he launched a series of TV ads accusing Davis of "pandering to special interests," because the bill would make it easier for "terrorists" to get a California license.

In one fell swoop, what had been seen as an important civil rights issue was converted into a special interest claim that, if allowed, would aid the cause of terrorists. This ignored the fact that even major law enforcement officers, including LAPD chief Bratton, supported the bill, and that supporters had promised to try to address legitimate security concerns. In sounding the alarm of national security and linking it to the issue of the rights of undocumented immigrants, Arnold was tapping into a powerful vein, invoking the security interest to further reinscribe racial difference.

The more explicit version of this argument was taken up by right-wing talk radio, specifically by Hedgecock, who had been a loud voice during the recall, exhorting his 350,000 listeners to sign recall petitions, and leading the conservative faithful to Schwarzenegger's camp in the closing weeks of the election. Relentlessly linking the issue of illegal immigration to national security, Hedgecock asserted that "the ease with which people can cross our border and penetrate our most secret and vital institutions renders this country open to further terrorism." As insightfully reported by Mike Davis, author of the seminal *City of Quartz*, Hedgecock's racist hysteria culminated by arguing that the driver's license bill marked "the end of American democracy, the end of fair elections. Vast numbers of operatives are enlisting newly ID'd immigrants to cast thousands of illegal ballots to keep Davis in power. San Diego is slated to be invaded by trade unionists from LA who are going to tear down pro-recall signs and seek to otherwise intimidate the pro-recall vote." Hedgecock urged locals to defend their homes and resist the hordes of illegals in the spirit of 1776.

While Schwarzenegger never made the argument against the driver's license bill in such explicit racial terms, the subtext was clear: this bill would open the floodgates to the hordes, and I, Arnold, have come to say, "I will not let it happen."

To be sure, my argument does not seek to conflate Schwarzenegger with his supporters' excesses, as at one level it's important to Schwarzenegger that he not enrage the Latino community the way his close advisor Pete Wilson did with the racist demagoguery of Proposition 187. That tactic actually backfired on Wilson and resulted in a huge jump in Latino naturalization and voter registration. Hence Schwarzenegger keeps stressing a kinder, gentler form of racism, in which he constantly points to his immigrant roots. But in invoking the language of national security and denouncing the arguments in favor of the driver's license bill as another example of special interest politics, he rhetorically isolates the immigrant community, most specifically the Latino/Latina community, as unsavory players in the political process who must be checked.

This theme was further reiterated when Schwarzenegger launched another set of ads, this time denouncing the Indian gaming industry. The ads claimed that "Indian tribes operating casinos play money politics in Sacramento, contributing $120 million to politicians in the last five years. Their casinos make billions, yet pay no taxes and virtually nothing to the states. Other states require revenue from Indian gaming, but not us. It's time for them to pay their fair share. All other major candidates take their money and pander to them. I don't play that game." This ad, while clearly a slap at his Democratic opponent for accepting large donations from the Indian gaming industry, is far worse than the rhetoric on the driver's license bill. First, it's a blatant misrepresentation of the facts. Tribal gaming revenues are operated under tribal authority, not state governments. While tribes can make compacts with the states, they are independent entities. Most importantly, the claim that the tribes owe the states ignores California's shameful history with regard to Native Americans beginning with statehood in 1850 when the governor explicitly called for their extermination. Only in recent years, as the gaming industry has brought some degree of financial stability to some tribes, has the pattern of exclusion and political powerlessness begun to turn. The question of Indian gaming is an extremely complex one; it is in fact highly controversial within the Native community. My point is that now, in effect, Native Americans in California are being told that their right to participate in the political process is subject to a different set of presumptions. That is, their money is unsavory, and they have somehow unfairly benefited from it. It's racial scapegoating of the most rank kind, designed to provoke resentment toward a highly vulnerable group at a time of economic instability.

While Schwarzenegger's racial rhetoric may not be as crass as that of his sponsor, Pete Wilson, it invokes an image of "insider" and "outsider" in sufficiently racialized terms to be clearly recognizable and comprehensible within current racial discourse, particularly through an interest convergence analysis. The shape-shifting nature of national security, cutting in on the one instance in favor of limited racial reform and then in the same election in favor of polarizing political agendas, reveals the salience of interest convergence. On the one hand, national security promotes limited racial justice in *Grutter* and, at the same time, justifies the denial of members of immigrant community access to a driver's license.

Interest convergence has helped to keep me from going crazy. It has allowed me to identify an insight that not only speaks of tragic limits, but, by insisting on the interconnectedness between the interests of racially subordinated people and whites, the theory describes a potential intervention in our current racial geography. The challenge of interest convergence is that it invites us to look for the nodes, the sites, and the spaces where the fates of oppressed minorities and non-elite whites are joined, as opportunities to engage in social action. It also stands as a reminder that such opportunities may be very difficult to locate and hard to sustain, as coalition building may first require demolition of the coalition among whites, built amid both perceived and actual white racial privilege as sustained by major societal institutions. The definition of interest is a process filtered through the lens of race. This simple fact both poses a great challenge and is a source of a more modest hope that we begin to understand race as an opening for change.

9

Envisioning Abolition: Sex, Citizenship, and the Racial Imaginary of the Killing State

KENDALL THOMAS

2004

Kendall Thomas is the Nash Professor of Law and co-founder and director of the Center for the Study of Law and Culture at Columbia Law School. His past appointments include visiting professor at Stanford Law School and Princeton University. He received his BFA from Yale College and his JD from Yale Law School. His teaching and research interests include U.S. and comparative constitutional law, human rights, legal philosophy, feminist legal theory, Critical Race Theory, and law and sexuality. Thomas was an inaugural recipient of the Berlin Prize Fellowship of the American Academy in Berlin and a member of the Special Committee of the American Center in Paris. Thomas is a co-editor of Critical Race Theory: The Key Writings That Founded the Movement *and* What's Left of Theory?

For most of its history, the academic literature on the U.S. system of capital punishment has concerned itself with policy analyses of death penalty law and its administration. In recent years, however, the traditional policy paradigm has been supplemented (if not displaced) by scholarly investigation of the *cultural* register of death penalty jurisprudence and the regime of "state killing" of which it is a part. At the center of this "cultural turn" in death penalty scholarship is an interest in the symbolic dimension of capital punishment. In the words of one of its most accomplished proponents, the cultural study of the death penalty attends to the ways in which the death penalty "create[s] social meaning and thus shape[s] social worlds."

If the death penalty is part of a larger cultural imaginary that it helps shape, contemporary advocates for the abolition of the death penalty cannot hope to transform our national conversation about race and capital punishment without first taking the full measure of the *cultural* challenge that the abolitionist movement faces. That challenge, in a word, is this: because the death penalty serves important symbolic functions in the wider culture of the twenty-first-century United States, the continuing, if conflicted, civic consensus in favor of state killing is no longer responsive (if it ever was) solely to the logic of the better argument and the persuasive power of empirical proof. If we are honest with ourselves, we have to reckon with the fact that the current terms of the discourse of civil society in this country on race and the death penalty throw us up against the limits of liberal political legalism, with its faith in the well-ordered rhetoric of reason and rule-governed rationality, and above all, in the American political theology of individual constitutional rights.

The popular American discourse on the death penalty operates through cultural mechanisms that do their work at the level of the unconscious, or more specifically, at the level of what might be called the "racial unconscious." If we are to envision abolition of the death penalty, what we need, then, is a critical conceptual vocabulary that places the cultural phenomena of racial desire and racial fantasy at the heart of popular American discourse on capital punishment.

To work toward that end, I examine the production and circulation of cultural "meanings and symbols and representations" in the capital case of Wanda Jean Allen. Allen, poor, black, mentally impaired, and lesbian, was put to death by the State of Oklahoma on January 11, 2001. I pursue two overlapping concerns. The first is an interpretive account of the trial and appellate records in Allen's case, together with a documentary film about the final three months of her life, *The Execution of Wanda Jean*. I argue that the project of social meaning and social world making in the Allen case proceeded largely through the state's strategic manipulation of the psychic or "subjective side of social relations," above all through the deft, unspoken appeal to fantasy and the mobilization of the politics of racial and sexual enjoyment.

My other mission is methodological. Here, I advance the following propositions. First, the Allen case demonstrates the limits of the "rationalist" or "reformist" understandings of and arguments against capital punishment that have thus far characterized the cultural study of the death penalty. Second, a critical cultural analysis of the "irrational rationality" of the death penalty system should be seen as a crucial task for those of us who are trying to map the complex relationship between race and state killing at the beginning of the twenty-first century, a moment some have argued will be remembered as the dawn of a new era of "post-racial" racism. Between and alongside these two, I develop a third argument, which has to do with the productive possibilities of staging an encounter in this theater of analysis between Critical Race Theory, queer theory, and a political conception of psychoanalytic theory.

On December 2, 1988, Wanda Jean Allen shot her lover, Gloria Leathers, during an argument in the parking lot of a suburban police station just outside Oklahoma City, Oklahoma. Four days later, Allen was arrested in connection with the shooting. Shortly afterward, Gloria Leathers died from her wounds. Allen was eventually tried and convicted under Oklahoma law of murder in the first degree and the felonious possession of a firearm after former conviction of a felony. After deliberating for only two hours, the jury recommended that Allen be sentenced to death for the murder of Gloria Leathers and given a ten-year prison sentence for the felonious possession of a firearm. After exhausting her state and federal appeals, Allen sought and was denied clemency by the Oklahoma Pardon and Parole Board. On Thursday, January 11, 2001, Allen was killed by lethal injection at the Oklahoma State Penitentiary in McAlester. Wanda Jean Allen was the first woman to be executed by the State of Oklahoma and the sixth woman to be executed in the United States since the administration of the death penalty was resumed in 1977. Allen was the first black woman executed in the United States since 1954, the year the U.S. Supreme Court rendered the landmark *Brown* decision, a fact that, as I will argue, should not be ignored.

In the briefs filed with various courts during the appellate process, a number of arguments were offered on Allen's behalf. Relying on evidence that Allen had been found as a teenager to have an IQ of 69, Allen's counsel argued that she was mentally retarded and thus unable to control her actions. The appeals briefs charged, further, that her trial attorney, who had never represented a client in a capital case, had improperly been forced to remain on the case despite his request to have competent counsel appointed. Finally, Allen's appellate counsel argued that her initial conviction and the jury's recommendation of the death penalty at the sentencing hearing were the result of prosecutorial misconduct. The briefs placed particular emphasis on what they characterized as the prosecution's continual "distortion" of evidence regarding the relationship between Allen and Leathers, who had met and become lovers while they were both serving time in prison. These distortions, argued Allen's lawyers, included the depiction of Wanda Jean as the "dominant" person in the relationship, testimony by Gloria Leathers's mother that Allen was the "man" in the relationship, the introduction of testimony about greeting cards Wanda Jean had given Gloria on which she had signed her name "G-e-n-e," and other characterizations that, in the words of Allen's counsel, "unduly emphasized that [Allen] was engaged in a homosexual relationship with Leathers" and "tended to humiliate [Allen] in the eyes of the jury."

The tone of the Oklahoma Court of Criminal Appeals was typical of the opinions issued by both the state and federal courts that reviewed Allen's conviction. After stating that the first issue before it was "whether the sentence of death was imposed under the influence of passion, prejudice or

any other arbitrary factor," the Court of Criminal Appeals concluded, inter alia, that the lower court committed no error in allowing presentation
of "evidence [that Allen] was the 'man' in her homosexual relationship with
the decedent. . . . It was used to show [Allen] was the aggressive person in
the relationship, while the decedent was more passive." In the words of the
presiding judge, "The evidence would help the jury understand why each
party acted the way she did both during the events leading up to the shooting and the shooting itself. . . . Under these circumstances, its probative
value was not substantially outweighed by its prejudicial effect . . . and the
evidence was properly admitted." The Court of Criminal Appeals did not
address the argument of the lone dissenting opinion, which took exception to the notion that

> the majority finding the appellant was the "man" in her lesbian rela-
> tionship has any probative value at all. Were this a case involving a
> heterosexual couple, the fact that a male defendant was the "man" in
> the relationship likewise would tell me nothing. I find no proper pur-
> pose for this evidence, and believe its only purpose was to present the
> defendant as less sympathetic to the jury than the victim.

In *The Execution of Wanda Jean*, an assistant attorney general for the
State of Oklahoma, Sandra Howard, defended the verdict and sentence imposed on Allen. After summarizing Oklahoma law on the concept of pre-
meditation, Howard offered the following remarks about Allen:

> Wanda Jean was just a very domineering person. Their relationship
> was very turbulent over the years. Police had been called out numerous
> times and, you know, there was really no doubt from the testimony at
> trial that Miss Allen was the dominant person in the relationship.
> The state introduced into trial two different cards that Wanda Jean
> had sent to Gloria that were very threatening. One of them looks very
> innocent on the front, shows someone talking about, you know, being
> in Wanda's prayers and says also, you're also in most of my confessions.

But then Wanda Jean puts the P.S. on the card, "I'm the type of person who will hunt someone down I love and kill them. Do I make myself clear Gloria?" and it's signed "Gene." And then a second card shows a gorilla on the front, it says, "Patience, my ass, "I'm gonna kill something" and when you read the back, Wanda has written to Gloria, "Try and leave and you'll understand this card more. Dig, for real, no joke. Love, Gene" and she signed it "G-E-N-E," Gene. Wanda would sometimes sign "G-E- N-E." That's when she considered herself to be the male figure in the relationship, if there is such a thing in these types of relationships.

Media accounts, particularly in the gay and lesbian press, seized on Allen's case as evidence of a pattern in capital prosecutions of men and women who are gay or lesbian. In this perspective, the conviction and sentencing of Wanda Jean Allen are a blatant example of homophobia in the criminal justice system generally and in capital cases specifically. In a representative article entitled "Queer on Death Row," journalist and social critic Richard Goldstein lists the Allen case as one of a number of recent capital murder convictions of gay men and lesbians in which "stereotypical beliefs about homosexuals . . . may have sealed their fate."

Although Goldstein concedes that "race, class, and reduced mental capacity all play a major role in capital punishment," the heart of his discussion of Wanda Jean Allen centers on the ways in which "Allen's sexuality was never far from the case." While I agree that the Allen prosecution is a textbook example of the legal uses of homophobia in capital murder cases, I also believe that a standard "lesbigay studies" (to use a term coined by William Eskridge Jr.) perspective minimizes or risks altogether ignoring another, equally meaningful aspect of the case. This is the obvious, though unacknowledged, significance in the Allen prosecution of race and racism, which, if we hope to understand it, demands a more complex interpretation of the case than is possible through the language of lesbian and gay studies. However, what I have said about the limited value of a conventional lesbigay studies framework also holds true for any approach to the Allen case that uncritically relies on standard post–civil rights understandings of race and racism in U.S. death penalty law. Racial inequality is alive and well throughout the criminal justice system: in the composition of the bench and prosecutorial bar, in the demographics of grand and petit juries, and in the incidence and severity of punishment. Nonetheless, the now regnant ideology (both in and outside the courts) that racism may be said to exist only when consideration of race is explicit and purposeful (and not always then) has all but knocked the political wind out of standard race-based critiques of the criminal justice system, generally, and the administration of the death penalty, in particular.

Given the enfeebled state of the mainstream discourse, then, we can expect little traction in a simple shift of critical attention from something called "sexuality" or "sexual orientation" to something called "race" or vice versa. The intellectual challenge, rather, is to think the questions of race and racism raised by the case around, or, if you prefer, *inside* the axes of sex, sexuality, and sexual orientation. In the words of Wahneema Lubiano, we might say that the story of Wanda Jean Allen's trial and execution is a story of the "places where race no longer talks about race" precisely and paradoxically by talking about it through something else and elsewhere. "What," asks Lubiano, "might race help us think about that race does not name, but to which it is nonetheless connected?"

Jacques Derrida once famously argued that there is "no racism without a language. The point," he goes on to insist, "is not that acts of racial violence are only words but rather that they have to have a word." My question is this: Does that "word" have to be the word *race*? Are there circumstances in which racial meaning making takes place through recourse to other words or, indeed, through the language of image and symbol, without the use, that is, of any words at all? What does the Allen case tell us about the ways in which race and racial representation figure in the U.S. legal and political discourse on capital punishment in our putatively "post-racial" age?

The Racial Imaginary

The interpretive strategy toward which I am gesturing is suggested in part by Paul Kahn in a brief but brilliant polemic, *The Cultural Study of Law*. Kahn's stated goal is to outline the program of a scholarly legal method that abandons the reformist ambitions that have historically guided the practice of legal criticism. "The legal academic is the captive of law. If a discipline is to emerge that actually studies law as an object for theoretical description and elaboration, the scholar must first free herself from the law." Kahn issues a call for legal scholarship that undertakes the systematic study of the language and logic of "law's rule." This "cultural discipline of law" aims to elaborate the "genealogy" and "architecture" of law whose chief object is a critical understanding of the "legal imagination": "To understand the power of law," Kahn argues, "we must stop looking so much at the commands of legal institutions and start looking at the legal imagination."

Kahn's urged investigation of the "legal imagination" is provocative and potentially productive. Nonetheless, a thick description of the implication of law and culture in the trial of Wanda Jean Allen demands a more radical and a more radically interdisciplinary understanding of what we mean by the idea of "imagination" than Kahn himself provides. The cultural study of how legal actors and institutions "imagined" the trial and execution of Wanda Jean Allen must find a language to describe the burden of representation that was borne in the Allen case by the "racial imagination" or the racial imaginary.

A first step in the effort to specify the relationship between the legal and racial imaginations might be to consider the ways in which the racial imaginary occupies a region or site in the broader constellation that philosopher and social theorist Charles Taylor has denominated the "social imaginary." For Taylor, the term is meant to capture the ways in which people imagine "their social existence, how they fit together with others, how things go on between them and their fellows, the expectations that are normally met, and the deeper normative notions and images that un-

derlie these expectations." Taylor notes that the work of the social imaginary "is not often expressed in theoretical terms," but is rather conveyed
and "carried in images, stories, and legends."

We might say that the raw material of the social imaginary consists of
pictures, rather than propositions. This imaginary field reflects and refracts
the "largely unstructured and inarticulate understanding of our whole situation, within which particular features of our world show up for us in the
sense they have." This understanding "can never be expressed in the form
of explicit doctrines because of its unlimited and indefinite nature. That
is another reason for speaking here of an imaginary and not a theory."

Although he does not discuss the idea of race, Taylor's concept of the
"social imaginary" takes us a step further in mapping the movement of the
modem racial imaginary. Extrapolating from Taylor, I would emphasize two
distinctive modal dimensions of the social imaginary that is "race." First,
the racial imaginary differs from other social imaginaries in the way it
emerges from, indeed, may be said only to exist in, a field of vision and
visualization that exceeds the boundaries of language and discourse. Second, the racial imaginary operates in and through mental mechanisms that
are not only unstructured and inarticulate, but *unconscious*. No deep understanding of the work of the unconscious in and on the racial imaginary
is possible without serious, sustained engagement with psychoanalysis.
The psychoanalytic account of "how we acquire our heritage of the ideas
and laws of human society within the unconscious mind" offers an indispensable resource for a critical cultural study of the psychic life of race
in law.

My point of entry into the intersection of the legal and racial imagination via the psychoanalytic approach is the idea of "racial castration," which
David L. Eng has elaborated in a book by the same name. Eng's study offers a sophisticated revision of Freud's theory of fetishism. According to
Freud's classic account, fetishism is a story about the trauma of sexual
difference. The male fetishist, as it were, disavows what in Freud's theory is
thematized as female castration. Instead, he "[sees] on the female body a
penis that is not there to see." From the Freudian perspective, this imagined

penis is a fetish—a surrogate penis, projected onto the female body or sym-
bolically displaced onto a substitute object, such as a lock of hair, a pair of
undergarments, a shoe.

In a probing psychoanalytic reading of David Henry Hwang's play
M. Butterfly, Eng offers an account of this psychic process when it is faced
with the trauma of racial difference. In Hwang's drama, a French diplomat falls in love with a Chinese opera male diva/transvestite/spy. Instead
of seeing on the female body a penis that is not there to see, the French
diplomat refuses to see on his lover's male Asian body a penis that most
definitely is there. In Eng's account, this "racial castration" of the lover's
body "suggests that what is being negotiated in this particular scenario is
not just sexual but racial difference." It is a psychic operation that unfolds
under the jurisdiction of Orientalist law: an Asian man "could never be
completely a man." As Eng reads it, *M. Butterfly* thus demonstrates "the
impossibility of thinking about racism and sexism [and I might add ho-
mophobia] as separate discourses or distinct spheres of analysis."

As Rey Chow has similarly reminded us, "Race and ethnicity are . . . co-
terminous with sexuality, just as sexuality is implicated in race and ethnicity. To that extent, any analytical effort to keep these categories apart
from one another may turn out to be counterproductive, for it is their
categorical enmeshment—their categorical miscegenation, so to speak—
that needs to be foregrounded." The challenge is to elaborate a concept of
the erotic that remains alert to the social fantasies that animate the psychic life of racial and gender violence. If writers such as Rey Chow and
David Eng are right about the need to attend to the "categorical miscegenation" of race, sexuality, and ethnicity, we must be prepared to come to
grips with the possibility that political fantasies are indistinguishable from
psychic realities of the sexual imagination.

Two further points must be emphasized straightaway. First, the acting
out of the violent racial and sexual fantasy on whose erotic kernel I have
been insisting need not find its aim and end in the experience of pleasure
we associate with sex. To the contrary. At its extremity, sexual and racial

violence can find satisfaction only in a realm of psychic pain that lies, as it were, "beyond the pleasure principle."

The second point returns to the problem of the death penalty, to a consideration of the ways in which the relationship between *eros* and *thanatos* underwrites the political imaginary of the state and of the law that legitimates state power. The erotic economy is not limited to the social enactment of racial and gender violence commonly categorized as crime. The history of Africans in America is replete with instances in which sex and sexuality have been deployed as tools in the arsenal of racial violence. In this context, the death penalty, particularly, calls for an analysis that seeks to understand how the production of death that is state-sanctioned killing is a kind of "political erotics," a triangulated affair between the state, the citizen, and the condemned.

A critical account of cases such as that of Wanda Jean Allen must place the question of the erotics of racial power and violence at the very center of its analysis. How does the Wanda Jean Allen case implicate social values and psychic investments in a libidinal economy that is not merely similar to, but parasitic on those we ordinarily associate with the political economy of sex?

In the Allen case, the prosecution pursued a strategy of "lesbian fetishism" (the term comes from Elizabeth Grosz, although I use it in a quite different sense here). Over the course of the trial, Allen's body became the imagined site of a penis "that [was] not there to see." From this perspective, Allen was subjected to a psychic (and cultural) mechanism of social homophobia. Allen's lesbian identity and desire were "masculinized": she was the "dominant figure" in her relationship with Leathers; she was the "husband" to Leathers as wife; she was the woman masquerading as a man who dared to walk around the house with her breasts bared in the company of men, who defiantly refused her given (feminine) name.

I do not mean to deny the force in Allen's case of the prosecutorial uses of the figure of the murderous lesbian, a stock stereotype with an infamous and long pedigree. My intention rather is to indicate why the act of "legal imagination" that animated the prosecution's strategy in the Allen case was not merely or primarily the homophobic projection of the lesbian body. It was already also a racist projection, a fantasy of the *black male* body in which Allen's masculinized lesbian body was conscripted to serve as a screen for the dangerous, deadly hypermasculinity that remains the iconic image of the black presence in white America: "She is a hunter when she kills," as the prosecutor put it at Allen's trial. "She hunts her victims down and then she kills them." By the end of the trial, Allen had been remade into the apotheosis of the figure of black "female masculinity," to use Judith Halberstam's phrase. Allen's rage (which the prosecution recounted so frequently during her trial that it became virtually identic) was insistently invested with racial meanings the prosecution never had to articulate explicitly. One might say that the state effectively played the race card; what the prosecutor did in fact was to make racist use of a homophobic hand.

Stereotypical representations of homosexuality operated freely in the Allen trial as a simultaneous point of transfer for psychic processes of sexual and racial fetishism. Sexuality became the site of a kind of surplus semantic value, which made race and racial meanings available as technologies of state power while silently masking the latter's operation. What a reading of the record suggests was a scrupulous adherence to the formal protocols of a putatively color-blind criminal law regime was, in the event, not color-blind at all. In this respect, the Allen trial fits seamlessly into the critical framework of Slavoj Žižek's notion of "ideological fantasy," whose basic logic is disavowal.

I suggested earlier that the field of vision and visibility is an important theater of racial representation. As Kalpana Seshadri Crooks has reminded us, "although race cannot be reduced to the look," it is nonetheless "fundamentally a regime of looking" or visualization. This visualization is not strictly epidermal or corporeal. In the United States, the fetishistic regime of the racial gaze has long been part of the metaphysical, deep structure of our law. A few examples will suffice to underscore the centrality of this cultural form in the political unconscious of American legal thought. Seen in visual terms, the law of hypodescent (more colloquially known as the "one drop of blood" rule) ascribed a power to the specular field of whiteness, a power that could see past the folds of flesh that cover the black body; Article I, Section 2, clause 3 of the U.S. Constitution could visually amputate three-fifths of the black slave body and ignore the unrepresented remainder; and we are all familiar with the masterful projection of scopic power (I am thinking of Harlan's dissent in *Plessy v. Ferguson*) that declared that the "eyes of our Constitution" could be "color-blind" precisely because "every one knew" that the "dominance" of the "white race" was secure "for all time."

In *The Execution of Wanda Jean,* the continued refusal of the "racial solipsistic" among us to see and thus to know the intersubjective relationship of racial equality is poignantly evident in the clemency hearing granted to Wanda Jean Allen a few months before her death. A viewer of the documentary cannot help but be struck by the deafening silence that follows Allen's statement to the clemency board at the end of the hearing. On the standard account, the purpose of a clemency hearing is to provide representatives of the state who are not judges or lawyers to consider the human costs and consequences of the decision to execute a convict who has been sentenced to death. The hearing is not the place to engage in adversarial legal argument (for example, about race-based or sexual-orientation-based discrimination in the administration of capital punishment—arguments that, as I have noted, the U.S. Supreme Court has effectively foreclosed). Rather, its purpose is to stage a performance of abjection by the convicted felon: in short, the purpose, meaning, and effects of the contemporary clemency hearing are all directed at the production of affect and emotion (in this regard, they are the flip side of the victim-impact statement that, in recent years, has witnessed such a lively resurgence). With the loss of her voice—a literal loss—Allen is deprived of the communicative means necessary to convey her humanity to the parole board. The progressive and quite literal phonic dematerialization of her voice perversely affirms her infrahumanity, to use Paul Gilroy's term.

The Allen clemency hearing reveals another aspect of the racial politics of capital punishment in the United States: the death penalty is not merely about the literal liquidation of the black body, but about its antecedent reduction to the mere biological existence that Giorgio Agamben has called "bare life." The body of the death row inmate stands in effect as a specific instance of the more general figure of the black civic condition in the contemporary U.S. political order. From this perspective, Negro citizenship is not the active, robust political personhood of Madisonian republicanism, but a species of what Russ Castronovo has aptly denominated "necro citizenship," a civic status in which political life and identity are constructed on an ideological foundation of death. Again, this death is not always literal: the racial thanatopolitics of the modern "post-racial" era concerns not only the actual biological death of black citizens, but the strategic subjugation of living black bodies through the mode of discipline that Michel Foucault has called biopower. The biopolitical practices that consign African Americans to the liminal sphere of civic half life or virtual death are not primarily material, but symbolic. This is a form of political death dealing that proceeds primarily through the exercise of semiotic state power, for example, the "racist color blindness" that holds that official affirmative reference to or recognition of race in the contemporary post-racial moment is by definition racist.

Race, State, *Jouissance*

It would be a mistake, however, to see the Allen prosecution solely as a public staging of the psychic and physical degradation that awaits the bodies of those black and brown ethnic irritants who refuse, in Randall Kennedy's approving phrase, to adhere to "the established moral standards of white, middle-class Americans." The suffering and death inflicted on Wanda Jean Allen's imagined male body operates simultaneously as a conduit for organization and the expression of racial and sexual enjoyment.

By "enjoyment," I refer to the English rendering of *jouissance*, a term introduced into the psychoanalytic literature by Jacques Lacan. However, while at one level of meaning, *jouissance* is a cognate of the English word "enjoyment," both in the ordinary language "sense of deriving pleasure from something, and in the legal sense of exercising certain property rights," for French speakers, *jouissance* conveys a second, specifically sexual connotation, since it is also an idiomatic expression for orgasm. The substance of what I am calling "racial sexual enjoyment" and of the violent political and social fantasies that underwrite it are in many ways indistinguishable from the psychic realities that inform the sexual imagination.

What do the trial and state killing of Wanda Jean Allen tell us about the politics of racial enjoyment? Reading the transcript and opinions in the Allen case or watching the documentary film on her execution, one is struck by the smug but barely concealed delight Oklahoma officials seemed to take in the abjected figure of Wanda Jean Allen as a "dead citizen" (to adapt Lauren Berlant's vivid phrase). Before she is actually killed, Allen is conscripted to play the role of "dead citizen walking" in a bureaucratic spectacle that enacts her social and civic annihilation.

Slavoj Žižek's account of the "ethnic moment" of the nation as the "surplus" or "leftover" of the universalizing project of the nation is particularly pertinent here. For Žižek, nationalism is "the privileged domain of the eruption of enjoyment into the social field," a materialization of *jouissance* as a collective political fantasy:

What is at stake in ethnic tensions is always the possession of the national Thing: the "other" wants to steal our enjoyment (by ruining our "way of life" and/or it has access to some secret, perverse enjoyment. In short, what gets on our nerves, what really bothers us about the "other," is the peculiar way he organizes his enjoyment (the smell of his food, his "noisy" songs and dances, his strange manners, his attitude to work—in the racist perspective, the "other" is either a workaholic stealing our jobs or an idler living on our labor). The basic paradox is that our Thing is conceived as something inaccessible to the other and at the same time threatened by him; this is similar to castration which, according to Freud, is experienced as something that "really cannot happen," but whose prospect nonetheless horrifies us.

That prospect also fascinates us. This "package deal" of horror and fascination goes some way toward explaining the persistently high level of support for the death penalty in this country. Wanda Jean Allen is the projected representation of the specter of the dangerous black masculinity that threatens the political utopics of a harmonious, "more perfect" (if not perfectible) union. She embodies, by proxy, the long nightmare that haunts the phantasmatic dream of our criminal justice system as an enlightened exercise in rational participatory democracy: the ugly arc of racial antagonism without which there would be no "national Thing."

The trial and execution of Wanda Jean Allen demonstrate that contemporary racism in the United States is characterized by a number of the features David Halperin has observed about American homophobia: it has no fixed propositional content and no determinate discursive form. In the Allen case, the mobilization of homophobia as an alibi for racism ought not obscure the degree to which racial fantasy and the psychic politics of racial enjoyment will remain a critical pillar in the architecture of the emerging "post-racial" state. In mapping the relationship in the Allen case between the death penalty and the politics of enjoyment, I align myself with writers such as Michael Taussig, who has called for critical attention to the symbolic economy of state fetishism: "Like the Nation-State, the fetish has a deep investment in death—the death of the consciousness of the signifying function. Death endows both the fetish and the Nation-State with life, a spectral life, to be sure. The fetish absorbs into itself that which it represents, leaving no traces of the represented. A clean job."

Without specifying the role of the racial imaginary in the collective psychic processes by which the U.S. nation-state binds its subjects to the political fantasy of a "post-racial" multicultural citizenship, the play of life and death to which Taussig refers can be only partially understood. The "death of the consciousness of the signifying function" of race in no way entails the death of race itself. To borrow the words of Daniel Patrick Moynihan, the execution of Wanda Jean Allen stands as a case study in "semantic infiltration," a linguistic operation by which racial meanings are secreted through the interstices of language that has nothing to do with race. In order to describe this "splitting off" of racial signifiers and racial signifieds, we must move beyond an abstract, general account of the formal "*figure* of state fetishism" to consider the "politics and historicity of jouissance" that is its material social ground.

In a discussion of the publication by Benetton of a January 2000 book of photographs and interviews of U.S. death row inmates, *We, on Death Row*, Austin Sarat suggested that the Italian clothing company's catalog of portraits of condemned prisoners "misses the mark." Sarat argues that in thinking about the death penalty, "the faces we should be looking at are our own. The question to be asked about state killing is not what it does for us, but what it does *to* us." For Sarat, to pose this question is to reckon with "the cost of state killing to our law, our politics, our culture." On Sarat's account, "state killing diminishes us by damaging our democracy, legitimating vengeance, intensifying racial divisions, and distracting us from the challenges that the new century poses for America."

Sarat is surely right. The costs of the death-dealing market in capital punishment are great indeed. Yet this rationalist reckoning of the price we pay to have the death penalty tells only part of the story. In making the case for the fundamental irrationality of capital punishment, Sarat's analysis overlooks the political, cultural, and psychic *benefits* of the dance of state death for the U.S. racial and sexual polity. In the Allen case, the production of death that is state killing involves a fetishistic transubstantiation of value. The Allen case involves an irrational rationality in which values are reversed, costs become benefits, and the laws of objective interest and rational calculation give way to the transvaluative law of an irrational but by no means illusory enjoyment. David Cole has noted that the American criminal justice system "affirmatively depends on [the exploitation] of inequality. Absent race and class disparities, the privileged among us could not enjoy as much constitutional protection of our liberties as we do; and without these disparities, we could not afford the policy of mass incarceration that we have pursued over the past two decades."

The claim that state killing is at odds with America's enlightened democratic self-image is both true and beside the point. A thick-descriptive or normative account of the dance of state death must attend to the libidinal economy of capital punishment, to the miasmatic politics of a racial and sexual enjoyment that eludes the assumptive logic of rationalist policy analysis. The death penalty in the United States evokes Achille Mbembe's account of the public execution in 1987 of "two malefactors" in Douala, Cameroon. Mbembe suggests that the economy of power in the postcolonial state "is an economy of death—or, more precisely, it opens up a space for enjoyment at the moment it makes room for death, a space in which power procedurally mediates the transformation of pleasure into a site of death."

Contesting Criminal Justice as a Racial Project: *McCleskey v. Kemp*

The case of Wanda Jean Allen not only highlights the fetishistic character of state killing and its perverse, peculiar pleasure in the projected figure of the murderous, masculinized black lesbian body, the operation of state power in the "post-racial" state in which a growing number of commentators in and outside law have begun to say we now live or must aspire to live. It demonstrates the relevance in understanding the operation of racial power in the "post-racial" state of the question "What does the practice of capital punishment do for (some of) us?" Answering that question should remain an urgent task for anyone who is committed to contesting this nation's necrophilic romance with the death penalty.

In my view, abolitionist activists cannot afford to ignore the lesson we should have learned from Justice Antonin Scalia's now-infamous memorandum to the Conference in *McCleskey v. Kemp*, a 1987 case that has been described as "the Dred Scott decision of our time." In *McCleskey v. Kemp*, the U.S. Supreme Court was asked to rule on a federal constitutional claim by Warren McCleskey, an African American who had been convicted and sentenced to die by a Georgia jury for the murder of a white police officer. Relying in part on statistical evidence of systemic interracial and intraracial disparities in the state's administration of the death penalty, McCleskey

maintained that Georgia was using capital punishment in a racially discriminatory fashion in contravention of the Equal Protection Clause of the
Fourteenth Amendment to the U.S. Constitution.

Replying to an early draft of what would become the majority opinion
in the case, Justice Scalia wrote:

> I disagree with the argument that the inferences that can be drawn
> from the Baldus study are weakened by the fact that each jury and
> each trial is unique, or by the large number of variables at issue. And
> I do not share the view, implicit in [Justice Lewis Powell's draft lan-
> guage], that an effect of racial factors upon sentencing, if it could
> be shown by sufficiently strong statistical evidence, would require
> reversal.

"Since it is my view," continues the memorandum, "that the unconscious
operation of irrational sympathies and antipathies, including racial, upon
jury decisions and (hence) prosecutorial [ones], is real, acknowledged by
the [judgments] of this court and ineradicable, I cannot honestly say that
all I need is more proof."

Much might be said about this extraordinary document. The first and
most important observation has to do with Scalia's "breathtaking" admission that race and racism are constituent components of our criminal justice regime. In conceding that racism is an "ineradicable" and (by a strange
twist of logic) constitutionally inconsequential fact defining who and how
we criminally punish, the Scalia memorandum in effect concedes the extent to which, in Stephen Bright's words, our criminal courts "are the institutions in the United States least affected by the civil rights movement
that brought changes to many American institutions in the last forty years."
Criminal justice is a racial project; the United States is a racial state.

What chiefly interests me here, however, is the passage in which Justice
Scalia traces the roots of these "race effects" to "the unconscious operation
of irrational sympathies and antipathies." In raising the question of the
"unconscious" and "irrational" determinants of the death penalty, Scalia's

analysis puts its finger on the very heart of the problem with which opponents of capital punishment must reckon. How might attention to the unconscious and irrational dimensions of the popular discourse on race and the death penalty help the abolitionist movement fashion a strategy to break the current consensus in favor of capital punishment?

First, the Scalia memorandum directs our attention to the way in which, at its core, the question of the relations between race, crime, and capital punishment must be approached from at least two distinct but related directions: as a legal question, but also as a *political* question. The continued consensus in favor of the death penalty rests on the state's manipulation of racial anxiety and animus in the service of a project that has very little to do with the actual perpetrators or the actual victims of crime. Its central object is to entrench and extend the technology of modern state power that Jonathan Simon calls "governance through crime." We would do well in this regard to remember the legal realist insight that law is the continuation of politics by other means. The fact that the popular public discussion of the death penalty and racial justice continues to be framed with reference to law and the rule-of-law state does not divest that discourse of its political character and consequences.

Moreover, it should be said straightaway that the political dimension that concerns us here is most emphatically *not* the formal institutional politics of reasoned debate and deliberation. This brings me to a second implication of Scalia's argument. To say that the public discourse on and the state practice of capital punishment is riven by unconscious and irrational forces is to argue for a distinctively cultural conception of death penalty politics. In its cultural register, political mobilization against or in favor of the death penalty is not only or not primarily about penal policy and practice. The production and circulation of "meanings and symbols and representations" of crime and punishment addresses the "subjective component of political being" or the "psychic life" of politics. In insisting on the presence and power of the "unconscious" and "irrational," Justice Scalia is in effect arguing that capital punishment is a political field of image, identification, and association. Like politics generally, the popular politics of the death penalty is a politics "in which the way that people 'imagine' themselves occupies a crucial place."

A number of recent studies have noted the extent to which "the statistical overrepresentation of African Americans among violent offenders and victims provides much less of a basis for white fear than the images of black criminality fostered by the media and other sources." In the words of one commentator, the U.S. news media has come to play a decisive role in "increasing fear of crime," in "instilling and reinforcing racial stereotypes," and in "linking race to crime," not least through the sensationalist specularization of the black male body. Despite falling crime rates, the media's racialization of violent crime at the level of the image has fueled the shift to more punitive policies that has characterized our criminal justice system in the last couple of decades.

The task of the abolitionist movement is to break the imagined connection between black Americans and crime (a connection, I might note, to which African Americans themselves are by no means immune). The goal, as I see it, is to "manufacture dissent"—to contest the deadly ideological fantasy that underwrites the racial thanatopolitics of the popular discourse on capital punishment. If they are to meet the resistance to abolition on its own ground, activists opposing the death penalty must begin to take political fantasy seriously. Put another way, the strategy of this abolitionist movement should be to produce new images and identifications that, on the one hand, deracialize crime and, on the other, decriminalize race.

Stephen Duncombe comes very close to the argument I am advancing here in his *Dream: Re-imagining Progressive Politics in an Age of Fantasy*. Although he does not explicitly address the politics of capital punishment, Duncombe urges progressive political activists to learn how to "build a politics that embraces the dreams of people and fashions spectacles which give these fantasies form—a politics that understands desire and speaks to the irrational; a politics that employs symbols and associations; a politics that tells good stories."

Given what I have said here about the phantasmatic representation of black masculinity in the white American mind and how U.S. death penalty law and politics use the black masculine to imagine crime and inflict punishment on black people across the sex-gender-sexuality line, the challenge is clear: the most pressing task of the abolitionist movement is to build a constituency for a new, anti-racist vision of our body politic and a new corporal politics that not only reimagines black bodies, but recognizes and revalues black lives.

10

And We Are Still Not Saved: Twenty-First-Century Constitutional Conflicts

DERRICK BELL

2005

Derrick Albert Bell Jr. was an American lawyer, professor, and civil rights activist. In 1971, he became the first tenured African American professor of law at Harvard Law School, and he is often credited as one of the originators of Critical Race Theory. He was a visiting professor at New York University School of Law from 1991 until his death in 2011. He was also a dean of the University of Oregon School of Law. Bell wrote extensively about the progress of racial reform in the United States across a range of genres, from fiction to legal analysis to autobiography. He contributed key writings that helped form the Critical Race Theory movement, such as Faces at the Bottom of the Well, *and his casebook,* Race, Racism, and American Law, *is used widely in law schools across the country. In addition to his far-reaching impact as a teacher and scholar, Bell championed the cause of civil rights outside the classroom. He leveraged his positions as the first tenured African American professor at Harvard Law School and the first African American dean of the University of Oregon School of Law to challenge law schools around the country to embrace diversity in their hiring practices. After graduating from*

the University of Pittsburgh School of Law in 1957, he worked with the Civil
Rights Division of the U.S. Department of Justice, the only African Ameri-
can among thousands of lawyers. He left after two years when the govern-
ment asked him to resign his membership in the NAACP and then went on
to become first assistant counsel at the NAACP Legal Defense and Educa-
tional Fund under Thurgood Marshall, supervising more than three hundred
school desegregation cases in Mississippi.

Bell is survived by his wife, Janet Dewart Bell, his three children, Derrick,
Douglass, and Carter, and three siblings.

This lecture's title is a variation on the theme of the first of my four books, featuring my quasi-fictional heroine, Geneva Crenshaw. Published in 1987, that book recognized how much needed to be done to achieve the racial equality we once felt was within reach as a result of the civil rights gains made through the courts, the Congress, and in the streets during the 1960s and 1970s.

The title, borrowed from the prophet Jeremiah's lament that "The harvest is past, the summer is ended, and we are not saved," acknowledged the inadequacy of our progress, but suggested that further effort would strengthen gains realized and open new horizons. Now, almost two decades later, the rationale for optimism is seriously diluted by a range of catastrophic conditions facing all Americans and endangering black Americans to an unprecedented degree.

I always hoped that my admittedly dire insights about America and racism would prove to be wrong. The subtitle of *Faces at the Bottom of the Well* is "The Permanence of Racism." It reflects my view, not that all whites are evil, but that the social stability of the free enterprise system, with its great disparities in income and wealth, gains stability by the presence of an outgroup whom the majority can feel are their inferiors. My much-criticized position flew in the face of Gunnar Myrdal's explanation, set out in his 1944 study, *An American Dilemma,* in which he insisted that racism reflected in slavery and segregation was "a terrible and inexplicable anomaly stuck in the middle of our liberal democratic ethos." Myrdal assured us that standard American policy-making was adequate to the task of abolishing racism. White America, it was assumed, *wanted* to abolish racism.

But my "racism is permanent" position was simply a further step beyond that taken by Princeton professor Jennifer Hochschild. She disagreed with Myrdal's anomaly assessment, finding instead that racism is a crucial component of liberal democracy in this country. The two, she said, are historically, even inherently, reinforcing, or, as she puts it, the apparent anomaly is an actual symbiosis.

Professor Lani Guinier asserts: "Race in the United States is a by-product of economic conflict that has been converted into a tool of division and distraction. It is not just an outgrowth of hatred or ill will. Racism has had psychological, sociological, and economic consequences that created the separate spheres inhabited by blacks and whites in 1954 but extended well beyond them."

"Well put," you may say, "but Bell, those statements about racism are hardly headline news." True enough, but the continuing vitality of racism, albeit in less overt forms than at earlier times, when combined with current political and economic conditions, poses special dangers that justify a new look at a prediction by Professor Sidney Willhelm in his 1970 book, *Who Needs the Negro?* Professor Willhelm, a sociologist who has studied and written about racial issues for many years, asserts that slavery and segregation rested on the need to exploit black labor, but whites now produce wealth through the exploitation of technology, and I am sure he would add continuing job bias, and the importation of foreign labor while outsourcing manufacturing jobs that helped many blacks and whites gain middle-class status.

Not needing black labor, Willhelm maintained that society felt free to offer them "equal opportunity." But, he warned, the myth of equality within a context of oppression simply provides a veneer for more oppression. Blacks are increasingly being disgorged from the labor force as surplusage in the modern, computerized economy. For eyewitness evidence of the numbers of unemployed black men of working age, simply walk down 125th Street or watch the frantic basketball games in the play yard at 6th Avenue and West 3rd Street.

Willhelm warns that the redundancy of blacks in the marketplace, and the growing socioeconomic gap places the continued existence of black life in America at risk. With blacks relegated to being outcasts in the labor market, and poverty-stricken in the midst of plenty, predictable future ghetto uprisings, born of frustration, could provide the excuse for police and other officials to eliminate those who resist military rule over the communities. And, warns Willhelm, military retaliation will not recognize class distinctions. All blacks, regardless of class, will be viewed as and treated like the enemy.

Rather than dismiss Professor Willhelm's three-decades-old prediction as simply proof that a white man can suffer a form of racial paranoia as serious as mine, I want to examine three crises, two that are current and one that the first two can set off. The crises, I contend, support Willhelm's apocalyptic prophesy.

First, the country is in crisis. Second, black people are in crisis. Third, policymakers will be tempted—as they have in the past—to resolve or shift the responsibility for Crisis One by sacrificing the interests of blacks who, because of the conditions in Crisis Two, will be unable either to respond effectively or resist.

Crisis One: There are certainly major reasons for fear and anxiety in our country today that justify designating them as a crisis. The country's leaders, as a response to the most horrendous attack our nation has ever suffered, and against the advice of the United Nations and long-term allies, launched a preemptive war against a small nation, Iraq, justified with fabricated information.

The war is currently costing $216 billion and counting, and has been the cause of the deaths of thousands and the maiming in body and mind of many more. It has enraged enemies who can reap great destruction on us, even without owning nuclear submarines, supersonic planes, and smart bombs. We know from the Israeli experience that Homeland Defense—

even if competently run and appropriately funded—is no guarantee of protection against suicide bombers. Meanwhile, the Democratic Party has redefined the term "loyal opposition" with an emphasis on the loyal, and far too little focus on the opposition.

The budget surplus built by the supposedly "tax and spend" Democrats has been transformed by Conservative Republicans into the largest budget deficit in history, both to pay for the war and to provide tremendous tax breaks to the already rich. The government avoids bankruptcy by borrowing huge sums from Asian nations who could weary of watching the dollar's decline compared to other currencies, thereby precipitating an economic crisis—the government equivalent of bankruptcy.

Supposedly to ease the budget deficit, but actually to reflect opposition to big government for the needy, social programs are being cut and Social Security and Medicare are targeted for revisions from which neither may survive. Walmart, utilizing employment tactics right out of the late nineteenth century, is now the nation's largest employer, with other major firms striving to adopt its labor exploitive model. As a result, fewer and fewer jobs are secure, and more and more families are experiencing or at risk of financial disaster.

Fiscal experts warn us that the stock market is as unstable as it was just prior to the crash of 1929, and for the same reason. Corporate executives who now receive 500 times the income of their average worker appear insatiable when it comes to profit. Outsourcing and downsizing are thinly veiled synonyms for putting employees in the unsavory positions of dismissal on Friday or picking up the slack on Monday morning. Shaky business deals are common and often illegal, as indicate by the financial pages that on many days read like a criminal docket of inquiries and indictments. Insider trading is common, and accounting companies who prepare the financial data that is supposed accurately to reflect companies' well-being, have gained and deserve the reputation of used car dealers.

As reported by Roger Lowenstein in a recent *New York Times Magazine* article, the pension plans that both corporations and elected officials were ready to offer employees, often in lieu of higher wages, now leave a great many private and public funds horribly underfunded. The federal Pensions Benefit Guaranty Corporation is $23 billion in the red, which could mushroom to $100 billion, as more companies use bankruptcy to rid themselves of pension plans that were not adequately funded or from which funds have been taken to shore up businesses. Public pension plans are in no better shape and are underfunded by a total of $300 billion and arguably much more. One wonders how much average citizens know of this. They certainly won't learn much about the economic dangers they face from the corporate media unless there is scandal involved.

It is a far from happy fact that most Americans do not read the newspapers, and in many regions the papers give them precious little of real substance to read. Television news programs, where many seek the news, are more committed to crime, scandal, sports, and the weather, in that order, than to solid news coverage about matters that substantively affect our lives. In fact, entertainment is the *name* of the news and profit is the *game* of the news. Profits come from a torrent of expensively presented commercial messages that monopolize a third of the news programs, offering cures for all manner of bodily ills and disfunctions.

Much of the media is blatantly partisan or so committed to "neutrality" that criticism of those in power is rare. How many truly progressive voices— Noam Chomsky, Howard Zinn, the editorial writers and editors of *The Nation, In These Times*, or *American Prospect*—appear on even public radio or television? As a result, Americans hear (and, alas, want to hear) far more about the latest sex-related criminal trial or in-depth coverage of their favorite sports team than a balanced discussion of the issues of health, employment policies, schools, and taxes that so determine our economic condition in a system that provides socialism for the wealthy while hailing the virtues of free enterprise capitalism for the rest of us.

Watching football stadiums holding upwards of 100,000 fans fill each week, or being inundated by some of the estimated two million Halloween revelers that jammed New York's Greenwich Village recently, I wonder, Do these people understand the troubles facing their country? What would it take to get two million people jamming Greenwich Village streets to protest the war or any of several social inequities that are endangering the lives of so many of us?

Meanwhile, Congress is so gerrymandered and the incumbents so well-funded by and responsive to corporate contributors to their campaigns that there is little hope that a revitalized Democratic Party can recapture control. Then, there are the environmental depravations, the unchecked petroleum prices that are providing oil companies with huge profits and bringing thousands of businesses to their financial knees while requiring consumers to cut back on food in order to buy the gas needed to get to work and keep their families from freezing. The number of Americans without any health coverage now exceeds 45 million, with millions more participating in plans that are woefully inadequate in case of serious illness of injury. But let's move on to how the disasters on our doorsteps affect African Americans.

Crisis Two: There is a growing economic gap between blacks and whites in every measure of well-being. There are an increasing number of black people living below the poverty line, and the consequences of their poverty are obvious. Black households today earn only about 59 cents to the white household's dollar. Sociologist Thomas Shapiro argues that while income is an important element, it is far less important than wealth—all of the assets and resources that a family has at its disposal.

The median white family in 1999 had $81,000; the median black family had only $8,000. Thus, in terms of wealth, blacks have less than 10 cents to the white dollar. Focusing on children instead of families, 26 percent of all white children grew up in asset-poor households in 1999, compared to 52 percent of black children and 54 percent of Hispanic. Thus, the rate for blacks is twice as high as it is for whites—though the figures for all are a national disgrace.

Employment at every level for all groups has gotten more difficult in recent years because of layoffs due to corporate mergers, bankruptcies, and other business practices, most of which are designed to get rid of employees, reduce their salaries and health benefits, and otherwise improve corporate profit margins—if not their reputations for ethical functioning. Predictably, blacks are harmed by traditional "last hired, first fired" policies, but also are likely the chosen sacrifices where managers must make staff reduction choices.

At the unskilled job level, studies show that employers prefer white or immigrant workers over blacks, particularly black men. In New York City, surveys show employers prefer white men who have spent up to two years in prison over similarly qualified blacks with no prison time. A Northwestern sociology experiment found that the disadvantage of being a young black male job applicant was "equivalent to forcing a white male to carry an 18-month prison sentence." Additionally, while acknowledging a criminal background cut white applicant chances by half, acknowledging a criminal background cut a black applicant's chances by two-thirds.

Nor are black women exempt from job bias based on supposition. Economists at MIT and the University of Chicago found that putting a white-sounding name on a resume is worth as much as an extra eight years of work experience. Black women with names like Tanisha and Jaronda are passed over for callbacks in favor of women with more traditionally American names like Betty and Jean. White names received 50 percent more callbacks for interviews than did African American names. The amount of discrimination is uniform across occupations and industries. Federal contractors and employers who list "Equal Opportunity Employer" in their ad discriminate as much as other employers. We find little evidence that these results are driven by employers inferring something other than race, such as social class, from the names. These results suggest that racial discrimination is still a prominent feature of the labor market. Title VII of the 1964 Civil Rights Act protecting against employment discrimination is still on the books, but judicial interpretations have narrowed its value so much that civil rights groups and private lawyers are reluctant to represent those who have experienced discrimination.

Despite continuing patterns of discrimination, a great many of us are in better positions than was the case for virtually all of us almost fifty years ago. There is now a substantial black middle class who earn good incomes, live in attractive residential areas, send their children to good schools, drive nice cars, have money in the bank, and generally enjoy lifestyles, if not of the rich and famous, then of those who, as the TV sitcom described them several years ago, are "moving on up."

(Alas, we in the middle class are not immune from the notion that escape from subordinate status can be achieved through a fixation on consumer spending. According to Target Market, a company that tracks black consumer spending, blacks spend huge amounts on depreciable products—clothes, cars, electronics, and furniture.)

Black people such as Senator Barack Obama, Supreme Court Justice Clarence Thomas, Secretary of State Condoleezza Rice, Brown University president Ruth Simmons, and dozens of sports and entertainment figures including Oprah Winfrey, Bill Cosby, Tiger Woods, Denzel Washington, Sean "P. Diddy" Combs, Kanye West, O.J. Simpson—whether respected or despised—are household names. Consider as well the black people working in executive-level positions, including heads of major corporations such as Ken Chennault at American Express, Richard Parsons at Time Warner, and Stanley O'Neal at Merrill, Lynch. Even conceding my still controversial assertion that racism in the United States is permanent, you will assure me and comfort yourselves that black people can survive racism and some can achieve impressive success.

Acknowledging these success stories, though, confirms rather than refutes my Interest-Convergence Principle that asserts that relief from racial discrimination, when it comes, requires that policymakers perceive the relief we seek will provide a clear benefit for the nation or portions of the populace beyond African Americans. No matter how harmful, exploitative, or life-threatening a racist policy or practice is, petitions for reform are *recognized and implemented only so long as they advance the nation's interests.* Thus, slavery, segregation, and patterns of murderous violence were insufficient to stir any branch of government to corrective action. A perception of self-interest among policymakers, including those on the Supreme Court, was, in my view, the major motivation for outlawing racial segregation in 1954, as opposed to the many earlier opportunities. The decision provided a real boost in our competition with communist governments abroad and the campaign to uproot subversive elements at home.

This was not a fortuitous coincidence. The list of similar race-related motivations for advancing or sacrificing black interests in freedom and justice is a lengthy one. Thus, again, without in any way wishing to diminish the accomplishments of blacks who have achieved measurable success in a wide range of fields in recent decades, I simply point out that political conditions moved white policymakers to ease restrictions that made some success possible and for the talent and hard work of some blacks—far from all—to be recognized and rewarded. Were these restrictions not in place, blacks at an earlier time would have achieved no less impressive success. For we know that many of our parents and grandparents had ambition and worked very hard, but were denied opportunity. Their aspirations, their drive to achieve were frustrated by discriminatory barriers that were obvious and, for most, unbreachable.

Worthy of mention is the fact that a great many blacks in seemingly enviable positions are doing so at a high price, and sometimes a price not worth paying. As they climb the ladder of success, they may be required to leave their values on the rungs and "arrive" well-heeled and moderately respected by nearly everyone but themselves. They learn the hard way that success does not shield them from the myriad forms of racial subordination.

The Rage of a Privileged Class by journalist Ellis Cose is based on dozens of interviews with educated black people holding impressive positions in corporate and government offices. They are embittered because success does not shield them from being bypassed for promotions that sometimes go to people they trained. Pushing for the hiring of other people of color can be a frustration, particularly when it becomes apparent that those doing the hiring are not interested as long as you are there.

Those blacks seeking success in the business world may decide not to protest the discrimination that clouds their lives. No such options are available to many young, black males who, despite having more opportunity for success than any of their forebears, are stumbling through life. In *The Envy of the World,* Ellis Cose surveys their status.

If we brought them together in one incorporated region, the black males who are now in prison would instantly become the twelfth largest urban area in the country. A recent study shows that in 2002, 10.4 percent of black men ages 25 to 29, or 442,300 people, were in prison. By comparison, 2.4 percent of Hispanic men and 1.2 percent of white men in the same age group were in prison. Marc Mauer, the assistant director of the Sentencing Project, a prison-change research and advocacy group, said of the continuing high number of young black men in prison that "the rippled effect on their communities, and on the next generation of kids growing up with their fathers in prison, will certainly be with us for at least a generation."

When Cose adds to the prison population the black males ravished by AIDS, murder, poverty, and illiteracy, the widening gap separating the black elite from the so-called underclass, makes for a paralyzing pessimism. Out of his many interviews, Cose constructs a mosaic of the temptations of the street, its powerful allure, it seduction: young, black males feel it is "offering us a place to belong, the only place—or so we are made to believe—that we alone can own." "From the moment our brains are capable of cognition, we are primed to embrace our presumed destiny." Their perception of reality is shaped by movies, television, and the radio, all portraying the black man as a "street-wise, trash-talking operator, as the polar opposite of the refined, cerebral white male, who, coincidentally, many control the world but lacks our style and soul."

These are the models for many young people who, overcome by the obstacles of poverty and racism they view as insurmountable, determine to flout social conventions, ignore education, and live so as to "keep it real." For many, the results are a disaster that inevitably leads to death or imprisonment.

Crisis Three—This potential crisis grows out of Crisis One, the troubled economic condition of the country, and Crisis Two, the vulnerability of black people, both as a result of that economic condition and because much of the progress made can be attributed to the interest convergence phenomenon. One would hope that racial progress would be linear, that the gains of today would lead to further gains in the future. But, as I have tried to show, racial progress is cyclical. Gains that appear secure in one period are rolled back in the next.

Remember the remarkable progress former slaves made in about a decade during post–Civil War Reconstruction, all with precious little help from the federal government and all manner of opposition from Southern whites. And remember as well how those gains were wiped away after the Hayes-Tilden Compromise, when the Republicans whom blacks had strongly supported literally bartered black freedom and their safety away in order to secure Hayes's elevation to the presidency.

Yes, this sellout happened in 1877, but didn't the Supreme Court similarly sacrifice black rights in the second *Brown v. Board* decision with its "all deliberate speed" decision? Whites strongly opposed what the Court had held just a year earlier, and with no support from the executive or congressional branches, the Court, its reputation at risk, and with the concurrence of much of the country, in effect, reversed itself. For not the first time, black struggles for racial equality were rewarded with nice words but inadequate and quickly expiring substantive enforcement.

Affirmative action policies, willingly adopted by policymakers as a response to the urban rebellions of the late 1960s, opened many positions previously closed to blacks and women. Over time, widespread opposition rendered any acknowledged use of race in such programs suspect and presumptively invalid.

Today, the administration that controls the White House, the Congress, much of the judicial system, and even the corporate media, is in trouble. The polls show the president is losing support steadily. Hurricane Katrina revealed incompetence at high levels, and the ValerieGate cover-up has led to one indictment, with perhaps more to come.

While some of us—particularly blacks, only 2 percent of whom, according to recent polls, support the president—are rather enjoying the administration's squirming, we would be well advised not to celebrate too soon.

This is the party that came to power in the South (recall Ronald Reagan launching his campaign with a speech in Philadelphia, Mississippi, near the site where the three civil rights workers were murdered in 1964), and then flourished through much of the middle of the country by insinuations that their party would not protect "special interests," read blacks. They have kept those promises through general opposition to civil rights, particularly affirmative action. At election time, they have resorted to blatant tactics (recall the Willie Horton ads), or more blatant (see the practices preventing blacks from voting in Florida in 2000, and in Ohio in 2004).

In terms of basic rights, this administration summarily deported thousands of Middle-East persons with minor visa issues, while ignoring reports of extremely suspicious behavior by the 9/11 plane hijackers. Even now, despite widespread criticism of policies of uncivilized treatment and torture of those held without charges in Guantánamo and other sites, it is debating whether its standards for handling terrorist suspects should comply with Geneva Convention rules.

The Democratic Party, which relies heavily on black support, particularly in presidential elections, is so concerned about alienating white voters that it hardly mentions continuing racial discrimination, affirmative action, or civil rights. Black voters are supposed to understand and accept this silence, but what are we to think when the Democrats fail to mount court challenges after literally thousands of blacks are excluded from the polls in Florida in 2000? And in 2004, Senator Kerry conceded while blacks in Ohio were demanding a recount of votes because of flagrant election violations, charges that if sustained would have given Kerry the presidency.

There is, then, little indication that the Democratic Party will provide much opposition if the Republic administration determines to shift the blame for their failures by exploiting, further, the still virulent sense among so many that this is and should remain a white country; and the unconscious sense of some that this would be a far better country if blacks did not exist.

In a recent *Washington Post* column, Jabari Asim commented on the suggestion by radio host and former education secretary William Bennett that if all black babies were aborted, the crime rate would go down. Asim wrote:

> While much has been said about Bennett's bizarre warbling, little comment has been made about the tradition to which is belongs. His hypothetical vision of a United States without black criminals has its roots in a dream of a country without any blacks at all. This particular neurosis is as much a part of our national tradition as baseball, racism, and the rewarding of lusterless loyalists with important and powerful positions.

Mr. Asim reminds us that George Washington expressed the wish to be rid of Negroes whom he deemed idle and not worth the cost of keeping them healthy enough to work in his fields. Thomas Jefferson shared that view and actually proposed sending all blacks back to Africa. Abraham Lincoln did the same.

Throughout the nineteenth century and beyond, the myth of black laziness and criminality persisted and our inferiority as human beings provided a basis for fame to a number of social scientists, down to the bestselling author of *The Bell Curve*. Writing in 1970, Ralph Ellison observed that "the fantasy of an America free of blacks is at least as old as the dream of creating a truly democratic society."

My most popular story, "The Space Traders," builds upon this dream by imagining huge ships from another planet landing on the shores of the United States and offering all manner of riches if the country would allow it to take away all its citizens designated as black. Given a few weeks to decide, I imagine the debate that takes place and the decision of a conservative administration to put the question to the people in a national referendum. They well know the outcome when the rights of minorities are placed on the block of a general election. And they prove right. Americans vote for the trade by a 70 to 30 percentage. The final paragraph of the story reads:

> Dawn on the day of the trade presents an extraordinary sight. In the night, the Space Traders draw their strange ships right up to the beaches and discharge their cargoes of gold, minerals, and machinery, leaving vast empty holds. Crowded on the beaches are some thirty million silent black men, women, and children, including babes in arms. As the sun rises, the Space Traders direct them, first, to strip off all but a single undergarment; then, to line up; and finally, to enter those holds which yawn in the morning lights like Milton's "darkness visible." The black people look fearfully behind them. But, on the dunes above the beaches, guns at the ready, stand U.S. guards. There is no escape, no alternative. Heads bowed, armed now linked by slender chains, black people leave the new world as their forebears had arrived.

When I used to read this story to audiences and then ask whether it could happen here, most blacks quickly responded, Yes. Whites were more uncertain. I then told them that I was not interested in how they might personally vote, but wanted them to think of whites in the communities they knew best. Imagine, I asked them, whether they felt that a majority of these whites would vote for the trade were they to do so in the privacy of a voting booth. Slowly, almost painfully, most whites raised their hands.

In his novel *The Plot Against America*, Philip Roth imagines how an American idol, in this instance Charles Lindbergh, might be elected president and, based on his high regard for the Nazis, affect policies of humiliation and anger against American Jews through a government program whereby Jews would be placed, family by family, across the nation, thereby breaking up their neighborhoods—ghettos—and removing them from each other and from any kind of ethnic solidarity. Roth illustrates how easily people can be persuaded by self-interest to abandon morality.

An oft-repeated theme in the mammoth Holocaust history, reflected in *A Holocaust Reader*, edited by Lucy Dawidowicz, is that "The final solution would not have been possible without the pervasive presence and the uninterrupted tradition of anti-Semitism in Germany. The exposure of the German people for generations to conventional anti-Semitism in its manifold forms—political, nationalist, racial, cultural, doctrinal, economic—eventually rendered them insensitive to Hitler's radical and deadly brand of anti-Semitism."

Can we be certain that the anti-Semitism that made the Holocaust possible is that different from the racism that could provide the same preconditions in America, if leaders feel the need to designate the traditional scapegoat as the cause of their policy failures? As I have tried to show, though, a general roundup of all black people is not needed. We need only consider the conditions I have all too briefly recounted here. And then imagine new policy initiatives that would further what is already well under way.

In my book *Gospel Choirs*, for example, I imagine enactment of a Freedom of Employment Act under which all jobs held by blacks are rendered vulnerable because of a strong presumption they were obtained through considerations of race. Black employees can be replaced by persons not eligible for affirmative action, who can show they had stronger traditional qualification at the time the job was filled. Given the strong opposition to and deep resentment of affirmative action policies, it is not difficult to guess how this measure would be received and enforced.

These, then, are the current crises that give content to Professor Wilhelm's predictions and my concerns. The challenge of apocalyptic prophesy is just that: a warning without easy resolution. Our uncertainty about the level of danger, the degree of decline might be measurable. Nuclear scientists designed a doomsday clock to represent how near government policies were to bringing us to nuclear disaster. We need an Index to Racial Attrition, one that would input data on a range of conditions and produce a single number reflecting that we are moving toward or veering away from the catastrophic fate that Professor Willhelm predicted and that so many of us too quietly fear.

A racial attrition index, prepared by social scientists and computer-oriented statisticians, would provide a dramatic rendering of our social progress and decline. In effect, it would offer a periodic technological prophesy, one calling on the essence of our humanity to take action needed by all. For, as Lani Guinier and Gerald Torres point out, blacks are like the canaries that alerted miners to a poisonous atmosphere. Issues of race point to underlying problems in society that ultimately affect everyone, not just minorities. Addressing these issues is essential. Ignoring racial differences—race blindness—has failed. Focusing on individual achievement has diverted us from tackling pervasive inequalities that, beyond the camouflage of race, affect us all.

Ralph Ellison suggested that we're a race of Jeremiahs, prophets calling for the nation to repent. The Index of Racial Attrition, then, will serve as a monitor of our status and that of the country. In a different form, blacks will continue to play a role in this society that Ralph Ellison eloquently describes:

"Blacks, of the many groups that compose this country, suffered the harsh realities of the human condition. Because of our past fate, for blacks, there are no hiding places down here, not in suburbia or in penthouse, neither in country nor in city. They are an American people who are geared to what *is* and who yet are driven by a sense of what is possible for human life to be in this society." Disagreeing with those who feel this would be a better country without blacks, Ellison predicts that the nation could not survive being deprived of blacks' presence because, "by the irony implicit in the dynamics of American democracy, they symbolize both its most stringent testing and the possibility of its greatest human freedom."

Ellison adds, "it is the black American who puts pressure upon the nation to live up to its ideals. It is he who gives creative tension to our struggle for justice and for the elimination of those factors, social and psychological, which make for slums and shaky suburban communities. . . . Without the black American, something irrepressibly hopeful and creative would go out of the American spirit, and the nation might well succumb to the moral slobbism that has ever threatened its existence from within."

What Ellison wrote in 1986 is no less true today, and yet his position is a minority view. Our survival as a people and a nation may depend on transforming the vision of a minority into a consensus acknowledged and embraced by the majority.

11

Racism as the Ultimate Deception

JOHN CALMORE
(LECTURE DELIVERED BY DERRICK BELL)
2006

*John Calmore, who passed away in 2009, was the Reef C. Ivey Professor of
Law at the University of North Carolina. He received his BA from Stanford
University and his JD from Harvard Law School. A former staff attorney at
the National Housing Law Project and Director of Litigation for the Legal Aid
Foundation of Los Angeles, among other positions, Professor Calmore taught
and wrote about civil rights, Critical Race Theory, local government law,
social justice lawyering, and torts. He was a co-author, with Martha Mahoney
and Stephanie Wildman, of the widely adopted law school text* Social Justice:
Professionals, Communities, and Law.

Hurling "racism!"—at a group or an individual—as an epithet is both common and easy to do. Seriously getting to the roots of racism—that is, the
favoring of one group, the white, over minority groups—and pulling up

---

In 2006, University of North Carolina School of Law professor John Calmore was
scheduled to give the annual Bell lecture; when he took ill, Derrick Bell delivered the
lecture from notes provided by Professor Calmore. The transcription provided is of
Derrick Bell's words.

those roots to eradicate them is, however, extraordinarily difficult. This is so despite the progress that supposedly has been made in race relations in this nation since the Emancipation Proclamation became effective in 1863.

Professor John Calmore explores the seemingly indestructible phenomenon of racism via Thomas Mann's fictional confidence man, who is adept at succeeding in the world through his ability to fulfill people's expectations of him in whatever role he is playing, whether waiter or aristocratic youth. Utilizing this character enables Calmore to convey his sense that racism is a sort of racial phantasm, one that plays all too effectively on the self-interest of varying groups of people, their differing motivations, ideologies, egos, and greed, whether white or black, whether well-meaning and trying to do the right thing or actually racist. This phantasm has the effect of maintaining the invidious disparity between white society and minority groups in order to stabilize society for the benefit of those in power, who, not surprisingly, insist that the world is and should be entirely color-blind.

Thus, however easy it may be to identify overt racism, it is very difficult to discern its more subtle and destructive activity and, in turn, to act against it. It is quite like the fictional Shadow of the long-ago radio series, a detective who had the power to cloud human minds. The racism phantasm undermines common sense, making us—proponents and opponents of racism alike—all too likely to advocate policies that, in the short or long run, will disappoint rather than fulfill our fervently sought-after outcomes.

Given the often dire outlook, racial equality advocates too readily embrace research with predictions of positive outcomes. The economist and sociologist Gunnar Myrdal concluded in his massive mid-twentieth-century study, *An American Dilemma*, that while racism was "a moral lag," it was merely an odious holdover from slavery—"perhaps the most glaring conflict in the American conscience and the greatest unsolved task for American democracy." Following Myrdal, more than two generations of civil rights advocates accepted his politically comforting rationale and worked hard to fulfill his predictions.

Unfortunately, the reality turned out to be more in line with the earlier, 1903 view of Dr. W.E.B. Du Bois, who began seeking the truth about race in America rather early in his long life. He asserted, without optimism, that "the color-line" would prove to be the major problem of the twentieth century. The continued importance of race in a new century gives added credence to Dr. Du Bois's prediction, such that, at this point, it is more of a prophesy.

Forty years after Myrdal, in 1984, Professor Jennifer Hochschild wrote— with more accuracy than Myrdal, but to much less acclaim—that far from being an anomaly, racial division is a rather crucial component of liberal democracy. The two are "historically, even inherently, reinforcing"; that is, as she puts it, "the apparent anomaly is an actual symbiosis."

Considering the racial issue from a theological perspective, George D. Kelsey, a professor of Christian ethics, explains why so many people who practice racial discrimination are also sometimes devout, even born-again Christians. He acknowledges that while racism initially served as an ideological justification for the constellations of political and economic power expressed in colonialism and slavery, "gradually the idea of the superior race was heightened and deepened in meaning and value so that it pointed beyond the historical structures . . . to human existence itself." Although contrary to the fundamental teachings of Christianity, belief in a superior race became the center of value and an object of devotion, enabling every white person to gain a "power of being" through membership in that race.

As a complete system involving—as does religious faith—meaning, individual value, and loyalty, this belief enables the most economically and culturally deprived white man to feel so superior to any black that the former feels entitled to justify ignoring such a basic Christian admonition as "love thy neighbor as thyself." So great a conflict between belief and action may only be explained as the work of the phantasm of racism.

John Calmore has written that:

race and racism are always concepts in formation. Our notion of race and our experience with racism do not represent fixed, static phenomena. Racism is more than the intentional behavior of the occasional bad actor. Racism mutates and multiplies, creating a range of racisms.

We must be able to bring up issues of race and racism without the terms always leading to fear, alienation, and off-point debate.

As a result, we fail to appreciate the shifting parameters that mark the consideration of race—"how group interests are conceived, status is ascribed, agency is attained and roles performed."

Hochschild, Kelsey, Calmore, and many other observers seek to home in on racism's actual functioning and effects. Unfortunately, their efforts are either rarely heard or are ignored in favor of voices proclaiming what many people—some blacks and many whites—find more comforting: that racism, if it ever existed, is no more than an excuse made by some colored peoples who do not want to work and forge ahead in this free society the way most whites and a few blacks are doing and have done. Stephan and Abigail Thernstrom, for example, claim that "the serious inequality that remains is less a function of white racism than of the racial gap in levels of educational attainment, the structure of the black family, and the rise in black crime."

Such conclusions that confuse the causes of racism with its effects—doubtless the work of Calmore's phantasm of racism—are comforting rationales that the man or woman in the street is all too ready to accept. Some people accept and act on these views even though they doubt them. They are like the fellow trying to win at three-card monte: at some level, he knows he cannot beat the card shark, but the possibility of ultimately succeeding keeps him playing until he has lost both money and dignity. This racial sleight of hand has mesmerized a great many white Americans for more than three hundred years.

Early in American history, when African slavery took root in the middle of the seventeenth century, working-class whites readily accepted it. Along with their successors, they identified with white wealthy planters and supported their policies—even though they were and would remain economically subordinate to those able to afford slaves. In turn, the large landowners, with the safe economic advantage provided by their slaves, were willing to grant poor whites a larger role in the political process. Although black slavery appeared to lead to greater freedom for poor whites, it actually greatly limited their chances of advancing economically beyond bare survival.

Slave owners were, for their part, easily persuaded that the profits of slavery were worth its costs in aggravations, fears, and moral gymnastics. Their sense of racial superiority over their slaves blinded them to the advantages of the more efficient labor system evolving in the North from early in the nineteenth century. In 1856, as hostility grew between pro-slave states—with their plantation system—and Northern states—with their increasingly competitive industrial system—Chief Justice Roger Taney handed down the *Dred Scott* decision. He found that blacks, whether slave or free, could not be citizens. In doing so, he succumbed to the enticing notion that the Framers had not resisted seventy years earlier: that otherwise nonnegotiable differences on the slavery issue could be settled by sacrificing the interests of blacks. Taney's ruling failed to settle the issue because, where he saw slavery as the game, it was only its name; what was really at stake was the industrial versus the plantation system. When slavery was challenged economically as well as morally, the South's secession led to four years of bloody conflict in which almost 400,000 Confederate soldiers, most from the working classes who did not own slaves, were killed or wounded. They fought and died for a way of life that kept them in a subordinate condition. Nonetheless, in the wake of defeat, they and their former slave owner superiors continued to support political policies and extra-political violence to ensure the continuation of the failed system they had come to know so well. The fact that these working classes thought only blacks were the victims again illustrates that a force beyond stubbornness and pride of place was at work.

After the Civil War, according to historian C. Vann Woodward, Southern leaders in the post-Reconstruction era enacted segregation laws mainly at the insistence of poor whites who, given their precarious social and economic status, demanded these barriers in order to retain a sense of racial superiority over blacks. As Woodward observes, "[i]t took a lot of ritual and Jim Crow to bolster the creed of white supremacy in the bosom of a white man working for a black man's wages."

Northern white workers, all too appropriately referred to as "wage slaves," fell prey to racism's blandishments as well. Race was a major facilitator of the acculturation and assimilation of European immigrants during the late nineteenth and early twentieth centuries. Horribly exploited by the mine and factory owners for whom they tolled long hours under brutal conditions for subsistence wages, their shared feeling of superiority to blacks—the racism phantasm—was one of the few things that united them.

Other facilitators included the blackface and racially derogatory minstrel shows of that period, which savagely disparaged blacks. These propaganda pageants facilitated the acculturation and assimilation of immigrants by inculcating a nationalism whose common theme was the disparagement of blacks. Given these imposed—and too readily accepted—racial barriers, there was little possibility that white immigrants would cross racial lines to unite with blacks in resisting exploitation and deprivation by the powerful who, then as now, did not respect any color line.

Clinging to their white racial status, labor unions refused to admit blacks to their ranks and thus undermined organizing efforts when strikes were subverted by factories that hired otherwise unemployed blacks to replace the striking workers. As for the economic masters of the working class, the industrialists, their desire for wealth and power under the factory system was so great that they willingly faced the often swiftly swinging pendulum of an unregulated market that could bring ruin as well as riches. Assuming that exploitation of the working class was essential to their way of business, corporate owners resisted by every available means the efforts by organized workers to get them to share their profits with those whose labors—under conditions of indignity, dirt, and danger—made the profits possible.

This resistance led to terrible labor strife, and only the Great Depression of the 1930s brought about some reform, which proved temporary for a multitude of reasons. Today, corporate leaders, whose memory of the past is clouded by their unswerving focus on the "bottom line," are again placing short-term profit over all else. This time, they and the governments they are so instrumental in putting into power have placed what once was the world's richest economy in debt to foreign nations that have historic reasons to become exacting creditors.

Even today, in the twenty-first century, many whites remain vulnerable to arguments contending that social reform programs are "welfare programs for blacks." They ignore the fact that poor and working-class whites (the terms are virtually interchangeable as more and more Americans have incomes at the poverty level while working full-time) have employment, health, education, and social service needs that barely differ from those of a great many blacks. Dismissing their attitudes and actions as racist is easy enough. It is not inaccurate, but viewed from the perspective of Calmore's thesis, it is insufficient. Can it be that group identification with blacks, even on issues of importance to both, undermines the sense of superior status that is a major component of their self-esteem?

Once, during the question period at a lecture I gave, a black man told me that racism makes white folks stupid. Just, I thought, as Calmore's racism phantasm does, and has in the past, to people of all colors, white as well as black, leaders and followers both. How does one better comprehend what motivated those who presided over the birth of this nation to sacrifice proposals to ban slavery in favor of surrendering their principles of freedom? Why would they seek to maintain the support of slave owners and slavery profiteers that brought about a birth that proved unstable precisely because of those arrangements? That original sacrifice of black—and human—interests sets a pattern that has been repeated, in one way or another, throughout our history.

Given that history, might there have been a similar influence, no less contrary to basic interests, that moved Frederick Douglass—an escaped slave and self-educated man of great intelligence who became the leading black abolitionist and one of the great orators of his time—to persuade President Lincoln to include a provision in the Emancipation Proclamation authorizing the enlistment of escaped slaves into the Union forces? We know that Douglass felt that the slaves' participation in the war would win the nation's respect and bring them full rights as American citizens. But, given his all-too-direct knowledge of America's racial hostility, what led him to urge that men, only recently having freed themselves from the viciousness of slavery, be allowed to enlist and face almost certain death in an army that did not want them, refused for a long period to pay them, and sent them again and again on what were—even on the killing fields of that brutal war—essentially suicide missions?

And what led roughly 179,000 black men who served as soldiers in the U.S. Army and another 19,000 who served in the Navy—nearly 40,000 of whom died over the course of the war—to believe that their valor as Union troops would be, or could be, rewarded with other than cursory thanks and, ultimately, rejection? The question I pose here of Frederick Douglass— and of the thousands of soldiers he helped recruit for the Union army— can be just as appropriately put to most black leaders who have followed him into the present.

Certainly, black leaders and those they led had a vision, but it was not a vision emanating from either history or their lived experience. It is as though the racism phantasm was taking advantage of the freedom they longed for to lure them into pushing for programs that—albeit under new and promising names—would in fact ensure the maintenance of the subordinate status they sought to escape.

The post–Civil War amendments to the Constitution—much like the earlier Emancipation Proclamation and the later civil rights laws—promised black people much more than they could deliver, or more than whites were willing to permit them to deliver, while each amendment served to further what policymaking whites felt would be in at least whites' short-term interests.

From Biblical times to the present, the power that has enabled a few to see through sham to truth has gained them rebuke and worse. The accolade of prophet is bestowed only long after their truths have been ignored and disaster has rendered them self-evident. Thus it was with Dr. Du Bois in the 1930s when the National Association for the Advancement of Colored People (NAACP) leaders, despite a bleak judicial record of racial hostility, convinced themselves that Negroes could effectively challenge racial segregation in the courts. Dr. Du Bois, one of the organization's founders, while not opposed to, and recognizing the potential benefits of, integration, was well aware of the continuing force of racial hostility. Seeing economic development as the prerequisite of rights—not as an automatic reward after those rights were gained—he urged development of strong neighborhoods and schools, and the building and supporting of black business.

In the area of education, Dr. Du Bois conceded, "Other things being equal, the mixed school is the broader, more natural basis for the education of all youth. It gives wider contacts; it inspires greater self-confidence; and suppresses the inferiority complex." But, he warned, "A mixed school with poor and unsympathetic teachers, with hostile public opinion, and no teaching of truth concerning black folk, is bad." He concluded, "[T]he Negro needs neither segregated schools nor mixed schools. What he needs is Education."

Despite Dr. Du Bois's reputation as the foremost intellectual in the racial field at the time, not only was his advice ignored, but his continued effort to propound it cost him his position in the NAACP. We all know of the two decades of litigation efforts culminating in the Supreme Court's 1954 decision in *Brown v. Board of Education.* And we know as well of the long years of efforts to overcome the fierce resistance of whites to that decision. In many areas, they fought to keep black children out of schools that were often hardly better as educational entities than were their usually underfunded black counterparts.

Today, a half century after *Brown,* most black and Latino children attend schools that are primarily black and Latino and that, with some notable exceptions, provide a wholly inadequate education. We need to figure out what led so many civil rights leaders and lawyers to assume, again against all history, that equal educational opportunity for black children could be obtained—only attained according to some—in racially integrated schools.

Looking back on my own years of deep involvement in the school desegregation campaign, I myself have wondered how I and others could allow our dream of an integrated society to cause us both to ignore Dr. Du Bois's admonition and, more importantly, to fail to recognize that better schooling, not integrated schools, was what the black parents we represented needed and wanted. I realize now that we were misled by a force beyond our vision: that, despite our idealism, we were rendered vulnerable because we failed to recognize the deviousness and pertinacity of the forces against us.

That force remains viable, as is obvious with the Supreme Court's *Parents Involved* decision. In two districts, some white parents challenged school board policies intended to ensure a degree of school integration. In the functioning of these policies, their children were denied admission to their chosen schools. Here, it is easy to see how the smooth tongue of the racism phantasm could convince the white parents that priority for black or Latino children over theirs, whatever the school boards' goals, cannot be in keeping with their sense of racial priority and thus must be unconstitutional. With the current composition of the Court, these parents and their view prevailed.

The two courts of appeal that earlier heard the cases approved both school boards' plans as worthwhile means of maintaining a degree of racial diversity in the school systems. The dozens of amicus briefs filed by liberal groups focused on this theme. They urged the application of the Supreme Court's closely divided decision in *Grutter v. Bollinger*, the 2003 University of Michigan Law School case involving the role of diversity in law school admissions. The amicus briefs, however, did not consider in any depth whether the special educational needs of black and Latino students are being met in these school systems where the emphasis is on diversity and educational quality is simply assumed.

It is, of course, this assumption of an otherworldly racial phantasm influencing decisions that is perhaps most appropriately applied to politicians in general, and this country's current leaders in particular, who tend to operate through the racism phantasm, playing on the self-interest of various social groups, pandering to their greed and arrogance, and preying on the fear and ignorance of much of the population. The use of race to generate that fear has been an essential part of their modus operandi.

As a phantasm, of course, racism is the combination of many factors. Harvard Law professor Lani Guinier asserts:

Race in the United States is a by-product of economic conflict that has been converted into a tool of division and distraction. It is not just an outgrowth of hatred or ill will. Racism has had psychological, sociological, and economic consequences that created the separate spheres inhabited by blacks and whites . . .

All coalesce into persuasive influences that render us all—racists and anti-racists alike—subject to forces seemingly beyond our control and even our understanding. Here is a further explanation of my long-held view that racism is permanent: not because so many whites are evil, but because the large and growing disparities between the "haves" and "have-nots" in our economic system will continue to require racism to stabilize the disparities and to reassure many white people that, despite their lowly status, they are better than, and deserve priority over, those minority groups whose color makes them easily recognizable and thus all too readily dismissed.

This diagnosis of racism is not meant to make us despair. Rather, we need to keep our eyes not just on the prize of racial justice, but on the carefully focused plans and action that are necessary to confronting the barriers that stand in its way. We need to act with the attitude of the farmer who left his fields in order to join the voting rights march from Selma to Montgomery. Along the march, when he was asked whether he thought the marchers would be able to win in Montgomery, he responded directly and simply: "We won when we started." The farmer understood that the challenge of life is to move beyond passivity in the face of power and take action against injustices small and large. He understood that, as Ray Charles reminds us in one of his songs, "[u]nderstanding is the best thing in the world."

However fearsome understanding may be, it may also be the prerequisite for a willingness to risk speaking and acting in ways that fly in the face of consensus thinking. Such actions—taken in the knowledge that they may bring scorn, rejection, and retaliation, and taken from a perspective that rises beyond race—can often defy the efforts of the racism phantasm and even encourage others to emulate the risk taker in the search for truth.

Truth expressed in the language of poetry can offer beauty and reassurance as well. Thus, in one of his articles, John Calmore quotes a passage from Patricia Williams, the poet laureate of the Critical Race Theory movement:

> I think that the hard work of a nonracist sensibility is the boundary crossing, from safe circle into wilderness: the testing of boundary, the consecration of sacrilege. It is the willingness to spoil a good party and break an encompassing circle, to travel from the safe to the unsafe. The transgression is dizzyingly intense, a reminder of what it is to be alive, . . . to survive the transgression is terrifying and addictive. To know that everything has changed and yet nothing has changed; and in leaping the chasm of this impossible division of self, a discovery of the self surviving, still well, still strong, and, as a curious consequence, renewed.

We surely need more persons like Dr. Du Bois, whose willingness to see truth beyond the contrary consensus may be the only antidote to the racism phantasm. Israeli author David Grossman, whose son was killed in the 2006 war in Lebanon, is a contemporary model of such truth telling. Speaking at a rally in Tel Aviv to mark the eleventh anniversary of the murder of Prime Minister Yitzhak Rabin and presented in the presence of Israel's current prime minister, Grossman's speech provided an example of the truth telling we need so badly. Two paragraphs stand out as applicable as much to the United States, Israel's chief ally, as to Israel itself:

> There was a war, and Israel flexed its massive military muscle, but also exposed Israel's fragility. We discovered that our military might ultimately cannot be the only guarantee of our existence. Primarily, we have found that the crisis Israel is experiencing is far deeper than we had feared, in almost every way.
>
> From where I stand right now, I beseech, I call on all those who listen, the young who came back from the war, who know they are the

ones to be called upon to pay the price of the next war, on citizens, Jew and Arab, people on the right and the left, the secular, the religious, stop for a moment, take a look into the abyss. Think of how close we are to losing all that we have created here. Ask yourselves if this is not the time to get a grip, to break free of this paralysis, to finally claim the lives we deserve to live.

Here is a further indication that the only defense against the racism phantasm as it operates in the real world is absolute honesty about our actions, our desires, our goals, or as close to that ever-elusive dream as we can come. Even with our best efforts, we are easily misled; false steps are more easily taken than retraced. And admission of error is particularly hard. Yet only the honest seeking of truth can protect us from being victimized by the racism phantasm that has done so much harm to individuals and to the nation we all share.

12

Like a Loaded Weapon

ROBERT A. WILLIAMS

2007

Robert A. Williams Jr. is the Regents Professor, E. Thomas Sullivan Professor of Law, and faculty co-chair of the University of Arizona Indigenous Peoples Law and Policy Program. Professor Williams received his BA from Loyola College and his JD from Harvard Law School. He was named the first Oneida Indian Nation Visiting Professor of Law at Harvard Law School, having previously served there as Bennett Boskey Distinguished Visiting Lecturer of Law. Williams has received major grants and awards from the Soros Senior Justice Fellowship Program of the Open Society Institute, the MacArthur Foundation, the Ford Foundation, and the National Endowment for the Humanities. He is the author of The American Indian in Western Legal Thought: The Discourses of Conquest, *which received the Gustavus Myers Human Rights Center Award as one of the outstanding books published in 1990 on the subject of prejudice in the United States. He has also written* Linking Arms Together: American Indian Treaty Visions of Law and Peace, 1600–1800 *and* Like a Loaded Weapon: The Rehnquist Court, Indian Rights, and the Legal History of Racism in America.

There is a very telling *Far Side* cartoon by Gary Larson that I like to share with people whenever I'm asked to talk about the history of Indian rights in America. The cartoon depicts an Indian in buckskins and full feathered-headdress regalia standing next to a teepee, addressing members of his tribe. They're all sporting either feathers or braids in their long black hair. The Indian standing in front of the group, obviously the leader of this tribe, is shown holding up a necklace made of a few tacky beads. In the cartoon bubble above his head, he proudly proclaims to his assembled little band, "To begin, I'd like to show you *this*! Isn't is a beaut'?" The caption below the cartoon simply reads, "New York 1626: Chief of the Manhattan Indians addresses his tribe for the last time."

A good number of folks always seem to think they get the joke in this cartoon right away. After their laughter and chuckles subside, I like to ask them why they think they get it. Typically, they say something like, "It's all about the Indians selling Manhattan to the Dutch for a bunch of worthless beads and trinkets." Some of them can even tell me exactly how much the Indians supposedly were paid by the Dutch for the sale of Manhattan. If you let them go on, they'll say that everybody knows that Indians usually got ripped off in their treaties with the white man. "Common knowledge," they'll say. "Come on, you're the one who's supposed to be the expert."

I want to know more about this core organizing belief that so many people seem to have about Indians and their worthless treaty deals. What types of iconic symbols and mythical metanarratives are evoked in their minds by the infamous story of the Indians selling Manhattan to the Dutch, of all people, for twenty-four dollars in lousy beads and trinkets? Why is it that so many people seem to believe that Indians had this relatively primitive, unsophisticated way of life that supposedly made them clueless as to the "real" value of what they were selling when they made treaties with the white man for their lands? No one can ever seem to remember exactly where or how they acquired this type of cultural metaknowledge about Indians. It's just one of those things a person somehow picks up along the way while growing up in America, or so I'm told. It's all part of our racial imagination.

Once I get people to confess their basic ideas about Indians, Indian lands, and stupid Indian treaty deals, it's relatively easy to deconstruct this cartoon for them. The reason they think they get it, I explain, is because of a commonly held, long-established negative racial stereotype about Indians in the American racial imagination. Most people in this country believe that Indians were a primitive people when the white man finally "discovered" them in the New World. That's why the tribes were totally clueless as to the real value of the real estate they gave up in their treaties. They were savages.

Though his readers may not be precisely aware of it, Larson is subversively playing up on this basic stereotype that he knows most people in America have about Indians, iconically represented by the apocryphal tale of the sale of Manhattan. If the Indians were too primitive and savage to appreciate the true value of their land, then why are they about to get rid of their chief for selling Manhattan for a bunch of lousy beads? Get it?

Larson's cartoon works precisely because it plays against this long-established racial stereotype of Indians as unsophisticated savages, making us reimagine the Indians' actual reaction to news of the sale of Manhattan from a different, nonstereotyped perspective. The cartoon's somewhat jolting view of what happened to that Indian chief when he reported back the news to his tribe conflicts with our commonly held stereotypes of Indians as too uncivilized and ignorant to know what an idiot their chief was for selling Manhattan for twenty-four dollars. Maybe they weren't so savage, ignorant, and uncivilized after all. Maybe they just had a stupid chief who made a bad deal for their land, which offers a whole new perspective on a very old story about a very old treaty. Now they're not so sure if they really did get the joke in the cartoon, or if it got them instead.

Here's one way to tell if Larson's cartoon let your stereotypes get the best of you. Ask yourself this question: Can you say anything knowledgeable about any other Indian treaty, besides the treaty for Manhattan?

I know it makes some people uncomfortable, being confronted for the first time with their negative racial stereotypes of Indians. But the fact that so many people respond to this racialized image of Indians as uncivilized, easily duped savages—and the fact that there is not much to counter that pervasive, clichéd stereotype in their minds—is just one illustration of the continuing, organizing force of a long-established, well-known way of talking, thinking, and writing about Indians in the American racial imagination. There is, in other words, a language of racism in America directed at Indians, and most of us, whether we are conscious of it or not, are very familiar with it.

What most people are not very familiar with are the scores of legal battles Indians have fought throughout American history to protect their rights to their lands and other important legal interests guaranteed in literally hundreds of treaties with the United States. Most people don't bother to familiarize themselves with the fact that Indians still regard these treaties and their ancient promises as solemn and perpetual pledges of peace and protection between two peoples, pledges that create a sacred relationship of trust.

I'm not accusing any of my fellow Americans in general of being "racist" just because they chuckled at a *Far Side* cartoon that let them see their own clichéd stereotypes about Indians at work in their minds. I do, however, tell people that even if we ourselves make a conscious choice, or at least the effort, to refrain from doing anything that helps keep this tradition alive in our daily lives and interactions with others, such a choice doesn't mean that this familiar way of talking, thinking, and writing about certain minority groups in our history doesn't continue to affect the world we live in today. It does, in very subtle and sometimes very dangerous ways. The negative racial stereotypes, apocrypha, and other forms of racial imagery that we all know about are part of the history of racism in America. That history is an important part of our cultural memory and continues to define who we are and how we got that way as a people.

The Long-Established Tradition of Negative Racial Profiling of Indians as Stereotypical Savages in the Supreme Court's Indian Rights Decisions

Given our cultural heritage as a settler-state nation of different peoples whose history has been defined, to a significant degree, by questions of race and racism, no one should be at all surprised to discover that a number of long-established and well-known languages of racism in America can be found reflected in many of the Supreme Court's most important decisions on minority rights under the Constitution and laws of the United States. Given the persistence and pervasiveness of Native racial stereotypes and hostile racist imagery in shaping our history, these languages have inevitably found their way into that part of our national heritage involving the written decisions of the Supreme Court. For the most part, after all, the justices were born and raised here in America and were exposed to these languages. They know what these languages are all about: these languages are about the use of negative stereotypes, racial images, and apocryphal tales to justify the stigma of inferiority attached to certain racially subordinated groups in our society. In fact, you can tell the justices know all about the language of racism historically directed against Indians in America simply by reading their opinions on Indian rights.

During the Marshall Court Era

Indians, for example, are unembarrassedly referred to as "heathens" and as "fierce savages, whose occupation was war, and whose subsistence was drawn chiefly from the forest," by Chief Justice John Marshall in his 1823 opinion in *Johnson v. McIntosh*, one of the most important Indian rights cases ever handed down by the Supreme Court. Nor was this an isolated incident of legalized racial profiling by the man whom most historians and legal scholars revere as the greatest chief justice of all time.

In the landmark opinions on Indian rights that John Marshall wrote for the Supreme Court in the early nineteenth century, Indians were routinely referred to as a racially inferior group of people who were living as savages at the time of the coming of the white man to America. The case of *Cherokee Nation v. Georgia*, for example, is another leading Supreme Court decision authored by Marshall. In that oft-cited, landmark case on Indian rights, Marshall described Indians as constituting a race of people who were "once numerous, powerful, and truly independent" but who had gradually sunk "beneath our superior policy, our arts and our arms." They sought redress for their legal grievances, Marshall explained, not by going to a court of law like white people do, but by appealing to the "tomahawk." And in *Worcester v. Georgia*, one of the most cited, celebrated, and relied upon Supreme Court Indian law cases of all time, Marshall, writing for the Court, referred to Indians as a people who "had made small progress in agriculture or manufactures, and whose general employment was war, hunting, and fishing."

It's not surprising to find that Indians lost more times than not, at a ratio, in fact, of two to one, during this "heroic age of the Supreme Court" when the greatest chief justice of all time talked about them this way. How would you as a lawyer like those odds, arguing for the rights of your Indian client before a justice of the Supreme Court who said the types of things Marshall said about Indians in his seminal opinions on Indian rights? You might feel that such a justice was highly prejudiced against Indians as a group and therefore probably biased against your client's rights and interests in the case. To avoid even the appearance of impropriety, such a justice ought to be recused in a case involving an Indian tribe.

Throughout the Nineteenth-Century Supreme Court's Decisions on Indian Rights

Unfortunately for tribes and their lawyers, the odds of encountering justices on the Supreme Court who have talked the same way about Indians that Marshall did have always been pretty high. Lots of Supreme Court justices have followed the precedent set by Marshall and have used this same type of colorful, oftentimes overwrought, occasionally even over-romanticized, but always thoroughly racist language of Indian savagery in their opinions on Indian rights.

The Supreme Court, in fact, used to routinely rely on this type of racist language in deciding important, precedent-setting cases on Indian rights. Throughout the nineteenth century and even well into the twentieth century, the justices seemingly couldn't help themselves from talking about Indians as if they were hostile savages who deserved to disappear from the American cultural landscape. They talked this way about Indians, in fact, *even* in cases where Indians were directly involved as litigants pleading their rights before the Court. Whenever one of those old Supreme Court decisions set out an important precedent that defined Indian rights under the Constitution and laws of the United States, it seems that the justice writing the opinion couldn't help but go off on some crazy tangent, calling Indians these backward, ignorant, lawless, warlike, lazy, or drunken savages and claiming they were getting just what they deserved under our Constitution and laws.

No one should be surprised or upset about it. It's just the way Indian law was back then. You'll be reading a Supreme Court decision on Indian rights, and all of a sudden you think you've hit upon the website for one of those Ku Klux Klan or Aryan Nation hate groups. Out of nowhere, the Court's opinion will start saying gratuitous, hateful things: that Indians were separated from the white race "by the instincts of free though savage life," that they had been conquered and were now governed by "superiors of a different race," that the white man's civilized rule of law was "opposed to the traditions of their history, to the habits of their lives, to the strongest prejudices of their savage nature," or that attempting to measure "the red man's revenge by the maxims of the white man's morality" would offend basic norms of civilized justice and basically be a total waste of time. It's crazy, I know, even disturbing at times, to encounter this type of legalized racist hate speech directed against Indians in a U.S. Supreme Court opinion, but it's there in just about all of those old Indian rights cases. Some of the most hostile racial attitudes in nineteenth-century America toward Indians can be found in the Indian rights decisions of the Supreme Court.

For instance, one of the most important Indian rights decisions issued by the late nineteenth-century Supreme Court is *United States v. Kagama*. *Kagama* uses this judicialized form of racist hate speech against Indians and their rights to justify the unilateral imposition of federal criminal law on tribes even though the Constitution, as the Court itself admits in the case, nowhere expressly delegates such a power to Congress. The justices of the *Kagama* Court nevertheless unanimously declared that under U.S. law, Indians were regarded legally as "wards of the nation." Because they were "dependent on the United States—dependent largely for their daily food; dependent for their political rights"—these "remnants of a race once powerful, now weak and diminished in numbers," were under the plenary authority of Congress. The United States could therefore impose "its laws on all the tribes" if it wanted to, regardless of whether Indians liked it or not, and it really didn't matter what the actual text of the Constitution might have to say on the issue.

Despite its nineteenth-century racist language and antiquated notions of Indian racial and cultural inferiority, *Kagama* is still regarded as a leading precedent in the Supreme Court's Indian law. The case, decided in 1886, is unembarrassedly cited and relied upon, for instance, by the twenty-first-century justices of the Rehnquist Court as still good authority on Indian rights in America today.

Still Crazy After All These Years: The Maintenance of a White Racial Dictatorship in the Supreme Court's Post-Brown-Era Indian Rights Decisions

Of course, back in the nineteenth century when the justices of the Supreme Court were issuing opinions like *Johnson*, *Cherokee Nation*, *Worcester*, and *Kagama*, America, racially speaking at least, was a much different type of place. It really was crazy back then, with things like slavery, lynchings, and forced military relocations of entire Indian nations, not to mention the horrible stuff that was done to the Chinese, Japanese, and Mexican people who came here in search of the American dream. There are some historians who look at America back then and say that it was basically a "racial dictatorship," with white people on top and all the colored ones on the bottom.

Now, for some folks, calling America a white racial dictatorship might be going too far. But as a general rule, white people in America used to do some pretty crazy things to people of color back in those days. And "those days" really weren't all that long ago. It wasn't until 1954, after all, the year Elvis Presley cut his first hit record and, at least according to some, changed everything about white America's racial imagination, that the Supreme Court finally decided that blacks should be treated the same as whites under the Constitution of the United States in the landmark civil rights case *Brown v. Board of Education.*

Most people seem to assume that because Elvis and *Brown* revolutionized America's racial imagination when it came to blacks, the story must have gotten better for all the other minority groups in America after that. At least that's the lesson they've been taught to believe: Everything got better in America, racially speaking at least, after Elvis and *Brown.*

For Indians, though, it really didn't get that much better, at least in terms of keeping all the hostile nineteenth-century racial stereotypes of Indian savagery out of the Supreme Court's opinions on Indian rights. Every schoolchild in America learns that the justices decided the landmark civil rights case of *Brown v. Board of Education,* finally removing the long-established badge of legalized racial inferiority and recognizing black Americans' equal rights as citizens of the United States, in 1954. What most Americans don't know is that the Court issued one of the most racist Indian rights decisions of all time, *Tee-Hit-Ton Indians v. United States* the very next year! The Court's 1955 *Tee-Hit-Ton* decision unembarrassedly embraced the same basic racist language of Indians as culturally and racially inferior, wandering, ignorant savages that the justices of the nineteenth-century Supreme Court routinely used in their decisions on Indian rights.

"Every American schoolboy knows," Justice Stanley Reed declared for a six-person majority in *Tee-Hit-Ton,* "that the savage tribes of this continent were deprived of their ancestral ranges by force and that, even when the Indians ceded millions of acres by treaty in return for blankets, food and trinkets, it was not a sale but the conquerors' will that deprived them of their land." In other words, in 1955, the year *after* the Supreme Court's landmark civil rights decision in *Brown,* a majority of the justices expressly relied on the same racist stereotype of Indians and their worthless treaty deals that the cartoonist Larson relied on in his *Far Side* cartoon. The difference was that Larson used this racial imagery as the basis of a subversively intended joke that played on our stereotyped racial beliefs. There was nothing funny about the way the justices used this negative racial stereotype of Indian savagery in *Tee-Hit-Ton*: they turned it into a generalized interpretive

principle for understanding the legal history of all the treaties ever negotiated by any Indian tribes with the United States. Based on their racial profiling of the Indians who brought the *Tee-Hit-Ton* case, the Court held that
the indigenous tribes and other Native groups of Alaska had no right to
be compensated under the Fifth Amendment of the Constitution when the
United States unilaterally took their lands away from them.

As *Tee-Hit-Ton* demonstrates, the legally sui generis nature of the language of racism used by the Supreme Court to decide Indian rights cases
throughout American history was unaffected by the holding of *Brown*.
Brown's paradigm of equality of rights applied to black Americans was not
applied by the Court to Indians. And the reason is plainly stated in *Tee-
Hit-Ton*: Indians were savages at the coming of the white man to American, and their lands were taken by a superior civilization.

Even after the *Tee-Hit-Ton* case, decades following the great civil rights
struggles of blacks and other minority groups for racial equality in America, we see Supreme Court justices who persist in relying upon and citing
cases and legal precedents replete with hostile racist stereotypes of Indians as inferior savages with lesser rights than other Americans. As crazy
as it may seem, the language of racism directed at Indians that was so popular with the justices in the nineteenth century is still being perpetuated by
the Supreme Court in many of its most important decisions on Indian rights
in the post-*Brown* era.

Take the case regarded by the Rehnquist Court as one of the most
important Indian rights decisions of the twentieth century, *Oliphant v.
Suquamish Indian Tribe*. Written by then associate justice William
Rehnquist in 1978 (the year after Elvis died, by the way), *Oliphant* has
been unwaveringly cited and adhered to by the justices as the leading precedent of the Court on the critical issue of tribal jurisdiction over non-
members on the reservation.

Oliphant holds that an Indian tribe lacks criminal jurisdiction over non-
Indians committing crimes on its own reservation, even if the crime was
committed against the tribe's *own members*. Rehnquist's opinion cited and
quoted more than a dozen nineteenth-century Supreme Court precedents,

executive branch policy statements, and congressional legislative enactments and reports to justify the decision in *Oliphant*. Virtually every text Rehnquist uses from this period of white racial dictatorship in America consistently and unembarrassedly stereotypes Indians as lawless, uncivilized, unsophisticated, hostile, or warlike savages. As Rehnquist's opinion in *Oliphant* clearly demonstrates, these precedents show conclusively that in the nineteenth century Indians were uniformly regarded by the dominant society and by the justices of the Supreme Court as an inferior race and as therefore entitled to lesser rights than whites. And according to *Oliphant*, a case decided almost a quarter century after the landmark civil rights decision in *Brown v. Board of Education*, that's precisely the way the Court is going to keep on treating Indians and their rights in present-day America.

For example, at a very early point in his opinion in *Oliphant*, Rehnquist relies upon a rarely cited 1891 Supreme Court Indian law case, *In re Mayfield*. Rehnquist not only resurrected this obscure nineteenth-century Indian law case as a reliable precedent in his opinion, he actually used its blatantly racist nineteenth-century judicial language of Indian savagery and white supremacy to justify the Court's holding that Indians have always possessed diminished and inferior rights compared to the white population under United States law:

> In *In re Mayfield*, the Court noted that the policy of Congress had been to allow the inhabitants of the Indian country "such power of self-government as was thought to be consistent with the safety of the white population with which they may have come in contact, and to encourage them as far as possible in raising themselves to our standard of civilization."

Based on this nineteenth-century racist stereotype of Indian cultural inferiority embedded in the reasoning of the *Mayfield* decision, Rehnquist's opinion in *Oliphant* held that the Court had no choice in 1978 but to deny Indian tribes this privileged form of self-governing power over non-Indians committing crimes upon tribal members on the reservation today:

while Congress never expressly forbade Indian tribes to impose criminal penalties on non-Indians, we now make express our implicit
conclusion of nearly a century ago [in *In re Mayfield*] that Congress
consistently believed this to be the necessary result of its repeated
legislative actions.

This is not the only instance in which Rehnquist cited and even directly
quoted a nineteenth-century text containing overtly racist stereotypes of
Indians in support of his twentieth-century holding in *Oliphant*. Throughout his opinion, Rehnquist perpetuates a nineteenth-century language of
racism to justify the Court's holding in *Oliphant*. For instance, he quoted
from an 1834 congressional report issued at the height of the genocidal Removal era of U.S. Indian policy to support *Oliphant's* general "principle"
that Indians do not have criminal jurisdiction over non-Indians. This
"principle," he writes,

> Would have been obvious a century ago when most Indian tribes were
> characterized by a "want of fixed laws [and] of competent tribunals of
> justice." . . . It should be no less obvious today, even though present day
> Indian tribal courts embody dramatic advances over their historical
> antecedents.

Throughout *Oliphant*, Rehnquist repeatedly cited and quoted from a
large number of nineteenth-century texts that expressly displayed an overtly
hostile, racist attitude toward Indians and Indian tribal culture. And *Oliphant* is simply one of many instances in which a Supreme Court justice,
post-*Brown*, relied on a long-established tradition of negative racist stereotypes, apocrypha, and images of Indian savagery to justify the Court's decision in an important Indian rights case. *Oliphant* is simply part of a
much larger legal history of racism directed at Indians, perpetuated by the
racist nineteenth-century precedents and accompanying judicial language
of Indian savagery found in leading decisions of the U.S. Supreme Court.
The justices continue to uphold a form of legalized racial dictatorship dating

from the nineteenth century and in doing so give legal sanction to a long-established language of racism directed against Indians in America.

The Legal History of Racism Against Indians in America as Perpetuated by the Supreme Court's Indian Rights Decisions

I believe that one of the major reasons why the justices have been able to continue to perpetuate this long-established tradition of racial profiling of Indians with little expression of surprise, much less embarrassment, by most Americans is that most Americans themselves continue to believe, "deep down," in this deeply entrenched national mythology of Indian savagery. Most Americans, including the present-day justices of the Supreme Court, are simply unable to think about Indians and Indian rights without calling upon and invoking in their own minds such long-established stereotypes, images, and apocryphal tales of Indian tribalism as an inferior and fatefully doomed way of life in comparison to the superior European-derived civilization that colonized and conquered America.

Aside from Indians and their lawyers, most Americans generally express little concern or notice, and virtually no discomfort at all, when the Rehnquist Court issues an important legal opinion that stigmatizes Indians as being too backward to enjoy the same rights to property or self-government, for example, as do non-Indians. No headlines scream out from our nation's leading newspapers, "Rehnquist Court Holds That Indians Have Inferior Rights to Self-Government Because They Once Were Savages" or "Court Continues Its Racist Old Ways in Indian Law," even though these are precisely the types of things the Rehnquist Court is in fact doing in many of its present-day Indian rights decisions.

Getting "Practical": The Hard Trail of Confronting the Justices with Their Racial Profiling Techniques in Indian Rights Cases

I am *not* arguing for a theoretical approach to protecting Indian rights that suggests to Indian people that they would be better off "ignoring the Supreme Court." I do not believe that the Court is a hopelessly racist institution that is incapable of fairly adjudicating cases involving the basic human rights to property, self-government, and cultural survival possessed by Indian tribes as indigenous peoples. I would never attempt to stereotype the justices in that way.

Nor does the discourse-based approach to reforming Indian rights that I argue for mean to suggest that Indians should focus their primary legal energies on nondomestic legal and political forums, such as the international human rights system. As a "practical matter," having worked for Indian clients and Indian rights both in the domestic courts of the United States and within the international human rights system, I have no illusions about the intractability of the deeply entrenched racist attitudes and stereotypes that surround the discourses of indigenous peoples' rights in both of these forums.

I'm also aware that the U.S. Supreme Court will not soon surrender its interpretive privilege as prime arbiter of Indian rights in this country, no matter what the international human rights system has to say about indigenous peoples and their treatment under U.S. law. The Court simply *cannot* be ignored by Indian rights advocates. It's the proverbial eight-hundred-pound gorilla that blocks the way of every legal struggle aimed at protecting Indian rights in the United States today. And as every international human rights lawyer knows, you certainly can't ignore the Supreme Court if you want to use the international human rights system's adjudicatory processes to protect Indian rights. Domestic remedies normally have to be exhausted first to even get a hearing in that system.

I believe that Indian rights lawyers and scholars must engage these entrenched racist attitudes and stereotypes "on all fronts by whatever means necessary." In theory *and* as a practical matter, I recognize that the Supreme Court is one of the most important of those fronts. What I do urge is adoption of a strategy of direct confrontation that challenges the continuing use of racial stereotypes, racial profiling techniques, and spurious racist imagery and apocrypha in thinking and talking about Indian rights by the

Court, by the U.S. Congress, by the international human rights system, and even by Joe Six-Pack down at the local bar.

My argument on the need for this type of confrontational strategy that focuses on identifying and bringing to the fore the nineteenth-century racist judicial language of Indian savagery used by the present-day Court in its major Indian rights decisions does entail one axiom of belief and Native knowledge: Indian rights will never be justly protected by any legal system or any civil society that continues to talk about Indians as if they are uncivilized, unsophisticated, and lawless savages. The first step on the hard trail of decolonizing the present-day U.S. Supreme Court's Indian law is changing the way the justices themselves talk about Indians in their decisions on Indian rights.

Let me also say at the outset that I know this will not be an easy task. As one of the justices recently conceded, the Court is a reactive institution; "real change comes principally from attitudinal shifts in the population at large. Rare indeed is the legal victory—in court or legislature—that is not a careful byproduct of an emerging social consensus." Although I sense a subtle but demonstrable attitudinal shift in the society at large that does seem to signal an emerging consensus that the use of any racial stereotype depicting Indians as savages is inappropriate in present-day U.S. society, I also recognize that there is a lot of work that needs to be done to make this slowly crystallizing consensus palpable to the justices on the Court.

It's a hard trail that lies ahead. The salutary effects of the growing number of high schools and colleges that have abandoned the use of stereotyped Indian mascots and insignia, for instance, are instantaneously diminished in a singularly reinforcing jolt to the American public's racial imagination by a single, widely reported decision, issued by a federal district court judge sitting in Washington, DC, reversing the U.S. Patent and Trademark Office Appeals Board's 1999 ruling that the Washington "Redskins" trademark is racially disparaging to Indians, and must therefore be canceled. The less stereotyped and less demeaning way that schoolchildren in America are taught about Indian culture and history today as opposed to just a generation ago is instantaneously overwhelmed by a simple click of the mouse and the mass marketing cultural force of "Kaya," the American Girl Indian doll, who "draws strength from her family, the legends her elders tell her, and the bold warrior woman who is her hero." While there are signs of a general shift in the way we talk about Indians in this society, such countersigns as these tell us that we're not there yet. The hard trail that must be traveled as a society in ridding ourselves of these types of degrading and diminishing stereotypical images of Indian savagery, primitivity, and alien otherness has only just begun.

We can all participate in making this reformulated vision of racial justice more palpable to the justices of the U.S. Supreme Court by engaging in any number of subversive and even overt practices. A law clerk to one of the justices, for instance, can leave a copy of this lecture lying around next to the watercooler at work. Lawyers representing tribes before the Court can point out in their briefs and also during oral argument that opposing counsels' precedents and case citations routinely refer to Indians in these negative stereotyped terms and ask the justices to make them stop.

Law professors can get together and write a huge legal treatise showing the justices why Indian law needs to be purged of the negative racial stereotypes and images that support so many of the Court's leading precedents. Journalists and maybe even the Fox News Channel might be persuaded to give fair and balanced coverage to an important emerging question in the American legal academy and Indian bar: Should the Supreme Court be relying at all upon cases from an era of white racial dictatorship in deciding Indian rights cases in the twenty-first century?

Congress, lobbied by Indian tribes to reject the archaic stereotypes and images, can pass legislation overturning or at least modifying what Indians and their advocates regard as the Rehnquist Court's most racist and dangerous decisions on Indian rights in America.

And, of course, the justices themselves (at least five of them) can come to the realization that they are relying on and perpetuating outmoded nineteenth-century racist precedents and legal language. They can walk away from that watercooler and decide that even without a societal consensus condemning such anarchaic, racist language, they can find better, less-stereotyped ways, more consistent with the Constitution's egalitarian spirit and values, to decide Indian rights cases.

"A Winning Courtroom Strategy"

To the contrary, the legal history of racism in America teaches us that the most successful minority rights advocates of the twentieth century recognized that the real waste of time was trying to get a nineteenth-century racist legal doctrine to do a better job of protecting minority rights. It is useful to recall Thurgood Marshall's response to those many sincere, well-intentioned, and experienced legal advocates who told him, when he was legal counsel for the National Association for the Advancement of Colored People (NAACP), that it was impractical to expect the Supreme Court to abandon the nineteenth-century constitutional law doctrine of "separate but equal" enshrined in *Plessy v. Ferguson*. Asking the Supreme Court to overturn *Plessy*, Marshall steadfastly believed, was indeed a winning courtroom strategy.

Indians, their lawyers, and that segment of the American legal academy that teaches and writes about their rights have a lot to learn from the history of the racial paradigm shift represented by *Brown*, from Marshall's heroic example as the most successful minority rights advocate of the twentieth century to argue before the Supreme Court, and from the many other human rights stories of resistance, struggle, and triumph in America. These stories are the most important parts of the more general story of the legal history of racism in America and the Supreme Court's role in perpetuating it. The history of the civil rights movements for blacks, for example, quite clearly teaches us that one does not successfully advocate for a historically oppressed minority group's rights by writing legal briefs or legal treatises showing the justices how to get the racist principles and doctrines of the past to work better in protecting minority rights in the present-day United States.

I believe that one of the most important lessons taught by *Brown* and its legacy is that the justices must be continuously confronted with the pernicious, persistent, and continuing effects of a long-established language of racism in America. As the Supreme Court itself recognized in rejecting the "separate but equal" legal discourse of *Plessy* in *Brown*, the practical real-world impact of such a language is far greater when it "has the sanction of law." As the Court recited in *Brown*, such language affects "hearts and minds, in a way unlikely ever to be undone." Removing this form of legal sanction by repudiating the precedents that perpetuate racist language in the Supreme Court's Indian law opinions is a first critical step that must be taken on the long hard trail of bringing about a major paradigm shift in the way the Supreme Court approaches its job of protecting the basic human rights of Indians in America. Any approach that ignores this step, I believe, is ultimately going to be the real waste of time.

I am *not* advocating an approach that is focused purely on revealing the use of racist language and its harmful effects and then waiting for a resulting, inevitable transformation in the justices' racial attitudes. I am not, in other words, being insufficiently attentive to Derrick Bell's famously stated "interest convergence dilemma," which holds that minority rights are only recognized by the dominant society when that society perceives that it is in its own best interest to do so. In fact, I view a discourse-based approach to protecting Indian rights as being preparatory and partial but nonetheless integral to the much harder task of discovering those points of convergence that might exist between the interests of the dominant society and Indian tribes in protecting important Indian rights.

Having been well schooled by Professor Bell himself when I was a young, affirmative action–oriented law student at Harvard and he was developing and testing his seminal materialist thesis upon those of us who were fortunate enough to have him teach us about race and racism in American law, I have always regarded myself as a long-practicing and ardently committed racial realist when it comes to the task of protecting Indian rights. I recognize that civil rights advances seem to come about only when it's in the perceived self-interest of the dominant majority society to recognize minority rights. I certainly do not want to be accused of making the jejune mistake of believing, in the words of Richard Delgado, that "minority misery is unnatural and certain to be corrected once pointed out to those

LIKE A LOADED WEAPON

in power." I know, indeed, that we are not saved simply because the Court has changed the way it talks about a particular minority group in its opinions on that group's rights.

I know as well that as a basic strategic principle, showing the non-Indian majority, in society and on the Court, that it's in the broader public interest to protect Indian rights will materially improve Indian rights lawyers' chances of winning their cases.

But before that type of racial realist showing according to the prescriptions of Bell's interest convergence paradigm is even attempted, the lessons of *Brown* strongly suggest that the long-established racial stereotypes and imagery in the Court's decisions and precedents must be first exposed and then attacked.

My "Singularity Thesis" for Protecting Indian Rights in America

Indian rights are much different from the types of minority rights that were and remain at the center of the continuing struggle for racial equality represented by cases like *Brown*. As the noted Indian law scholar and advocate Charles Wilkinson has argued, "The most cherished civil rights of Indian people are not based on equality of treatment under the Constitution and the general civil rights laws." Ultimately, what Indians are seeking from the Court is something much different. They are arguing for a right to a degree of "measured separatism"—that is, the right to govern their reservation homelands and those who enter them by their own laws, customs, and traditions, even when these might be incommensurable with the dominant society's values and ways of doing things.

This seemingly balkanizing, separatist aspiration for a measured degree of indigenous self-determination and cultural sovereignty thus situates most Indian rights questions upon difficult and very "unfamiliar intellectual terrain" for most of the American public. It's much harder, in other words, to secure recognition and protection for highly novel forms of Indian group rights to self-determination and cultural sovereignty in American society than for the far more familiar types of individualized rights that most other minority groups want protected.

My singularity thesis for protecting Indian tribal rights recognizes, as a matter of both strategy and tactics, the inherent difficulty of convincing the American public that it is in its material interests, no matter how broadly defined, to recognize a measured right of Indian tribes to rule themselves on their reservation homelands by their own laws, customs, and traditions, particularly when that right appears to interfere with or threaten the dominant society's interests or values. It also recognizes that advocating for Indian rights to self-determination and cultural sovereignty requires addressing what I take to be the sincere and legitimate concerns of the Court, Congress, and Joe Six-Pack about the theoretical incommensurability and the real-world material consequences of recognizing, let us say, that Indian tribal courts can exercise criminal and civil jurisdiction over non-Indians on the reservation without affording them the precise protections of the Constitution's Bill of Rights.

Once we recognize the singularly problematic nature of Indian rights claims, we also come to realize the importance, as a preparatory matter, of the language that the American public and the justices themselves use in talking about Indians and their asserted rights to a degree of "measured separatism" under the Constitution and laws of the United States. If we continue to let the Court talk about Indians as if they are uncivilized and unsophisticated savages and use racist precedents that define their rights accordingly, we are not likely to make much headway in developing a winning courtroom strategy that convinces the justices that it is in the American public's interests to recognize an admittedly highly problematic and exclusive set of Indian rights to a degree of measured separatism in this country.

13

A Hip-Hop Theory of Justice

PAUL BUTLER

2008

Paul Butler is the Albert Brick Professor in Law at Georgetown University Law Center and a legal analyst on MSNBC. He has also served as the Bennett Boskey Visiting Professor at Harvard Law School. He previously served as a federal prosecutor with the U.S. Department of Justice, where he specialized in public corruption. Professor Butler is a graduate of Yale University and Harvard Law School. He was awarded the Distinguished Faculty Service Award three times by the Georgetown Law graduating class. He is the author of Let's Get Free: A Hip-Hop Theory of Justice, *winner of the Harry Chapin Media Award, and* Chokehold: Policing Black Men, *a finalist for the NAACP Image Award.*

I fell in love with hip-hop on a crowded dance floor at Yale. Everyone was screaming the chorus to the old-school classic, "Rapper's Delight": "Hotel, motel, Holiday Inn. If your girl starts acting up, then you take her friend!" It was not the most socially responsible moment for me or hip-hop, but both of us have evolved since then. We've each grown up to become experts on American criminal justice—from the inside out.

Imagine criminal justice in a hip-hop nation. Believe it or not, the culture provides a blueprint for a system that would enhance public safety and treat all people with respect. Hip-hop has the potential to transform justice in the United States. Who would have thought that hip-hop—the most thuggish art—could improve law and order?

For some time the debate about criminal justice has been old-school. Different slogans—"three strikes," "broken windows," "zero tolerance"—accede to prominence, and then lose their luster.

Hip-hop offers a fresh approach. It first seems to embrace retribution—the old-fashioned theory of "just deserts." The "unwritten law in rap," according to Jay-Z, is that "if you shoot my dog, I'ma kill yo' cat . . . know dat / For every action there's a reaction."

Next, however, comes the remix. Hip-hop takes punishment personally. Many people in the hip-hop nation have been locked up or have loved ones who have been. Punishment is an exercise of the state's power, but it also gets in the middle of intimate relationships. "Shout-outs" to inmates—expressions of love and respect to them—are commonplace. You understand criminal justice differently when the people that you love experience being "locked down all day, underground, neva seein' the sun / Vision stripped from you, neva seein' your son," as Beanie Sigel says in "What Ya Life Like."

Hip-hop exposes the American justice system as profoundly unfair. The music does not glorify lawbreakers but it also does not view all criminals with disgust. A hip-hop theory of justice acknowledges that when too many people are locked up, prison has unintended consequences. Punishment should be the point of criminal justice, but it should be limited by the impact it has on the entire community.

Now, in a remarkable moment in American history, pop music is weighing the costs and benefits of going to prison. As we listen to the radio, watch music videos, dance at clubs, surf the internet, or sport the latest fashion, we receive a hard-core message from what Public Enemy's frontman Chuck D has called the "black CNN."

Hip-hop already has had a significant social impact. It is one of the best-selling genres of music in the world. Hip-hop transcends rap music: it includes television, movies, fashion, theater, dance, and visual art. Hip-hop is also big business: estimates of its contribution to the U.S. economy range to the billions. Increasingly, hip-hop is also a political movement.

Hip-hop foreshadows the future of the United States—one in which no racial group will constitute a majority. It is the most diverse form of American pop culture. The most commercially successful hip-hop artists are black, though there are popular white and Latino acts as well. The consumers are mainly non-black. The producers are Asian, black, Latino, and white—and combinations of all of those. The Neptunes, among hip-hop's most acclaimed producers, consist of Chad Hugo, a Filipino American, and Pharrell Williams, an African-Korean American.

At the same time an art form created by African American and Latino men dominates popular culture, African American and Latino men dominate American prisons. Unsurprisingly, then, justice—especially criminal justice—has been a preoccupation of the hip-hop nation. The analysis of crime and punishment comes from the people who best know those features of life in the USA.

Bold, rebellious, often profane, the music has multicultural detractors as well as fans. One need not like hip-hop, however, to appreciate its potential to transform. In the history of the United States, it is hard to recall another major form of pop culture that contains such a strong critique of the state.

Many seem to be listening. The hip-hop generation is gaining political power, and seems more inclined to use it than has historically been the case with either youth or artists. I do not suggest, however, that hip-hop fans will be a potent voting bloc in the near future. My claim is more ideological. Hip-hop culture makes a strong case for a transformation of American criminal justice: it describes, with eloquence, the problems with the current system, and articulates, with passion, a better way.

Hip-hop was born in one of the poorest and most crime-ridden communities in the United States: the South Bronx, New York. In the 1970s the South Bronx was a place of a desperate, hard-knock creativity, as evidenced by the way its citizens talked, dressed, and danced. Even the teenagers who drew graffiti on subway cars thought of themselves as artists, though the police had a different point of view.

A man who spun records for parties—DJ Kool Herc, he called himself—tried using two turntables to play copies of the same record. Herc used the turntables like a musical instrument and made his own songs from other people's recordings. Sometimes Herc would speak rhythmically to his beats (a technique borrowed from his Jamaican heritage). He taped these "raps" for boom boxes, and the music became popular all over New York City.

Herc's work inspired other DJs, including Afrika Bambaataa. Bambaataa expanded Herc's musical tracks from disco and house music to virtually any recorded sound, including rock music and television shows. DJs "battled" (engaged in artistic competition) at city parks, and dancers performed in an athletic, bone-popping style called "break dancing."

For the criminal-justice-minded, three features of the birth of hip-hop are striking. First, many artists took what scholars call an "instrumentalist" view of the law: they didn't let it get in the way of achieving their goals. So the trespass law did not deter the graffiti artists, the copyright law did not stop the DJs from sampling any music they wanted, and the property law did not prevent DJs from "borrowing" electricity from street lamps at public parks. Second, virtually every hip-hop artist renamed himself or herself; "slave" or "government" names were seldom used to describe the artists. Many hip-hop artists named themselves in ways that seem to comment on the criminal law. A short list includes rappers and groups such as Big Punisher, Bone Thugs-N-Harmony, Canibus, Missy "Misdemeanor" Elliott, Mobb Deep, Naughty by Nature, OutKast, and Public Enemy. Third, rappers were compared, almost from the beginning, to African griots, who also "dropped science"—i.e., communicated wisdom—with drumbeats and words.

In the late 1980s, rap music took two radically different directions, both with consequences for criminal justice. In one, many artists addressed political issues, resulting in, according to the *Journal of Black Studies*, "the most overt social agenda in popular music since the urban folk movement of the 1960s." A classic album of this era is Public Enemy's *It Takes a Nation of Millions to Hold Us Back*.

The other direction of rap, however, drew more attention, and sales. "Gangsta rap," which unapologetically depicted outlaw conduct in the inner city, became popular. The group NWA (Niggaz With Attitude) received widespread media attention for its controversial song "Fuck da Police."

Hip-hop music continues to exemplify a dichotomy between the political and the pleasurable. The *Washington Post* has described "two faces of hip-hop," one a "conscious" side "where political, social and cultural issues are hashed out in verse." The other side is "the bling-bling, the music that embraces the glamorous life, the live-now-I-got-mine attitude found in countless hits, and in flashy videos where hootchy mamas bounce their backsides and Busta Rhymes exhorts, 'Pass the Courvoisier.'"

Conscious hip-hop is critically acclaimed, with Lauryn Hill's *The Miseducation of Lauryn Hill* becoming the first hip-hop album to receive a Grammy award for Album of the Year in 1999. Since then, OutKast has also won top honors. Gangsta and "bling bling" rap, on the other hand, have been derided as materialist, sexist, and homophobic. Still, these forms of hip-hop have their defenders. They assert that the lyrics are accurate reflections of some people's experiences. Anyway, one person's "conscious" rapper might be another person's gangsta rapper. Bestselling artists 50 Cent, Lil Wayne, and Young Jeezy are described by some critics as gangsta rappers and by others as artists whose music comments, critically, on the costs of violence and materialism.

Rap pioneers like DJ Kool Herc and Afrika Bambaataa probably did not foresee the extraordinary success their art form would have with suburban consumers. Market studies indicate that about 70 percent of people who buy hip-hop music are white. Hip-hop has also had a major impact on style. Rap stars like P. Diddy and Jay-Z preside over houses of fashion that produce top-selling menswear sold at Macy's and Bloomingdale's. Hip-hop fashion started as an homage to the loose, baggy clothes that inmates wear. It was even the style, for a while, to wear shoes with no shoelaces—also in tribute to prisoners, whose laces are taken away so they won't use them to hang themselves.

Some members of the hip-hop nation have explicitly embraced politics. The most prominent is Russell Simmons, the multimillionaire co-owner

of Def Jam, a hip-hop record label. Simmons created the Hip-Hop Sum-
mit Action Network (HSAN), a nonprofit organization "dedicated to har-
nessing the cultural relevance of Hip-Hop music to serve as a catalyst for
education advocacy and other societal concerns fundamental to the well-
being of at-risk youth throughout the United States."

HSAN has emphasized reform of the criminal justice system, including
the "total elimination of police brutality and the unjust incarceration of
people of color and all others." HSAN's focus has been the repeal of New
York's Rockefeller drug laws. These laws, enacted in 1973 during Governor
Nelson Rockefeller's administration, require long prison sentences for
drug crimes. The organization's "Countdown to Fairness" campaign is specifically intended to accomplish repeal of the Rockefeller laws.

What happens when many of the leaders of popular culture are arrested
and incarcerated? For the hip-hop nation, this is not a theoretical question. It's happened to many of its most prominent artists. Both the New
York and Miami police departments have acknowledged targeting hip-hop
artists.

A revealing example of the role of punishment in hip-hop was seen in an
issue of *Source* magazine, which calls itself the "bible" of hip-hop. The
March 2004 cover featured the tagline "Hip-Hop Behind Bars: Are Rappers
the New Target of America's Criminal Justice System?" The cover showed
mug shots of ten hip-hop stars who are incarcerated or awaiting trial.

The statistics about rap artists reflect the statistics about African American and Latino men. In the mid-1990s, one study found that one in three
young black men were under criminal justice supervision. An African American man born in 1991 has a 29 percent chance of being imprisoned, compared with a 16 percent chance for a Latino man, and a 4 percent chance for
a white man. There are more young black men in prison than in college.

The reaction of artists in the hip-hop community to mass incarceration
has been to interrogate the social meaning of punishment. Prison, as depicted in rap music, is a placement center for the undereducated, the unemployed, and, especially, aspiring capitalists who, if not locked up, would
successfully challenge elites. Big L, for example, complains that the police

"wanna lock me up even though I'm legit / they can't stand to see a young brother pockets get thick."

In order to maintain their self-esteem, the African American men who dominate hip-hop send the message that any organization composed primarily of people like them must be kind of cool; it matters not whether that organization is Howard University, the National Basketball Association, or the state penitentiary. So when people say that hip-hop glorifies criminals, it is more accurate to think of it as respecting African American and Latino men. It rejects the stigma that the criminal justice system puts on them. Since these men wield significant influence over what the nation's youth think is cool, it may be only a matter of time before punishment loses its stigma with other Americans as well.

Martha Stewart is not a member of the hip-hop generation, but when she did her prison bid, there was a hip-hop effect. She was hardly stigmatized by her incarceration; she walked out of prison and right back to her TV show, magazine, and huge corporation. It's the hip-hop view: prison is a bad thing that happens to some people, but it doesn't mean anything about their morality or worth as a person.

To say that hip-hop destigmatizes incarceration understates the point: prison, according to the artists, actually stigmatizes the government. When a large percentage of the people you know, respect, and love get locked up, then being locked up seems to say more about the state than about the inmate. We are supposed to be disgusted with people the law labels as criminals, but that would mean we are disgusted with one in three black men. The hip-hop community consists of these young men and other people who know and love them. It does not find them to be disgusting people. Just the opposite.

In a culture that celebrates rebelliousness, prison is the place for unruly "niggas" who otherwise would upset the rich and powerful. In this sense, inmates are heroic figures. In "A Ballad for the Fallen Soldier," Jay-Z sends a "shout-out to my niggaz that's locked in jail / P.O.W.'s that's still in the war for real . . . But if he's locked in the penitentiary, send him some energy / They all winners to me."

While idealizing outlaws is certainly not limited to hip-hop, the culture's depiction of the criminal as a socially useful actor is different from, say, movies about the Old West. Hip-hop politicizes crime. Breaking the law is seen as a form of rebelling against the oppressive government. Rappers who brag about doing time are like old soldiers who boast of war wounds. The hip-hop slang for being arrested demonstrates the culture's view of the almost arbitrary nature of criminal justice: one "catches a case." The language connotes the same combination of responsibility and happenstance as when one "catches" the common cold.

Some of the most exciting new thinking in criminology focuses on the role of "social norms" in preventing crime. The idea is that culture (or subculture) is more important than law in influencing how people behave. We care more about how people in our "hood" label us than how the government does. Criminal law, then, is most effective when it supports social norms that contribute to public safety. It fails when it subverts those norms. The best example is the fact that when incarceration is not sufficiently stigmatized, it loses its value as deterrence.

Hip-hop suggests that American punishment is not designed mainly to enhance public safety or for retribution against the immoral. Rather, its critique of punishment echoes that of the philosopher Michel Foucault, who argued that prison is designed to encourage a "useful illegality" that benefits the state by increasing its power. The scholar Robin Kelley notes that "most rappers—especially gangsta rappers—treat prisons as virtual fascist institutions."

In "All Things," Pep Love, of the rap collective Hieroglyphics, laments, "The pen [penitentiary] is an inkwell, niggaz is slaves / Even if we not locked up, we on our way." When prison is thought of as a rite of passage, it has lost its potential to keep us safer. If incarceration is to be meaningful, it must be reinvested with stigma. We could accomplish this by using punishment less frequently and more effectively. Hip-hop suggests a way.

Every society has seen the need to punish. The hip-hop nation is no different. Three core principles inform hip-hop's own ideas about punishment. First, people who harm others should be harmed in return. Second, criminals are human beings who deserve respect and love. Third, communities can be destroyed by both crime and punishment.

How would these ideas contribute to a theory of punishment? In a sense, the hip-hop nation, and especially its black and Latino citizens, are best situated to design a criminal justice system. The philosopher John Rawls suggests that law is most just when it is made by people who don't know how they will fare under it. Imagine having to create a justice system not knowing whether you are white or black, male or female, rich or poor, citizen or alien. Since minority members of the hip-hop nation are both the most likely to be arrested and incarcerated for crimes *and* the most likely to be victims of crimes, they arguably come closest to Rawls's ideal lawmakers. Their theory of punishment will value both public safety and fairness to lawbreakers.

I do not mean to suggest that hip-hop culture has explicitly constructed a theory of punishment. The claim is more limited but still, I hope, profound. Thousands of hip-hop songs consider crime and punishment. These voices are worth listening to; they evaluate criminal justice from the bottom up. Our current punishment regime has been designed from the top down, and that, in part, explains why many perceive it to be ineffective or unfair.

We should not look to hip-hop culture for an entirely new justification of punishment. Hip-hop culture does not create out of whole cloth, and neither do the philosophers, scholars, and politicians who have articulated the current punishment regime. The art of hip-hop is in the remix. Thus some hip-hop overtly responds to trendy theories of punishment. For example, the "broken window" theory of law enforcement, in which the police arrest for any minor crime, has had a profound impact on the ghetto and thus on hip-hop culture. Other elements of hip-hop can be interpreted as unconscious shout-outs to scholars of whom the artists probably are not aware. Foucault's influential history of the prison reverberates throughout hip-hop theory, as does the new criminal law scholarship on third-party interests in criminal law and the effects of mass incarceration. Hip-hop culture, though, is post-postmodern. In fact, some of its characteristics, especially its embrace of retribution, seem startlingly old-fashioned.

Our criminal justice system would work better if the ghetto philosophers and the classic philosophers met. They address many of the same issues in punishment, including causation, harm, responsibility, excuse, and justification. We would see that Erykah Badu, Snoop Dogg, and Jeremy Bentham have a lot in common. Immanuel Kant and Jay-Z would get along well, but their differences would be instructive. Not all of the artists are brilliant theorists, although some of them are. They represent, however, a community that has borne the brunt of the world's two-hundred-year experiment with prisons. That community knows much, has laid it down on tracks, and now attention must be paid.

Hip-hop abides by a strong conviction that wrongdoers should suffer consequences for their acts. The culture abounds with narratives about revenge, retaliation, and avenging wrongs. The narrator in Eve's "Love Is Blind" kills the man who abuses her close friend. Likewise, Nelly warns, "If you take a life, you gon' lose yours too."

At the same time, the culture embraces criminals. In Angie Stone's "Brotha," for example, she sings, "To every one of y'all behind bars / You know that Angie loves ya." The Lost Boyz rap, "To all my peoples in the pen, keep ya head up." This kind of warm acknowledgment of the incarcerated is commonplace in hip-hop, and virtually unheard of in other popular cultures, which largely ignore the more than two million Americans in prison.

The most important civic virtue in the hip-hop nation is respect. One of the culture's contributions to the English language is the verb *dis*, which means "to disrespect." To dis someone is worse than to insult them—it is to deny his or her humanity. Hip-hop vocabulary also includes the term *props*—to give props is to afford proper respect. While the misogyny and homophobia in some hip-hop makes it difficult to claim that the culture universally values respect for all persons, virtually all hip-hop connotes a respect for the dignity of lawbreakers.

In attempting to reconcile hip-hop's impulse to right wrongs with its respect for dignity—even the dignity of criminals—a criminal law scholar immediately thinks of retribution. This justification of punishment is premised on the idea of "just deserts." When one harms another, justice requires that she be harmed in return. Retributivists believe that punishment communicates respect for the criminal by recognizing him as a moral agent and respect for the victim by avenging his harm.

The Bill of Rights codifies the retributive concern for the criminal's humanity. The Eighth Amendment prohibits the state from punishing criminals in a manner that is inconsistent with their dignity. The Supreme Court has also interpreted the Eighth Amendment as requiring that criminals not be punished disproportionately to their crime, although it has given lawmakers wide latitude in determining what proportionate punishment is.

How would a profound respect for the humanity of criminals change the way we punish them? We would be more concerned about the punishment fitting the crime. Now our sentences for drug crimes seem mainly designed to put away offenders for years. Hip-hop culture, like retributive philosophy, emphasizes the importance of moral autonomy and free agency. Both suggest that people who freely choose to do wrong should be punished. Where hip-hop theorists and traditional philosophers diverge, however, is on how to determine responsibility.

In the hip-hop view, the choice made by a poor person to sell drugs has a different and less blameworthy social meaning than the choice by a middle-class person to engage in, say, insider trading. In "Dope Man," Jay-Z raps, "I grew where you hold your blacks up / Trap us, expect us not to pick gats [guns] up / Where you drop your cracks off by the Mack trucks / Destroy our dreams of lawyers and actors / Keep us spiralin', goin' backwards."

Hip-hop culture emphasizes the role of environment in determining conduct, whereas classic retributivist theory focuses on individual choice. In essence, hip-hop culture discounts responsibility when criminal conduct has been shaped by a substandard environment. OutKast, for example, asserts "knowing each and every nigger sellin', but can you blame / The fact the only way a brother can survive the game."

The hip-hop analysis does not deny that the underprivileged are moral agents; it does, however, require us to consider thoughtfully how free some people's choices really are. In the words of NWA:

[A] nigga wit' nothin' to lose
One of the few who's been accused and abused
Of the crime of poisonin' young minds
But you don't know shit 'til you've been in my shoes

Hip-hop culture advocates retribution, but not at all costs. The rapper Makaveli notes, "My homeboy's doin' life, his baby mamma be stressin' / Sheddin' tears when her son finally ask that question / Where my daddy at? Mama why we live so poor?" If the consequence of making people pay for their crimes is the decimation of a community, then retribution is less important. Punishment should be reduced when it harms people other than the criminal.

Reducing punishment based on its effect on others sounds radical—until we look at the practice in other contexts. Under federal sentencing law, prosecutors can decline to hold corporations accountable for crimes when that would be bad for shareholders or employees. In Canada a similar analysis applies to the sentencing of native people—i.e., Canadian Indians and Eskimos. The judge is supposed to consider the effect on the entire ethnic group.

Hip-hop culture suggests broad support for such an approach in the United States, especially as applied to minority communities. In practice, consideration of collateral effects might lead to criminal sanctions other than incarceration—for example, probation or community service. When prison is appropriate, sentences might be shorter, or family leave could be allowed. Prisoners might be allowed to work to support their families. The goal would be criminal justice targeted not just to the individual offender, but to his entire community.

Who's Bad?

Consider the following fact: in the United States, approximately half of the people in prison are African American. If punishment is being allocated properly, this statistic suggests that half of the most dangerous or immoral Americans are black, even though African Americans make up only about 12 percent of the population. The person who has confidence in the American criminal justice system probably has an unfavorable view of blacks and Latinos, and a more positive view of whites.

The hip-hop nation rejects this view. It does not see morality or dangerousness as allocated along the race and class lines that the prison population suggests. A frequent theme in hip-hop is that the law does not correctly select the most deserving candidates for punishment. Specifically, the law does not properly weigh the immorality posed and danger caused by white elites. Rather, it exaggerates the threat posed by the poor and by minorities. From this perspective, blameworthy conduct by privileged white people or the government often goes unpunished.

Thus Ice-T jokes that "America was stole from the Indians / Show and prove, what was that? A straight up nigga move." Immortal Technique complains that "families bleed because of corporate greed."

Hip-hop artists sometimes accuse the state of complicity in crime. In "Gun Music," Talib Kweli raps, "You know who killing it, niggas saying they militant / The only blood in the street is when the government spilling it." In another song, Kweli provides an example: "[The police] be gettin' tips from snitches and rival crews / Doin' them favors so they workin' for the drug dealers too / Just business enforcers with hate in they holsters / Shoot you in the back, won't face you like a soldier."

Of course, complaints that criminal law is selectively enforced against blacks and other minorities are familiar, and not only in hip-hop culture. Hip-hop's indictment of criminal justice goes further; it identifies bias in the way that crime is defined as well as the way that the law is enforced.

Some hip-hop artists have suggested that lawmakers define crime in a way that does not challenge powerful corporate interests, even when corporations cause harm. KRS-One, in "Illegal Business," explains: "In society you have illegal and legal / We need both, to make things equal / So legal is tobacco, illegal is speed / Legal is aspirin, illegal is weed." It is legal for a corporation to make a gun. Nicotine and alcohol distributors are licensed by the government; in the case of tobacco there are even government subsidies for growers. Sellers of other drugs, including arguably less harmful ones, are punished. Hip-hop suggests that some of the existing distinctions between legal and illegal conduct, and between crimes and torts, are unprincipled.

Hip-hop sometimes presents poor minorities as relatively powerless in the grand scheme. "Right or wrong . . . I don't make the law," Erykah Badu explains to her criminal-minded lover in "Danger." In this view, the real bad dudes—including people who profit from widespread alcoholism, tobacco sales, and the demand for guns—are politically powerful. The fact that their injurious conduct is not punished helps explain hip-hop's lack of confidence in American criminal justice.

In hip-hop culture, the idea that minorities are selectively prosecuted sometimes seems to border on paranoia. In the case of drug offenses, however, this perception is accurate. According to statistics compiled by the U.S. government, blacks represent about 14 percent of monthly drug users. Yet they account for more than 56 percent of people incarcerated for drug use. Just because you are paranoid, the old joke goes, doesn't mean they're not out to get you.

The fact that drug offenses are selectively prosecuted in the African American community informs the hip-hop perspective on drug criminalization, but it is only one factor among many. Some people say that hip-hop glorifies the use of illegal drugs. This is partly true.

Hip-hop culture suggests that recreational drugs like marijuana and Ecstasy enhance the quality of life and that they are fun. Hip-hop stars Ja Rule, Missy Elliott, and Tweet collaborated on a song called "X," which extols the virtues of having sex under the influence of Ecstasy. The Notorious B.I.G. raps: "Some say the x, make the sex / Spec-tacular."

Marijuana, especially, is the hip-hop nation's intoxicant of choice. In a classic song, Snoop Dogg raps about the pleasure of riding through his neighborhood sipping alcohol and smoking weed. The scholar Michael Eric Dyson describes marijuana as "the necessary adjunct to ghetto fabulousness. . . . Getting high is at once pleasurable and political: It heightens the joys to be found in thug life while blowing smoke rings around the constraints of the state."

There are more hip-hop songs critical of the harm posed by alcohol than by other soft drugs. The most vilified drug might be the "40-ounce." Public Enemy, for example, compared this large can of malt liquor that is sold almost exclusively in poor neighborhoods to a "gun to the brain."

Hip-hop offers a more nuanced, and less consistent, perspective on "hard" drugs. The sellers are accorded more respect than the users. Rapper 2Pac (aka Tupac Shakur), for example, criticizes his addict parent for being a "part-time mutha." In another song, however, he praises street-corner dealers for raising him when his father was not present.

Other hip-hop artists are angrier at drug sellers. Ice Cube raps, "And all y'all dope-dealers . . . You're as bad as the po-lice—'cause ya kill us." He goes on to castigate dealers for "exploitin' us like the Caucasians did / For 400 years—I got 400 tears—for 400 peers / Died last year from gang-related crimes." Still, there is sympathy for why some people sell drugs. Biggie Smalls facetiously dedicated his autobiographical song "Juicy" to the people who called the police when he was "just tryin' to make some money to feed my daughters." Kanye West raps about being "forced to sell crack" because there "ain't no tuition for having no ambition / and ain't no loans for sittin' your ass at home."

Ultimately, hip-hop acknowledges the terrible consequences that some drugs have for individuals and communities. The culture is not as quick as some scholars to label drug crimes "victimless." Acknowledging these costs, however, does not necessarily lead to a belief that drug offenders should be punished. The hip-hop consensus seems to be against punishment of drug offenders, because of (1) the selective enforcement of the drug laws in minority communities; (2) the social factors that contribute to drug use and sales; (3) the fact that the government allows the sale of harmful drugs like tobacco and alcohol; (4) the government's perceived complicity in the availability of drugs in the ghetto; and (5) the collateral consequences of punishment in minority communities. In this view, the state may have a legitimate interest in controlling the use and sale of some drugs. First, however, the government must prove that it can enforce the drug laws in a nondiscriminatory way and that the benefits of regulation will not be outweighed by the costs.

The idea of using prison to punish people is only about two hundred years old. It was intended to be more humane than the then-prevailing methods of punishment: killing criminals, harming their bodies, or banishing them from the country.

How successful has the experiment been? The hip-hop nation is better situated to answer the question than virtually any other community in the world. The United States incarcerates more people per capita than any country in the world. The majority of its inmates are African American and Hispanic. Hip-hop became popular during the same period that the prison population experienced its greatest expansion.

The experiences of the over two million people now incarcerated in the United States have been documented more in hip-hop than in any other medium. The portrait is ugly. To Nas, prison is "the belly of the beast" and "the beast love to eat black meat / And got us niggaz from the hood, hangin' off his teeth."

The universal view is that punishing people by locking them in cages for years is a miserable public policy. Incarceration is cruel because it is dehumanizing. It is counterproductive because, as discussed earlier, it has been used so promiscuously in minority communities that it has lost its value as deterrence. The scholar Robin Kelley summarizes the hip-hop perspective as follows: "Prisons are not designed to discipline but to corral bodies labeled menaces to society; policing is not designed to stop or reduce crime in inner-city communities but to manage it."

The artists put it more poetically. In the words of Dead Prez, "Behind enemy lines, my niggas is cellmates / Most of the youth never escape the jail fate / Super maximum camps will advance they game plan / To keep us in the hands of the man locked up." Immortal Technique says that "sleeping on the floor in cages starts to fuck with your brain / The system ain't reformatory, it's only purgatory." DMX describes "the frustration, rage, trapped inside a cage."

Hip-hop often depicts incarceration as being driven by profit rather than public safety. Its analysis is that it is socially expedient to warehouse people whose problems are difficult or expensive to treat, especially when there are economic benefits to the (largely white and rural) communities where prisons frequently are situated.

The hip-hop perspective is reminiscent of the philosopher Immanuel Kant's concern that it is immoral to punish people as a means of benefiting society. According to some artists, that is the real meaning of the punishment regime. Gang Starr complains: "The educational system presumes you fail / The next place is the corner then after that jail." Mos Def suggests a "prison-industry complex" that supports a "global jail economy." Ras Kass explains: "It's almost methodical, education is false assimilation / Building prisons is more economical."

Hip-hop culture ascended to national prominence in the post–civil rights era. For the hip-hop nation, one of the enduring lessons of the Civil Rights Movement is that the criminal law was used as an instrument of racial subordination. Images of civil rights activists getting locked up, or beat up by the police, are common in hip-hop culture, especially music videos.

Hip-hop artists express some of the same concerns as do traditional civil rights activists about criminal justice. Both vigorously protest racial profiling by police. Unlike civil rights culture, however, hip-hop is not focused on proving respectability to elites. As an NAACP civil rights lawyer, Thurgood Marshall, based on this "politics of respectability," refused to represent black men accused of raping white women, even when he thought they were innocent. Hip-hop doesn't care as much about what the rich and powerful think. It champions the human rights of those society chooses to call criminals as enthusiastically as the rights of the falsely accused. It is as concerned with fairness for drug sellers as for law-abiding middle-class people who are stopped by the police for "driving while black" or "driving while brown."

One serious deficiency in hip-hop is its endemic sexism and homophobia. Can any credible theory of justice be based on a culture that routinely denigrates more than half the population? The answer must be "no." For hip-hop to command the moral authority that, at its best, it deserves, it must address subordination within the hip-hop nation. The problem besmirches hip-hop's extraordinary aesthetic achievement and detracts from its important evaluation of criminal justice. Hip-hop music and videos, especially, contain the kind of depictions of gender and sexuality that we might expect of adolescent boys.

The increasing prominence of women rappers provides limited cause for hope. Hip-hop has a long way to go, however, before its constructive political analysis is not compromised by lyrics, visual images, and attitudes that put down a considerable portion of its own community.

In hip-hop culture there is a tradition of answer raps—of provocative responses to provocative words. I look forward to those responses.

14

Between Slavery and Freedom: The Deep Racial Roots of the 2008 Financial Crisis

EMMA COLEMAN JORDAN

2009

Emma Coleman Jordan is the J. Crilley Kelly and Terry Curtin Kelly Professor of Business Law at Georgetown University Law School. She is best known for establishing the field of economic justice in legal theory, and for her work in financial services and civil rights. She is a past president of both the Association of American Law Schools and the Society of American Law Teachers. She has served as chair of the Financial Institutions Committee of the California State Bar, and she organized the Financial Institutions and Consumer Financial Services section of the Association of American Law Schools. Professor Jordan is the recipient of the American Bar Association's Margaret Brent Award, the American Lawyer Lifetime Achievement Award, and the Clyde Ferguson Award for Outstanding Scholarship, Teaching, and Service. With Angela P. Harris, she co-authored Economic Justice: Race, Gender, and Identity.

A year and eight weeks ago, here in New York City, there was the financial crisis of 2008. We all know that crisis: CNN Breaking News, MSNBC,

CBS, NBC—it was all over the news. Bear Stearns had fallen in the spring, and then, in the month of September, Lehman Brothers, Fannie Mae, Freddie Mac, AIG. The world as we knew it was falling apart.

On a weekend in late September, Congress met to authorize the Troubled Asset Relief Program. And in the first vote, it was voted down. People were outraged that those who had caused a crisis that brought the United States to the edge of financial collapse should receive money from taxpayers. By October 3, with a number of sweeteners, including Hollywood contracts that were put in as riders, the Emergency Economic Stabilization Act passed.

But the crisis did not begin in 2008. In 2000, Ed Gramlich, a member of the Board of Governors of the Federal Reserve, told Alan Greenspan that "there are subprime loans that are growing in their scope. And there's no federal regulation."

By 2005, 23 percent of all subprime mortgages were originated by banks and thrifts, 25 percent were originated by finance companies affiliated with banks and thrifts—subsidiaries of bank holding companies that could have been regulated by the Federal Reserve under the Home Ownership and Equity Protection Act (HOEPA)—and 52 percent were originated by companies with no federal supervision—primarily mortgage brokers and standalone finance companies. When Gramlich brought this issue to Fed Chair Alan Greenspan's attention, Greenspan ignored a proposal from Gramlich to subject subprime lenders to the added scrutiny that might have helped to curtail questionable lending practices that are now blamed for the soaring defaults. So you may think the crisis began with the collapse of Bear Stearns, with the near insolvency of Citibank and the Bank of America. But I'm here to tell you that the crisis began with the explosion of subprime loans that were marketed disproportionally to communities of color.

The story that we are told about this crisis is curiously ahistorical. So I begin at the beginning—not in 2005 or 2000, but a period of time where we can construct a cultural history and the meaning of home ownership for African Americans. That date is 1865, and the context is the freedom that came at the end of the Civil War.

Ownership of land has always defined true freedom for African Americans. From the end of the Civil War to the middle of the subprime crisis, the psychic dividing line between slavery and freedom has been ownership of land. A modern sheriff's eviction pales in comparison to the risks to life and liberty that newly freed slaves boldly encountered in the days immediately after the Civil War.

One version of community for former slaves was the deeply held aspiration for membership in the community of white property owners. The paradox of this definition of community is that the move from slave status to citizen, at the same time, also encompassed the prospect of individualism. Slaves could define and establish their agency with the move from being the subject of property to becoming the owners of property. The dreams of individual ownership created the possibility of carving a uniquely personal identity of family, culture, and custom, and legal authority to exclude others from that place called home.

This was a legally protected space to which the newly freed slaves aspired. So that while individualism and community are often in tension in liberal, social, and political theory. Property ownership provided a place where former slaves could emerge with a new identity as individuals, persons in the law, and members of a community of landowning citizens with all the rights and privileges that land ownership could confer.

I have adopted the year of the end of the Civil War, 1865, as the starting point for my discussion of the impact of the financial collapse of 2008 on black wealth, in order to situate the modern conversation about financial institutions, securitizations, and predatory lending in its racial historical context. Much of the popular account of the role of race in the subprime crisis has been strangely devoid of historical foundations, and is wrong. People who were duped, people who were not smart enough to figure out that they shouldn't sign these contracts, signed them. In this telling, they were propelled by greed or ignorance to seek something that they should have known they couldn't have: land ownership.

What caused this thirst, this craving beyond rationality, for ownership of land?

My project turns on this narrative, and I emphasize the magnitude and the intensity of the cultural meaning of the ownership of land as a starting point. Because it is only through the prism of the fractured, yet persistent black obsession with ownership of land that one can truly make sense of the economic justice claims of homeowners who signed predatory agreements that featured contractual trapdoors beneath a noose of predatory terms.

Historian Leon Litwack, who wrote *Been in the Storm So Long* and *Trouble in Mind*, on black life in the American South in the years after the Civil War, provides a vivid portrait of the expectations, courage, and disappointment surrounding land ownership, and the fragile moments of transition from slavery to freedom. The struggle to convert the promise of land made by General Sherman, and transmuted into a firm economic reliance by the ensuing heated rhetoric at the end of the Civil War. This economic expectation is as much today, as it was then, a defining heart of the struggle for black freedom.

Litwack combed the archives of the New Deal Federal Writers' Project of the Great Depression to locate interviews with more than two thousand ex-slaves. Men and women who were by then eighty years old were asked to recall their experience of freedom at the end of the Civil War in interviews conducted in the middle of the Depression.

One police chief in Duplin County, North Carolina, had this to say about the newly freed slaves of 1865: "Some of them are declaring they intend to have lands, even if they shed blood to obtain them. Some of them are demanding all of the crop they have raised on the former masters' lands. And in some cases, so obstinate are they in these demands, that I have had to arrest them before they would come to terms."

The coercive force of law soon became a reliable tool to mediate the imagination of former slaves longing for the tangible confirmation of freedom that the promise of ownership of land conferred.

According to Litwack, "These former slaves reserved their most loving labor for small individual garden plots, which they had once tended and cherished as slaves. Many freedmen had heard enough of the postwar rhetoric of land distribution to imagine these modest plots expanded to 40-acre farms." Litwack concludes that these modest gardens "remain the most exciting prospect of all." These were plots that exceeded in importance, in emotional investment, any question of wages. So that by 1865 one Freedman's Bureau in Mississippi reported that the passion of land ownership was as fixed, as earnest, and as strong as any belief a man can ever have.

Black aspiration to own land soon collided with the firm conviction of whites that the land belonged to them. One South Carolina plantation owner wrote to his daughter that he was having difficulty raising crops, because laborers went about "stuffed with the idea of proprietorship. You cannot beat it into their thick skulls that the land, and everything else, does not belong to them."

The conflict between freedmen and plantation holders predictably intensified, so much so that in one stretch of Savannah, blacks took over two major plantations, citing their expectation of forty acres and a mule, and the implementation of that promise. It took federal troops to dislodge them.

Let's move forward to 1925, to Detroit, Michigan. Dr. Ossian Sweet, who was a medical doctor, was a Florida native, a graduate of Howard University Medical School, who served his post-medical internships in Vienna and Paris before he returned to Detroit in 1924 to accept a position at the Dunbar Hospital. He began saving money for a home, and by the spring of the next year he had saved $3,500. Sweet used the $3,500 for a down payment on an $18,500 house located on Garland Street in East Detroit. The Sweet house is a one-and-a-half-story brick house built in 1919, typical of many homes in working-class Detroit neighborhoods. It's a bungalow-style structure with a full basement and open porch on the first floor and an enclosed sun porch on the south side. The second story is covered with shingling, and atop the house is a gabled roof. This house still stands today.

This house was the subject of Dr. Ossian Sweet's deeply held passion for home ownership. He wanted to move his wife and daughter into a new location. He had worked hard to achieve a higher economic station. But, by

September 1925, a group of neighbors in the community, aware of Sweet's imminent arrival, had vowed to keep blacks out of the neighborhood, stating that they intended to maintain the neighborhood's present "high standards."

Sweet knew of the neighbors' hostility and vowed to his brother that he was prepared to die like a man. He invited some friends and relatives to bring guns and ammunition to this house in Detroit. He sent his wife and daughter away. The neighborhood was tense. Groups of people gathered in front of Sweet's home. The Detroit police, anticipating racial violence, posted officers at the scene day and night. The NAACP's Walter White stated that "in the two years prior to 1925 90 percent of the new recruits to the Detroit police force were Southern recruits, susceptible to Klan propaganda."

On September 9, Sweet and his friends left the house to go to work. When they returned, the crowd had grown into a mob, throwing rocks and bottles. A Detroit news reporter said that four hundred to five hundred people had gathered, throwing stones that hit the house like hail. This lasted until around 10 p.m., when shots rang out from the second-floor window, killing one of the men in the crowd and wounding another. The police arrested all of the occupants of the house and charged them with murder.

The NAACP promised to help, and they brought Clarence Darrow as chief counsel. Darrow was assisted by Arthur Garfield Hays and Walter M. Nelson. Frank Murphy was the presiding judge who was deeply committed to conducting a fair trial. Darrow built an impressive case. In the end, the jury in Sweet's trial was hung. Sweet's brother was later tried, and that trial ended in a not-guilty verdict. There's a plaque on the front of this house marking this dramatic fight by a black doctor defending his home ownership against a white mob.

I want to move further down the timeline now to 2005 and Williamsbridge in the Bronx. The Williamsbridge area of the Bronx is a representative ground zero for the subprime devastation that has wracked the nation. This northeast Bronx neighborhood is home to working-class families.

Sixty-five percent of its residents are black. Many are first-time homeowners who are immigrants from Nigeria, Ghana, and Jamaica.

Today, in 2009, there is block after block of broken windows and abandoned homes with multiple foreclosure and auction notices plastered on the doors. The empty buildings, the loss of jobs, decreased business and tax revenue all speak to the broken dreams of families who thought they were moving up the ladder of life to grasp their share of future family stability.

The concentration of foreclosures is intense in this area of the city. This created a new community of subprime deficit, where the foreclosures created an algorithm of financial loss that imploded on these families, who lost not only that 1865 dream of home ownership, but found that the community and their individual identities were in fact erased by these losses.

The 31 percent ownership rate in Williamsbridge nearly equals the average for the entire city. But these high rates of ownership masked deeper financial defects in the loan products that residents used to become homeowners. Traditional banks had once avoided these areas. The foreclosure patterns in the Bronx, outside of Williamsbridge, affect the same places that have histories of redlining. The hunger for housing was fueled by Federal Housing Authority ("FHA") Depression-era policy, when African Americans were not permitted to receive FHA government-subsidized loans.

As a result of this policy, in Levittown, Pennsylvania, there were no African American residents. The "thin red line" term comes from the red line first initiated as a racially exclusionary policy by FHA economist Homer Hoyt in 1932. His racist color-coded classification system precluded FHA loans to qualified black applicants living in segregated neighborhoods. So we can see that the algorithm of economic inequality began in slavery and was formalized by a government agency, the FHA.

In the years 2000 to 2007 unregulated mortgage brokers and subsidiaries of the biggest banks saw an opportunity in these property-starved communities to fill the void created by years of redlining. They filled it with high-cost loans, products with unconscionable terms designed to fail.

If you look at subprime market share by race, you can see that in 2004 African Americans had the largest share of these defective loans, at slightly above 25 percent. For whites the share was very, very low, less than 10 percent. The best way to describe these loan products is that they were home ownership mirages, where people thought for two years that they were going to own a home for thirty years. Loan products such as the variable rate 2/28 loan, for example, had a stable, fixed rate for the first two years. In the third year, however, that loan rate escalated sharply, making the loan unaffordable.

These high-cost loans were not an accident. They are the product of the anti-regulatory philosophy that governed America at the time, allowing Alan Greenspan to ignore Ed Gramlich in 2000, when Gramlich warned of disaster on the horizon because of the way these loans were structured. Greenspan relied instead on the work of Richard Posner, a legal scholar, and Gary Becker, an orthodox winner of the Nobel prize in economics. Both theorized that markets will self-correct.

That philosophy was then coupled with the idea that racial discrimination is simply a preference like any other preference—the way some people like chocolate, some people like vanilla, and some like strawberry ice cream. Some people simply do not like to live next to black people. The argument went that these neutral preferences will play out in the marketplace and the marketplace should be left unchecked to distribute housing and other goods without government intervention. However, it was not simply a question of a neutral distribution of subprime loans.

These loans were targeted at African Americans using high-pressure tactics and were compelled by the algorithm of inequality. African Americans wanted land, they wanted individuality, they wanted community. Ownership of land was the dividing point between freedom and slavery. For these descendants of slaves and immigrants, defective subprime loans became yet another elusive possibility for ownership.

In addition to targeting first-time homeowners, lenders also targeted the poorest neighborhoods with subprime refinancing. Grandmothers and grandfathers who'd raised children in their homes were encouraged to take out loans on the family homestead. Of subprime refinances, 44 percent were in the poorest neighborhoods; for black neighborhoods the figure was 51 percent, versus 9 percent for white neighborhoods.

For the residents of Williamsbridge, these loans were a devastating economic disaster. As billionaire investor Warren Buffett has described, the loans and the process by which they were generated were "weapons of mass destruction." The destruction was not the destruction of Bear Stearns, Citibank, Bank of America, AIG, Fannie Mae, and Freddie Mac. It was the destruction of the dreams, the hopes, and the aspirations of the residents of Williamsbridge, who live in a community that is now boarded up.

Lawsuits brought by the NAACP and the City of Baltimore against Wells Fargo survived a motion to dismiss in federal court because an affidavit of a high-ranking vice president of Wells Fargo recounted that she had been told to target African American communities in Baltimore. Her commission income in 2006 was $900,000. Her commission skyrocketed because of the algorithm of racist inequality.

These loans were distributed with a structure that I call the inequality machine. In the inequality machine, an independent, unregulated mortgage broker could use affinity groups, churches, and other avenues of access to tap into the preexisting hunger for identity and membership in the community of property owners that began in 1865.

The convergence of multiple layers of structural risk then created an interconnected global glue through the magic of securitizations. The world headquarters of Citibank and Williamsbridge are two miles apart, but they were bound together by the calculated complexity of the securitization process. When most of us got our first mortgage, somebody sat down with you and asked for your W-2. They did everything but call your momma to find out who you were and who your people were before you got a loan.

In the new model of securitization, loans were pooled into a securitization trust with a securitization trust agreement, where investors were promised returns, through the magic of credit rating agencies. Standard & Poor's, Moody's—all of these credit rating agencies—should have their names changed to Hansel and Gretel credit rating agencies. They made it up.

After groups of high-risk, subprime mortgages were put into securitization trusts, Moody's, Standard & Poor's, and Fitch agencies gave slices of those trusts AAA ratings, based on fictional algorithms about cash flow coming from the borrowers based upon the rising value of their homes.

It turns out, when you pierce the algorithm, the model was GIGO: garbage in, garbage out. All of the assumptions about home values were taken from the middle of the bubble. All the data used for credit rating agencies to rate the likelihood of default came from the period before subprime loans were issued and the higher third-year rates kicked in, causing massive defaults.

Yet for every one of those loans, there was a mortgage broker who got a commission. The 2/28, the 3/27, the no-option, "pick a pay" loans with exit fees—all of these abusive loan products were sold into these communities by commission. The "originate-to-distribute" model was an inequality machine because everybody at the bottom got the bad mortgages, and along this inequality machine, fees were generated. The credit raters got their fees. The Wall Street securitization got its fees. And we know that the people at the top of Citibank, the people at the top of Merrill Lynch, the people at the top of Bank of America got paid extremely well.

We're now in an uproar about executive pay at firms that have been rescued by taxpayers with no conditions on these bailouts. Ken Lewis, the chief executive of Bank of America, stepped down just recently under pressure from shareholders. He was stripped of one of his titles, chair of the board of Bank of America. And the pressure continued, stock price fell. The Bank of America had acquired Merrill Lynch in an expansion. Bank of America had acquired one of the largest subprime lenders in the United States. Under Lewis's leadership, Bank of America acquired Countrywide Mortgage and Merrill Lynch, investment brokers, become sources of grief for Bank of America. The Merrill Lynch acquisition is now the subject of investigation by New York Attorney General Cuomo. Cuomo has been aggressive in going after the information about how these decisions were made to make these acquisitions, who's getting paid, and how the pay is being distributed.

Eventually these problematic features—high bonuses, high compensation and commissions, and bad loan products—came to be seen as toxic assets. The toxic assets were placed in portfolios with fairytale credit ratings and sold to the world. The Bank of Iceland fell because they bought the fairytale ratings of the subprime loan securitization process. This produced what I like to call boomerang contracts. When these contracts were initiated, the loan brokers thought, "I'll take my commission and run. After two years these people will default, and if they don't default I can come back and get another commission to get them to refinance. And they'll go for another few years and I'll get another commission."

This process of flipping and turning loans was also a part of this inequality machine. This is a boomerang contract because the loans came back to hit the very institutions that initiated them. They thought that the risk was being externalized. It was not. One surprise of the subprime crisis is that the homes in Williamsbridge were connected to the Bank of Iceland. And that very interconnection is what produced the market failures.

Credit default swaps, another piece of this puzzle, where bets taken on the likelihood of performance of various agreements, were completely unregulated. The Derivatives Act of 2000 was passed explicitly for the purpose of protecting credit default swap, investors' contractual insurance against loss, from government regulation. It was the credit default swaps in the Structured Finance Unit of AIG that brought AIG to its knees and to 80 percent ownership by the taxpayers. We own AIG. Aren't you feeling rich?

The theoretical and legal foundations for this shift in wealth came from ideology. And the ideology came from three sources: the legal scholars, the regulators (Alan Greenspan being the most prominent and the most powerful), and the economists, including Becker and Posner. These are the strict, orthodox free-market adherents.

But, Alan Greenspan did have an epiphany. Under questioning by Congressman Waxman, in the House Government Oversight Committee hearings. Greenspan elaborated on his failure to respond to Gramlich, to intervene when these racially targeted loans first became accelerating parts of the global securitization machines. Greenspan, under pointed questioning, explained the economic ideology shaping his regulatory choices. In one especially telling exchange, Greenspan conceded the flaw in his ideology, and he acknowledged that this flaw led him to fail to respond to earlier warnings.

Waxman begins: "You had an ideology. You said that, 'I do have an ideology. My judgment is that free competitive markets are by far the unrivaled way to organize economies. We have tried regulation, none meaningfully worked.'

"You had the authority to prevent irresponsible lending practices that led to the subprime mortgage crisis," Waxman continued. "You were advised to do so by many others. Do you feel that your ideology pushed you to take decisions that you wish you had not made?"

Mr. Greenspan answered, "Well, remember, though, whether or not ideology is a conceptual framework, it is the way people deal with reality. Everyone has one. You have to. To exist, you need an ideology. The question is not whether it exists or not, it is whether it is accurate or not."

Waxman: "Are you saying that you made a mistake?"

Greenspan: "Yes. I found a flaw. I don't know how significant or permanent it is, but I've been very distressed by that fact. I found a flaw in the model that I perceived as the critical functioning, ah, structure, that defines how the world works."

Waxman: "Your ideology was not right. It was not working."

Greenspan: "Precisely. That's precisely the reason I was shocked, because I had been going for forty years or more with very considerable evidence that it was working exceptionally well. Those of us who have looked to the self-interest of lending institutions to protect shareholders' equity, myself included, are in a state of shocked disbelief."

The crisis did not begin in 2000. It did not begin in 2005. It began in 1865, 1925, and the redlining government of 1932. It began with a systematic set of circumstances in which some people had houses and land and some people did not. The inequality machine created a backdrop in which wealth was erased, where blacks hold eight cents for every one dollar that whites hold. So, we have wide and devastating wealth gaps that stretch from slavery to segregation to subprime loans. Between 1998 and 2007, the wealth gap between blacks and whites increased exponentially to just over a hundred thousand dollars in 1998. By the end of the subprime crisis, that wealth gap was over $140,000. So the crisis is increasing the wealth gap. There is also a big divide in home ownership, with blacks below 50 percent, whites above 70 percent, and Asians at about 48 percent.

Home equity is your life cushion. That's how a middle-class kid can go to college. That is how you're going to retire. And this crisis has wiped out home equity for many. How many people have looked at 401(k)s lately, or 403(b)s? Last January, when things were very, very tense, 30 to 40 percent of the value of that major investment was wiped out by the subprime loans crisis. The failure to stop a few originations that began in the African American community morphed, following an infectious disease model. Remember, Williamsbridge is connected to Citibank, is connected to the Bank of Iceland, is connected to China. These home ownership patterns and innovations in subprime mortgages are important.

My work in economic justice tries to address the deficit in theory, extend the vocabulary of outrage, and establish mechanisms for combatting these changes. Bonuses for bankers are defended as contracts. Securitization agreements are defended as contracts. And I am here to say that we do have tools in the toolkit of the common law that can help us listen to the economic justice claims of our communities. Recovery will be slow and painful. There was no bailout for black homeowners seeking to cross the bridge between slavery and economic freedom.

In the Greenwich financial case, securitization investors challenged Bank of America in a class action lawsuit brought by the attorneys general of sixteen states, led by Jerry Brown, the attorney general of California, leading to a settlement of $85.4 billion for victims of predatory loans.

On the other hand, the revenue is coming into the securitization trust. And investors in the trust are saying, "You can give away your $85.4 billion, but you owe us $85.4 billion face value of houses, many of which are in foreclosure or underwater. You've got to pay us." And a court is deciding this issue as we sit. Technical processes have been used to move it from state court to federal court: now it's back in federal court. The first decision simply said a contract is a contract and the securitization holders must be paid.

I say economic justice requires that these public contracts, in an enterprise that has benefited from $12 trillion of taxpayer subsidies to keep these businesses from failing, requires an adjustment of the securitization agreements. Going beyond theory, people are beginning to rise up. We've got squatters. We've got judges and sheriffs who are nullifying. And we've got judges who are finding that some of these enforcement efforts are not properly documented. And so, as they say, reality and formality bites.

We've got an uprising, a way of pushing back with the claims of economic justice, from people who are saying enough and no more. The development of the economic justice theory that is my work and my life's passion involves identifying the ways in which adhesion contract theory, unconscionability theory, good faith and fair dealing theory all require us to modify the contract claims of people who have benefited from the originate-to-distribute model with large bonuses, who are using the contract as a shield to keep profits that came at the expense of communities that have been historically starved.

And so today is a new day. We do have an opportunity to go forward with theory, with claims, and with hope for the future, so that Ossian Sweet and those South Carolina sharecroppers who wanted their plot of land, who wanted their individuality and their community, will not have fought in vain.

15

After Obama:
Three "Post-racial" Challenges

DEVON W. CARBADO

2010

Devon W. Carbado is the Honorable Harry Pregerson Professor of Law at UCLA School of Law and the former Associate Vice Chancellor of BruinX for Equity, Diversity and Inclusion. Professor Carbado writes in the areas of employment discrimination, criminal procedure, implicit bias, constitutional law, and Critical Race Theory. He has won numerous teaching awards, including twice being elected Professor of the Year by the UCLA School of Law classes. Professor Carbado was an inaugural recipient of a Fletcher Foundation Fellowship and of an Atlantic Philanthropies Fellowship for Racial Equity. He is the co-author, with Mitu Gulati, of Acting White: Rethinking Race in Post-Racial America.

Being an African American in a predominantly white institution is like playing a small but visible part in a racially specific script. The main characters are white. There are one or two blacks in supporting roles. Survival is always in question. The central conflict is to demonstrate that one is black enough from the perspective of the supporting cast and white enough from the perspective of the main characters. The "double bind" racial performance is hard and risky. Failure is always just around the corner. And there is no acting school in which to enroll to rehearse the part.

Yet, blacks working in white institutions act out versions of this "double bind" racial performance every day. It is part of a broader phenomenon that Mitu Gulati and I call "Working Identity." Working Identity is constituted by a range of racially associated ways of being, including how one dresses, speaks, styles one's hair; one's professional and social affiliations; who one marries or dates; one's politics and views about race; where one lives; and so on and so forth. The foregoing function as a set of racial criteria people can employ to ascertain not simply whether a person is black in terms of how she looks but whether that person is black in terms of how she is perceived to act. In this sense, Working Identity refers to both the perceived choices people make about their self-presentation (the racially associated ways of being listed above) and the perceived identity that emerges from those choices (how black we determine a person to be).

Paying attention to Working Identity is important. Few institutions today refuse to hire any African Americans. Law expressly prohibits that form of discrimination and society frowns upon it. Indeed, most institutions profess a commitment to diversity, so much so that "diversity is good for business" is now a standard corporate slogan. Companies that invoke that mantra will have at least one black face on the company brochure or website. Moreover, employers want to think of themselves as "color-blind." That perception is hard to sell if all the employees are white. Finally, to the extent that there are some blacks in the workplace, the employer can use them as a shield against charges of racism or racial insensitivity: "How can you say we are racist? Obviously, we wouldn't adopt a policy that would hurt our African American colleagues."

The reality today, therefore, is that most firms want to hire some African Americans. The question is, which ones? Working Identity provides a basis upon which they can do so. Employers can screen their application pool for African Americans with palatable Working Identities. These African Americans are not "too black"—which is to say, they are not racially salient as African Americans. Some of them might even be "but for" African

Americans—"but for" the fact that they look black, they are otherwise in-distinguishable from whites. From an employer's perspective, this sub-group of African Americans is racially comfortable in part because they negate rather than activate racial stereotypes. More generally, the employer's sur-mise is that these "good blacks" will think of themselves as people first and black people second (or third or fourth), they will neither "play the race card" nor generate racial antagonism or tensions in the workplace, they will not let white people feel guilty about being white, and they will work hard to assimilate themselves into the firm's culture. The screening of African Americans along these lines enables the employer to extract a diversity profit from its African American employees without incurring the cost of racial salience. The employer's investment strategy is to hire enough Afri-can Americans to obtain a diversity benefit without incurring the institu-tional costs of managing racial salience.

Acting like Obama

Americans understand the dynamic of being black on stage more than they might even realize. Barack Obama's ascendancy to the forefront of Ameri-can politics has put the phenomenon into the public domain. Obama ra-cially acted his way into the most significant role in the world, president of the United States. To do so, he successfully performed the racial "double bind," persuading white voters that he was not "too black" and black voters that he was "black enough."

Obama's persuasion techniques are almost always subtle. His perfor-mances are rarely racially didactic. Perhaps this is because we, his ever-watching political audience, are often (but as we shall see, not always) subtle about the racial roles we expect him to play. It is difficult for us to talk openly about a person's degree of blackness, as though racial identity were a thermometer. Few want to be accused of suggesting that a "real" black person should act one way or another. Leave it to late-night televi-sion to dispense with that worry. A *Saturday Night Live* sketch featured cast members playing Jesse Jackson and Al Sharpton discussing whether

America is ready for a black president. Their answer: it depends on the person's degree of blackness, or "scales of soul." They then proceed to ask whether Obama's degree of blackness will change as America gets to know him. Different social factors move Obama up and down the scales. The fact that his name is Barack moves him up to a higher degree of blackness. But that he was called Barry in high school moves him down. That he was raised by a single mother moves him up, but the fact that he was raised in Hawaii moves him down. His marriage to a black woman moves him up—and so does the fact that in the past he dated white women.

One can challenge the accuracy of both the biographical elements of Obama's family history and personal associations and whether they move people up and down some scale of blackness along the lines the skit suggests. Nonetheless, the skit reflected a phenomenon about which people were (sometimes only quietly) talking. In none of these discussions did anyone assert that Obama was white, though some emphasized that his mother was white and argued that the public discourse about his race obscured that fact. The issue was almost entirely about Obama's degrees of blackness. Both black and white voters were taking his racial temperature.

For Hollywood stars, such as Sarah Jessica Parker and George Clooney, Obama's racial temperature was just right: not too hot (which is to say, not "too black") and not too cold (which is to say, not "too white"). Other white voters read Obama's racial temperature that way as well. Two decades ago, when we were in law school and Obama had just finished his stint as the president of the *Harvard Law Review*, it was inconceivable to us that it would someday become fashionable for Hollywood stars to get behind a black man for president, let alone Barack Obama. Who would have thought that whites would be lining up to offer their support, leading the "yes, we can" charge and proudly bearing Obama bumper stickers on their cars—even before many in the black community joined the effort? Who would have thought that a significant part of the Democratic political machinery would pick Obama over Hillary Clinton? This was all unimaginable. And yet all of this actually happened. The explanation—or at least part of it—was that Obama was not "too black," but still "black enough."

On Being Not "Too Black"

Obama is biracial—the son of a black man from a small village in Kenya and a white woman born in Kansas. He grew up largely with the white part of his family in Hawaii. His professional and academic credentials are impeccable: Harvard Law School graduate, president of the *Harvard Law Review*, law professor at the University of Chicago, among other accomplishments. From Obama's very early public appearance at the Democratic National Convention in 2004, he seems to have understood that his political future would turn on his ability to work his identity for a white audience. He seems to have understood that he could not enact a racial performance that his white audience would perceive as being "too black." He pitched his speech at the Democratic convention to avoid being racially pigeonholed in that role:

> Now even as we speak there are those who are preparing to divide us, the spin masters, the negative ad peddlers who embrace the politics of anything goes. Well, I say to them tonight, there is not a liberal America and a conservative America—there is the United States of America. There is not a Black America and a White America and Latino America and Asian America—there's the United States of America. We worship an awesome God in the Blue States, and we don't like federal agents poking around in our libraries in the Red States. We coach Little League in the Blue States and yes, we've got some gay friends in the Red States. We Are One People.

The speech created a buzz. His audience loved it. Applause could be heard for days. Yet nothing Obama said was particularly remarkable. Granted, the speech was delivered with rhetorical flare, elegance, and grace. But what was striking about Obama's performance, particularly from the perspective of a white audience, was that a black political figure was talking passionately about American politics without making them feel racially uncomfortable or racially guilty. At least some white Americans could have interpreted Obama's performance as offering them a kind of racial cover ("we are not racist, because we support Obama"). This is not hyperbole. There are discrimination cases in which the defendant's response to the allegation of discrimination is basically to say: "I supported Obama for president, therefore I cannot be a racist."

But even if white Americans were not experiencing Obama in terms of racial cover, they were certainly experiencing him in terms of racial palatability. Nothing in Obama's comments hinted at racial division, racial antagonism, or racial conflict. Indeed, nothing in his speech hinted at civil rights. This was not the Reverend Jesse Jackson. This was not Congressman John Lewis. This was not Al Sharpton. Then–presidential hopeful Joseph Biden pretty much said as much. He described Obama as "the first mainstream African American who is articulate and bright and clean and a nice-looking guy." For *Washington Post* columnist Eugene Robinson, much of Biden's description was code for Obama's racial palatability to white voters. According to Robinson:

> There was a sharp reaction, mostly focused on Biden's incomprehensible reference to personal hygiene. For my part, I never made it past "articulate," a word that's like fingernails on a blackboard to my ear. Will wonders never cease? Here we have a man who graduated from Columbia University, who was president of the *Harvard Law Review*, who serves in the U.S. Senate and is the author of two best-selling books, who's a leading contender for the Democratic presidential nomination, and what do you know, he turns out to be articulate. Stop the presses. . . .
>
> Yes, I'm ranting a bit. But before you accuse me of being hypersensitive, try to think of the last time you heard a white public figure described as articulate. Acclaimed white orators such as Bill Clinton and John Edwards are more often described as eloquent. What's intriguing is that Jackson and Sharpton are praised as eloquent, too— both men are captivating speakers who calibrate their words with great

precision. But neither is often described as, quote, articulate. Apparently, something disqualifies them. . . .

I realize the word is intended as a compliment, but it's being used to connote a lot more than the ability to express one's thoughts clearly. It's being used to say more, even, than "here's a black person who speaks standard English without a trace of Ebonics."

The word articulate is being used to encompass not just speech but a whole range of cultural cues—dress, bearing, education, golf handicap. It's being used to describe a black person around whom white people can be comfortable, a black person who not only speaks white America's language but is fluent in its body language as well.

Biden recognized that he had committed a faux pas and apologized for any offense his comments might have caused. He had "no doubt that Jesse Jackson and every other black leader—Al Sharpton and the rest—will know exactly what I meant." Jackson was forgiving, Sharpton less so. When Biden called Sharpton to apologize, Sharpton began the conversation with a note about his personal hygiene: "I told him I take a bath every day." For Sharpton, Biden's comments were less a verbal gaffe and more an effort on Biden's part to "discredit Mr. Obama with his base" by distinguishing him from political figures like Sharpton and Jackson. It was an effort to demonstrate that Obama was not "black enough."

Obama, for his part, considered Biden's comments "unfortunate" and "historically inaccurate." According to Obama, "African-American presidential candidates like Jesse Jackson, Shirley Chisholm, Carol Moseley Braun and Al Sharpton gave a voice to many important issues through their campaigns, and no one would call them inarticulate." This might well be so. But little if anything about Obama's campaign linked him to these political figures. More to the point, white voters continued to draw an intra-racial line between Obama, on the one hand, and other black political actors, on the other. Obama was a different kind of black politician, a new category of black. He was racially palatable. He was racially comfortable. He was not "too black."

On Being "Black Enough"

But was he black enough? The fact that he lived on the South Side of Chicago, attended a black church, and married a black woman all helped to shore up his racial authenticity. His relationship to basketball helped too. Obama seems to love the sport. And at least he thinks he is pretty good at it. Moreover, he prefers the Carolina Tar Heels to the Duke Blue Devils. What's the relevance of that?

Well, race may have absolutely nothing to do with Obama's preference for Carolina. Perhaps when he lived in Chicago, he became a Michael Jordan fan. Any Chicago Bulls fan worth his salt knows of MJ's Carolina pedigree. Or maybe this was simply an election strategy and had nothing to do with race. Obama needed to win North Carolina. His team would have known that there are more Tar Heel fans among the voters in that state than Blue Devil fans.

But, just maybe, Working Identity is implicated here as well. Recall the *Saturday Night Live* skit. It would not have escaped Obama and his advisers that the basketball program at Duke has long been accused of pursuing only those black players who some argue "act white," whereas Carolina has long been perceived as the more authentically black team. Retired basketball player Jalen Rose made this point about Duke in an ESPN documentary: "I hated everything I felt Duke stood for. Schools like Duke didn't recruit players like me. I felt like they only recruited black players that were Uncle Toms."

Preferring the Tar Heels would help with the black vote without alienating whites because UNC–Chapel Hill is more popular in the state anyway (it is the flagship state university). Picking Duke, on the other hand, could have compounded the extent to which some African Americans already perceived Obama to be insufficiently black—indeed, the kind of black who, according to Rose, Duke sought to recruit, the kind of black person who is not "black enough."

For comedian and television personality Bill Maher, Obama is at times exactly that kind of black person. Expressing disappointment with Obama's handling of the British Petroleum (BP) oil spill, Maher commented that Obama "is a little professorial. He saw someone [on the Gulf Coast] and said 'I have been briefed on your pain.'" Pulling no punches, Maher went on to add: "I thought when we elected a black president we were going to get a black president. This [BP oil spill] is where I want a real black president. I want him in a meeting with BP CEOs, you know, where he lifts up his shirt so they can see the gun in his pants. That's [in a "black" man's voice] 'we've gotta motherfu**ing problem here?' Then shoots someone in the foot."

Maher was not the first to ask whether Obama is authentically black or black enough. Author Debra Dickerson commented that Obama is not "black" from an American political and cultural viewpoint because that term refers to those descended from West African slaves. Obama—who she says is "as black as circumstances allow"—has not experienced the burdens of the legacy of slavery. Princeton professor Cornel West also raised questions about Obama's racial identity and commitments. He did so in the context of criticizing Obama's decision to announce his presidential candidacy from the location where Abraham Lincoln's political career began, the Old State Capitol in Illinois, rather than from the State of the Black Union, Tavis Smiley's annual gathering. According to West, Obama "speaks to white folks and holds us [African Americans] at arm's length." The Reverend Al Sharpton, who is now a staunch Obama supporter, was, at the time of Obama's presidential run, even more pointed: "We cannot put our people's aspirations on hold for anybody's career, black or white." "Just because you are our color doesn't make you our kind." For Sharpton, the fact that Obama looked black (in the sense of having "our color") didn't mean that he acted black (in the sense of being one of "our kind").

To be fair to both West and Sharpton, one could say that they were simply noting that it was less than clear whether, if elected president, Barack Obama would be focused on the various dimensions of black inequality. Neither was concerned about whether Obama acts black or white per se. But a black person's political commitments and connections to the black community are factors some African Americans employ to ascertain whether a person is sufficiently black. Just ask Supreme Court Justice Clarence

Thomas. It is largely because of his political commitments and relationship to the black community that some African Americans continue to
use the unfortunate term "Uncle Tom" to describe him. West and Sharpton
were not suggesting quite this much in their 2008 criticism of Obama,
but they were commenting on the extent to which they perceived Obama
to be authentically black. While neither West nor Sharpton even implicitly raises questions about Obama's blackness today (though West has been
consistently critical of Obama's presidency), both deemed it appropriate and
important at the time to comment on what Russell Robinson might call
Obama's perceived "authenticity deficit."

The issue has not gone away. There is now a literature exploring aspects
of Obama's racial authenticity. For example, Angela Onwuachi-Willig and
Mario Barnes have argued that "[p]art of Obama's campaign strategy
seemed to include an active disregard of race or 'racial' figures, even when
they seemed difficult to ignore." As evidence, they point to the fact that
"when Obama accepted the Democratic nomination for the presidency on
the forty-fifth anniversary of Dr. Martin Luther King, Jr.'s 'I have a Dream'
speech, he never spoke the Reverend's name or even inserted the words
'black' or 'African American' during his speech." Similarly, Eduardo
Bonilla-Silva and Victor Ray maintain that Obama "distanced himself
from most leaders of the civil rights movement, from his own reverend,
from his own church, and from anything or anyone who makes him 'too
black.'" Finally, Fredrick Harris has weighed in, provocatively raising the
question of whether Obama's racial distancing suggests that we might
"still [be] waiting for our first black president." His point, at least implicitly, is that in terms of political commitments, Obama is not black enough.

Getting the Double Bind Racial
Performance Right

Part of what intrigues us about Obama's Working Identity is that, quite
apart from Obama's "true" behavioral inclinations, whatever those might
be, he likely makes conscious choices about how to work his identity. When,

for example, he learns about the BP oil spill or the plans to build a Muslim community center near Manhattan's Ground Zero, he can react with emotion, anger, erudition, and so on. These are choices. But Obama exercises these choices under enormous constraints. As noted, he has to negotiate a racial "double bind." He has to be black enough to get buy-in from African Americans, but not so black that he loses the white vote. The difficulty for Obama is in knowing beforehand what racial performances will satisfy these two racial demands. When he gets this right, the results are striking.

Recall candidate Obama's now-famous speech on race. Many describe it as one of the greatest American speeches. It signaled the audacity of hope and stressed that we can become a more perfect union through racial healing, responsibility, and cooperation. The enthusiastic response to his speech, while understandable, obscured that Obama's racial "double bind"—the fact that he could afford to be neither "too black" nor "not black enough"—is precisely what produced the historic address. More specifically, the speech was a reaction to what came to be known as Reverend Wright's "God Damn America" speech, in which Wright said: "The government gives them the drugs, builds bigger prisons, passes a three-strike law and then wants us to sing 'God Bless America.' No, no, no, God damn America, that's in the Bible for killing innocent people. God damn America for treating our citizens as less than human. God damn America for as long as she acts like she is God and she is supreme."

The endless circulation of Wright's words, spoken four years earlier, created a firestorm of controversy. Obama was potentially in trouble. For more than twenty years and up until that moment, Wright had been Obama's pastor. In addition to marrying the Obamas, he had baptized their two daughters. Obama's initial reaction was to explain that Wright "is like an old uncle who says things I don't always agree with." This did little to squash the controversy. More was required. Few would have predicted that the "something more" would be a major speech on race. Such a speech could render him not simply "the candidate of race" to borrow the words of Rush Limbaugh, but the black candidate of race. The circulation of Wright's statements changed the calculus. The statements essentially blackened Obama. At least initially, when Obama was still suffering from an authenticity deficit, he could not simply have repudiated Reverend Wright. That would have made him not "black enough" in the eyes of some black voters.

Obama negotiated these competing racial demands—that he be "black enough" but not "too black"—by giving a speech in which he engaged race in both historical and contemporary terms. In the context of doing so, he condemned and contextualized the minister's fiery comments. While Obama made clear that some of Wright's sermons reflect "a profoundly distorted view of this country—a view that sees white racism as endemic, and that elevates what is wrong with America above all that we know is right with America," he also pointed out that Reverend Wright's church, "like other predominantly black churches across the country . . . embodies the black community in its entirety. The church contains in full the kindness and cruelty, the fierce intelligence and the shocking ignorance, the struggles and successes, the love and yes, the bitterness and bias that make up the black experience in America."

Moreover, Obama specifically discussed ongoing racial inequality; noting that American schools are still segregated "fifty years after *Brown v. Board of Education*, and the inferior education they provided, then and now, helps explain the pervasive achievement gap between today's black and white students." Racism, he maintained, is not something that resides "in the minds of black people"; it is a real problem that must be addressed "not just with words, but with deeds."

That Obama criticized, but did not repudiate, Wright, and at the same time spoke unequivocally about the persistent problem of race, reduced the likelihood that people (especially blacks) would consider him not "black enough." Indeed, among the blacks who welcomed the speech, some worried that it might have made him "too black" in the eyes of whites.

This did not happen. Obama's poll numbers had dipped after Wright's comments became public, but the candidate recovered his ground after the speech. This political recovery was not just a function of the fact that Obama's speech reflected his now-familiar rhetorical signature—elegance, sophistication, and balance—but was also because, in addition to calling attention to racism, he spoke of our collective capacity to beat it. Moreover, he urged African Americans to link their "particular grievances—for better health care, and better schools, and better jobs—to the larger aspirations of all Americans—the white woman struggling to break the glass ceiling, the white man who's been laid off, the immigrant trying to feed his family." He called for racial solidarity, not racial balkanization, and racial unity, not racial division. Further, he admonished blacks to take "full responsibility for our own lives—by demanding more from our fathers, and spending more time with our children, and reading to them." The themes of racial cooperation, racial unity, and black social responsibility throughout his speech reduced the likelihood that people (especially whites) would consider him "too black."

According to the *New York Times*, Obama directed members of his staff to devise a strategy, based on existing research, for how he should manage the question of race throughout the campaign, but also for how he should make Americans "comfortable with the idea of putting a black family in the White House." In this sense, Obama's staff was advising him not only on matters of policy but also on how he should work his identity. Whether Obama continues to receive or request such advice is hard to know. What is clear is that his Working Identity is always on the political table.

Consider the case of Trayvon Martin, a seventeen-year-old black male who was shot and killed by George Zimmerman, allegedly in self-defense. The story quickly became headline news and required Obama to work his identity in response. Trayvon was wearing a hooded sweatshirt at the time, and some attributed his death to that fact. According to Geraldo Rivera, for example, the hoodie was "as much responsible for Trayvon Martin's death as George Zimmerman was." From Rivera's perspective, in effect, the hoodie took away Trayvon's innocence and turned him into a "bad" black.

Initially, Obama said nothing. Then, in response to pressure from leaders in the black community (who pointed out that he had not hesitated to reach out to the Georgetown law student whom Rush Limbaugh had called a "slut"), he intervened, observing that: "If l had a son, he'd look like Trayvon." This carefully crafted statement reminded all Americans that Obama is black and reminded African Americans that Obama conceives of himself as black. Moreover, the statement signaled that, because Obama exists within a black family context, he and his family are vulnerable to racism. Essentially, Obama was saying: If I had a son, he'd be black; as such, he would be subject to the kind of risk that resulted in Trayvon Martin's death. All of this subtle signaling solidified Obama's connection to African Americans. In that moment, he was "black enough."

At the same time, Obama's comments did not alienate white Americans. This is because they were not explicitly racialized. Few quarreled with Obama's statement "If I had a son, he'd look like Trayvon." How could they? It is descriptively accurate, at least in the sense that if Obama had a son he would indeed look black. This is hardly a controversial claim and, at any rate, is not the kind of statement that would make Obama "too black." Like his speech on race, then, this was another successful "double bind" racial performance.

Much is at stake with respect to whether Obama successfully performs the racial "double bind." Small missteps in acting "too black" or not "black enough" can negatively impact the public's reactions to his domestic and foreign policy initiatives. How Obama works his identity shapes and is shaped by the positions he takes on Iran, the Middle East peace process, the financial crisis, immigration reform, and marriage equality. Newt Gingrich repeatedly referred to President Obama as the "food stamp president," forwarding the idea of Obama as the "welfare president." Were white Americans to perceive Obama in that way, it could move him up the scales of blackness, rendering him "too black."

From the other side of the "double bind," Obama will likely continue to contend with questions about whether he is "black enough." In this respect, one can query whether his recent position supporting marriage equality for gay and lesbian couples will move him down the scale.

Beyond Obama

Obama is not alone in his dilemma. African Americans in predominantly white institutions experience similar performance pressures all the time. They, too, have to negotiate a racial "double bind." They, too, are black on stage. Although "double bind" racial pressures in the workplace can take a variety of institutional forms, perhaps the best example is the employer who wants his African American employee to be black enough to function as racial window dressing for the firm (for example, by serving as the African American representative on important committees) but not so black as to create racial conflict or discomfort in the workplace (for example, by agitating for robust diversity initiatives within the institution).

That many African Americans find themselves negotiating the line between being "black enough" but not "too black" suggests that they are not passive objects of discrimination, waiting for the experience to happen to them and complaining about it after the fact. They proactively work their identities to avoid discrimination in the first place. This is what Johnny Williams did in the context of his job search subsequent to completing his MBA degree from Booth School of Business at the University of Chicago. After a miserable time in the 2010 job market, Williams embarked on a set of strategies to increase his market appeal. One involved removing all references to race from his resume. "His membership, for instance, in the African American business students association? Deleted." According to an article by Michael Luo of the *New York Times*, Williams's logic was this: "If they're going to X me, I'd like to at least get in the door first."

Williams's account was part of a more general story the *New York Times* ran about the racial gap in employment opportunities for white and black college graduates. Roughly a week later the *Times* ran another article by Luo, "'Whitening' the Resume." It focused on the resume-whitening strategies African Americans employ to minimize the salience of their blackness. These strategies are not about "passing" in the sense of presenting oneself as white to escape the burdens and disadvantages of being black. Indeed, because some institutions are expressly interested in diversifying their ranks, it is sometimes helpful to be identifiable as black. The question is, how black? In whitening his resume, Williams was not denying his race. He was trying to appear less black "to at least get in the door."

Decision-makers—whether voters, employers, law enforcement officials, or school admissions officers—implicitly or explicitly demand that African Americans work their identities to satisfy decision-makers' racial expectations. Failure to work one's identity can result in losing elections, unpleasant and even deadly interactions with law enforcement, losing out on jobs, being passed over for promotions, and denial of admission to educational institutions. The disadvantages are not a product of simply being black. They are a product of how black a decision-maker perceives a particular person to be. In this respect, the problem I have been describing is not so much an interracial discrimination problem (decision-makers preferring whites over blacks) but rather an intra-racial discrimination problem (decision-makers preferring some blacks over others).

16

Justice Undone: Color Blindness After Civil Rights

IAN HANEY LÓPEZ
2011

Ian Haney López is the Earl Warren Professor of Public Law at the University of California, Berkeley, Law School, where he teaches in the areas of race and constitutional law. He obtained his BA from Washington University and his JD from Harvard Law School. Professor Haney López is the author of Merge Left: Fusing Race and Class, Winning Elections, and Saving America, *and* Dog Whistle Politics: How Coded Racial Appeals Have Reinvented Racism and Wrecked the Middle Class, *as well as two other books and two anthologies. He was a recipient of an Alphonse Fletcher Fellowship, co-founded the Race-Class Narrative Project, and co-chaired the AFL-CIO's Advisory Council on Racial and Economic Justice.*

Clearly I think we all have a sense that justice is yet unfinished in the United States, but I mean undone in the sense of dismantled. The gains we made during the Civil Rights Movement have been systematically undone, dismantled, removed, and defeated, through the doctrine of color blindness. That's the idea that I explore.

The current state of equal protection is abysmal. Let's start with the question: How well does equal protection protect people of color from racial discrimination today? Well, the test under the court is that you must identify a particular state actor who has acted with a state of mind akin to malice in order to establish unconstitutional discrimination. But proving malice on the part of an individual state actor is not the hard part. The hard part is that you need direct evidence.

What does direct evidence mean? It means you can't rely on circumstantial evidence. For example, if you were, say, Warren McCleskey, a black man convicted of having killed a white man, and you were in Georgia, and you had evidence that somebody like you, a black defendant convicted of killing *another black person*, was twenty-two times less likely to be put to death, would that be enough to show malice on the part of the state of Georgia? Would that be enough to impugn the Georgia state legislature that maintains this death penalty regime? That extreme a disproportionality in terms of death sentencing has to be something like malice. Yet the Supreme Court said, "Well, that's a disparity that appears to correlate with race, but that's not enough. You have to show malice with direct evidence."

So what's direct evidence? Direct evidence seems to require a confession. You need somebody to put it in writing. You need somebody to tell it to a journalist: "Yes, I'm here discriminating against black people." You need somebody to make a videotape of themselves. Now, I know and you know that people make videotapes of themselves doing extraordinary things. But that shouldn't be the constitutional test.

Since the Supreme Court articulated this test in a couple of cases in 1979 and 1980, the Court has never, not once, not one single time, found discrimination against non-whites. Not since 1979. The Court reduces the test to the idea that an *express* use of race is unconstitutional. That's the first half of color blindness.

Now a quick aside: anti-discrimination law is much more than what the Supreme Court does. It's much more than what the Constitution provides. So what if you're looking beyond the Supreme Court? And what if you're not looking just at the Constitution?

Here's a dismaying statistic: for all plaintiffs seeking to litigate discrimination claims in federal court, whether based on race or gender or nationality or disability or age, the chance of success is 5 percent. Only 5 percent of people who litigate claims of discrimination *on any basis* in any federal court succeed. The number of those who succeed for race discrimination claims is even lower. So in effect, when we ask, "To what extent does equal protection protect?" it does not protect non-whites. Indeed, the law itself is largely now unavailing as a source of protection against discrimination. That's the first half of color blindness.

Now to the second half. If the first half is that only the express use of race will be held unconstitutional, the second half is that *all* express uses of race will be held unconstitutional. We just said nobody's saying race expressly. Well, nobody who's trying to *harm* non-whites is saying race expressly. But the state, when it tries, and all of us, when we're trying to address racism, when we try to *repair* racism, we often use the word *race* expressly. And the Supreme Court has effectively said, "Whenever the state uses the term *race* expressly, that's immoral. That's likely to be unconstitutional." So this is where we are now. Since the late 1980s, in every affirmative action case to come before the Court except one, the Court has said, "That's unconstitutional, you can't do it."

Now you're thinking, okay, this is the doom and gloom part. No, this is the "so things are bad now but they're going to get worse" part.

Because we haven't seen how bad it's going to be in terms of the law. The law's going to get worse. First, I think there's a good chance that the Supreme Court is going to agree to hear a case coming out of Texas challenging affirmative action. If it does, there are five votes on the court to strike down affirmative action in higher education by this June. The one case that has been an exception to date was *Grutter*, the 2003 case that allowed affirmative action in higher education. But *Grutter* is unlikely to survive this year.

Second, you think about the logic of the Court. In one of its recent decisions, in *Parents Involved*, the logic goes well beyond simply banning affirmative action. It seems to suggest that the Court—or at least four justices of the Court, with Justice Kennedy temporizing—is prepared to say that the government can never consider race at all, even in the context of general policymaking. So if you want to think about the government trying to shape policies with respect to housing, or with respect to where to site schools, or with respect to how to provide health care, at least four justices, maybe five, seem on the cusp of saying that government is prohibited from ever affirmatively considering race.

More than that, the logic of *Ricci*, the anti-anti-discrimination case—that case dramatically narrowed the reach of federal anti-discrimination law. That was bad. But even worse, the logic of that case suggests that private actors, subject to federal anti-discrimination law, will soon not be able to engage in race-conscious efforts to avoid discrimination against non-whites.

So the Court now interprets the Constitution to ban affirmative action at the state level. But the logic of the *Ricci* decision suggests that *federal anti-discrimination law* will soon be understood to ban affirmative action. And if it does, that means large private employers could not engage in affirmative action. Foundations could not engage in affirmative action. Private educational institutions could not engage in affirmative action. That's the logic.

So how did we get here? Now, in law typically we answer that question by saying, What does the Court say? The Court says some truly ludicrous things. For instance, the Court says, "Well we have to strike down affirmative action because it would be elitist to think you could tell the difference between affirmative action and Jim Crow." Now that's just absurd. But that's a majority opinion.

One of my favorites is: "Affirmative action is unconstitutional because it's divisive." I'm like, well, hold on one second. We're trying to resolve majoritarian oppression of a minority, and we're going to make a test of that whether 100 percent of the majority supports this? Of course it's going to be divisive, it's majoritarian oppression of a minority. And the Court is an institution that's supposed to protect minorities from majorities. How can the test possibly be whether it's divisive? If it weren't divisive, we wouldn't need it.

So this logic is laughable. It's nevertheless very important to engage with what the Court has said, because the Court for the last forty years has played a very important role in our society in elaborating justifications and in legitimizing the shift to a sort of color-blind racism.

But I'm going to go outside of law. Derrick Bell is one of the founders of Critical Race Theory, and I think one of his most fundamental insights was that in order to understand race and law, you've got to step outside law. You can't understand what's happening in race and law within the parameters of the Court decisions themselves. So we're going to step outside law and ask about electoral politics, and try and figure out how we got here. The short answer is, through the Southern Strategy, which is better understood as the rise in popularization of color-blind racism. Let's begin with George Wallace.

The image that most people probably have of George Wallace is from his January 1963 inauguration, where he vowed to stand in the schoolhouse doors and block integration at the University of Alabama, and he proclaimed, pounding his fist, "Segregation now. Segregation tomorrow. Segregation forever." But the George Wallace I'm interested in is the George Wallace before and after that moment. Before, because in 1958 George Wallace was, by Southern standards, a racial moderate. Indeed, he sat on the board of the Tuskegee Institute. But in campaigning for governor of Alabama in 1958, he ran against a racial reactionary, and he lost. And sitting in the car with his cronies, smoking cigars, just before giving his concession speech in 1958, he said to his friends, "Well, boys, no other son of a bitch is ever gonna out nigger me again." And by that he meant, I'm going to the right on race. I'm going to be the racial reactionary. And that's who he was in 1962, which allowed him to win the governorship of Alabama and to give that inaugural speech.

And I'm also interested in the George Wallace who comes after that inaugural speech. Because in June 1963, he made good on his promise to stand in the schoolhouse door. But it was a carefully scripted event. The national media was there, and Wallace put away his most inflammatory racial rhetoric, and instead, while banning two black students from entering the University of Alabama, Tuscaloosa, George Wallace said, "This is about fighting an overreach on the part of the federal government. This is about an illegal usurpation of power by the central government."

Now, this was carefully scripted. The federal government quickly mobilized the Alabama National Guard, and the students were integrated into that school within a couple of hours. But George Wallace went home, and over the next week 100,000 letters and telegrams arrived at his office, half of them from outside the South. Condemning him: 5 percent. Celebrating him: 95 percent. And George Wallace had an epiphany, or three. In an interview with a reporter, the reporter used these terms to explain Wallace's first epiphany: "They all hate black people. All of them. They're all afraid. All of them. Great God, that's it, they're all Southern, the whole United States is Southern." That was his first epiphany.

His second epiphany was more dangerous. George Wallace had figured out how to tap into that hatred, and the key was to use non-racial language that stoked racial fears but allowed people to tell themselves they weren't motivated by racism. In the words of the historian Dan Carter, "Wallace pioneered a kind of soft porn racism in which fear and hate could be mobilized without mentioning race itself, except to deny that one is a racist."

So this becomes a standard move in every George Wallace speech. After this, George Wallace would later insist, "I have never made a speech or statement in my life that reflected on any man because of his race, color, creed, or national origin." Yeah, right.

So what's epiphany number three? That he could run for president, that he could compete on a national scale with his ability to mobilize white voters through these coded racial appeals, and that brings us to 1968, and why George Wallace is relevant tonight. In 1968, George Wallace has already lost the Democratic primary so he's running as an independent. And he's taking votes away from Richard Nixon. Richard Nixon sees what's going on, sees that he's losing votes to George Wallace, and Nixon understands that to win the presidency he needs to out-Wallace Wallace. And that's what Nixon does.

In his 1968 campaign, especially late in the campaign, Nixon begins to emphasize racial issues, such as neighborhood stability. Such as forced bussing. Such as welfare. And more than anything else, law and order. As he emphasizes all of these social issues, he's always very, very careful never expressly to mention race, but to keep hammering away at these issues that he understands trigger racial fears. In one of his campaign ads, he links civil rights to protest, to violence, and to crime. Images of protests, of rioters, of police, of violence flash across the screen while a deep voice intones, "Let us recognize that the first civil right of every American is to be free from violence, so I pledge to you we shall have order in the United States."

Nixon, watching that commercial in private, exults, "That's it. That hits it right on the head. It's all about law and order and those damn Negro and Puerto Rican groups." Nixon knows it's about race, but he never admits it in public. Instead, he puts out all of these different issues that code as race but that allow people to deny that they're motivated by race.

Nixon barely wins in 1968, but Nixon and Wallace together get 57 percent of the popular vote. And the next year, a Nixon operative named Kevin Phillips generalizes the lesson of 1968. In a book called *The Emerging Republican Majority*, Phillips says that Republicans can win if they can break the New Deal coalition that put together white members of the working class, northeastern elites, and blacks, and they can do that through coded racial appeals to the whites. He also says that Republicans don't need black votes to be elected, so there's no cost to the coded racist appeals. And that is the Southern Strategy, a term that Phillips uses to describe how the Republicans are going to achieve this new Republican majority.

Fast-forward to Ronald Reagan, when he secures the Republican nomination. Reagan holds his first campaign event at a county fair outside Philadelphia, Mississippi, where three civil rights workers were killed during the civil rights era. And in that context, for the first time, Ronald Reagan endorses states' rights. In going to that county fair, he was taking the advice of the Mississippi Republican Party member who'd assured him that the Neshoba County Fair, outside Philadelphia, Mississippi, was an ideal place for winning George Wallace voters. By invoking states' rights, Reagan is harking to George Wallace's vow to fight illegal usurpation of power by the central government. That's the same language.

Reagan actually provided more colorful language—all the language about the Chicago welfare queen with eighty names and thirty addresses and four deceased husbands who's making over $150,000 a year. My personal favorite is Reagan talking about welfare, specifically food stamps. "The food stamp program," Reagan said, "is a program that allows some strapping young buck ahead of you to buy a T-bone steak while you're waiting in line to buy hamburger." And he says it over and over again at all these campaign events, "Some strapping young buck." A little too close, right? He was subjected to a lot of criticism, so he backed off to "some fellow ahead of you." But he knew the racial imagery that he was drawing on, and his audience understood that racial imagery. He was clearly engaged in this sort of Southern Strategy, this use of coded language.

Then Bill Clinton was elected, so what happened to the Southern Strategy? It became normal politics. Bill Clinton was elected by embracing the Southern Strategy. He embraced it during his campaign when he criticized Sister Souljah at Jesse Jackson's Rainbow Coalition event. He embraced it when he traveled back to Arkansas so that he could oversee the execution of a mentally impaired black man, Ricky Ray Rector, so impaired that he asked that the dessert from his final meal be saved for him for the next day. And Clinton, after traveling back to Arkansas for this execution, said, "No one will ever criticize me for being soft on crime."

But Clinton did more than just embrace the Southern Strategy as electoral politics. He also embraced it as policy. So it's Clinton who ends welfare as we know it, and it's Clinton who adopts a federal three-strikes law, and who lobbies for a dramatic increase in the number of death-worthy crimes under federal law, and who pushes for $30 billion to fund Reagan's war on crime. As one report found, the Clinton administration's tough-on-crime policies resulted in the largest increases in federal and state prison inmates of any president in American history. By Clinton's time, the Southern Strategy had ceased to be the Southern Strategy. It is now just the basis on which politicians—Republicans and Democrats—compete to be elected in the United States.

It is frequently said, perhaps apocryphally, that when Lyndon Johnson signed the 1964 Civil Rights Act he said, "We've lost the South for a generation." He was so wrong. Because they didn't just lose the South for a generation; they've lost it permanently. And more than that, the Democratic Party has lost white majorities. No Democratic candidate for president has won a majority of the white vote since Lyndon Johnson in 1964, not even Bill Clinton. And certainly not Obama. Obama finished 12 points behind in terms of white voting. Throughout the South, Obama won 30 percent of white votes. In Alabama, he won 10 percent.

Now back to the judiciary. What are we to make of the Southern Strategy and what has happened in equal protection? The first and easiest answer is: this is all about judicial appointments. The Southern Strategy was looking for coded phrases: *crime, welfare, activist judges*. Why activist judges in the 1970s? They pushed civil rights too far. They coddled criminals. They allowed affirmative action. They were responsible for forced bussing.

If you think about the other social issues that are part of what's broadly termed the southernization of politics, courts are deemed responsible for permissive laws with respect to pornography, they're responsible for gay rights, for abortion, for women's rights. All of these issues are laid at the doorstep of "activist judges" by conservative politicians—which is to say, by this point, politicians competing for white votes on the basis of the Southern Strategy. When these politicians get elected, it's with a mandate to appoint conservative justices.

Twenty-eight of the forty years between 1968 and Obama's election in 2008 were under Republican administrations, and during that time fourteen Supreme Court justices were appointed, twelve of them by Republican administrations. These include Burger, Powell, Rehnquist, O'Connor, Kennedy, Scalia, Thomas, Alito, and Roberts. Those are the individuals who are consistently rendering equal protection into a doctrine that won't protect minorities but *will* strike down affirmative action.

I've got O'Connor and Kennedy in there, and I know a lot of people are primed to think: swing vote moderates. Well, they're swing votes, but they're not moderate. They're really quite conservative on the issue of race, and to the extent that O'Connor and Kennedy are understood as moderate, it's simply another testament to how far to the right the Court has gone on race.

During his eight years in office, Ronald Reagan reshaped the federal judiciary to a degree matched only by Franklin Roosevelt. He named five Supreme Court justices, 78 appeals court justices, 290 district court judges: more than half the federal judiciary. Collectively, his appointees were economically conservative, youthful, white, male, and uniformly hostile to affirmative action.

We could tell the story of what's happened to equal protection simply in terms of the politics around the Court, and the appointments of judges hostile to affirmative action. But there's another really important element that I want to stress here. The Southern Strategy is really a version of color-blind racism. It's *color-blind* in the sense that it never makes a formal reference to race, except of course to deny that racism is an issue. It's *racism* in that it constantly seeks to stoke racial animosity.

So if you just change vocabulary for a minute, it's color-blind racism that creates a court that is about to enact color blindness. And when you put it that way, what happens with intent doctrine, with this whole creation of a malice standard, begins to sound like returning a favor to racism. Because it's the intent standard that says, "Hey, it's only racism if you make an express reference to race." But these justices were all put onto the Court by people who were racist without an express reference to race. When Nixon appointed Burger and Powell and Rehnquist, racism had already changed to a non-express form.

So when those justices turn around and say, "Racism is only when you mention race expressly," it no longer seems like, well, they misunderstood how racism really works, they didn't really get it. Now it looks like an effort to make sure that the racial politics of the candidates who put them there could never be indicted. Not literally under the doctrine, nor culturally, nor popularly. Because the Court was saying, what the guys who put us here are doing doesn't count as racism at all. That's how the intent doctrine now begins to relate to the color-blind racism of the Southern Strategy.

When the Court begins to announce that it needs to be suspicious of every use of race because you can't tell the difference between affirmative action and Jim Crow, it's saying that at the historical point where the only express uses of race are *in the context of affirmative action.* They already know that, because they've been put on the Court by a politics that has stopped expressly referring to race. And so now we begin to understand this color blindness doctrinally. It's not just that the justices get there through color-blind politics, but that the color blindness that they enact is in a sort of close and exculpatory relationship with the politics that put them there.

What does this have to do with race today if we think about color-blind racism as normal politics in the United States? Four quick points:

Point number one, widely accepted: even those people who seek to oppose this sort of racial politics embrace the basic structure, the basic legitimacy of that politics. It's so hegemonic that even those who oppose it really end up embracing colorblindness. Even Barack Obama. Now Barack Obama really has to worry about the Southern Strategy. He has to worry that he's going to be racialized and all these code words are going to be used against him. He's got a real interest in opposing it. So how does he relate to race as a discourse?

In his 2006 book *The Audacity of Hope,* he says, "Rightly or wrongly, white guilt has largely exhausted itself in America. Even the most fair minded whites, those who would genuinely like to see racial inequality ended, and poverty relieved, tend to push back against suggestions of racial victimization or race-specific claims based on the history of race discrimination in this country." And from this he goes on to conclude that it makes good political sense that efforts to remediate racial injustice should be couched in universal language, not in the language of race, but, for example, in the language of class. And so he goes on to say, "Proposals that solely benefit minorities dissect Americans as us and them. We must instead make universal appeals." So he's saying, we're going to do something different than the Southern Strategy. We're going to try these universal remedies.

But listen to the language he uses when he talks about white guilt and racial victimization; those are the frames of the conservatives who talk about the need for repair as simply a function of white guilt, and who cast the gross injustice of racism as racial victimization. He's already using their frame. And he's doing more than using their frame, he's coming to their conclusion. He's ratifying their color-blind aesthetic, because he's telling us that we will solve racism's harms by never talking about race. That is color blindness, right? I guess it deserves a different term. I guess we could call it post-racialism, because it's slightly different. It's democratic color blindness. So let's call it post-racial. But it's basically the same thing. That's how widely accepted this new approach to race is.

Point number two: it's not just elections, it's policy, and it's policy that over the last forty years has deeply skewed, indeed has remade America. If you think about education, if you think about housing, if you think about welfare, you see that that's true. Perhaps you see that most powerfully with respect to racialized mass incarceration. In 1970, 200,000 people were in prison and in jail; now, it's over 2 million, with another 4.7 million on probation or parole. This is outrageous. The United States has 5 percent of the world's population and 25 percent of the world's prisoners. Two-thirds of those are black and brown.

In *The New Jim Crow: Mass Incarceration in the Age of Color Blindness*, Michelle Alexander says—and it has just incredible poignancy to it—that there are more black men in prison, on probation, or on parole now than were held under slavery in 1850. It's just unbelievable what we've done as a society. We incarcerate five times as many people as the European country with the highest rates of incarceration. In turn, this suggests that four out of five people in our prisons do not belong there.

And the Obama administration, too, is participating in this politics. Every year now the Obama administration is deporting 400,000 people, more people than we've deported ever before, with every likelihood that that number will go up next year, because it's a campaign issue.

In terms of wealth, median family household wealth for whites is twenty times that of blacks, and eighteen times that of Latino households. In terms of poverty, 39 percent of black children live in poverty, 36 percent of Latino children live in poverty, and 12 percent of white children live in poverty.

Point number three: the reigning ideology of government has changed over the last forty years, because what's driving conservative politics— certainly what's funding it—is a laissez-faire libertarian politics around big business.

But nobody is saying in public, "We really want to go back to survival of the fittest. If you're powerful and you make good, good for you, and if not, it's right and proper you should starve to death." That's just not popular. So instead, what they say is, "We need to make libertarianism popular— populist—by tying it to social issues." And what are those social issues? Crime, welfare, abortion rights, gay rights, marriage, activist courts, race. What we've really seen over the last forty years is the reemergence of a libertarian philosophy of governance that we thought we defeated back in the late 1920s. But it's come back, and libertarians are using social issues—most powerfully coded racial appeals—to get people to sign on to their economic agenda and their politics. And they've been tremendously successful. The wealthiest 1 percent now control more than 20 percent of the nation's wealth. And that's a function of the racial politics of our coun- try over the last forty years.

Fourth point: Color-blind racism hasn't just changed our policies and our governing ideology, it's changed the meaning of race itself. Up through the 1960s, race was always biology-plus-culture: brown and lazy, black and las- civious, or black and criminal. The big innovation has been to hive off the biological part, and to focus simply on the cultural or the behavioral part. With the biological part there, lurking in the background, but denied when- ever you need to deny it. That's the big move of color-blind racism.

What do you get out of that? The first thing you get is the ability to blame minorities for their position in society, because now it's dispositional: it's black pathology and brown laziness that explains why browns and blacks are so disproportionately poor. At the same time, you exonerate whites. The plight of black and brown people doesn't have to do with situational factors, and it certainly doesn't have to do with ongoing racism. And you get to celebrate whites, because you get to say, "Well, why are whites wealthy? It must be that they have a culture that allows them to do well under meritocratic competition."

The second thing color-blind racism gives us is a new racial discourse in popular culture that works a lot like the intent doctrine, in the sense that you can never find racism anymore. As long as people never use a race word, as long as they're talking only about behavior and defective culture, they can't possibly be racist. Take all the hysteria about Mexicans and immigration and all these laws that target illegal aliens, for example. The Klan is heavily involved. White supremacist groups are heavily involved. Neo-Nazis are heavily involved. That sounds a lot like racism to me. But they retort that illegal is a crime, it's not a race.

As long as they keep using the phrase *illegal alien*, whatever they say or do can't possibly be racist. That's the way the new racial discourse works to insulate racism. As long as they don't say "spic," they can't possibly be racist. When in Alabama they prohibit intermarriage between someone with lawful status and someone who's an illegal alien, Alabama is essentially reenacting anti-miscegenation laws. But don't worry, illegal is a crime, not a race, right?

There's also a parallel to affirmative action. Remember that the Court has ruled that using the word *race* in the context of affirmative action is racism. So in our cultural politics today, who are the racists? I've been talking a lot about race, so I must be the racist. Or this is even better: here's the Tea Party writing to the NAACP after the NAACP raises a concern about racism within elements of the Tea Party: "It is nothing less than hate speech for the NAACP to be smearing us as racists and bigots. We believe, *like Dr. Martin Luther King Jr.* [emphasis added!], in a color blind, post racial society, and we believe that when an organization lies and re-sorts to desperate tactics of racial division and hatred, they should be publicly called out for it." Which is what the NAACP thought it was doing.

Finally, this new racial discourse has not only changed the way in which we talk about race, it has changed racial categories themselves. Racial cat-egories used to be fairly rigid at their boundaries, defined again by the importance of biology, either in terms of morphology—what you look like—or in terms of ancestry. Even if you looked white, if you had black ancestry you were black. That has changed over the last forty years. Now, racial cat-egories are defined to a large extent in terms of behavior or imputed behavior—culture and whatnot—in a way that facilitates the rise of what I'm going to call honorary white status. Apartheid South Africa invented the term *honorary white*. Basically, they wanted to do business with Japan, and it turned out that under their racial ideology, the Japanese were racial cockroaches. But people won't do business with you if you think they're a racial cockroach, right? So the white South Africans said, okay, we'll give you honorary white status, and you can visit the country and function as if you're white. Just don't move here, because then: cockroach.

We do the same thing in the United States. We now have an honorary white status, and to whom do we give that? Well, we give that to people who, through education, through wealth, through professional accomplish-ment, are now allowed to function as if they're white. This honorary white status is still color dependent. The lighter you are, the more likely you are to achieve this status, and this is both within racial groups and between racial groups. Lighter racial groups—lighter non-white groups—have eas-ier access to whiteness, so it's still partly color dependent. And the status is fragile. If you want to lose honorary white status, all you have to do is say, "Race matters."

If you just talk about race—how dare you!—you're going to lose your honorary white status. So it's fragile. But ideologically, it's incredibly impor-tant, because the presence of honorary whites helps make the claim that race has ceased to matter for everybody. This is the incredibly important role of Obama. It's also the important role of those non-whites who are willing to say, "Race no longer matters"—Clarence Thomas, Herman Cain, et al.

Racial categories have eased in the sense that if you were considered non-white in the 1960s, now—if you're light enough, and if you're well enough educated and have professional accomplishments, and if you keep to this pact of silence about the relevance of race—you can now function as white in a way that you would not have been able to do forty years ago, and in a way that seems to legitimate the sort of racial changes that we've undergone.

It seemed that there was so much promise in the Civil Rights Movement. So much seemed poised to change in 1968. Indeed, for some of us, things did change. Things did remarkably improve. But racism adapted remarkably quickly. It took the language of civil rights, of color blindness, it took the legal tools of civil rights, of equal protection, and it turned that very language, those very tools, into weapons that preserved the status quo, and indeed weapons that actually allowed libertarianism and concentrations of power and great inequalities of wealth to come back into our society.

I was a student of Derrick Bell's when he was drafting *Faces at the Bottom of the Well*, where he wrote about the permanence of racism: "Black people will never gain full equality in this country. Even those Herculean efforts we hail as successful will produce no more than temporary peaks of progress, short lived victories that slide into irrelevance as racial patterns adapt in ways that maintain white dominance." I first heard that as a student, and, I gotta tell ya, I thought it was silly. I thought he was patently wrong. And what was the best evidence? His presence at Harvard Law School. My presence at Harvard Law School. I mean, clearly, things had gotten better.

It's taken me a long, long time to recognize the fundamental genius of Derrick Bell. When he was talking about the permanence of racism, he wasn't talking about me. He wasn't talking about us. Not those of us who are privileged now. The fundamental genius of Derrick Bell was that he could talk about the poor and the hungry, the incarcerated, those who are working as exploited labor. He could talk about the women who are excluded, even from positions at Harvard Law School. And more than that, he could see the connection between the them and the us, between the subordinated and the privileged, between the ways in which we were all of us sometimes subordinated and sometimes privileged, and the way that made us all human, and interconnected, and mutually responsible.

It's when you think about all of us, what's happening to *all of us* in this society, that Derrick Bell seems prescient in 1991 writing about the permanence of racism. Because the great promise of the Civil Rights Movement has slid into irrelevance. It was a temporary peak of progress, but race reconsolidated in a way that ultimately *did* maintain the racial status quo, and in fact made *everyone* worse off in our society.

Should we despair that this is where we find ourselves sixty years after *Brown v. Board of Education*? I want to give Derrick Bell the last word here. In his epilogue, entitled, "Beyond Despair," he wrote:

> I am reminded that our forebears, though betrayed into bondage, survived the slavery in which they were reduced to things, property, entitled neither to rights nor to respect as human beings. Somehow, as the legacy of our spirituals make clear, our enslaved ancestors managed to retain their humanity as well as their faith, that evil, and suffering, were not the extent of their destiny, nor of the destiny of those who would follow them. Indeed, we owe our existence to their perseverance, their faith. In these perilous times, we must do no less than they did: fashion a philosophy that both matches the unique dangers we face and enables us to recognize in those dangers, opportunities for committed living and humane service.

17

Critiquing the Family Tree:
White Supremacy in the Writing
of History

ANNETTE GORDON-REED

2012

Annette Gordon-Reed is the Charles Warren Professor of American Legal History at Harvard Law School and a professor of history in the Faculty of Arts and Sciences, as well as Carl M. Loeb University Professor, at Harvard University. She obtained her BA from Dartmouth College and her JD from Harvard Law School. A MacArthur Fellow and Guggenheim Fellow, Professor Gordon-Reed is the author of Thomas Jefferson and Sally Hemings, *as well as* The Hemingses of Monticello, *winner of a Pulitzer Prize for History and a National Book Award for Nonfiction.*

One of the reasons I went to law school, and I think a reason that prompts a lot of people to go to law school, was my sense of justice. I and others have a belief that law is a way of making a difference in the world. I wanted to try to combine my love of history with the kind of passion of law professors and lawyers and people who think about the world and analyze problems in a particular way—to bring this project to history.

One of the things I noticed in historians' writing about the relationship between Thomas Jefferson and Sally Hemings, was the way Jefferson biographers first wrote about them. For instance, I saw that the authors dis-counted the words of African American enslaved people who said that this liaison took place. At the same time, they treated the word of Jeffer-son's family—white, upper-class, slaveholding people—as if they were sac-rosanct. There was a clear bias in the way they were viewing this matter. I also noticed that historians very often talked about the subject in legal terms: they'd say, "Well, if this were a legal case, Jefferson would be found innocent. He would be found not guilty." And they would say that "the bur-den of proof is on Madison Hemings. The burden of proof is on these en-slaved people who are saying this." I thought, "All right, if you think that this is like a legal case, let's play the game. Don't beat up on an ex-slave, somebody who's dead and who you think you can make fun of with impu-nity. Let's play the game, and see how this goes."

It was a perfect kind of case, I believed—a perfect way to do the kinds of things that law professors and lawyers do. When the book was published, my publisher decided to hire a publicist. They wanted to sell the book by making it like a trial, as if I were trying a case against Jefferson. Well, I was never a trial lawyer. I have no firsthand knowledge about being a trial lawyer. That's not what I thought that I was doing in the book. I saw my-self as doing the kind of critical thinking that I learned how to do when I was at Harvard Law School, and the kind of critical thinking that I try to do as a law professor with my students, walking them through a case, walk-ing them through a controversy, and having them weigh evidence.

When the book was published, I was criticized by some historians and others, who used the fact that I had been trained as a lawyer and prac-ticed law against me. Detractors said, "You're just a lawyer. And lawyers lie. You know, lawyers make up stories and lawyers will only see their side of the case." But *good* lawyers cannot operate that way. They have to know all of the information. They have to know the other side's case as well as they know their own. It's not enough to just think about what you want to say. You have to know the strengths and weaknesses of your own position. What I saw myself doing was taking the information about Jefferson and Hemings, subjecting it to scrutiny, seeing the weak points and the strong points in the narratives of people who were saying the story about them was true, and doing the same for the other side.

Now, I should say I was not primarily interested in proving Thomas Jefferson and Sally Hemings had an affair, or whatever this relationship was. But I did want to talk about the way historians discussed this question. How they discussed this matter suggested that the legacies of slavery were still with us; that even though these historians would not see themselves as having the same kind of attitude as slave holders, they were still thinking about things in the same way. To them, the words of black people still weighed less than the words of white people.

Certainly, in colonial Virginia, when slavery was beginning, enslaved people could not testify at all. They were not thought of as oath-worthy, and they couldn't give testimony, because people didn't think that they would tell the truth. The phrase that was used was *naturally mendacious*; black people lied just as part of their nature.

Eventually, there was an evolution to saying, "Well, black people can testify, but they can testify against other free blacks because there was no concern for the interests of that disfavored group. Blacks couldn't testify against enslaved people, and you can think about why that would be the case. Enslaved people were property. The person testifying could be affecting the interests of a white person. Later on, blacks could testify against slaves, but there had to be what was called "pregnant circumstances"—effectively, extreme circumstances. This system of law was reifying white supremacy. I remember reading the phrase *Negro news* in the papers of a planter, said as if it were a common phrase. When talking about a report of something happening they would say, "Oh, I heard that said, but I just thought that was Negro news," meaning it was something that was not worth believing, obviously.

So, when reading history, I was looking at these and other kinds of dismissive statements in letters and other documents from whites in the eighteenth and nineteenth centuries, and I saw the way enslaved people's words were treated. Then I was looking at historians who were writing in the twentieth century about Jefferson and Hemings, and they were doing pretty much the same thing. They were saying, in effect, "We can't trust these people." At the same time, there was the story from Jefferson's family about why all of Sally Hemings's children looked just like Jefferson. They looked just like him, two of his grandchildren said, because they were the children of his nephews.

Historians accepted that story, even though the letters and the documents they were relying on to make the case that one of Jefferson's nephews fathered Hemings's children were riddled with errors. To begin, the two grandchildren named two different nephews as the father of all of Hemings's children. I suspected the historians had some inkling that these people were making stuff up. But the question was not whether or not they believed it. The question was whether or not they were prepared to say, "These black people are telling the truth, and these white people are lying."

The way historians were handling this story was a bigger issue to me than whether or not Tom and Sally had children together. I grew up in Texas and I knew about slavery. Black people in the South know that there were blended families. White men had children with their enslaved women. The existence of that phenomenon was just not a big deal. That's something that was a well-known fact. I wasn't really interested in proving that. I was interested in proving how white supremacy infected the writing of history, and in particular, the writing of the history of a subject that is enormously important to all Americans, but especially important to African American people who were the objects of the oppression of slavery.

So, I did the comparison of the evidence, and I asked and answered three questions: What is the likelihood that Madison Hemings, who said that he was the son of Thomas Jefferson and Sally Hemings, was telling the truth? And I determined that there was a high probability that he was telling the truth.

The second question was: What is the likelihood that the Jefferson family story, which said, "It's not Thomas Jefferson; it's the nephew, Sam Carr, or the nephew Peter Carr" is true? And I said that the likelihood was not very high at all. In fact, that this story was almost certainly untrue.

And the third question was: What is the likelihood that a man named Thomas Woodson was the son of Thomas Jefferson and Sally Hemings? There is a family of Woodsons who believe that they are descendants of Thomas Jefferson and Sally Hemings. And looking at all the evidence that I could find, I said that this story was not likely true.

I made these bold claims. And I have to say, my book was received very well—much better than I thought it was going to be received. People often ask me, "What was it like when this book came out and you were subjected to all this scorn and everybody came with their torches to get you and all?" But it was nothing like that. Some people reacted with hostility, but in the main, it was well received.

Then one day, I was giving a talk in Charlottesville, and a woman raised her hand and said, "We're going to have an answer to this." And I said, "Oh? How are we going to do that?" And she said, "We're going to do a DNA test." I found out later that she really didn't know *how* they were going to do a DNA test. She had first thought about digging Jefferson up, which is never, ever going to happen.

But they hit upon this idea of doing Y chromosome testing, which was a very, very well-established way of testing for patrilineal lines. Every man has a Y chromosome, and your Y chromosome is the same as your great-great-great-great-grandfather's, and if you have sons, it's the same all the way down. So, you could test a line of Jeffersons, a line of Hemingses, a line of Carrs (the alternative father theory), and a line of Woodsons, to see if the Woodsons were part of it.

Sure enough, they decided that they were going to do this test. And a man named Eugene Foster went around gathering blood from all of the relevant families and sent it to three separate labs. I think two of them were in England and one was in France. Just think about this major effort to determine whether or not this man was the father of this woman's children.

I had to sit for a year waiting, after having said these things very boldly. It's not very often that historians make claims and then science comes to answer them. At the end of October in 1998, I got a phone call from a reporter at the *Wall Street Journal* who asked, "What would you say if the

DNA came back and it said there was a connection between the Hemings descendant and the Carrs?" And I said, "Well, you know, blah, blah, blah." She asked what I would say if it came back and there was a connection between the Hemings descendant and the Jeffersons, and I responded. She then said, "Well, it hasn't come back." That was not true. In fact, a couple of days later, I found out that the DNA had come back, and what I had written about all of this had been corroborated. The likelihood that Hemings and Jefferson were connected was high, because there was a match. There was no match with the Carrs and there was no match with the Woodsons. I was quite obviously relieved, having staked my whole professional career on this very spectacular statement that law professors and lawyers can do it better than the way the historians had done it.

It was quite a relief for me to get that answer. People say there is such a thing as "thinking like a lawyer," but it's really just critical thinking. Applying critical thinking to this problem, and moving away as much as I could from any kind of prejudice—certainly any kind of racial prejudice— to answer this particular question, was the best way to an answer. This process was, overall, about historians. Because if I did this, historians could have done it. I didn't use anything that was not available to historians all along. This question should have been handled differently from the beginning.

That was one phase of my thinking about this particular question. And I felt vindicated by it, and my life changed after that. I decided I wanted to do something different. Looking at law and history and the way they intersect, it occurred to me that one of the reasons people did not pay attention to, or did not give credence to, the Hemings family story, is that they didn't know anything about members of the family. I decided to write another book introducing the Hemingses to the world, having readers think about them as individual people; not as an enslaved man and an enslaved woman, but as Elizabeth Hemings, Sally Hemings, James Hemings, Robert Hemings—as individuals.

There's a tendency, I thought, to see enslaved people as a monolith, in much the same way that black Americans today are too often seen as a monolith. One day, my daughter told me she was watching a marathon of a show called *Scrubs* and then another marathon of another show that had black characters. And she said, "You know, the black characters are always the same. You know exactly what they're going to do." There are stereotypes of white characters, too, but the range of things that white people can be—their personalities—is much wider than it is for black people, for whom it's the same stuff over and over again.

You see that in the writing about slavery, which I believe helps construct attitudes about white supremacy and race. And you see it today. I wanted to do a book that changed the way people saw enslaved people. And that's why I decided to write *The Hemingses of Monticello*.

As I was working on it—this is strange, because with my whole focus on law, there was something that I had not thought about when I was working on my first book, where there was just sort of a glimmer of an idea—I was reminded forcefully when I was writing about the Hemingses of the ways in which law helps construct our understanding of what we think family is. And the question I had to ask was: What does it mean when we take an entire group of people, in this case enslaved people, and remove the protections of law from their families?

Enslaved black men and women could marry on their own terms, but their marriages weren't legally recognized. Obviously, enslaved parents did not have the control over their children in the ways we think normal, because children didn't belong to them legally. They belonged to the person who claimed legal ownership of them. If a woman was raped in slavery, that was considered a trespass against her owner, not rape. There was no such thing as rape as we think of it. Forced sex was treated as if it did not implicate the feelings or interests of the victimized woman.

How do you think about a group of people, how do I write about a family's story, when the kinds of shorthand that law typically provides, like protections of marriage, legitimacy, the notion of legitimacy of children, did not and could not apply? It all seems like chaos. So, when people talk about the Hemings family, and when people talk about Sally Hemings, they feel no compunction about giving new fathers to her children willy-nilly.

Because she didn't have a legal husband, she didn't have that protection, the cloak of law, that marriage would have provided.

And so, if you try to say, "This is this particular family's story," even if you have the corroboration of other kinds of circumstances, other people's testimony, if you don't have that license, then it's as if you don't—and can't—know anything.

On the flip side, consider the writings about Jefferson and his first wife, Martha, who died in 1782. Because Jefferson destroyed all of her letters, we have no letters between the couple. Only two letters from her, that are not substantive, survive. But because they were married, historians write about them as if they know them. The marriage gives people license to fill in the blanks, and act as if they know how they felt about each other and what their relationship was like.

People use that shorthand to give protection to Martha Jefferson that Sally Hemings will never have. If I were to say, "Look, we don't have any DNA evidence that Jefferson was the father of his children with his wife," people's blood pressure would rise. But the fact is, we don't know. We really don't know anything about that. We think we know, because they were legally married. And I think that's a good thing socially. But as a historian, you have to understand that law has its own purposes. Family law has its own purposes. The rules are put in place to figure out who gets this guy's stuff when he dies, who has the right to a child's labor, and who can be put on the hook for maintenance of a child. It's not a biological question. If a woman is married to somebody, the presumption is that the children of the marriage belong to the husband. And that *is* a presumption, because we don't want to say, "Well, you know, everybody thinks that, but I saw this guy coming over and blah, blah, blah." You don't want to open that inquiry. The law gives you the shorthand that allows you to know things, or to act as if you know things, that you don't really know.

The marriages of white people are protected. For enslaved families, where you don't have the protections of law, it's all chaos. We can't know anything at all about them. That was one of the real difficulties in writing the book. I try to reconstruct this notion of family, of the Hemingses, by talking about the ways that enslaved people worked to keep their families together. For example, they named their children after their relatives.

In *The Hemingses of Monticello*, I had to have a family tree, because there are a lot of Sallys and there are a lot of Marys, lots of Roberts and Jameses. They were all naming each other after one another, to keep those kinds of connections alive. Some of the Hemingses became free, and at the moment when Jefferson died and many of the people at Monticello had to be sold, free members of the Hemings family pooled their resources and bought relatives. They did things that suggested, really showed, that they did have these family feelings. The only thing they didn't have was this legal protection that white families had.

In looking at the Hemingses of Monticello, and trying to make the case for them as people who were credible witnesses about their families, I had to go through and piece together as much as I possibly could to counteract the presumption that nobody knows anything about them, because they were born out of legal wedlock and they were—the phrase that was used is *filius nullius*—the child of no one. In those days, it was as if children born outside of marriage had dropped out of the sky.

Of course, everybody's the child of somebody. Everybody has a biological mother and a father. But I think the lack of legal protection for marriages and family was another reason that historians could dismiss the stories of enslaved people. And I hadn't really thought about that enough when I was writing my first book. I was thinking mainly about testimony, and how to weigh the testimony in a different way. I didn't see how this utter dismissal of the notion of family could come about because of the ways law creates its own kind of reality. Historians, rather than being creative in the way that Derrick Bell was creative in thinking about things in a different way, were just using the shorthand of law to say that these families should be protected, and those families should not be protected, and we can't know anything about Sally Hemings. The father of her children could be anybody in the world, because she was an unmarried woman. It doesn't matter that she had children named for Jefferson's best friends and relatives—children who all looked like Thomas Jefferson. Or that she conceived children only when he came back home. When he was in office as vice president and president, he would come home, and nine months later, she had a baby. This happened over and over. The alternative fathers were living in the area, but could never manage to get her pregnant when he was not there. It was all timed to him. One of Jefferson's best friend talks in his diary about Jefferson's connection to Hemings. But without Jefferson's explicit acknowledgment and without a marriage, it's as if these children could belong to anybody in the world.

This is something that I hadn't thought about enough before. It gave me a different understanding about some of the things that historians may have been feeling, and some of the things that Jefferson's legal family feels now; the legal white family. You know, we all draw circles around our family. If somebody were to come to me and say, "I'm a member of the Gordon family," for example, I'd say, "Um, really? What's the story with that?" We are, to some degree, put in a defensive posture once we have drawn the circle. We think we know who the members of our family are.

The difference with Jefferson's descendants today is that if somebody were to say to me that my great-great-great-great-great-grandfather had a mistress and children with her, I don't think it would bother me that much. I'd say, "Oh, that's interesting." But I gather that for some number of Jefferson's legal descendants, he has sort of been collapsed to a grandfather. If it were my grandfather, it might make a difference. Or even my great-grandfather. But he looms much larger in their lives than I think the typical seventh or eighth grandfather would loom in most peoples' lives.

I think now that's the reason for a good part of the hesitancy about this, a fateful reason that the historians felt that they had to be protective. It's not just racism, which I definitely think was a part of what they were doing. There's also this notion of how we feel about our families, and how law tells us we're supposed to feel about our families, and how we're supposed to feel about families that don't have those protections of law.

The Hemingses of Monticello adds to this by discussing this issue of law and how it shapes reality, and I tried to find other ways to substitute for the shorthand of law. One of the things you can do to show this is the way

I end the book, talking about the story of Peter Fossett, who was a member of the Hemings family. He was the grandson of Elizabeth Hemings.

When Jefferson died in 1826, he was $107,000 in debt. That's a lot of money now, but it was then equivalent of a couple million dollars in that period. Everything had to be sold, including 135 people. And Peter Fossett was put on an auction block and sold at the age of eleven. His father, Joseph Fossett, had been freed by Jefferson, but his mother Edith had not been freed. The father went into the community to some members of the Hemings family, but also to members of the white community, and asked them to buy his children. He promised that when he saved enough money, he would buy them back. You don't need a marriage license for that. You don't need a legal structure to tell people to have the sort of feeling of family that this man had.

He worked and saved his money and he did buy back his children. But the man who bought Peter refused to sell him. He reneged on the deal. The family stayed in Virginia for a time, trying to persuade this man to sell Peter back to them. Eventually when things got really bad in Virginia after the Nat Turner Revolt, they left and went to Ohio. And there's sort of a happy ending, as much as these kinds of endings could be happy; in slavery, there aren't that many happy endings.

When Peter Fossett was older, he bought his freedom and he joined his family out in Cincinnati, Ohio. Some members of the family worked on the Underground Railroad. Peter became a prominent caterer and a minister, and he founded a church that is still in operation today. So, this family, these people who in slavery didn't have what we call law to protect them, nevertheless managed to be cohesive enough to create something and to never forget one another. They worked for years for this, so that they could be together.

This whole notion that family feeling did not exist among enslaved people certainly was never true. And historians never should have thought that it was true and treated enslaved people as if they did not have families that should have been respected.

Ending my book with this story was my way of saying that family existed, whether it existed in law or not, and of showing the tragedy of the separation of enslaved people, which was the thing that they feared the most, because they did not have the protections that most people today feel and take for granted.

That's how I've tried to make a mark in the way that Derrick made a mark, by doing something in the spirit of what law professors and lawyers do, which is trying to make the world better, to advance it in any way that I can.

18

Badges and Incidents: Lingering Vestiges of Slavery and the Thirteenth Amendment

WILLIAM CARTER JR.

2013

William Carter Jr. is a professor at the University of Pittsburgh School of Law, where he previously led the school as dean for six years. He is the recipient of a Robert T. Harper Excellence in Teaching Award, a Leadership Excellence Award from the National Diversity Council, and has been named twice in Lawyers of Color Magazine's *Annual "Power List." He obtained his BS from Bowling Green State University and his JD from Case Western Reserve University School of Law. His scholarship focuses on the areas of constitutional law, civil procedure, political and civil rights, and litigation.*

The Thirteenth Amendment's text is rather brief. It provides that "neither slavery nor involuntary servitude, except as a punishment for crime whereof the party shall have been duly convicted, shall exist within the United States, or any place subject to their jurisdiction." The amendment clearly outlaws chattel slavery or similar forms of forced labor. As discussed below, its framers also intended the amendment to eliminate what they called "the badges and incidents" of slavery: that is, the laws, customs, and social structures that supported slavery or arose therefrom.

Properly defining the content and scope of the Thirteenth Amendment's prohibition on the badges and incidents of slavery requires understanding slavery as its Reconstruction framers did. Slavery involved more than forced labor, unequal treatment, and the property law rights and status of the owner and the owned. All of these were fundamental aspects of the slave system, but they were not its sum total. Rather, as revealed by the surrounding historical context and the debates leading to the adoption of the Thirteenth Amendment, the amendment's framers understood slavery to also include the surrounding infrastructure of customs, practices, and systemic forms of racial subordination that supported an ideology of white supremacy, which enabled the system of slavery to prosper and persist. Beyond simply outlawing chattel slavery, the framers also intended for the amendment to provide the federal government with the power to eliminate the lingering vestiges of the slave system.

Based on my research into the Thirteenth Amendment debates in Congress and the historical context in which the amendment was adopted, I believe that the Thirteenth Amendment's proscription of the badges and incidents of slavery should be interpreted with regard to both its immediate purposes and its broader intended reach. First, in interpreting the Thirteenth Amendment, I suggest that we must begin by understanding slavery as did the amendment's framers. They recognized that only one racial group was systematically subjected to the horrors of American chattel slavery and that their descendants are therefore most likely to suffer the continuing impact of the legacies of the slave system. However, notwithstanding the amendment's immediate focus on enslaved African Americans, the Thirteenth Amendment also reaches beyond the descendants of the enslaved and extends, as per its framers' intent, to eliminating the badges and incidents of slavery wherever and in whatever form they be found, even if the victim is not African American.

The contemporaneous historical context illuminates the Thirteenth Amendment's framers' intent and concerns. The predominant view of anti-slavery whites and the early Republican Party in the antebellum period was that slavery should not be extended beyond the places where it already existed and would eventually wither on the vine in those places where it did exist. The center of gravity in anti-slavery dialogue and action subsequently shifted toward full and immediate abolition, however, in reaction to a series of events in the decades immediately preceding the Civil War. Most acute were the "Bleeding Kansas" dispute and the *Dred Scott* decision, which helped drive anti-slavery activists toward the belief that the time had come for the country to make a clean and complete break with the system of slavery. That sentiment culminated and crystallized in the proposal that became the Thirteenth Amendment.

By the time of the final debates in Congress regarding the Thirteenth Amendment, congressmen of both parties generally recognized that the legal institution of chattel slavery would end with the North's anticipated military victory in the Civil War. The congressional debates therefore focused less upon whether slavery would or should end than they did upon two other main themes regarding what would follow the end of slavery. The first theme involved the issues of federalism and "states' rights," that is, whether the central government or state and local governments would be responsible for defining and protecting the freedmen's rights after the end of chattel slavery. By establishing that "Congress shall have power to enforce this [amendment] by appropriate legislation," the Thirteenth Amendment gave a clear answer: the primary power and responsibility regarding the freedmen's civil rights was to rest with Congress, not the states.

The second main theme of the congressional debates involved the question of which affirmative rights, if any, the freedmen would or should have after the end of chattel slavery. This portion of the debates provides the greatest insight into defining the badges or incidents of slavery the amendment's framers intended the Thirteenth Amendment to prohibit. Some of the Thirteenth Amendment's supporters identified particular legal disabilities that they recognized as incidents and legacies of the slave system. For example, Senator Harlan spoke of disenfranchisement from the civil court system, the inability to serve on criminal juries, the inability to own property, and the violation of conjugal and familial relationships as badges and incidents of slavery. More typically, however, the amendment's framers and supporters spoke in terms of broad, natural rights that would evolve as needed to eliminate the legacy of slavery entirely. Senator Henry Wilson of Massachusetts, one of the amendment's primary advocates, stated that the Thirteenth Amendment was designed to "obliterate the last lingering vestiges of the slave system; its chattelizing, degrading, and bloody codes; its dark, malignant, barbarizing spirit; all it was and is, everything connected with it or pertaining to it." Senator Charles Sumner of Massachusetts, another leading advocate of the Thirteenth Amendment, articulated similarly broad goals, stating that the amendment "abolishes slavery entirely, everywhere throughout this country. It abolishes it root and branch. It abolishes it in the general and the particular. It abolishes it in length and breadth and then in every detail."

Notwithstanding these broad proclamations of purpose by the Thirteenth Amendment's framers, for nearly a century, the Supreme Court treated the amendment as a historical curiosity with little contemporary effect, consistently holding that the amendment prohibited only chattel slavery or modern instances of literal involuntary servitude. As a result of the court's narrow early Thirteenth Amendment jurisprudence, the amendment largely lay dormant until the 1960s when it was revived in *Jones v. Alfred H. Mayer Co.* In *Jones*, the plaintiffs were an interracial couple seeking to buy a home in St. Louis. The plaintiffs claimed that the defendant refused to sell a home to the couple because the husband was African American. The plaintiffs sued under 42 U.S.C. § 1982, which was originally enacted as part of the Civil Rights Act of 1866 and was based on Congress's Thirteenth Amendment power to eliminate the badges and incidents of slavery. The defendant argued that Congress's Thirteenth Amendment power did not reach private racial discrimination and was instead limited to enforcing the prohibition of literal enslavement.

The Supreme Court upheld § 1982 as a reasonable exercise of Congress's power to abolish all badges and incidents of slavery, whether imposed by governmental or private action. The Court reasoned that:

Just as the Black Codes, enacted after the Civil War to restrict the free exercise of [the freedmen's] rights, were substitutes for the slave system, so [too] the exclusion of Negroes from white communities became a substitute for the Black Codes. And when racial discrimination herds men into ghettos and makes their ability to buy property turn on the color of their skin, then it too is a relic of slavery.

Jones seemed to open the door to an expansive vision of constitutional authority to redress the lingering vestiges of slavery and consequent forms of systemic inequality in ways that equal protection doctrine does not. The Supreme Court, however, moved quickly to close that door. *Palmer v. Thompson* is one example of the Supreme Court's post-*Jones* reluctance to broadly apply the Thirteenth Amendment. *Palmer* arose when the City of Jackson, Mississippi, refused to comply with an order to integrate its swimming pools, even after reluctantly agreeing to integrate its other public facilities. As Judge Leon Higginbotham explains in his seminal book *In the Matter of Color,* stereotypes about black cleanliness and black dangerousness—particularly the perceived threat of sexual violence to white women—and the stigma attached to commingling of the races in intimate settings such as swimming pools had produced in whites a deep and visceral aversion to sharing public swimming facilities with blacks. The *Palmer* plaintiffs sued the city to force it to allow black residents to have access to the public pools. They alleged, inter alia, that the city's actions were tantamount to an official public statement of proclamation of African Americans' inferiority to whites and that such stigmatization imposed a badge or incident of slavery in violation of the Thirteenth Amendment. The Supreme Court summarily rejected the Thirteenth Amendment argument, stating that the plaintiffs' claim, if accepted, "would severely stretch [the amendment's] short simple words and do violence to its history." Although the *Palmer* Court refused to find that the Thirteenth Amendment standing alone created a self-executing cause of action for badges or incidents of slavery, the court did reaffirm *Jones* in holding that Section 2 of the Thirteenth Amendment empowers Congress to legislate in order to remedy or prevent the badges or incidents of slavery. While the *Palmer* Court signaled its own discomfort with adopting a badges and incidents of slavery remedy as a matter of judicial interpretation, it left the door open to appropriate congressional action.

Congress, however, has infrequently exercised its power under Section 2 of the Thirteenth Amendment. The most notable recent examples of federal law passed pursuant to the Thirteenth Amendment involve federal hate crimes legislation. Two federal courts of appeals have recently upheld these statutes against constitutional challenges. The first case, *United States v. Nelson,* arose out of the Crown Heights riots. Existing tensions between black and Jewish residents of the neighborhood exploded into riots after two African American children were struck and severely injured by a car driven by a Jewish person. Shortly after the traffic accident an angry crowd gathered, some of whom attempted to attack the driver. After the driver and the children were removed from the scene, the two defendants, who were African American, participated in inciting a mob to attack Yankel Rosenbaum, a man visibly identifiable as Jewish by his Orthodox garb. He was stabbed and subsequently died of his injuries. The defendants were prosecuted for violating 18 U.S.C. § 245, which makes it a federal crime to "injure[], intimidate[] or interfere[] with . . . any person because of his race, color, religion or national origin." The defendants argued that the convictions could not be sustained because the statute, as applied, exceeded Congress's Thirteenth Amendment power. Their arguments were twofold. First, the defendants argued that even if the Thirteenth Amendment authorizes Congress to proscribe the badges and incidents of slavery, such power only extends to protecting *racial* groups from such vestiges of slavery. Because Jews in contemporary America are not considered a separate "race," the defendants argued that the Thirteenth Amendment's protections could not extend to them. Second, the defendants argued that even if Congress's Thirteenth Amendment power could extend protection to Jews, it would be inconsistent with the amendment's purposes to apply federal hate crimes law to punish African American defendants, since blacks were the original beneficiaries of the Thirteenth Amendment's protection.

The *Nelson* Court rejected the defendants' arguments. The Court acknowledged that Jews are not considered a separate race in contemporary American society and that African Americans were the Thirteenth Amendment's original intended beneficiaries. Nevertheless, the Court reasoned that the victim's race is not determinative of the scope of Congress's Thirteenth Amendment power to redress the badges and incidents of slavery. The Court's view was that slavery and its cognate institutions distorted American society as a whole by embedding pro-slavery laws, customs, and norms into American law and culture. One aspect of the social control essential to maintaining the slave system was that the legal system allowed private actors to inflict violence with impunity upon members of an identifiable racial group. The *Nelson* Court held that, because the framers of the Thirteenth Amendment intended to give Congress the power to eliminate all vestiges of slavery, Congress could rationally use this power to enact the federal hate crimes statute and identify, prevent, and punish such violence today as a badge or incident of slavery.

United States v. Hatch is the second recent case involving the Thirteenth Amendment and federal hate crimes law. In *Hatch*, the defendants kidnapped a developmentally disabled Native American man, assaulted him, and branded a swastika into his arm using heated metal. The defendants were prosecuted and convicted under the federal James L. Byrd and Matthew Shepard Hate Crimes Act. The defendants appealed their convictions, arguing, inter alia, that the Act exceeded Congress's Thirteenth Amendment power. The Tenth Circuit affirmed the convictions and upheld the Act, holding that "Congress's enforcement power under Section 2 [of the Thirteenth Amendment] extends to eradicating slavery's lingering effects, or at least some of them." The Court reasoned, similar to *Nelson* and in reliance upon *Jones*, "Congress could rationally conclude that physically attacking a person of a particular race because of animus toward or a desire to assert superiority over that race is a badge or incident of slavery," given the key role that such private violence against a despised and subordinated racial group played in supporting the system of slavery.

Hatch, along with a similar constitutional challenge in *United States v. Cannon,* has attracted considerable attention from advocacy groups that oppose federal hate crimes law and seek to return Thirteenth Amendment jurisprudence to its pre-*Jones* scope. Such groups have filed amicus briefs seeking to overturn defendants' convictions in both cases. These cases are of tremendous importance, inasmuch as, if a circuit split develops, the Supreme Court may well reexamine the scope of Congress's badges and incidents of slavery power.

Finally, it is worth exploring the potential benefits of a more robust application of the Thirteenth Amendment. First, the Supreme Court has consistently held that the Thirteenth Amendment, unlike the Fourteenth, does not have a state action requirement. Thus, the Thirteenth Amendment, unlike the Equal Protection Clause, can be applied to the actions of private individuals that inflict a badge or incident of slavery, thereby reaching forms of subordination that currently lack any constitutional remedy. Second, the Supreme Court has also left open the possibility that the Thirteenth Amendment embraces disparate impact discrimination, in contrast to the Court's interpretation of the Equal Protection Clause as reaching only purposeful discrimination. Thus, forms of systemic and structural subordination or individual discrimination arising from unconscious bias, which are effectively immunized from serious equal protection review due to the absence of purposefully discriminatory action, would be subject to constitutional scrutiny under a Thirteenth Amendment disparate impact theory.

There remain a variety of barriers to greater legislative and judicial enforcement of the Thirteenth Amendment power to redress the badges and incidents of slavery. For example, in a recent article drawing upon Professor Bell's work, I argued that one reason for the continued judicial reluctance to employ the Thirteenth Amendment to address the legacies of slavery may be a perceived lack of interest convergence. At the risk of some oversimplification, Professor Bell's interest convergence theory posits that advances in civil rights seldom happen solely out of altruism; rather, dramatic and/or durable advances in civil rights occur only when such advances, although putatively on behalf of minority groups, also advance the interests of the privileged majority. If interest convergence theory is correct, we should not be surprised that the full intent of the Thirteenth Amendment has never been fully realized, inasmuch as the Thirteenth Amendment's original genesis in advancing black liberty makes it seem that its contemporary applicability would have little relevance to privileged racial groups. Thus, as I have written elsewhere, "to the extent that the badges and incidents of slavery theory is perceived [as only benefiting blacks], it would seem to have little utility to white elites. Interest convergence theory would therefore suggest that it is unlikely to be successful" in capturing the public, judicial, and legislative imagination.

To be clear, I believe that the proper interpretation of the badges and incidents of slavery requires focusing on the legacies of slavery and understanding that those legacies are primarily felt by the descendants of those enslaved (i.e., African Americans). However, a full understanding of the system of slavery and the oppressive structures it created reveals that the amendment's goal was to eliminate all of the vestiges of the slave system, some of which may be felt by persons other than African Americans. The Thirteenth Amendment's framers believed that slavery had become "the master of the Government and the people," and that the "death of slavery [would be] the life of the Nation." Slavery, for example, demanded the acquiescence of whites in black subordination, and slavery's laws and customs therefore severely punished whites who stood in favor of black liberty. Slavery infringed abolitionists' freedom of speech in opposition to slavery, freedom of worship when support of abolition was based on religious principles, freedom of assembly to gather in opposition to black enslavement, and freedom of travel to places where support of abolition was punished by law and by private action, and endangered their economic liberty and personal safety. Understanding the slave system's full reach and lingering contemporary effects may therefore help to illuminate that eradicating the badges and incidents of slavery is a project that benefits us all.

In closing, I believe that a robust Thirteenth Amendment jurisprudence directly furthers Professor Bell's legacy by bringing to light uncomfortable truths about lingering systemic subordination and forcing us to address them. Those entering the legal profession need to have a special resiliency to maintain a commitment to social justice in the face of a variety of distractions and enticements that will be presented throughout their career. I cannot guarantee that there is glory or even victory in the struggle for social justice, but I can tell you that it will be worthwhile and that there is a joy to the struggle itself, as shown through the life and work of Professor Bell.

19

The Criminal Injustice of Capital Punishment

STEPHEN BRIGHT

2014

Stephen Bright is the Harvey Karp Visiting Lecturer in Law at Yale Law School, and a professor of practice at the Georgia State College of Law. He has served in the roles of director, president, and senior counsel at the Southern Center for Human Rights in Atlanta over a period of thirty years. He has tried capital cases before juries in Alabama, Georgia, and Mississippi, and argued four capital cases before the Supreme Court. Subjects of his litigation, teaching, and writing include capital punishment, legal representation for poor people accused of crimes, conditions and practices in prisons and jails, racial discrimination in the criminal justice system, and judicial independence. He obtained his BA and JD from the University of Kentucky, and he is a recipient of both the American Bar Association's Thurgood Marshall Award and the National Association of Criminal Defense Lawyers Lifetime Achievement Award.

I want to provide a report from the field in terms of what is going on with this amazingly primitive punishment that we have: capital punishment. Specifically, I want to talk about the realities of it, about race and poverty.

I can summarize my talk pretty much with the case of one man, Glenn Ford, an African American man who was sentenced to death in Shreveport, Louisiana, and was released on March 11, 2014, after thirty years on death row at the Louisiana State Penitentiary, often called Angola, for a crime he did not commit. He is one of 147 people who have been sentenced to death and later exonerated in the last forty years. He was accused of robbing a jewelry store and committing a murder during that robbery. Because Ford had occasionally done some yardwork for the victim, he was accused. That's all it takes. I have had those cases myself, where the white person is dead, and a person who mowed the grass or had some tangential connection to the victim, based on nothing more than that, becomes the defendant in the case.

Ford was assigned two lawyers to represent him. One was an oil and gas lawyer who had never tried a civil or a criminal case. The second lawyer was just out of law school and did slip-and-fall cases. There was no money for investigation or experts. And, as so often happens in capital cases, the prosecution used its discretionary jury strikes to exclude every African American in the venire. The case was tried in Shreveport, Caddo Parish. In front of the courthouse is a huge monument to the Confederacy—it includes busts of four Confederate generals, Robert E. Lee, Thomas Jonathan "Stonewall" Jackson, Pierre Beauregard, and Henry Watkins Allen, a Confederate flag, and a soldier. Despite a weak case against him, Ford was virtually defenseless before an all-white jury. He was convicted and sentenced to death.

The courts reviewing the case in appellate and post-conviction proceedings over thirty years did not find that Ford was denied adequate counsel or that there was race discrimination in jury selection. It was only because Ford's lawyers persevered year after year with the claim that this is not the right man, that somebody else committed this crime, that finally the prosecution had to admit they had the wrong man. In that one case, race and poverty denied a man thirty years of his life.

We see many consequences of poverty in the criminal justice system. The one I want to focus on is the consequence of having a court-appointed lawyer for those who cannot afford a lawyer. Jerome Godinich, a lawyer in Houston, missed the statute of limitations for filing a petition for a writ of habeas corpus for two death-sentenced inmates in 2009. In Texas, trial and appellate judges are elected. They often fail to protect the constitutional rights of people sentenced to death. The Texas Court of Criminal Appeals is like the soldiers who come on the battlefield and shoot the wounded. So it is very important for people sentenced to death that the constitutional issues—the suppression of exculpatory evidence, race discrimination—be reviewed before life-tenured federal judges. But there was no review by the federal courts in these cases because a lawyer did not file his papers on time.

The Texas bar and the Texas courts did nothing to protect other people from being represented by this lawyer in the future. The Texas Court of Criminal Appeals, which keeps a list of lawyers who can take these cases, did not do anything. It did not take Godinich off the list. The Texas bar did not do anything. It had the responsibility to protect the public from lawyers who can't even file their papers on time. It doesn't get any more basic than that. If a lawyer prepares some papers, they must be filed on time or the lawyer might as well not have prepared them at all.

What about the judges in Houston where this lawyer practiced? Surely they would take this lawyer off the list of attorneys who get court appointments to represent poor people accused of crimes. And, at the very least, they should take him off the list of people who get assigned to represent people in capital cases. But at this time, Jerome Godinich is representing over 350 people in felony cases, including three capital cases. One of the three, Juan Balderas, represented by Godinich, was sentenced to death in Houston last March.

What conclusion can one draw, except that the judges do not care? They know how bad that lawyer is. They can't not know it. I raised this with the president of the Texas bar, who was a little embarrassed about this as he should have been. He said, "Nobody complained about it to the bar." And I said, "I read about it in the *Houston Chronicle*, and I would hope that maybe some of the people in the Texas bar might read the *Chronicle* as well."

Justice Ruth Bader Ginsburg said she had never seen a death case among the many that have come before the Supreme Court in which the defendant was well represented. And it is not just in Texas and Alabama, places where lawyers are appointed and cases may just take two or three days before you go from the presumption of innocence to death. In Florida, a major death penalty state, at least thirty-seven people condemned to death have been denied any federal review of their cases because their lawyers missed the statute of limitations. Thirty-seven death penalty cases. It is the same lawyers over and over. The bar is not doing anything about it and the courts are not doing anything about it. So this is the lot of the poor—to be represented by lawyers who are that bad.

There are a number of reasons for this. First, governments are not providing the funding that it would take to have a system that adequately represents people. Why would a state that is trying to convict and fine and imprison and kill people provide adequate funding for lawyers to defeat those very purposes?

People ask, "How is it that Texas has executed 550 people?" It is easy. There's no due process. It's amazing how quickly a case can move through the system without due process. A defendant is appointed a lawyer for trial who is a walking violation of the Sixth Amendment. One lawyer in Houston has twenty clients sentenced to death. That is larger than the death row of some states. There is a quick trial. The lawyer does not raise and preserve constitutional issues. The jury sentences the person to death. Then the court appoints an even worse lawyer to handle the appellate and post-conviction process. That lawyer may not even file his petition for habeas corpus on time. When a state does that, it can execute a lot of people in a short period of time.

When legislators and bar associations are considering the need for public defender offices or capital defender offices, one often hears, "Well, we want to have those offices. We know that it is the right thing to do, but, you know, we just don't have enough money to do that." One also hears: "We don't want a Cadillac. We just want a Chevy." I hear that comparison all the time. In Louisiana, Chevy, not a Cadillac. In Georgia, Chevy, not a

STEPHEN BRIGHT   281

Cadillac. In Texas, the same thing. When I hear that, I often think, we are talking about taking a person's life. We are talking about taking someone's liberty. Shouldn't we want a Cadillac? Shouldn't we at least have a little something better than what I have described?

One thing is for sure: there may not be enough money to defend cases, but there is always enough money to prosecute cases. Long before the military started giving out their leftover weapons to police departments as we saw in Ferguson, Missouri, police departments were already buying that kind of equipment, because they had so much money in federal grants that they didn't know what to do with it.

The Supreme Court sanctioned inadequate representation for the poor in the case of *Strickland v. Washington*, a decision that is not about ensuring competent counsel, but about covering up ineffective lawyering. The Supreme Court said that in reviewing a claim that a lawyer was ineffective, no matter how bad the lawyer, the court is to strongly presume that the lawyer is competent. No matter how clueless the lawyer, the courts are to presume that any decisions made were strategic decisions. In truth, some of the lawyers assigned to represent poor people haven't made a strategic decision since they got out of law school.

And, finally, no matter how deficient the representation, the courts can shrug their shoulders and say, "Well, we don't think it made a difference. There's not a reasonable probability that it affected the outcome." That is quite a departure from what Justice Murphy wrote for the Court in 1942 in the case of *Glasser v. United States*, when he said, "The right to the assistance of counsel is too fundamental and absolute to allow the courts to indulge in nice calculations as to the amount of prejudice arising from its denial." Now, the Supreme Court has said a crude guess is enough.

Robert Holsey, an African American man, was sentenced to death in Georgia at a trial where his lawyer was drinking a quart of vodka every day because he was upset and preoccupied because he was about to be indicted and disbarred for stealing client funds. (He ultimately was disbarred, convicted, and sent to prison.) The lawyer admitted that he gave little attention to Holsey's case. He did not present evidence that Holsey was intellectually limited and that during his childhood, as Judge Barkett said in her dissent, he had been "subjected to abuse so severe, so frequent, and so notorious" that people in his neighborhood called his childhood home the "torture chamber." A Georgia trial judge found that the lawyer had been ineffective and ruled that Holsey should get a new trial. But the Georgia Supreme Court reversed, saying that it did not think it made a difference. It did not defend drinking a quart of vodka a day and not putting on the evidence of intellectual limitations and abuse, but it concluded that Holsey would have been sentenced to death even if the evidence had been presented. And then on federal habeas corpus review, the Court of Appeals for the Eleventh Circuit held, 2–1, that there was not a reasonable probability that the outcome would have been different.

It is absolutely impossible for those courts to know whether it made a difference. The justices of the Georgia Supreme Court and the judges on the Eleventh Circuit weren't at the trial. They weren't on the jury. They didn't see the witnesses. They could not know whether it made a difference. And yet courts say in case after case that the deficient representation did not make a difference and so there is no ineffectiveness. Of course there is ineffectiveness in a case like Holsey's, but the law hides it by saying it would not have made a difference. It shows just how dishonest the law can be.

The Supreme Court has held that clients suffer the consequences of the mistakes of their lawyers because the lawyer is the agent of the client. But Jerome Godinich was not the agent for Johnny Johnson or Keith Thurman, the two men who were executed after he missed the statute of limitations for filing habeas corpus petitions for them, any more than he was my agent. What kind of law is this that takes the most incompetent, irresponsible, lackadaisical lawyer and tells a poor person who cannot afford a lawyer, "This is your agent, whether you like it or not"? Just imagine that that person is put in charge of your retirement, and the person doesn't even know there is such a thing as the New York Stock Exchange. And he may not even talk to you. But he is your agent. So everything he does binds you, no matter how misdirected it may be. At the end of the day after making all kinds of mistakes so that you don't have anything to retire on, this blithering incompetent goes on to be an agent for another person and ruins that person's life. That is what happens in capital cases. People under death sentence may be assigned a lawyer who is treated as their agent, but is so incompetent that he or she does not even file within the statute of limitations, leaving the client a dead man walking.

Let me make several points about race. The criminal justice system is the part of our society that has been least affected by the Civil Rights Movement. There has been a lot of change in the South since the Civil Rights Movement. People of color are serving on city councils, county commissions, and legislatures. John Lewis, who was beaten to within an inch of his life at the Edmund Pettus Bridge, in Alabama in 1965, is now a highly respected senior member of the U.S. House of Representatives. But at the courthouse, nothing has changed. It still looks like 1940 or 1950. The judge is white. The prosecutors are white. The court-appointed lawyers are white. And even in communities with a substantial number of African Americans, every person in the jury box is white. The only person of color in front of the bar of the courtroom is the person on trial.

The criminal courts have always played a role in racial oppression. The death penalty was critical to slavery. Michigan, Wisconsin, and Rhode Island could abolish the death penalty before the Civil War. Other northern states could limit it to just murder cases. But the states with slavery could not do that. The three states where there were more black people in slavery than there were white people could not limit application of the death penalty. And echoes of that history still live today. Over 80 percent of the executions since 1976 have been in the South. Well over half were carried out in just three states: Texas, Virginia, and Oklahoma.

In the South at the time of the Civil War, some crimes were punishable by death based on the race of the victim or the race of the defendant. After the war, slavery was perpetuated through convict leasing. Black people were arrested for loitering, vagrancy, or made-up charges, convicted in the courts, and then leased to the plantations, railroads, coal mines, turpentine camps, and other businesses. Douglass Blackmon's *Slavery by Another Name* describes how slavery was maintained in Alabama up until World War II through convict leasing.

Then there was also a relationship between the criminal courts and lynching, terrorism. People didn't get nearly as upset about terrorism back then as they do now. People who carried out lynching were almost never prosecuted in the courts. The United States Senate did not pass an anti-lynching bill in all of the time that people were being lynched. As Dan Carter, author of *Scottsboro: A Tragedy of the American South*, has pointed out, once southerners saw that lynchings were untidy and created bad press, they "were increasingly replaced by situations in which the Southern legal system prostituted itself to the mob's demand. Responsible officials begged would-be lynchers to 'let the law take its course,' thus tacitly promising that there would be a quick trial and the death penalty. . . . [S]uch proceedings retained the essence of mob murder, shedding only its outward forms."

Echoes of that history are visible today in selecting juries for capital cases. During jury selection prospective jurors are asked whether they are conscientiously opposed to the death penalty. Usually a number of African Americans raise their hands and say, "I'm opposed to the death penalty because the death penalty has been used to discriminate against African Americans." Then the prosecutor says, "And so you couldn't consider this case, could you? Because you are opposed to the death penalty. You think the death penalty was racist, don't you? Your honor, I move to strike the juror for cause." And that juror's struck and other African Americans are struck until there are few enough black jurors left that the prosecutor can use peremptory strikes to exclude the rest of the blacks in the jury venire, leaving an all-white jury.

The Supreme Court declared the death penalty unconstitutional in *Furman v. Georgia* in 1972, finding it arbitrary and discriminatory. Remarkably, just four years later, the Court upheld the death penalty statutes of three states: Georgia, Texas, and Florida. The Court held that just by tweaking the statutes—just by adding aggravating circumstances in some states, requiring a finding of future dangerousness in Texas, and requiring the consideration of mitigating factors—that that was going to overcome three hundred years of race history in this country.

That is what the court said in *Gregg v. Georgia* and its companion cases. But the death penalty before *Furman* and the death penalty today is a function of discretionary decisions made by law enforcement, prosecutors, judges, and jurors who are often influenced by the race of the victim as well as the race of the defendant, and by the success of prosecutors in excluding people of color from juries.

It is well documented that a person of color is more likely than a white person to be stopped by the police, more likely to be abused during that stop—put in a chokehold, thrown to the ground, have a knee in the back, have a gun pulled on them, handcuffed, and put in a police car—more likely to be arrested at the end of that stop, more likely to be denied bail when they get to court, more likely to get a more severe charge instead of a lesser one, and more likely to be sent to jail or prison instead of being put on probation.

The two most important decisions made in every capital case—the ones that decide whether they are going to be death penalty cases or not—are generally made by a single white man, the prosecutor. The first decision is whether to seek the death penalty—most prosecutors never seek the death penalty, but some do. Second is whether to engage in plea bargaining and resolve the case with a sentence less than death.

As a result of the exercise of discretion by prosecutors, just 2 percent of all the counties in the United States are responsible for a majority of the people on death row. That is, 62 of the 3,143 counties in the United States account for the majority of people on death row. Fifteen percent of counties account for all executions since 1976, and 20 percent of them account for all of the people on death row today. So, while thirty-two states have the death penalty on the books, 80 percent of the counties in this country have no one on death row. The combination of aggressive prosecutors and inadequate defense lawyers produces death sentences and executions. One county, Harris County which includes Houston, has sentenced 287 people to death since 1976. It has executed 121. That's more than any state except

Texas itself. It is more executions than either Oklahoma or Virginia, the only other states that have executed over one hundred people.

Experience and the statistics show that both the race of the victim and the race of the defendant play a role in who is sentenced to death. A defense lawyer who is evaluating the likelihood of a client being sentenced to death is going to ask, "What's the victim worth?" Is the victim Caucasian or a person of color, a person of status or a person who's poor, a person who's prominent in the community or a person who isn't? Once the lawyer knows that, the lawyer has a pretty good idea whether the prosecution is going to seek death, whether the prosecution will offer a plea bargain that takes death off the table, and whether the jury will impose death.

The Supreme Court acknowledged the racial disparities in the death penalty in the case of *McCleskey v. Kemp* in 1987. The Court even acknowledged racial discrimination throughout the system in rejecting McCleskey's challenge. Justice Powell wrote for the majority of the Court that McCleskey had not established a constitutional violation by presenting a sophisticated multiple regression analysis that showed that a black person convicted of killing a white person was 4.3 times more likely to get the death penalty. McCleskey's evidence showed that it was likely that McCleskey would not have been sentenced to death if his victim had been black. In rejecting the claim, Justice Powell expressed concern that accepting McCleskey's evidence could open the entire criminal justice system up to similar scrutiny. Justice Brennan called this the "fear of too much justice." The Supreme Court has prevented any litigation in this most critical area by adopting a standard for selective prosecution that is impossible to meet, and holding with regard to the Eighth Amendment that a death sentence is not arbitrary and capricious so long as there are procedures in place that minimize the risk. The Court does not look to see whether the procedures work. It just asks if the procedures are in place.

One of the procedures that supposedly minimizes the risk—although it was not in existence at the time of McCleskey's trial—was the standard to address discrimination in jury selection adopted by the Supreme Court in *Batson v. Kentucky* in 1986. Yet prosecutors continue to use their discretionary strikes to exclude people of color from juries. The Supreme Court purportedly prevented this in *Batson* by requiring in cases in which prosecutors strike a disproportionate number of people of color, that they give reasons for the strike and judges decide whether the strike was for a race-neutral reason or race. Thurgood Marshall was the only member of the Court who had tried cases. Gilbert King's great book, *Devil in the Grove: Thurgood Marshall, the Groveland Boys, and the Dawn of a New America*, describes Marshall's defense of a capital case in Groveland, Florida, in the late 1940s. Justice Marshall said that *Batson* was not going to work because any prosecutor can give reasons and either the prosecutor or the judge may have unconscious racial biases. Beyond that, any trial lawyer understands the dynamics at work: the judge presiding over a case may have been a prosecutor. Before he became a judge, he may have been the district attorney and the prosecutor before him may have been his chief assistant. When he became a judge, his chief assistant became district attorney. *Batson* asks the judge to make a finding that the prosecutor intentionally discriminated on the basis of race and lied about it by giving a pretextual reason for the strike.

Even if the judge and prosecutor do not have such a history, it is very difficult for the judge to make those findings. And reviewing courts almost always uphold the decision of the trial judge. The Eleventh Circuit upheld an Alabama death penalty case in which the prosecutor used twenty-one of twenty-one peremptory strikes against African Americans. He had a race-neutral reason for each of those twenty-one strikes.

In another case that came before the Eleventh Circuit, the prosecutor was asked to give a reason for striking a black woman. He said, "I struck her because she was an African-American woman and the man on trial is an African-American male." That is hardly race-neutral. But he was given a second chance; "I also was worried about her views on the death penalty." The court says that first reason wasn't permissible but the second reason was, so it upheld the strike and affirmed the conviction. Of course, this encourages prosecutors to give lots of reasons in hope that one of them sticks. In the case of *Foster v. Chatman,* the prosecutor gave seven or eight reasons for every strike of a black person. Surely one of them is going to hold up.

As Justice Marshall pointed out, *Batson* doesn't protect against unconscious racism of the judge or the prosecutor. A *Batson* hearing is widely regarded as a farce today. An Illinois appellate court said, after calling the process a charade, "Surely the new prosecutors are given a manual probably entitled, *Handy Race-Neutral Explanations,* or maybe *20 Time-Tested Race-Neutral Explanations.*" The court was being sarcastic, but that is exactly what prosecutors are doing.

It came out recently that the North Carolina Conference of District Attorneys had a statewide training program called "Top Gun 2." A one-page handout called "*Batson* Justifications—Articulating Juror Negatives" was handed out to those attending. It contained reasons they could give for striking black people. Before they had even seen the jury, they already had their reasons for their strikes. Among the reasons:

Attitude and air of defiance; you can bet which jurors the prosecutor is going to say have that air of defiance.

Lack of eye contact. The great thing about these reasons is that no one knows whether they're true.

Body language: arms folded, leaning away from the questioner.

Boredom. I think of all the juries I have picked, and I'm trying to think when we ever had one where people were riveted by all the standing around and waiting during jury selection.

A North Carolina court held that a prosecutor who went to that training— she denied she went to it but her CLE records showed that she did go to it—had used reasons that came right off the list verbatim. The court found that in capital cases in North Carolina, prosecutors strike African Americans at double the rate they strike other potential jurors. This is an absolute mockery of justice. *Batson* is one of those procedures that is supposed to minimize the risk, but, as I said, the courts don't look to see if it really works. It just says that *Batson* is available. Many lawyers don't even invoke *Batson* because they're too shy or too intimidated by the prosecutor to accuse them of race discrimination or they realize that it is hopeless. Justices Goldberg, Marshall, and Breyer all pointed out that if we want to end racial discrimination in juror selection, we have to end peremptory strikes. But there is no serious consideration of doing that.

In some jurisdictions, the prosecutors don't even have to use their jury strikes. Consider a case in Orleans Parish, Louisiana. If that case is tried in state court, the population of Orleans Parrish is 70 percent African American, so the jury pool is going to be roughly 70 percent African American. But if the case is prosecuted in the eastern district of Louisiana in federal court, only 20 percent of the jury pool will be African American. So some cases are being tried in federal court. In the parishes that are overwhelmingly white, prosecutors try their cases in state court. There are no black people there to get on those juries—discrimination took place long ago, when they were selling houses and so forth. It is the same thing in Richmond, Virginia; in Prince George's County, Maryland; and St. Louis, Missouri. Here we see the collaboration between the state and federal prosecutors to move these cases out to courts where there are the smallest number of African Americans to participate in the process.

Justice William Brennan had a remarkable sense of what it was like for a lawyer to talk to a client. In his dissent in the *McCleskey* case, he said that at some point Warren McCleskey probably asked his lawyer what was the likelihood that he would get the death penalty. A candid answer to that question, Justice Brennan said, would be very disturbing, because the lawyer would have to explain to McCleskey that neither his record nor his background nor even the crime he had committed would play as big a role in whether he received the death penalty as his race and the race of the victim. The lawyer would have to tell him that of all racial combinations, his combination, black on white, was the one in which the death penalty was most often imposed.

The story, he said, could be told in a variety of ways, but Warren McCleskey could not fail to grasp the essential narrative line. Race would play a prominent role in whether he lived or died. Justice Brennan observed that the *McCleskey* case would not change what lawyers told their clients about their chances of execution, and no matter how many criticisms there may be of the Court's decision, these painful conversations would serve as the most eloquent dissents of all.

There is no Supreme Court decision or legislative action that is going to change this. We will always be challenged by it. It will require our eternal vigilance. As W.E.B. Du Bois said, "We must complain, plain, blunt complaint, ceaseless agitation, unfailing exposure of dishonesty and wrong. This is the ancient, unerring way to reach justice."

One of Professor Derrick Bell's messages was that racism was permanent, but the struggle against it is worthwhile and valuable. We are not going to get a decision from a court that solves the problems of race relations so that everyone can live happily ever after. Poverty is not going to suddenly go away. These challenges are larger than any of us and they are going to be here for many years.

But there are encouraging signs. Some challenges to the lack of programs to provide competent lawyers to poor people accused of crimes have been successful. New capital defender offices in Virginia and other states have shut down the death penalty, because when people have good lawyers, it makes a difference. Six states have repealed their death penalty statutes. Three have governors that declared a moratorium on the death penalty in their states. And the number of death sentences imposed each year has gone down from around three hundred a year in the mid-1990s to fewer than eighty in these last few years. The constant agitation, the complaints, pointing out the incompetent lawyers, the racism, botched executions—all of these things have brought us closer to that day when we will make "Thou shall not kill" permanent, absolute, and unequivocable. But we are not there yet.

Finally, individual people are making a difference, no one more so than Bryan Stevenson, at the Equal Justice Initiative. EJI puts out information about judges overriding life sentences imposed by juries and giving people death sentences, about race discrimination, about prosecutors striking jurors—all this information that's contributing so much. These lawyers are like people who worked on the Underground Railroad who were getting one person at a time to safe passage until the larger issue, the issue of slavery, was resolved.

I will end by saying you have the opportunity to make a difference. Don't think that you can't make a difference. You can make a difference in saving a person's life—people are doing that every day. You can also make a difference by obtaining bail for a person who, if he or she goes to jail, will lose a job and a home. You can offer hope and comfort to people who have been neglected and mistreated and despised. You may not realize the value of that in law school. I was reading something by one of the doctors fighting Ebola. He said, "I learned as a doctor that at some point the medicine runs out, but that I still go on." That is true in the practice of law. The law runs out, but we still have to go on. We still have to comfort people. We still have to give them hope. We still have to hug them and their mothers and their children.

And so, any of us can be what Derrick Bell described as those who avoid wealth, fame, and prosperity and take on these things. And to be what Dr. Martin Luther King called drum majors for justice: those who are there in love and justice and truth and in commitment to others so that, out of this world, we can make a new one.

20

What's Left Out of *Brown*

SHERRILYN IFILL

2015

Sherrilyn Ifill is the seventh president and director-counsel of the NAACP Legal Defense and Educational Fund, Inc. (LDF). Among her successful litigation was the landmark Voting Rights Act case Houston Lawyers' Association v. Attorney General of Texas, *in which the Supreme Court held that judicial elections are covered by the provisions of Section 2 of the Voting Rights Act. She obtained her BA from Vassar College and her JD from New York University School of Law. She is the recipient of numerous honorary doctorates, the Society of American Law Teachers Great Teacher Award, and was an American Academy of Arts and Sciences Fellow. Her book* On the Courthouse Lawn: Confronting the Legacy of Lynching in the 21st Century *reflects her lifelong engagement in and analysis of issues of race and American public life.*

Every time a police officer kills an unarmed African American, or when I see the video of an officer killing a child or punching a woman in the face or choking an unarmed man to death, I spend time thinking about where we are as a country. After the Supreme Court's devastating decision in the Shelby County, Alabama, voting rights case—a case the NAACP LDF painstakingly litigated—or when the state of Texas imposed a new voter ID law that no longer allows students to use their university ID to vote, and no longer allows Native Americans to use their tribal ID to vote, but does allow for the use of a concealed gun carry permit as valid ID to vote, I spend time thinking about how we would challenge the law—in Texas, we did challenge the law, and won, although the federal court refused to suspend the voter ID law for last week's election. But I also spend time thinking about where we are on race in America, how we got here, and how we can do the extraordinary work of pushing us to where we need to go.

A lot of my thinking begins with 1954, because, of course, that's the beginning of our country as a nation free from legal apartheid. Last year, we celebrated the sixtieth anniversary of *Brown v. Board of Education*, so I spent even more time thinking about the road since *Brown*. With a background as a scholar and as something of a legal historian, I am like a kid in a candy shop at LDF, because we have about six thousand boxes of archives, several hundred of which will be cleared and available for scholarly review next year when we launch our Thurgood Marshall Institute. Our archivist and I have fun rubbing our fingers over tasty things that she finds in the archives. I've been reviewing materials, looking for clues that can help me understand where we are today in this country on the great issue of race, how we got here, and of course, always seeking insight into where we might be headed and how I might lead.

So, spoiler alert, I haven't figured everything out, but I want to share some of my thoughts, particularly about what I'm calling the predictive power of *Brown*. What I've discovered is that much of how we respond to issues of race today, much of our legal and political discourse, certainly much of even our physical landscape, has been shaped not by *Brown*, but by our reaction to *Brown*. And much of what we're seeing today was born and shaped in that crucible.

I want to examine what we knew and what we feared about the *Brown* decision, and how this country has been shaped by our responses to what we knew and what we feared. First, let's talk about what we knew. This is important because so much of what we understand about *Brown*, what we teach about *Brown*, what law students learn about *Brown* is the opinion itself. And I want to spend a little time talking about what is unsaid in the

Brown opinion, but what was very much part of the LDF's presentation to the Court in that case.

In the *Brown* opinion, Chief Justice Earl Warren and the entire court together united behind a singular monumental decision. The Court powerfully rejected the notion of segregation as a custom of preference, but instead recognized segregation as an affront to black citizenship, as a form of racial subordination. And one of the most important aspects of the opinion is the Court's recognition that education is one of the most important functions of state government and that it prepares young people for citizenship.

The story told by the Court in the *Brown* opinion became the dominant narrative about segregation. So it's worth remembering the Court's conclusion about *the harm* of segregation. What the Court said is, "Segregation of White and colored children in the public schools has a detrimental effect upon the colored children."

Let's sit with that for a moment, because it's a powerful statement, yet it's so glaringly asymmetrical. There's a missing part to the equation—a narrative that was and is as important and, I would argue today, with 20/20 hindsight, more important than the narrative about how segregation harms black children. The missing narrative is about the way in which segregation harmed and harms white children. There's no discussion of this harm in the *Brown* opinion, and yet it was part of the presentation of the case. In fact, the now-famous appendix to our brief, signed by thirty social scientists, including the great Kenneth and Mamie Clark, the creators of the doll test, whose work was cited in footnote 11 in *Brown*, contained the social scientists' powerful conclusions about how segregation harms white children.

I think today, sixty years later, we have to return to what those social scientists found. They warned, and I'm quoting now from their submission, "Children who learn the prejudices of our society are also being taught to gain personal status in an unrealistic and nonadaptive way. When comparing themselves to members of the minority group, they are not required to evaluate themselves in terms of actual personal ability and achievement. They often develop patterns of guilty feelings, rationalizations and other mechanisms, which they must use in an attempt to protect themselves

from recognizing the essential injustice of their unrealistic fears and ha-
treds of minority groups." They went on to say, "White children may experience confusion, conflict, moral cynicism, and disrespect for authority may
arise in majority group children as a consequence of being taught the moral,
religious, and democratic principles of the brotherhood of men, and the
importance of justice and fair play by the same persons and institutions
who in their support of racial segregation and related practices seem to be
acting in a prejudiced and discriminatory manner."

And they warned, "Some individuals may attempt to resolve this conflict
by intensifying their hostility toward the minority group. Still others react
by developing an unwholesome, rigid, and uncritical idealization of all authority figures, their parents, strong political and economic leaders. They
despise the weak, while they obsequiously and unquestioningly conform to
the demands of the strong whom they also paradoxically, subconsciously
hate. From the earliest school years, children are not only aware of the
status differences among different groups in the society, but begin to react to the patterns described above."

This is powerful stuff. The court reviewing the *Brown* cases was well
aware of this data, and yet none of it shows up in the opinion we all know
as *Brown v. Board of Education*, which is premised on the harm of segregation solely to black children. And the data were ignored by most of the
judges in the cases leading up to the Supreme Court.

One judge did not ignore these data. Judge J. Waties Waring, a federal
judge in South Carolina, was part of the three-judge panel that heard
Briggs v. Elliott, the South Carolina contribution to *Brown*. The South Carolina case, in many ways, had the most compelling facts of all the *Brown*
cases because of the conditions of segregated schools there. The plaintiffs
in that case suffered, perhaps, the worst reprisals, death threats, and economic devastation of any of the black parents in all of the *Brown* cases. In
fact, Mr. and Mrs. Briggs lost their jobs and livelihood and were destitute;
under threat of violence, they left South Carolina, never to return.

Judge Waring was an eighth-generation Charlestonian, a southern blue
blood. But beginning in the late 1940s, he presided over a series of cases

litigated by Thurgood Marshall. Marshall described his first trial before Waring, a teacher pay case, as the only time that Marshall said he tried a case with his mouth hanging open most of the time, because Judge Waring was so fair in allowing Marshall to present his case. It was unlike any experience Marshall had ever had in a southern courtroom up to that point.

By the time he sat as part of the three-judge panel hearing *Briggs*, Waring had decided several cases in Marshall's favor, including a case challenging the whites-only Democratic primary in South Carolina that mirrored Marshall's Supreme Court win challenging the Texas all-white primary, *Smith v. Allwright*, in 1944.

In each of the cases that Marshall tried before Waring, Waring grew increasingly harsh—and some would say strident—in his criticism of southern white supremacy, and *Briggs* was no exception. The three-judge court in *Briggs* upheld segregated schools in South Carolina, but Judge Waring dissented. And his dissent was regarded as a scathing denunciation of the society in which he was born and in which he flourished. The reprisals that he faced were so strong that he retired from the bench and moved to New York and never returned to South Carolina until he was buried there.

In his dissent, Judge Waring said, "The mere fact of segregation itself has a deleterious and warping effect on the minds of children. These witnesses testified as to their study and research and their actual tests with children of varying ages and they showed that the humiliation and disgrace of being set aside and segregated as unfit to associate with others of different color had an evil and ineradicable effect upon the mental processes of the young, which would remain with them and deform their view on life until and throughout their maturity."

And then he wrote the powerful lines, "This applies to White, as well as Negro children. These witnesses testified from actual studies and tests in various parts of the country, including in the Clarendon County, South Carolina, School District under consideration. They show beyond a doubt that the evils of segregation and color prejudice come from early training and from their testimony, as well as from common experience and knowledge and from our own reasoning. We must unavoidably come to the conclusion that racial prejudice is something that is acquired, and that that acquiring is in early childhood."

He continued, "When do we get our first ideas of religion, nationality and other basic ideologies? The vast number of individuals follow religious and political groups because of their childhood training, and it's difficult and nearly impossible to change and eradicate these early prejudices however strong may be the appeal to reason. There is absolutely no reasonable explanation for racial prejudice. It is all caused by unreasoning emotional reactions, and these are gained in early childhood. Let the little child's mind be poisoned by prejudice of this kind and it is practically impossible to ever remove these impressions however many years he may have of teaching by philosophers, religious leaders or patriotic citizens. If segregation is wrong, then the place to stop it is in the first grade."

And then he concluded with what became the most famous line of that opinion, "Segregation is per se inequality."

It has often been said that Chief Justice Earl Warren followed the template of Justice Waring's decision in *Briggs*, except for this one segment. He carefully adopted a more moderate tone and carefully walked around Judge Waring's discussion about the harms of segregation falling on white children. Chief Justice Warren walked around the testimony of social scientists on this point in his footnote citing the work of Dr. Clark and others.

So both the presentation of *Brown* and the dissent by a judge in perhaps the most compelling of the *Brown* cases talks about this phenomenon, but that narrative doesn't make it into the *Brown* decision. And this, I believe, is not inconsequential. In fact, I think it's monumental. The result is that the entire project of desegregation and of integration is described, understood, and internalized as a project to help black people, to help little black children with their self-esteem, to restore the dignity of black people. And certainly, that is part of it.

But it was never understood as critical to saving *white* children, to preparing white children for citizenship in a pluralistic society or as critical to the future of our united country. And I believe that sixty years later, we are still living with the fruits of this omission. We have never truly confronted how segregation harmed generations of white children and failed to prepare them for the pluralistic society in which we find ourselves.

As we watch these astonishing displays of indifference and violence and inhumanity in some of the videos that we have seen over the last year, I believe we must reckon with the reality that the record in *Brown* predicted with clarity not only what would happen to black children, but what would happen to white children if we failed to reckon with segregation. And I believe it's time for us to reengage the truth and the unexamined portions of the litigation we call *Brown*.

So, that's part of what we knew. What did we fear? Fear was palpable and toxic after *Brown*. And our response to that fear was truly extraordinary and must be examined as well. It shaped every institution in this country from schools to courts. Many of you know about massive resistance—the effort by members of Congress and by leaders in southern states to resist *Brown* at all costs.

You know about the closing of the Prince Edward County schools for five years just to prevent integration. And I really believe that those were the years in which we broke our covenant to provide quality public education for all of our children. I don't believe we ever returned from it.

One particular case demonstrates the kind of fear that existed in the year after *Brown* and, I think, shows how pervasive this fear was all the way up to the United States Supreme Court, which, after all, had just decided *Brown*. It's important to remember that in 1955, the year after *Brown*, it wasn't clear how fast these changes might come. In fact, we had *Brown* I and then we had *Brown* II. *Brown* I is the opinion with the soaring language full of promise, but also, sadly, with the omission I've just described. *Brown* II was a little pump of the brakes. That was the decision in which the Court hedged bets a little bit and said that desegregation would proceed with "all deliberate speed," and suggested that local courts and jurisdictions would be given the ability to determine how to begin to proceed with desegregation in a graduated way. Many of us know what the outcome of that was.

Brown II gave time for southern jurisdictions to marshal their strength, to develop massive resistance, to create private white academies, and to essentially create shadow school systems for white children in many jurisdictions. We look back on the *Brown* decision now and we see how it began to unravel legal apartheid, but in 1955 it wasn't clear what *Brown* would really mean.

In 1955, the subject of race and *Brown*'s reach was the text and subtext of a lot of cases that were making their way up to the Supreme Court. And in fact, in 1955, this fear about what *Brown* might mean became the focus of that year's Supreme Court confirmation hearing of Justice John Marshall Harlan II. I've argued elsewhere that the modern Supreme Court confirmation hearing was, in fact, born of *Brown*. Prior to *Brown*, confirmation hearings were fairly routine affairs, with one or two notable exceptions. Judge John Parker in 1934 had to answer questions about racist remarks made during his run for governor of North Carolina, and he ultimately withdrew (later to sit on that *Briggs* case that upheld segregation).

Justice Brandeis faced an ugly and drawn-out set of inquiries about his law practice and potential conflicts and, certainly, the hum of anti-Semitism vibrated below the surface, though was never explicitly expressed. But these were aberrations. Supreme Court confirmations were routine affairs. Normally, the nominee didn't even appear before the Senate Judiciary Committee. It was kind of all done on paper. What we've come to know as the modern Supreme Court confirmation hearing, where the nominee comes before the committee and answers questions over days about a range of their views on controversial topics, was born out of racial anxiety about *Brown*.

Justice Harlan II was no radical, no real profile in courage. He paled in comparison to the conviction and courage of his grandfather, the first John Marshall Harlan, who wrote the famous dissent in *Plessy v. Ferguson* in 1896. Harlan II was what they call "an able lawyer." *Brown* had been decided the year before, and there was some anxiety—and some might say hysteria—in the air. On the Senate Judiciary Committee led by Senator Harley Kilgore of West Virginia, the post-*Brown* anxiety centered itself on a case making its way up to the United States Supreme Court, *Rice v. Sioux City Memorial Park*. Senators—and we later learned some Supreme Court justices—feared that this case would get to the Court too soon and force the Court to take on a broad range of segregation issues in American life: parks and swimming pools, hotels, and, in the subject of this case, cemeteries.

The case involved the burial of a man named John Rice, who was killed in action in Korea in 1951 and whose body was flown home for his funeral. Rice received the Purple Heart, Bronze Star, and many other awards for his bravery. Several weeks before his burial, his wife, Evelyn Rice, had signed the contract with Sioux City Memorial Park for a plot in the cemetery where she would bury her husband. On the day of his burial, she and her three children, Pamela, Tim, and Jean, along with members of the extended family, assembled to bury John Rice. After they had the ceremony at the burial site, but before they lowered her husband's body into the ground, Evelyn Rice returned home with their children.

About an hour later, there was a knock at the door, and it was the owners of the cemetery. They came to tell her that, now that they had seen the people who came to mourn John Rice, they realized that they could not bury him there, because it was apparent that he was Native American. I've met and talked with Evelyn Rice, who was white, and she and her children, even though they were very young, remember very vividly the fear, confusion, and embarrassment they felt when they were told they would not be able to put John Rice in the ground.

But because he was a soldier and there were military men at the funeral, something different happened. These soldiers were actually quite disturbed and angry that the cemetery refused to bury John Rice. And they called Washington, DC, to talk about this terrible thing that had happened in Sioux City. Word got to President Harry Truman, who was outraged. He sent a cable to Mrs. Rice the following day telling her that her husband could be buried in Arlington National Cemetery, where he was ultimately laid to rest.

But before that happened, the members of the Sioux City Memorial Park came again to visit with Mrs. Rice and told her if she would just sign an affidavit saying that John Rice was white, they would be able to bury him. They didn't care that he wasn't actually white. Mrs. Rice was not a civil rights pioneer. She was not an activist. She was a devastated widow. But she refused to sign. She said she had no shame about him being Native American, and she couldn't understand why she would deny that he was Native American. In fact, she and her sister had grown up near the same reservation as John Rice, and she and her sister had married two brothers. She'd known John since she was a young girl, and he was truly the love of her life.

So she refused to sign, and her brother-in-law, John's brother, convinced her to see a lawyer. Although she was very reluctant and actually quite shy, she went, and they filed the case, which made its way up to the Iowa Supreme Court. The Iowa Supreme Court did not rule in favor of Evelyn Rice, and the case was headed to the United States Supreme Court at the time of the confirmation hearing of John Marshall Harlan II. On November 15, 1954, the same year as *Brown*, the Supreme Court essentially upheld the decision of the Iowa Supreme Court by splitting four to four, ruling that Mrs. Rice did not have the contractual right to bury her husband in that cemetery.

So this was in the air, and many of the senators were very distressed about the possibility that this case would go to the Supreme Court. They wanted to know, "Where do you stand, John Marshall Harlan, on this set of issues?" Senator Hart on the Judiciary Committee described it this way: "One of the country's greatest needs today is restoration of the Supreme Court to its historic stature. Its prestige has fallen to a low ebb. Too often in the past twenty years, the Court has become a political body. One example is the segregation decision, in which the Court usurps the functions of the Congress. Every nomination to the Supreme Court should therefore be considered in light of this need." I actually believe every nomination to the Supreme Court since then has been considered in light of that concern.

I came to learn about the *Rice* case because I was writing about Supreme Court confirmation hearings, and so many of the questions for Justice

Harlan were about the case. You might wonder, since I said he was just an able lawyer and not a profile in courage, why they were asking him all these questions about the *Rice* case. Well, in the *Rice* case, a brief had been submitted to the Supreme Court suggesting that the actions of the Sioux City Memorial Park, in addition to violating the Fourteenth Amendment, also violated the recently ratified UN Charter.

Justice Harlan had nominally made himself a part of an organization that was focused on promoting the UN Charter. When I say nominally, I mean that, as he testified, he just signed a sheet that somebody put in front of him. He'd never attended any meetings, and he didn't plan to. Yet this was enough to suggest to them that he might be one of those people who was interested in, you know, one world order. So that was the focus of their questioning.

Meanwhile, inside the Supreme Court, there was an effort not to deal with this issue. Although the Court had split four to four, they understood that the case was going to come back to them because there was an effort to seek a rehearing. Behind the scenes, Justice Frankfurter was deeply concerned about the Court getting what he would call "ahead of itself." He really believed that there needed to be moderation post-*Brown*, and he did not want the Court to step into this next phase of dealing with the issue of segregation. So many efforts were made to try and find procedural grounds on which to not hear the *Rice* case again.

Nevertheless, the case made its way back to the Supreme Court. John Marshall Harlan was confirmed in March 1955, when there was a petition for rehearing of the *Rice v. Sioux City Memorial Park* case. The Supreme Court did something kind of interesting. In May 1955, almost a year to the day after *Brown* I, the Court granted the petition for rehearing in *Rice*, and then they vacated their earlier decision on the grounds that cert had been improvidently granted the first time—they should never have agreed to hear the case. The reason they gave was that the state of Iowa had already passed a statute ending segregation in cemeteries. The Supreme Court had heard the *Rice* case, but in retrospect the Court said, in effect, "You know, we didn't really notice that we shouldn't have heard it. Now we can see that cert was improvidently granted." Thus, they were able to remove themselves from this very volatile situation.

There was a dissent from Chief Justice Warren, Justice Black, and Justice Douglas. But this case shows you how fearful the country was. Even the justices were worried about what integration might mean and about how quickly it might move. This fear of integration also changed the landscape of our country. As you know, it set off a kind of great migration of sorts, and an ignoble one I might add, but still, an exodus of whites from cities across the country. Unlike African Americans who fled the South seeking opportunity and jobs and fleeing the terror of lynching and violent white supremacy, the white migration to the suburbs involved opportunity. The creation of the white suburb was supported by massive government investments and coincided with the end of legal segregation, but it also involved a flight from the terror of the imagination, a terror conjured from ghost stories about integration and miscegenation, and the loss of white power and prestige.

White flight changed northern cities as powerfully as the great migration of blacks did the South. In fact, for a brief period of twenty years or so, both migrations were happening at the same time. Blacks were still coming up from the South to seek opportunity in northern cities in the 1960s and early 1970s, as whites were leaving cities for the suburbs to avoid integration.

The fear of integration began what became the abandonment of the public school system in this country—first through massive resistance, as I described earlier—and then through the bussing wars of northern cities in the 1970s, and ultimately as a matter of public policy. Truly, integrated schooling happened for a brief fifteen-year period after the passage of the Civil Rights Act of 1964 and ended soon after the Supreme Court's 1974 decision in *Milliken v. Bradley*, when the Court decided that city integration plans could not extend into the suburbs.

I, like perhaps many of you, was bussed to integrated schools during that brief period. Perhaps someday our story will be fully told, to contextualize the contemporary landscape of America: hyper-segregated, with development and white flight reaching further and further out as blacks moved into the suburbs, then moments of intense gentrification pulling whites back into pockets of major cities, with racially segregated, deeply distressed, poor black communities featuring public schools that are often upwards of 90 percent black. This landscape is the result not of *Brown* itself, but of the irrational and destructive fear of what *Brown* would mean.

So what shall we say to these things? I believe that we must return to the project of understanding integration, a word that is old-fashioned and perhaps sounds irrelevant these days. But if we're honest with ourselves, segregation is killing the fabric of this country. We do not know each other. We stand apart from each other. Our experiences are often too different. We don't understand the experiences of one another.

The integration I speak of is urgently needed. If we're ever to prepare our children for the exercise of responsible citizenship in a country that's increasingly diverse, it is urgent and essential that we deal with this, because economic integration follows racial integration. We cannot continue as a democracy with the vast chasms of income and wealth inequality in our country, or we will continue on this recurring reel from Detroit and Watts in 1966 and 1968, to Los Angeles in 1992 and Baltimore in 2015; from the killing of ten-year-old Clifford Glover by the NYPD in 1973, to the killing of twelve-year-old Tamir Rice by Cleveland police in 2014. After all, it's not only the killing of Tamir Rice, it's the officer who shackles Rice's teenage sister when she cries and screams as she sees her brother dying. It's when he says to the mother, "I'll arrest you too, if you don't stop screaming."

So what should the elements of this project be? First and foremost, we must return to the issue we grappled with before *Brown*: housing segregation. In the years before *Brown*, housing segregation was as much a preoccupation of the NAACP Legal Defense Fund as education became in the years after *Brown*. It was in *Hurd v. Hodge*—the case brought by Charles Hamilton Houston in 1948 successfully challenging racially restrictive covenants in Washington, DC, that we filed the first brief. This was a complex and detailed eighty-page brief that included economic and sociological data about the effect of racially restrictive covenants and housing deeds on the health and economic conditions of blacks living in the cities, on the strength of black families, on attitudes about race and racial prejudice, and on what was described in the brief as the international, national, and moral implications of this form of housing segregation.

That *Hurd* brief became the template for the brief of the sociologist in *Brown* and for hundreds of amicus briefs that we now file as a matter of course in the United States Supreme Court. *Hurd* led directly to *Shelley v. Kraemer*, which dropped down judicial enforcement of racially restrictive covenants in state courts. *Shelley* was a great win for LDF in 1948. Thurgood Marshall received telegrams from around the country, and all signs pointed to a continued focus on housing segregation.

In 1950, Marshall and the LDF team won a monumental case in the Supreme Court, *Sweatt v. Painter*, in which the Supreme Court rejected Texas's efforts to hastily establish a separate law school for black students, the Texas School for Negroes, as they called it. Instead, the Court determined that a separate law school for black students and the law school at the University of Texas could never be equal, that they were per se unequal. The LDF lawyers then saw that winning a challenge to segregated public school education in K through 12 was in sight.

In 1951, Barbara Johns in the eleventh grade led her fellow students in a walkout from her segregated high school in Prince Edward County, Virginia, and that courageous act of civil disobedience by a sixteen-year-old girl and her peers pushed attorneys Oliver Hill, Spottswood Robinson, and LDF to file *Davis v. County School Board of Prince Edward County*, the Virginia case that became part of *Brown*. The rest, as they say, is history.

It took nearly twenty years and the assassination of Martin Luther King for a concerted civil rights focus to return to the issue of housing segregation. The Fair Housing Act was passed in 1968, just six days after the killing of King, while cities all over the country burned in the wake of that terrible, terrible assassination.

Nevertheless, we remained deeply segregated, and I regard the segregation issue as one that is not only about law, but also about investments and

infrastructure, transportation policy, and so many other areas that we traditionally ignore or give little attention to in the civil rights space. The creation of the interstate highway system was a civil rights issue. We didn't
know it at the time, but it made the creation of the white suburbs possible. It was an investment in the creation of the white, segregated middle
class. And that investment, while a good thing in the abstract, meant that
the FHA, by supporting and encouraging the development of all-white en-
claves like Levittown, had as much to do with thwarting the promises of
Brown as the foot-dragging of timid federal judges. So we need a broader
lens for understanding civil rights challenges such as segregation.

We also need a candid and clear evaluation of how this country has benefited from even our tentative steps toward equality. The wealth that the
United States has amassed, and its leadership in the world, especially during the Cold War, as Derrick Bell wrote about in his interest convergence
theory—the leadership of American businesspeople and political leaders
in the world—has been enhanced by the story of America as a place of
equality and promise.

The very terms in which we describe ourselves as a nation were created
by the Civil Rights Movement and by civil rights litigation, and we've marketed those words and that image of our nation to leverage our economic,
political, and military might all over the world, at a great profit to many.
Civil rights lawyering and activism created a twentieth- and twenty-first-
century narrative about America that has quantifiable value. The case for
equality should be made on the basis of what it will do and has done for our
country, not just as a gift to racial minorities, or "free stuff," as they call it.

I'd like to see scholars do even more detailed work quantifying the equality dividend for our nation. This is what we gave America, and we get very
little credit for it. If we truly do care about our children, we must return to
the conclusions reached by the social scientists in *Brown*. Even if we don't
agree with all of the methodology, we must certainly admit that not just
black people, but white people, the soul of our country, the health of our
democracy, the integrity of every institution, all of these things have been
harmed by segregation and, as they said in the brief, related practices.

As we deal with the ongoing and stubborn issue of racial discrimination; as we grapple with police killings of unarmed African American men, women, and children; as we look at voter suppression and the vast economic equality gap between blacks and whites; as we wonder why the racism that we see today seems to be so stubbornly and disappointingly similar to the racism we encountered and thought we defeated years ago, I hope that we will reexamine *Brown* not only as a beginning of our democracy, but also as a crossroads, as a moment when we failed to take the necessary step of confronting the full measure of segregation's corrosive effect on our society, and when we allowed fear to overcome hope and possibility and the danger of doing that once again.

My work and our work at the Legal Defense Fund is focused on completing the unfinished work of *Hurd* and *Shelley* and *Brown*, and on using that broader lens I talked about to demand investments and infrastructure and supports that accompany our legal wins, to win cases, but also to follow the money and to take care that we attend to the narrative that we shape in our cases, and that gets reshaped or ignored by judges and scholars and the media.

I think often about the dignity and heroism of John and Evelyn Rice and their three children, who are some of the most extraordinary people I've ever met. Their dignity was challenged by fear, the fear of what integration would mean, the fear of true equality, the fear of a true democracy. But having met that courageous family and having heard them and talked with them, I still believe they won. I also believe that their courage, and the courage of the Briggs family and countless others who sacrificed for us by participating in these cases and taking these brave actions standing against fear, requires us to be brave enough to return to that which we know and knew—and, this time, to win.

21

The Society We Want

MICHELLE ALEXANDER

2016

Michelle Alexander is a visiting professor at Union Theological Seminary and an opinion columnist for the New York Times. *She is a former Ford Foundation Senior Fellow, a Soros Justice Fellow, and the recipient of a Heinz Award in Public Policy. She has clerked for Supreme Court Justice Harry Blackmun, and has run the ACLU of Northern California's Racial Justice Project. Professor Alexander is the author of* The New Jim Crow: Mass Incarceration in the Age of Colorblindness, *which was awarded an NAACP Image Award and named one of the Most Influential Books of the Last 20 Years by the* Chronicle of Higher Education. *For her Derrick Bell lecture, Professor Alexander was in conversation with Anthony Thompson of NYU School of Law. This chapter is an edited version of her remarks.*

The success of *The New Jim Crow* was a surprise to me and I think everyone around me. When I decided to write the book, I was teaching at Stanford Law School as a clinical professor and directing the civil rights clinics. I was fresh out of my work directing the racial justice project of the ACLU, where I represented victims of profiling and police brutality. I had recently been shaken into an awakening that our criminal justice system wasn't just another system infected with racial bias in our society, but was in fact operating as a thinly disguised form of racial and social control, eerily reminiscent of eras we left behind not so long ago.

Shortly after I arrived on the faculty at Stanford, I announced to a former mentor that I was planning to write a book arguing that our criminal justice system functioned much more like a racial caste system than a system of crime prevention or control. She said, "Are you crazy? You can't write that. Can't you write a case study about one of the cases you were working on at the ACLU? Can't you be reasonable just for a few years? If you switch tracks, you could get tenure, and then you can say any kind of crazy thing you want."

I have to say that there was a part of me that really, deeply wanted to succeed in that kind of traditional path. Stanford had never tenured a Black woman as law faculty. I felt it was important to have people on the law faculty who were committed to racial and social justice and who would carry on the scholarship and traditions of Derrick Bell and brilliant people like Kim Taylor-Thompson, Chuck Lawrence, Jerry Lopez, and Mari Matsuda—all of whom taught at Stanford Law School when I was a student. I had been taught by some of the most extraordinary people, and I wanted to be able to provide a similar kind of inspiration to students that they had for me, and so I was really torn. I think in part because of Derrick Bell's courageous example, walking away from Harvard Law School in protest of their refusal to hire an African American woman, I had to stop myself and ask, What's really more important?

"Making it" myself, or did I really feel called to speak a truth that needed to be spoken? And if I can't speak it here with the support of my colleagues, then maybe it's time to go. Nearly everyone I spoke to said that this was a terrible idea, a disaster, that I would be ruining my career.

When I decided to go to Ohio State, people said, "You're going to a lesser school. Where is it on the rankings compared to Stanford Law School?" I am so grateful to have had the kind of example that Derrick Bell offered of walking away from privilege, walking away from elite institutions, in order to do the kind of work that you truly believe is necessary and to stand for your principles.

I know Derrick Bell was criticized by many for his decision to resign from Harvard. Some said that it smacked more of chauvinism than chivalry. I understood why they offered that criticism. But for me, when I was a law student, what stood out was that he was willing to sacrifice privilege in order to stand for justice. And even though he might be wrong or make mistakes in that process, he was going to have the courage to stand up for his convictions. So I left Stanford Law School in order to write the book. Like many people, I didn't necessarily expect it to be successful.

In fact, in many ways it was published at the worst possible moment, because Barack Obama had just been elected our nation's first Black president, and our nation was awash in post-racialism. People were looking at me saying, "How can you say our nation has something like a caste system? We just elected Barack Obama." So I spent the first two years after the book was published speaking to half-empty church basements, to anyone who would listen. It took two years of screaming in the dark before the message began to resonate. So I can say yes, I'm surprised, but it's also what I hoped for.

I hoped and prayed that if people had access to the information and the stories and the history and the data, they might have their own awakening too. The book might help plant seeds right alongside all of the other seeds that have been planted by so many other civil rights lawyers, activists, and academics. I hoped that it might help inspire an awakening regarding the magnitude of the harm suffered in communities of color due to mass incarceration and the links to our racial history and our racial present.

In many respects, the success of *The New Jim Crow* is a vindication of Derrick Bell's interest convergence theory. Derrick Bell wrote, in one of the most influential law review articles for me, personally, that progress for African Americans cannot be explained by white morality, by appeals to justice, or by any other factor more than white self-interest, particularly economic interest.

Throughout our history, many of the greatest racial gains have been achieved for reasons that are best explained by whites' perceived interests as opposed to any other stated or imagined reasons. Although it seemed when my book was first published that it was coming out at the worst possible moment, in many respects it came out at the best possible moment, because our nation was dealing with the fallout of the housing market collapse.

State budgets across America were shrinking rapidly. States including California and Ohio were threatened with bankruptcy. Suddenly, across the nation, you had these former get-tough true believers like Newt Gingrich who were saying, "We can't possibly maintain this vast prison state we've created without raising taxes on the predominantly white middle class. Maybe it's time for us to reevaluate the system of mass incarceration we've constructed. Maybe it's time for a little bit of downsizing. Maybe it's time for us to shift course because we cannot afford to maintain this massive prison system." In recent years we've also seen an explosion of white drug addiction with the meth epidemic and heroin epidemic impacting white communities in ways very similar to the crack epidemic when it swept through Black communities. Now white folks are facing drug addiction and drug abuse; they're dealing with the prospect of their loved ones facing harsh mandatory minimum sentences and not getting the treatment and help they deserve.

Suddenly we hear politicians saying, "Now it's time for us to show greater care, compassion, and concern for those who are suffering from drug addiction. It doesn't help to simply lock people up and throw away the key." So in retrospect, I think we see that when this book came out it was not a moment when people across the political spectrum were having an awakening to the humanity of Black people. I don't think the recent turn in the national consciousness can be explained by a growing concern about the Black lives that have been shattered by mass incarceration. Instead, I think this sudden interest in criminal justice reform and the openness even among many conservatives to the message of my book was best explained by Derrick Bell's interest convergence theory.

When I graduated from law school and started out as a baby civil rights lawyer, I interpreted Derrick Bell's interest convergence theory rather narrowly to mean that we civil rights lawyers have to take advantage of these political opportunities and moments when they arise and squeeze what good we can out of them, and just keep doing that over and over. As Derrick Bell argued, actually achieving major transformational change is unlikely in our lifetimes. I was so idealistic as a law student and as a young lawyer that I didn't fully accept Derrick Bell's premise that racism is permanent. I bought into the idea that we should just keep looking for the short-term political opportunities.

When I was at the ACLU, I spent much of my time trying to squeeze as much as I could out of every political opportunity: lobbying legislators for relatively minor reforms, seeking data collection for law enforcement so that they would track the race and ethnicity of people who are stopped and searched by the police, filing lawsuits, arguing simply for data collection so that we could disprove law enforcement claims that racial profiling was just a figment of Black people's collective imagination. I spent many, many hours and lots of sleepless nights tinkering away at the machine, imagining that I was fulfilling the mandate of the interest convergence theory.

My views have changed a lot since then. After years of representing victims of racial profiling and police brutality and investigating patterns of drug law enforcement and attempting to assist people who have been released from prison, who were seeing one closed door after another—unable to find work, barred from public housing, denied access even to food stamps, saddled with hundreds or thousands of dollars of fees, fines, court costs, accumulated back child support—I came to see that what we were facing wasn't just a criminal justice reform problem, but the emergence of a new system of racial and social control. It became painfully obvious that none of this piecemeal reform work held any hope of dismantling the system of mass incarceration as a whole or birthing anything like a just criminal justice system.

As civil rights lawyers and advocates, we could spend the rest of our lives begging and pleading with politicians for a data collection law to be passed or signed or, "Won't you please, law enforcement, institute a slightly better use of force policy than the one you currently have?" We could spend the rest of our lives tinkering and tinkering, and generations would continue to be lost to this system.

When I think about the interest convergence theory now, I think it still has tremendous explanatory power. But I don't think our job as civil rights lawyers is simply to take advantage of political moments. Instead, I think our job is to help build movements that change the calculus regarding what is and is not in the interests of whites. So, for example, if you take a look at apartheid and why it finally crumbled, it wasn't because white folks one day woke up and said, "It's just not in our interest anymore to maintain this system of segregation and apartheid." No, it was because a movement was built to end apartheid, a divestment movement that changed the calculus of what was actually in the interests of whites in that nation. And it was a divestment movement that shifted global public opinion and turned South Africa into a pariah state that suddenly made it in the interests of whites in South Africa to say, "We have to end the system of apartheid if we're going to remain economically viable and maintain standing in the global community."

If I have any critique at all of the interest convergence theory, I would say that it sometimes does not give, in my opinion, as much credit as is due to the ability of advocates and activists and ordinary people to create the conditions in which change becomes necessary and unavoidable. And that is what I think we saw in the movement to end apartheid, and what we saw in the Civil Rights Movement. I believe we have within our power the capacity to build a truly transformational, even revolutionary movement that helps to change the culture of this country and create—proactively create—the kind of crisis that changes the calculus for those in power about what truly is in their interests.

Derrick Bell's article "Serving Two Masters" very boldly critiqued the civil rights establishment at the time, including the NAACP Legal Defense

Fund for its handling of school desegregation cases. It argued that civil rights lawyers were often so blindly committed to an integrationist agenda that they ignored or minimized the views of Black parents, who were far more interested in achieving quality education in their own neighborhood schools than having their kids bussed across town to schools that didn't want them, and where it wasn't at all clear that they were going to be receiving superior education. The courage that it took for Derrick Bell to write that piece at that time has to be noted. He was challenging his own friends and colleagues to think much more carefully about whether or not they were truly serving the interests of the communities they claimed to represent. He asked whether they were overly influenced by a commitment to an ideology that was supported and funded by white foundations and by people who didn't necessarily share the interests of poor communities of color, who wanted nothing more than for their kids to have a good education, and for their own communities and neighborhoods to be strong and to thrive.

That article primed me to be able to see my own complicity in the system of mass incarceration as a civil rights lawyer. When I was working at the ACLU and representing victims of racial profiling, it seemed like common sense to represent only the innocent, to identify those individuals who defied the worst racial stereotypes of African Americans and use them as named plaintiffs in the suits we were planning to file. This was a way of communicating to the white public that the police practice of stopping and frisking and searching Black folks disproportionately was motivated by race. It had nothing to do with criminality; it was about race.

When people called the hotline we'd set up to report racial profiling or discrimination by the police, we would send a form to them to fill out asking them a bunch of questions about their experiences with the police. And one of the questions was "Have you ever been convicted of a felony?" We literally asked people to check the box. People would turn in these forms, and those who checked the box, we would set aside, saying, "Well, they can't possibly serve as named plaintiffs in any suit we are planning to file against the California Highway Patrol or the Oakland Police

Department or the San Jose Police Department or any of the police de-partments." We knew that if we represented those people, law enforcement and the media would be all over us saying, "The police are supposed to keep their eye on them. They're the felons. They're the criminals. This isn't about race. This is about the police going after the bad guys."

So we deliberately excluded the very people who were most impacted by mass incarceration from the litigation. We denied them a voice at our press conferences. Instead, when we held a press conference about racial profil-ing, we would ask the schoolteacher who was stopped and frisked and made to lie spread-eagle on the pavement to speak.

We asked the military veteran who returned home and had his car searched and torn apart while his children were sitting in the back seat watching as the drug-sniffing dogs circled and barked. We asked a partner at a law firm who was stopped and pulled over, interrogated in his own driveway. We held these individuals out, the respectable ones, as the ones that America should care about. We argued in our litigation and publicly that the proof that this system is biased is the way these good people, these respectable people, have been treated.

I have shared a story many times about how I refused to represent a young man who told me he was innocent but had a felony record. And then I later came to learn that he had been telling the truth, and that he had drugs planted on him, and he had been beaten up by the Oakland Police Department. I hadn't listened to him and I hadn't believed him in part because he had been convicted of a felony.

When I came to see my own complicity and how, as a civil rights lawyer and advocate, I was in fact replicating the very forms of discrimination and marginalization and exclusion that I was supposedly fighting against, I could finally see how the civil rights community has time and time again found itself—not for reasons of any malice, but for reasons that are com-plicated and that need to be addressed—on the wrong side of some of the most important racial justice issues of our time. The awareness that those of us who think we're on the right side—the civil rights lawyers, the activ-ists who think that we're out there fighting the good fight—could well be part of the problem led me to write *The New Jim Crow*. Derrick Bell's example of writing scholarship that challenged his friends and his allies, saying we may be part of the problem rather than the solution, was a model for me and made it possible for me to write a book saying that the civil rights community has been quiet for too long.

We have allowed this human rights nightmare to occur on our watch. We have allowed ourselves to silence the very people who have been most harmed by the system. We are so committed to challenging this narrative that Black people are the criminals that we dismissed people most affected by the system as the wrong ones. In fact, this is the time when we have to be willing as civil rights advocates and activists to stand with those labeled criminals to tell their stories, to be willing to represent them and to challenge the routine criminalization of African Americans. We cannot protest only when one of the respectables is treated the wrong way.

When I started out as a young lawyer, I ignored Derrick Bell's message about the permanence of racism. I pushed it to the side; I didn't know if I could dedicate my life to working for racial justice if I didn't believe we might one day win. So I pushed that aside and thought, the road may be long but we'll get there one day, and it's up to me to do my part today.

I've seen enough now and learned enough to understand that the challenges we face are of a magnitude that I did not appreciate back then. I think Derrick Bell was absolutely right when he said that racism is just part of the DNA of this country. The United States was founded with a compromise over slavery embedded in the Constitution: Black people were defined as three-fifths of a human being. We have yet to come to terms with that racial history and it seems unlikely that our nation will ever do what is necessary to uproot the racism that is embedded in our political and economic systems and attempt to remedy it.

Where I may part ways with Derrick Bell is that I believe that revolutionary change is possible, because no empire lasts forever. If we acknowledge the basic fact that America is not going to exist in its current form forever, then the question becomes, What is going to replace it?

Our task as racial justice advocates is not to believe that our current political system or our current Constitution is the only America that can exist—certainly not our two-party system financed by corporate America, certainly not a Constitution that has a Thirteenth Amendment that provides an exception for "criminals," certainly not a Constitution that does not provide for basic human rights.

I believe that we as a people can bring into being a new nation, a new society. So the question is: What are we creating? What are we building? What kind of consciousness shifting must take place so that when that moment comes, when America as we know it no longer exists, we will be ready to build something new?

I understood Ta-Nehisi Coates, right alongside Derrick Bell, to have a racial realism about the limits of justice in America, given our racial history and our current political system and Constitution. I read with some despair the ending of *Between the World and Me*, where Coates says to his son that we must struggle, but don't imagine that the dreamers will ever fully wake up. The planet is heating up, and we're all likely to go down together in this great big ball of fire.

Coates may be right, but it's not inevitable. We have seen miracles happen in our own lifetimes: people whose lives have turned around in miraculous ways; people who have overcome just extraordinary odds; people who have overcome drug addiction; people who have gotten out of prison and dedicated their lives to ensuring that no one would ever have to go through what they've gone through; people who all over this country are standing up, speaking out, declaring that yes, Black lives matter, and we are still willing to build a revolutionary movement today.

I am not willing to concede that when this empire ends—and it will—we are not capable of building something more beautiful: a multiracial, multiethnic democracy in which every life and every voice truly matters, no matter who you are, where you come from, or what you may have done. I don't think this is utopian. I don't imagine that whatever comes after this empire will be a utopia, but I think we can create something radically better than what we have, something that defies our imagination even today.

It's with that hope and that certainty that America as we know it will not last forever that I am willing and able to continue working and organizing and speaking and imagining that all of our labors are not in vain.

I would encourage young people and activists today to be bold and act with courage. I think one of the truths about why we've had some difficulty in recent years making the kind of progress that many of us would like to see is that many of those who are running the show in civil rights policy reform organizations, or folks who have gone to good law schools, are people who follow the rules. I was admitted to law school not because I'd gotten bad grades or challenged authority, but because I was good at doing what was expected of me: following the rules and meeting the expectations of people in power.

But what it takes to be a good law student isn't necessarily what it takes to be a good revolutionary. So I think that's important to keep in mind. When you go out into the world and find yourself sometimes at odds with your colleagues, sometimes at odds with the organizations in which you may work, when you find yourself very lonely speaking a truth that others aren't necessarily ready to hear, you need to be willing to make mistakes and not play it safe all the time. Those are the traits that I think are required in addition to having a lot more compassion. Try to imagine that perhaps, despite all of the fabulous education and training you've received, maybe you have a lot to learn from people who haven't had the kinds of opportunities that you've had.

One of the greatest educations I received was when I was out of law school, working as a civil rights lawyer, and I finally figured out that I needed to slow down, stop and listen to the people who I claimed to represent. And it's not enough to listen. We also have to create space for those people—who know this system from the inside out, and who have dedicated themselves to ending the system of mass incarceration and bringing their knowledge, their expertise, their perspective, their understandings to bear in this time—to take leadership in this work and this movement. Let those people be your teachers, and recognize that after law school there is still much to learn from them as you work in common cause.

For my own next move, I've actually decided to walk away from the legal academy entirely. I recently accepted a visiting professor position at Union Theological Seminary. This is an odd move for me because I was not raised in a church. In fact, I was raised in a household that was deeply skeptical of organized religion. My mother is white, my father was Black, and they had difficulty finding a pastor who would marry them, in the early 1960s in Chicago. And so I was raised with an understanding that you don't necessarily find God in church, that churches are often on the wrong side of love and the wrong side of important social justice questions. We were raised with a deep sense of spirituality, but with a real skepticism about churches and organized religion. Yet I now find myself walking over to a seminary to study and teach in part because of my deep belief that the kind of truly transformational, revolutionary change that I hope to see and that I do believe is possible isn't a matter simply of changing laws or policy.

This kind of transformational, revolutionary change, at its core, raises profound moral and spiritual questions about who we are individually and collectively, what we owe one another, and what it means to be in relationship with one another. I don't think those kinds of deep, moral, spiritual, and philosophical questions generally get asked and answered in law schools.

Union Theological Seminary has a long history and tradition of asking precisely those questions. I'm looking forward to embarking on a new journey of learning about what many, many faith traditions and philosophers and cultures have to teach us about the meaning of justice and what kind of post-revolutionary society we ought to be working for.

22

A Tale of Two Americas

THEODORE M. SHAW

2017

Theodore M. Shaw is the Julius L. Chambers Distinguished Professor of Law and Director of the Center for Civil Rights at the University of North Carolina School of Law at Chapel Hill. Professor Shaw teaches Civil Procedure and Advanced Constitutional Law/Fourteenth Amendment. Professor Shaw formerly taught at Columbia University Law School, and was "of counsel" to the law firm of Norton Rose Fulbright, where his practice involved civil litigation and representation of institutional clients on matters concerning diversity and civil rights. Previously he was president and director-counsel of the NAACP Legal Defense and Educational Fund, Inc., for which he worked in various capacities over the span of twenty-six years. He obtained his BA from Wesleyan University and his JD from Columbia University School of Law, and he is the recipient of the Wein Prize for Social Justice and the Baldwin Medal, the highest honor given by Wesleyan University alumni for extraordinary service in the public interest. He has litigated education, employment, voting rights, housing, police misconduct, capital punishment, and other civil rights cases in trial and appellate courts, and in the United States Supreme Court.

Since Derrick Bell's passing six years ago in 2011, many of us have found ourselves in a time that challenges our souls. It is a time, increasingly, of madness. I've thought many times about the opening lines of Charles Dickens's *A Tale of Two Cities*, as I'm sure many of you have. If we can reimagine his opening lines for a moment, I think that it's appropriate to apply them to the present: It is the best of times, it is the worst of times. It is the information age, it is the age of fake news. It is the epoch of scientific knowledge, it is the epoch of scientific denial. It is the season of light, it is the season of darkness. It is the spring of hope, it is the winter of despair. We have everything before us, we have nothing before us. We are all going directly to Heaven; we are all going directly the other way.

We are in a post-racial America. We are in an America that is as infected and driven by racism as it has ever been. In short, the period is so unlike any other in our nation's history that many of us are unsure about the survival of American democracy as we know it. We have twice elected an eloquent and constitutionally steeped president of the United States whose signature achievement was comprehensive reform of our health care system. We have had an African American president who was respected as a leader throughout the world, who exemplified dignity and grace, who was a role model for tens of millions of African Americans and all American children, whose administration was remarkably scandal-free.

We presently have an administration that is bent on dismantling the Affordable Care Act, that has eroded our international standing, that is lead by a boorish bully who has stoked domestic division and cultivated a culture of nepotism and corruption.

These reflections are neither polemical nor partisan. Yet, a contemporary discourse about America on the cusp of the third decade of the twenty-first century is, by necessity, framed by partisan politics that are infused by race, if only because the Republican Party has embraced the politics of race. Even still, the relationship of the Democrats with black Americans is not without its own tensions.

Having said that, we have a mentally and emotionally unstable narcissistic president who has defended and harbored white supremacists, has unapologetically spewed racism and misogyny, who is insulting and crude, who openly disdains the rule of law, whose administration is oblivious to the ways that government and ethics operate, who forces us to explain things to our children that they shouldn't have to hear, especially from the president of the United States, who embarrasses us on the world stage, and who is unabashedly ignorant and uncaring about how our constitutional design was intended to work.

If Dickens were to return and write a tale about our country in the early twenty-first century, it might be entitled A *Tale of Two Americas*. One is the old America, which, for 232 years, elected an unbroken chain of white men to be president. The *new* America is reflected in the election in 2008 of our forty-fourth president, Barack Obama, to the first of his two terms. We appeared to be in an era in which it was finally true that any child in America could grow up to be president. Yet the current occupant of the White House owes his position in no small part to the fact that President Obama is an African American, and to the immense tidal wave of extraordinary opposition to the very legitimacy of his presidency and the idea that an African American could become president.

To be sure, not all of the opposition to Barack Obama's presidency was rooted in race. Bipartisanship and ideological opposition is a defining and largely healthy fact of life for every presidential administration. Bitter partisanship has marked politics throughout American history. Those who believe the United States is more divided today than ever before simply don't know history.

In the early days of our country, a sitting vice president of the United States shot and killed a former secretary of the treasury in a duel. All we have to do is think about, of course, the Civil War, which apparently is not yet over. Many Americans, I among them, believe that the United States may be facing an existential crisis. Some say that that's too pessimistic, too dark. I want to share with you something that I wrote on January 31, 2016:

In my early 20s, I read William Shirer's *The Rise and Fall of the Third Reich*. It is a massive documentation of how Hitler came to power in the Nazi era and how that era came to its end. Hitler fed on Germany's humiliation in the aftermath of the Treaty of Versailles and promised to make the German people strong and their nation great again.

He demonized and scapegoated minority groups, Jews, Roma (that is, gypsies), Africans, the disabled, gays and lesbians, and others, and rode a wave of alternate narratives and populism to power. In his early years, the National Socialist Party was not perceived to be a significant threat. They were a fringe group of extremists whose leader, Adolf Hitler, was a carnival barker, supported by a group of thugs. After all, Germany was a "civilized" nation, that, while on the losing side of World War I, had added a great deal to European culture. One of the most profound moral questions of the 20th century was how the Nazis came to power, and how one of the greatest European nations in modern times engaged in genocide and mass murder on an almost unprecedented scale. To be sure, genocide and mass murder in the name of nationalism, religion, and ethnic and racial superiority remain a hallmark of the human condition.

As Americans, however, we like to think of ourselves as immune from these threats. After all, we were on the "right side" of World War II, a "just war," and indeed it was true, as far as any war can be just. In any event, it was a necessary war. Now we find ourselves in another century in an even more technologically advanced civilization. The United States has seen the election of its first African-American president twice. The demographics of our country have changed so that its historical majority is being numerically overtaken.

Some take these changes in stride and even celebrate them as evidence of the strength of America's diversity. Some are deeply unsettled, some even unhinged. We are in uncharted territory. There are many who cry out to "take our country back" and who are ready to follow one who claims to be able to restore what they are told is America's lost greatness and strength. An American carnival barker has risen to be the front runner of one of our two major parties, which in recent years has increasingly become a party of intolerance, harboring racist ultra-nationalists and others who claim legitimacy at the expense of those from whom they differ.

At first, many did not take seriously the idea that Donald Trump was a political threat to win the Republican nomination for the presidency. His presence in the race was a crude form of political entertainment. Regardless of political differences, we told ourselves the Republican Party would assert itself and end this political circus and the unthinkable possibility of the Trump presidency.

Meanwhile, Trump has demonized Mexicans as criminals and rapists, called for building a wall on our southern border, engaged in racist rhetoric and innuendo aimed at our president, advocated banning all Muslims from entering the United States, called for violent treatment of anti-racism protesters at his public rallies, engaged in an ugly mocking and belittling rant against a disabled reporter who disagreed with him, demonstrated an extraordinary hostility to press and media who challenge him (including, incredibly, conservative outlets Fox News and the *National Review*), urged his supporters at yet another of his rallies to take the coats of protestors before physically ejecting them into subfreezing weather, threatened a bellicose foreign policy that masquerades as strength on the world stage, if elected president, and run a profane campaign, wholly devoid of any real substance.

As bad as it might be, it is one thing for a narcissistic egomaniacal public personality to engage in this manner as a private citizen. It's another thing when that individual is seeking to wield the power of the presidency of the United States of America, and it's yet another when that individual is the leading candidate of one of our country's two major parties. For some time now, I have believed that our nation is in real danger. I hope that I'm suffering from paranoia. I hope that I am proven wrong.

The threat we face does not have to be the same as that faced by Germany in the first half of the twentieth century. But as I watch events unfold, I am unsure where we are going and I keep thinking, "This is how it happens."

I wrote that on January 31, 2016. How much more is there to add since then? I can tell you that we are very much under assault daily. Every day there's something new. There's a new Twitter bomb. There's a new assault on individuals. We live in a country now where Nazis aren't only on a television network that looks back at World War II, but they're marching in our streets with Klansmen. Do you recognize America? The country that we live in now? I think that we can't be so sanguine about the fact that our country is being changed in many ways, largely as a reaction to the Obama presidency.

For decades, those of us who do civil rights work, those of us who are conscious of the continuation of racism in this country, have been told that we are paranoid, that we're stuck in the past. We've even been called, at times, race pimps. That we are making a living off of race because, presumably, we couldn't do anything else. We've said for so long that we're not done with the work of civil rights. I entered the Justice Department under the Carter administration and left under the Reagan administration because it was not a tenable place for me any longer. I did school desegregation cases, as Derrick Bell did. When I read Derrick's writings early on, some of them were hard for me to accept and process.

I was committed to doing school desegregation work. I believed that it was righteous work and that *Brown* meant something significant to all Americans. As I've often said, *Brown* was a dividing line, like the one between B.C. and A.D. Before *Brown*, African Americans were subordinated by race for hundreds of years. After *Brown*, at least under law, racial subordination was no longer legal, so *Brown* meant a great deal. It inspired new generations of civil rights lawyers. So when I heard Derrick say in his article "Serving Two Masters" that school desegregation has not worked out that well, challenging some of the assumptions that were sacred in the very places where I worked and where he used to work, I found that difficult.

I wrote something recently in which I acknowledged the fact that the accomplishments of the Civil Rights Movement sometimes, maybe even more often than not, came about in spite of, not because of, the relationships among those who worked for civil rights. There were some folks who were oil and water, and—talk about serving two masters—there were times when I felt no different than Derrick did when he was writing about school desegregation.

I knew different masters then. I chose not to make those my fights more often than not, and I thought Derrick was too cynical. I was much more optimistic. As it turns out, when Derrick talked about how race and racism are continuing facts of American life, that racism had not been eliminated, we didn't know the half of it. Maybe even Derrick did not know how bad it was.

I think it's very clear now that those who've been saying we've been in post-racial America are wrong. I do not know how they can continue to make those arguments, because there is nothing subtle about it. There are no dog whistles. There are sirens. These are difficult times. This is not democracy as we have envisioned it, and the idea that history is an irreversible march toward progress does not seem to be completely accurate.

In 2014, I moved from New York to North Carolina. Julius Chambers had urged me to come to North Carolina to accept an endowed chair in his name at UNC Law School and to run the UNC Center for Civil Rights. In time, I acceded because the "the twenty-first-century battle for North Carolina" is important. While I moved to North Carolina to teach, I have also learned. I had spent many years litigating civil rights cases across the South; it is one thing to parachute in to try a case. It is another to live in a southern state where a radically conservative legislature and Board of Governors holds power. Shortly after my arrival, the UNC Board of Governors launched an assault on the Center for Civil Rights. In September of 2017, the Board voted to strip the Center of its ability to bring cases on behalf of poor black and brown people who experienced discrimination. These cases provided experiential education opportunities for law students who would be the next generation of civil rights lawyers.

The proffered reasons for the Board of Governors action were thinly veiled. Some members of the board were, no doubt, intellectually conservative. Over decades of civil rights lawyering in which one had to prove discrimination, one develops a nose for pretext and discrimination. Many of the primary reasons advanced by Board of Governors members were grounded on antipathy to the civil rights of black people.

And that's what's been happening in North Carolina. The North Carolina legislature and the board of governors have acted in a range of ways that work against the interests of African Americans: a monster voter suppression bill, as it's been called, to strip voting rights from citizens in every way that they could, which the Fourth Circuit said attacked and targeted black voters with "surgical precision." Those are the words of the Fourth Circuit. The court found that the legislature intentionally worked to disempower black voters.

Those of us who litigated voting rights cases sought to create majority black electoral districts in order to desegregate democracy. Critics argued that we were wrong to seek majority-minority districts because they would hurt Democrats. But why should black people have to be the ballast for the Democrat Party? Given the persistence of racially polarized voting, why should black people have to sacrifice the opportunity to elect candidates of their choice especially those who come from their communities, to ensure the election of white Democrats? The problem with race in electoral politics, was not how black people voted. The overwhelming majority of candidates for whom they have voted have been white. The problem has been with how white voters have voted.

Whatever the merits of majority-minority districts, in the early 1980s, many legislatures went to the extreme, packing black voters into majority black districts in greater numbers than were necessary to guarantee the candidates of choice of black voters an opportunity to win, and leaving surrounding electoral districts overwhelmingly white and Republican. Black legislators were members of a racial and political minority groups in overwhelmingly white legislatures controlled by increasingly extreme conservatives.

In, North Carolina, the Republican legislature, dominated by the far right, appointed an overwhelmingly conservative, partisan Board of Governors of the state's higher education system. That is the source of the current regime's hostility to training a new generation of civil rights lawyers.

And the Board of Governors wasn't done with the Center for Civil Rights yet. An anonymous complaint was filed saying that the Center was engaging in the unauthorized practice of law. In spite of the fact that the state bar that processes these complaints certifies students to work in supervised settings which, up until then, had included the Center for Civil Rights, the Unauthorized Practice Committee retroactively determined that the Center had engaged in the unauthorized practice of law.

Some people ask, "Why stay in North Carolina?" My answer is: "Sometimes you run from fires, and sometimes you run toward them." North Carolina, in many respects, is ground zero, but it's also reflective of what's happening around the country. We can't escape racism in North Carolina and find an America that is racism free. We are in a country in which racism is ubiquitous.

Years ago, I gave a ride to a young man from Wales who was going to Ann Arbor from the airport in Detroit. I was asking him about his experience as a graduate student in the United States: "What do you think about our country?" I didn't know what I was going to hear; I wasn't fishing. He could have said, "I love it. It's the greatest place on earth." Instead, he said that what he was struck by is how in America, it seems that race is still the most important thing. He said, "It's like a Civil War that you hold under your breath." I've thought about that over the years. That's exactly what it is, except now it isn't even under our breath anymore. It's out in the open. When driving down the roads of North Carolina, Virginia, and elsewhere, I read historical markers—it used to drive my wife crazy, because I would have her stop the car every time. Now there's an app for the signs and you can read them without stopping. I also visit many of the places that were significant in American history. I've been to Harpers Ferry. I've seen where John Brown led his rebellion—John Brown, who was treated as if he were insane for rebelling against slavery. I've been to Gettysburg. I understand the loss of life at Gettysburg, how painful Gettysburg and the Civil War were, and how many Americans, from the North and the South, lost their lives. I understand that.

Just because you go and visit these places doesn't make you a racist. I've been to Fort Sumter to see where the first shots of the Civil War were fired, because I like history. I'm a student of history. There are some places, I think, that we all have to see if we really want to understand American history. But that doesn't mean that I venerate the statue of Silent Sam, who stands in the middle of the campus at UNC erected by the Daughters of the Confederacy and alumni to honor Confederate soldiers who fought in the Civil War (not the soldiers or the students from UNC who fought in the Union army, although there were many of them, too).

When the statue was dedicated, Julian Carr (Carrboro, North Carolina, next door to Chapel Hill, was named after him) talked about how when he came back from Appomattox, he horsewhipped a "black wench" who had fled to the campus for shelter after she had insulted a white woman in the quiet village of Chapel Hill. That statue stands on the campus in a central place, venerated and protected by recently enacted North Carolina law. Think about what that means. That statue is nothing if it is not a monument to those who fought to preserve slavery and white supremacy. So we're still fighting the Civil War. We were fighting in Charlottesville recently, and we're fighting it around the country and in the White House. I don't know where we're going as a country.

I know that Derrick Bell was a man of great principle, and sometimes I wonder whether I ought to do what Derrick did and resign from UNC. But I'm not Derrick. I don't claim to have what Derrick had. I know that I am fighting these folks and will fight them, with everything that I have. Derrick was, in many ways, conscious of these dilemmas, and he wrote about them in *Ethical Ambition*. The point is that each one of us has to, inside of us, find out what it means to us as individuals and to us collectively at this time to be in America, to see the madness that is occupying the White House right now and our government, and that is denied every day by people in media, by people in political parties, by people who frankly don't care about the issues that many of us care about.

What would Derrick do? I don't know what Derrick would do, but I know that he would tell us, because he's told us this already, to find out what's in each one of us, that little voice that tells you to stand up and speak against the day, as the saying goes. That's what we're called upon, right now, to do, to speak against the day, because this is not normal. It's not a good day. It's not the America that we committed ourselves to.

I know Derrick would, one way or another, be engaged in struggle every day in every way that he could against what's going on, and I urge all of us to do that. It's not just North Carolina, it's the entire country that's infected by a madness now. We can wait for the special prosecutor in hope, but I think that we have to raise our voices. We have to vote. We have to organize. We have to speak against this day and bend the course of history back to a path where it's something that we can be proud of.

23

The Boundaries of Whiteness: From Till to Trayvon

ANGELA ONWUACHI-WILLIG
2018

Angela Onwuachi-Willig is dean of and professor of law at Boston University School of Law. Previously, she served as Chancellor's Professor of Law at the University of California, Berkeley, School of Law, where she taught employment discrimination, evidence, family law, Critical Race Theory, and torts. Dean Onwuachi-Willig is the recipient of awards including the Association of American Law Schools (AALS) Clyde Ferguson Award, the AALS Derrick Bell Award, the Gertrude Rush Award from the Iowa Organization of Women Attorneys and the Iowa Chapter of the National Bar Association, and Law and Society's John Hope Franklin, Jr., Prize. She obtained her BA from Grinnell College and her JD from University of Michigan School of Law. She is the author of According to Our Hearts: Rhinelander v. Rhinelander and the Law of the Multiracial Family.

Today, far too many people argue that racism is a thing of the past. As proof of racism's disappearance, these individuals point to formal equality in the form of laws that prohibit explicit discrimination on the basis of race and that allow for the prosecution of individuals who engage in clearly racially motivated, violent attacks. Additionally, they note that most Americans

today would condemn the use of racial slurs, and most would profess a belief in racial equality.

However, as Derrick Bell so wisely taught us, the fact that racism operates in different ways today than it did in the past—the fact that racism is
more subtle than it was in the past or the fact that much racial discrimination, in some respects, is more likely to stem from non-conscious, rather
than conscious, bias—does not mean racism is not present. It does not
mean that racism is not a current and pressing problem in our society today.

Indeed, I argue that the same race-based forces and the same racist
tropes that worked in the past—a past that we do not and cannot deny was
steeped in the ugliest forms of race hatred—are still operating in contemporary society. I do so by taking what many view as an extraordinary
case about racial hatred from the 1950s, the Emmett Till murder and trial,
and comparing it to the Trayvon Martin killing and trial in 2012 and 2013.
In so doing, I show how the stereotypes that undergirded the Till case
remain quite ordinary today.

At the same time, I highlight a very subtle difference in the operation of
these forces and tropes by showing how the Emmett Till and Trayvon Martin cases reveal a movement from the Jim Crow era of protecting whiteness as property *in and of itself* to a post–civil rights era of protecting what
sociologist Elijah Anderson has called "the white space." In all, I argue that
the Till and Trayvon killings and trials centered on the policing of the
boundaries of whiteness.

Thereafter, I take a step back to very briefly examine another common-
ality between the Till and Trayvon cases: the cultural trauma, meaning
group-based trauma, experienced by African Americans due to the acquittals in these two trials and, more so, what I have identified as the
pattern of actions that repeatedly brings us to this form of cultural trauma
for African Americans. I ask and answer: "What is the cycle, if any, that
creates and re-creates the group-based trauma that African Americans
experience not only after police and quasi-police killings of nonthreatening or unarmed African Americans, but the trauma that arises after official legal responses that have consistently communicated to society that

black lives do not matter? I refer to this pattern or routine as "the new status quo."

Before I delve into my argument, however, I want to provide a refresher on the evil that found its way to Till in 1955. At approximately 2:30 a.m. on August 28, 1955, two white men, J.W. Milam and Roy Bryant, invaded the house of Preacher Moses Wright, an elderly black man who was hosting Emmett Till, his fourteen-year-old nephew from Chicago, Illinois, at his home in Leflore County, Mississippi. After hearing through the rumor mill that Till had allegedly whistled at Roy Bryant's wife, Milam and Bryant abducted the young Till with plans to teach him a good lesson. In fact, their "lesson" would be Till's last, because Milam and Bryant would beat, maim, and torture the young boy so badly that his father's ring, which Till wore during his trip to Mississippi, was the only clearly identifiable item on his person.

In her autobiography *Death of Innocence: The Story of the Hate Crime That Changed America*, Till's mother, Mamie Till-Mobley, described what she saw when she had to identify her only son's body. She wrote:

> When I got to his chin, I saw his tongue resting there. It was huge. I never imagined that a human tongue could be that big. Maybe it was the effect of the water, since he had been in the river for several days, or maybe the heat. But as I gazed at the tongue, I couldn't help but think that it had been choked out his mouth. I forced myself to move on, to keep going one small section at a time, as if taking this gruesome task in small doses could somehow make it less excruciating. . . . [S]tep by step, as methodically as his killers had mutilated my baby, I was putting him back together again, but only to identify the body.
>
> From the chin I moved up to his right cheek. There was an eyeball hanging down, resting on that cheek. It looked like it was still attached by the optic nerve, but it was just suspended there. I don't know how I could keep it together enough to do this, but I do recall looking closely enough to see the color of the eye. It was that light hazel brown everyone always thought was so pretty. Right away, I looked to the other eye. But it wasn't there. It seemed like someone had taken a nut picker

and plucked that one out. . . . Emmett always had the most beautiful teeth. Even as a little baby, his teeth were *very* unusual. . . . So I looked at his teeth, because I knew I could recognize them. Dear God, there were only two now, but they were definitely his. I looked at the bridge of his nose. . . . It had been chopped, maybe with a meat cleaver. It looked as if someone had tenderized his nose.

State officials in Mississippi tried to convince Till's mother to conduct his burial services in Mississippi. She refused, insisting that the state send her son's body to Chicago. Mississippi state officials complied with her demands, but ordered Till-Mobley not to open the casket that Till's body was sealed in. Hundreds of miles away in Chicago, Till-Mobley, whose family's roots were in Mississippi, but who lived in Chicago and gave birth to and raised her son in Chicago, defied their orders and opened up the casket. Horrified by what had been done to her son, Till-Mobley decided that she wanted the world to see what "race hatred" truly looked like. She held a four-day, open-casket memorial service in Chicago. More than 100,000 people chose to attend the service, with another 2,500 people attending the actual funeral. She also allowed the black press both to photograph her son's mutilated face and body and to publish the pictures in the pages of their magazines and newspapers. Images of the disfigured young man ran in *Jet* magazine, the *Chicago Defender*, the *Pittsburgh Courier*, the *New York Amsterdam News*, and the *Crisis*.

With such press, Till's murder garnered a significant amount of attention and outrage from both blacks and whites in the North. This outrage began to grow just about the same time as the unthinkable occurred: the September 5, 1955, indictment of Milam and Bryant, two white men, for the murder of Till, a black boy, by an all-white male jury in Mississippi, mostly consisting of planters.

Although Milam and Bryant admitted to kidnapping the young boy from his uncle's home, on September 23, 1955, an all-white and all-male jury in Tallahatchie County, Mississippi, acquitted the two white men of the murder charge for Till's death. Their decision took only sixty-seven minutes.

One underappreciated dimension of the murder of Emmett Till is that it occurred against the backdrop of the 1954 U.S. Supreme Court decision in *Brown v. Board of Education*. What the Till murder shows us is that *Brown* not only engendered anti-racist solidarity among blacks, it also produced racist cross-class solidarity among whites because of the property value of whiteness.

Emmett Till arrived in Mississippi during the summer of 1955 to visit family members only a year after the Supreme Court had issued its decision in *Brown* and, more importantly, in the middle of a southern revolt and backlash against the decision and the change it signified. Many whites were still reeling from the *Brown* decision, and to many white Mississippians, the northern Till, just by his presence, represented a threat to the social order. J.W. Milam and Roy Bryant were among those whites who were desperately fighting to maintain their way of life in Mississippi. As whites who were subsisting at a level just above white sharecroppers, Milam and Bryant had come to place a high value not only on the material benefits that their whiteness granted them over African Americans, but also on what W.E.B. Du Bois and legal scholars such as Cheryl Harris have defined as the psychological wage of whiteness—the compensation they received in the form of knowing that they would not fall to the bottom of the social hierarchy so long as all blacks remained there.

The best evidence of how the protection of whiteness and its attendant status and privileges served as part of the motivation for Till's murder came directly from Milam's mouth. After Milam and Bryant were acquitted, Milam bragged about murdering Till to journalist William Bradford Huie, who later published an article with the confession in *Look* magazine. Milam began his confession to Huie by expressing his desire to keep blacks in their place such that they would not exercise their right to vote. He proclaimed in part:

> I like niggers—in their place—I know how to work 'em. But I just decided it was time a few people got put on notice. As long as I live and can do anything about it, niggers gonna stay in their place. Nig-

gers ain't gonna vote where I live. If they did, they'd control the
government.

It is significant, but not surprising, that Milam referenced his troubles
with the idea of political participation by blacks in his confession. After
all, concerns about blacks voting in the area had been growing ever since
the *Brown* decisions. Although blacks made up the vast majority of residents in both Leflore and Tallahatchie Counties, whites had been able to
maintain control over both counties by preventing blacks from registering
to vote, including by killing those who dared to register to vote. In fact, no
blacks were eligible to serve on the jury in the murder trial against Milam
and Bryant because service on a jury depended upon eligibility to vote, and
no blacks were registered to vote in Tallahatchie County at all. In his confession, Milam revealed not only his concern with blacks voting in elections, but also his knowledge that blacks, given that they were numerically
the majority in Mississippi and specifically in his county, could control politics if they had the opportunity to actually vote.

The strongest evidence of Milam and Bryant's desire to protect the wages
of whiteness came near the end of Milam's confession, where Milam repeatedly referred to Till's being a northerner and where Milam complained over and over that Till simply refused to capitulate to the understood
racial hierarchy of Mississippi society. Milam ended his confession, declaring that he had no choice but to murder Till in order to make an example of him for northern blacks and any others who might even question the
way of life in Mississippi. Milam said:

What else could I do? . . . Me and my folks fought for this country,
and we got some rights. I stood there in that shed and listened to that
nigger [Till] throw that poison at me [Till's alleged talking back], and
I just made up my mind. *"Chicago boy," I said, "I'm tired of 'em sending
your kind down here to stir up trouble. Goddam you, I'm going to make
an example of you—just so everybody can know how me and my folks
stand."*

In fact, prior to that point in his story, Milam claimed that his and Bryant's original plan was simply to scare Till by taking him "to Rosedale, the Big River bends around under a bluff" that had a hundred-foot drop. In his article, journalist William Bradford Huie noted, "Big Milam's idea was to stand him up there on that bluff, 'whip' him with the .45, and then shine the light on down there toward that water and make him think [they were] gonna knock him in." According to Huie, Milam announced, "'Brother, if that won't scare the *Chicago* ____, hell won't.'" In other words, they purportedly planned only to scare Till until they realized that Till would not accept the idea of their being superior to him simply because they were white.

Even before that, Milam had subtly noted one way in which Till had already broken the unwritten rules of the South, a transgression that ended up depriving Milam and Bryant of one of the few signs of respect based on whiteness that they, as part of the white working poor, received in their daily lives: being addressed as "Sir" or "Mr." by blacks. Raised in the North as opposed to the South, Till was not accustomed to racialized means of communication between whites and blacks in Mississippi, such as referring to all whites, including white children, as Mr., Mrs., Miss, Sir, or Ma'am. As a result, when Milam and Bryant woke Till and his relatives up from their sleep at 2:30 a.m. on August 28, 1955, and shouted orders at them, a groggy Till, unlike his uncle, did not respond with the customary "Yes, sir" or "No, sir." Huie's retelling made it clear that Milam felt insulted by Till's failure to abide by these rules. Huie wrote:

> Big Milam shined the light in Bobo's [Till's] face, said: "You the nigger who did the talking?"
> "Yeah," [Till] replied.
> Milam: *"Don't say, 'Yeah' to me: I'll blow your head off.* Get your clothes on."

Making plain his measure of the psychological wage that whiteness offered him as well as his disdain for anyone who might even think to suggest that any black was as good as a white man, Milam proclaimed, "We were never able to scare him [Till]. They had just filled him so full of that poison that he was hopeless." If Milam's comment about his inability to rid Till of his "poisonous" thoughts were not enough, Milam's confession indicates that it was Till's alleged belief that he was equal to Milam that ultimately made Milam pull the trigger. Huie's tale explained:

> Big Milam ordered [Till] to pick up the fan.
> He staggered under its weight . . . carried it to the river bank. They stood silently . . . just hating one another.
> Milam: "Take off your clothes."
> Slowly, Bobo pulled off his shoes, his socks. He stood up, unbuttoned his shirt, dropped his pants, his shorts.
> He stood there naked.
> It was Sunday morning, a little before 7.
> *Milam: "You still as good as I am?"*
> *Bobo: "Yeah." . . .*
> *That big .45 jumped in Big Milam's hand. The youth turned to catch that big, expanding bullet at his right ear. He dropped.*

Intelligence collected during the FBI's investigation of the Till murder decades later corroborates this notion that Milam was most disturbed by Till's belief that he was equal to him. Years later, Milam would tell an undercover FBI interviewer that "[d]uring the beating Till was never respectful to the men and did not say 'yes sir' or 'no sir,'" and that "things got out of hand," and Till stated something to the effect of "he was as good as they are" before Milam shot him. In sum, Milam's own words serve as the best proof of how his desire to protect the status and privileges— the property—of his whiteness motivated him to kill Till. Like many other white Mississippians, Milam simply was not ready and willing to give up even the arguably meager compensation that whiteness provided him.

Much more was at stake than the protection of whiteness and its attendant privileges for these two men—Milam and Bryant. For white

Mississippians as a whole, whiteness and the social significance that it would have for their own place in the post-*Brown* world was in danger. Against the backdrop of change that the *Brown* decisions threatened to create, Till, or rather the criticism and attacks that came from northerners upon his death, ultimately came to represent a threat to white Mississippians' segregated way of life. To protect segregation and the benefits it yielded them, many white Mississippians, despite their initial reaction to distance themselves from Milam and Bryant, came around to protecting the two known murderers with the resources of a vigorous defense by all five attorneys in town and, ultimately, with their complicity in a "not guilty" verdict.

Further proof that white Mississippians were motivated more by their desire to preserve the property value of whiteness than any desire to protect Milam and Bryant as individuals was the manner in which white Mississippians deserted Milam and Bryant when they were no longer at risk of any further charges. Once white Mississippians were no longer worried that a conviction of Milam and Bryant could function as an indictment against their racially segregated way of life, they left the two men to suffer on their own. As Huie would report just one year later in another *Look* magazine article, entitled "What's Happened to the Emmett Till Killers?," both Milam and Bryant suffered severe personal consequences after their trial, though neither would ever suffer the ultimate consequence of the death penalty or incarceration. According to Huie, a year after the publication of Milam and Bryant's confessions in *Look* magazine in 1956, both men had "suffered disillusionment, ingratitude, resentment, [and] misfortune." First, boycotts by blacks resulted in the actual closing of all three stores that the Milam and Bryant families had operated for years—stores that had very much been "dependent on Negro trade." Upon his store's closing, Bryant "had trouble getting a job" and ultimately went to welding school, an act that Milam claimed would be of no help to Bryant and his family because "by the time you've learned it, you've ruined your eyes." Additionally, Milam, who, prior to the murder, had employed blacks to operate his mechanical cotton-picking machines, could not find any blacks who were willing to work for him after the Till murder and confession, so he was compelled to hire white men, whom he had to pay higher wages. In the end, Huie summed up the thoughts of Milam, who still, a year later, held no remorse for murdering the young Till, as follows:

> So Milam is confused. He understands why the Negroes have turned on him, but he feels that the whites still approve what he did. Why, then, should they be less co-operative than when they were patting him on the back, contributing money to him and calling him a "fine, red-blooded American."

Milam himself proclaimed, "I had a lot of friends a year ago. . . . Everything's gone against me—even the dry weather, which has hurt my cotton. I'm living in a share-crop with no water in it. My wife and kids are having it hard." In essence, once defending Milam and Bryant was no longer tantamount to defending the state's system of segregation, no white Mississippians cared about the fate the two men would suffer.

Like Emmett Till, Trayvon Martin, who had just turned seventeen years old in February 2012, found himself visiting family in a strange new town that same month. Following a ten-day suspension from his high school for having a baggie with marijuana residue on it in his school bag, Martin was brought by his father, Tracy Martin, to Sanford, Florida, four hours away from his mother Sybrina Fulton's home in Miami. The reason for bringing Martin to Sanford was to prevent him from using his time away from school during his suspension unproductively by simply hanging out with friends in Miami. On the night of the fatal shooting, Martin was a guest at the home of his father's girlfriend, Brandy Green, a black woman who was renting a townhome in a neighborhood called the Retreat at Twin Lakes in Sanford, Florida.

At approximately 7:15 p.m. on February 26, 2012, Martin was returning, after a run to the local 7-Eleven for candy and soda, to Green's home in the gated community. Likely due to the rain that night, Martin pulled the hood of his black sweatshirt over his head as he spoke to his friend Rachel Jeantel on the phone. At the same time, George Zimmerman, captain of the gated subdivision's neighborhood watch program, was driving to Target in his SUV. Upon spotting Martin in the rain, Zimmerman made a 911 call to report Martin as a suspicious person.

Despite being instructed by the 911 operator to remain in his vehicle, Zimmerman, who was carrying a gun, failed to follow the operator's directives, continued to follow Martin, and ultimately confronted the teenager. The next thing that Jeantel heard was Martin ask: "Why are you following me?" Then she heard a voice say, "What are you doing around here?" Following that, Jeantel heard what she believed was another person pushing Martin, Martin's phone crashing to the ground, "wet grass sounds," and then Martin saying, "Get off! Get off!" For a short while longer, Jeantel heard arguing in the background, and then the phone line went dead.

Only Martin and Zimmerman know what transpired after that point, but one undisputed fact is that Zimmerman shot and killed Martin, who was an unarmed guest of a resident in that same gated community. Martin had nothing on his person but his cellphone, an Arizona watermelon soda, a bag of Skittles, $40.15 in cash, a cigarette lighter, and some headphones.

Much like Till when he came to visit his relatives in Mississippi in 1955, Martin arrived at Sanford without any real knowledge of the racially tense environment that he was entering. What Martin did not know is that he was walking in a neighborhood where residents, much like white Mississippians in 1955, were fighting to preserve the whiteness of their neighborhood, or rather the meaning accorded to white spaces that their neighborhood had previously claimed. Additionally, Martin had no idea that he would encounter a person like George Zimmerman, who, like Milam and Bryant, may have been working to preserve his precarious status within the neighborhood's racial and class-based hierarchy because of his status as part-Latino and as a renter in a community that was hostile to renters.

As numerous studies have revealed over the years, whites are the most racially segregated group in the United States, and that reality is not by pure mistake or coincidence. On average, whites live in neighborhoods that are 74 percent white. This pattern for whites is distinct from that of racial and ethnic minority groups such as blacks, Latinos, and Asians, with blacks being the most segregated of all racial and ethnic minority groups. Unlike whites, "Blacks, Hispanics, and Asians . . . are willing to live in a neighborhood in which they are a numerical minority." However, for a variety of reasons, including discrimination and whites' preference to live among other whites, blacks live, on average, in neighborhoods that are 51 percent black; Latinos live, on average, in neighborhoods that are 48 percent Latino; and Asians live, on average, in neighborhoods that are 20 percent Asian, with the segregation of Asians increasing rather than decreasing over time.

More importantly, researchers have found that whites are the most segregated racial group in the country because they prefer to have only a few minority neighbors. For example, as the research of sociologists Maria Krysan and Camille Zubrinsky Charles has shown, prejudice is the strongest predictor of resistance to racial integration among whites, while fear of discrimination is the strongest predictor of blacks' avoidance of white neighborhoods. In fact, the work of scholars Richard Wright, Mark Ellis, and Steve Holloway reveals that "diversity is a 'turnoff' within White-dominated spaces for same-race White households." Moreover, another study by two professors in Seattle revealed that racial diversity was one of the strongest factors in terms of negatively predicting the degree to which whites viewed neighbor relations as harmonious. As Andrew Hacker explains in his book *Two Nations: Black, White, Separate, Hostile, Unequal*, many whites view living in neighborhoods with meaningful racial minority populations as being less than or inferior in terms of social standing.

At the time that Zimmerman killed Martin, the Retreat at Twin Lakes was undergoing a transformation. The downturn in the economy resulted in a change in the ratio of owners to renters like Zimmerman, with more and more foreclosures. Along with the foreclosures came a drop in the value of the townhouses in the neighborhood, with the homes that once cost buyers $250,000 falling to prices below $100,000. Additionally, a larger number of the townhomes in the gated subdivision went empty. The neighborhood also became more racially diverse.

By 2011, residents of the neighborhood began to report an increasing number of burglaries to the police. At that point, the tenor and pattern of

911 calls by Zimmerman, who had previously made many calls but without a racial pattern, began to change. All of a sudden, the suspicious individuals who became the subject of Zimmerman's calls had one thing in common: they were all black males. Zimmerman even called once to report the presence of a seven- to nine-year-old black male. Overall, the neighborhood watch residents began their efforts to preserve the whiteness of the Retreat at Twin Lakes, or at least the perception of the neighborhood as a white space. As Olivia Bertalan, a neighbor of George Zimmerman's, would later explain, "People were freaked out. It wasn't just George calling the police. . . . [W]e were calling police at least once a week." She continued:

> There was definitely a sense of fear in the neighborhood after all of this [the burglaries] started happening, and it just kept on happening. It wasn't just a one-time thing. It was every week. . . . Our next-door neighbor actually said if someone came into his yard he would shoot him. If someone came into his house he would shoot him. Everyone felt afraid and scared.

But the fact that only two of the neighborhood's forty-four burglaries, attempted break-ins, and suspected break-ins were confirmed to have involved black males supports the notion that the protection of whiteness—here, the protection of white spaces—and stereotypes of blacks were heavily guiding the actions of neighborhood watch participants like Zimmerman. It was not simply that Zimmerman and other neighborhood watch participants linked blackness with criminality, but that they viewed blacks who were in the spaces that they viewed as white as criminals, as outsiders who were up to no good. Indeed, long after it was shown that Martin, who had no criminal record, was simply walking back to the townhome where he was visiting his father's girlfriend that night, Frank Taaffe, a white resident of the neighborhood, insisted during a television interview that Martin was out of place in the neighborhood and should not have come near Taaffe's home while Taaffe was away from his townhome. Taaffe's interview proceeded as follows:

INTERVIEWER: Frank, what made him look suspicious—what made him look suspicious in your mind, just because he was walking through your yard?

TAAFFE: Because he was out of place. George knew he didn't live there. He was out of place. He was out of place.

INTERVIEWER: He had a right to be there, Frank.

TAAFFE: He's out of place. He's on private property. That's my property.

Although as many as eight burglaries within a year's time may reasonably concern many residents, in this instance, the concern seemed to be racialized in a way that was not corroborated by actual data, but rather by standard implicit biases. As Professor Song Richardson has explained, studies show that just "thinking about crime can trigger nonconscious thoughts about blacks, which in turn activates negative black stereotypes. . . . [And] disturbingly, not only does seeing a black individual bring negative racial stereotypes to mind nonconsciously, but simply thinking about crime triggers implicit thoughts about blacks in police officers and civilians alike."

Additional evidence of the role that the protection of whiteness played in Zimmerman's viewing Martin as suspicious, following him, and then killing the young boy lay in the perceptions and experiences of residents of color at the Retreat at Twin Lakes, who either did not perceive the same problems as Zimmerman and other neighborhood watch participants, or who became the targets of the policing by Zimmerman and other neighborhood watch participants. People like then-twenty-five-year-old Ibrahim Rashada, a black man, had to alter their daily rituals because they no longer felt free to roam about in the Retreat at Twin Lakes community once Zimmerman and the other neighborhood watch residents began their policing with a focus on black males. For example, instead of taking walks in his own neighborhood, Rashada took his regular walks downtown. As Rashada explained, "I fit the stereotype he [Zimmerman] emailed around. . . . 'A black guy did this. A black guy did that.' So I thought, 'Let me sit in the house. I don't want anyone chasing me.'"

In the end, much can be learned from comparing and analyzing the death and trials of Emmett Till and Trayvon Martin. Yes, we must acknowledge the advances that we have made in society since 1955. At the same time, we have to ask ourselves how far we have truly come when past injustices simply seem to emerge in new forms. The killing of Trayvon Martin and other police and quasi-police killings that have occurred in recent years are, in many ways, adapted forms of racism that previously resulted in tragedies like the lynching of Emmett Till. As Derrick Bell explained in his article "Racial Realism," understanding these patterns and adaptations of racism and repeated discrimination is necessary if we are ever to devise strategies for eliminating their effects in society. Bell directly contemplated the effects of repeated discrimination, explaining how we must acknowledge these realities as well as the limits of law if we ever want truly to change society. He wrote:

Unhappily, most black spokespersons and civil rights organizations remain committed to the ideology of racial equality. Acceptance of the Racial Realism concept would enable them to understand and respond to recurring aspects of our subordinate status. *It would free them to think and plan within a context of reality rather than idealism.* The reality is that blacks still suffer a disproportionately higher rate of poverty, joblessness, and insufficient health care than other ethnic populations in the United States. The ideal is that law, through racial equality, can lift them out of this trap. I suggest we abandon this ideal and move on to a fresh, realistic approach. Casting off the burden of equality ideology will lift the sights, providing a bird's-eye view of situations that are distorted by race. From this broadened perspective on events and problems, we can better appreciate and cope with racial subordination.

Taking these wise words from Professor Bell into account, I have begun to delve into a larger project that considers how police and quasi-police killings of unarmed African Americans and, more importantly, the legal outcomes in such cases, can deepen our understanding of what sociologists have defined as "cultural trauma" and the patterns of conduct that bring us to these group-based traumas. Sociologist Jeffrey Alexander of Yale University defines cultural trauma as group trauma that "occurs when members of a collective feel they have been subjected to a horrendous event that leaves indelible marks upon their group consciousness, marking their memories forever and changing their future identity in fundamental and irrevocable ways." As a group, African Americans have experienced cultural trauma not only in relation to killings like those of Emmett Till and Trayvon Martin, but also in relation to the acquittals that were handed down at the end of those trials.

One of the ways in which such killings, followed by repeated acquittals or non-indictments, have traumatized African Americans is that they have left so many of us with an expectation of injustice in our justice system. Consider the response of the family of Tamir Rice, the twelve-year-old African American boy who was shot and killed while playing with a toy gun in Cleveland, Ohio, after Timothy Loehmann—the police officer who shot the twelve-year-old child within two seconds of the officer's arrival on the scene—was not indicted for taking his life.

Sasha Ginzberg, one of the attorneys for the Rice family, responded to the non-indictment by proclaiming: "Tamir's family is saddened and disappointed by this outcome but not surprised." Others, such as Reverend Jawanza Colvin, an African American pastor at a Cleveland church who had pushed for Loehmann's arrest, expressed similar sentiments: "The fact that we are not surprised [by the grand jury's decision] is in and of itself an indictment of the culture of the criminal justice system."

Such responses by the Rice family and other African Americans could be read solely as a pessimistic outlook on the justice system in the United States. I feel they should instead be understood as measured responses to a sociological pattern of events and decisions that have developed in cases involving police and quasi-police killings of unarmed African Americans—a pattern that begins with a tragic killing or horrific beating of a nonthreatening or unarmed African American, that is frequently followed by an acquittal or non-indictment of the officer(s) or quasi-officer(s) who killed the unarmed victim, and that ends in cultural trauma and a sense of hopelessness and disappointment in the American legal system by African Americans.

Understanding these patterns of racism as they have evolved and are evolving over time is critical if we are to devise ways for combatting such structural and attitudinal problems in our society. As Professor Bell explained in his article "Racism Is Here to Stay," in spite of short-term advances in the Civil Rights Movement, black people, all people, must acknowledge how "racial patterns adapt in ways that maintain white dominance." Only then can we be "free to imagine and implement racial strategies that can bring fulfillment and even triumph." As Professor Bell explained, it is this "acknowledgement of racism's permanence, [which] far from an invitation to ultimate despair, [will] serve as [the] opportunity for new insight, more effective planning," and perhaps renewed victory.

24

Race, Violence, and the Word

KENNETH W. MACK

2019

Kenneth W. Mack is the inaugural Lawrence D. Biele Professor of Law and Affiliate Professor of History at Harvard University. He is also the co-faculty leader of the Harvard Law School Program on Law and History. He has taught at Harvard, Stanford, and Georgetown Universities, and the University of Hawaiʻi, and has served as Senior Visiting Scholar, Centre for History and Economics at Cambridge University. He obtained his BS from Drexel University, PhD in History from Princeton University, and his JD from Harvard Law School. Professor Mack's book Representing the Race: The Creation of the Civil Rights Lawyer *was a* Washington Post *Best Book of the Year, a National Book Festival Selection, was awarded honorable mention for the J. Willard Hurst Award by the Law and Society Association, and was a finalist for the Julia Ward Howe Book Award. Professor Mack was appointed by President Barack Obama to the Permanent Committee for the Oliver Wendell Holmes Devise History of the Supreme Court in the United States.*

In August 2014, protests broke out in Ferguson, Missouri, following the shooting death of an African American youth named Michael Brown by Darren Wilson, a local police officer. They quickly spread across the country and through the tendrils of social media, bringing one era of racial politics to a close. The protests, and the Movement for Black Lives that came to prominence in their wake, bookended a period that had lasted almost exactly ten years, beginning with the emergence of Barack Obama as a national figure.

Obama's meteoric ascent to the presidency had its source in his own professed politics of racial empathy—the claim that politics could be organized around the need to see the world through the eyes of others and in particular to see it across the fundamental political divide of race. But the new movement activists described a radically different world than Obama's, one that systematically discounted the values of black lives and in which government at all levels was complicit in racial violence. The movement made its black-oriented racial politics explicit, and birthed a new confrontational style of activism and indeed a new way of talking about race, where conversations about racial inequality must confront the continuing specter of violence.

We now live in a world where we can almost talk about racial violence in shorthand. All one has to do is recite a list of names—Eric Garner, Freddie Gray, Tamir Rice, Laquan McDonald, and of course Michael Brown—that serve as markers for our new language of race. One could recite another list of lesser-known names—Michelle Cusseaux, Tanisha Anderson, Aura Rosser, and Meagan Hockaday—as the legal scholar Kimberlé Crenshaw reminds us, names of women of color, which evoke the public and private violence often perpetuated against racial minorities that seems endemic to our times.

One could invoke Mother Emanuel African Methodist Episcopal Church in Charleston, South Carolina, or the Tree of Life Congregation in Pittsburgh. One could also invoke the names of political leaders and their allies in the media, both in the United States and in other countries, who regularly portray immigrants and refugees as part of an alien invasion and then have their rhetoric parroted by the purveyors of violence. Indeed, violence as the language of race is now so commonplace a theme that we might say there's a new literature, a new set of scholarship that places it at the center of the American narrative. The poet and essayist

Claudia Rankine, for instance, asks whether "The Condition of Black Life Is One of Mourning," citing "the daily strain of knowing that as a black person you can be killed for simply being black," and noting that none of us, at least none of us who can be marked as racial, ethnic, or religious outsiders, is immune from it.

In recent years, a spate of books has emerged with titles like *Mourning in America: Race and the Politics of Loss,* by David McIvor; *They Left Great Marks on Me: African American Testimonies of Racial Violence from Emancipation to World War I,* by Kidada Williams; *Killing African Americans: Police and Vigilante Violence as a Racial Control Mechanism,* by Noel Cazenave; and *New Worlds of Violence: Cultures and Conquests in the Early American Southeast,* by Matthew Jennings. Perhaps future historians will make some sense of it all as the emergence of a new canon of racial violence.

What does all of this have to do with law? The conventional view of the legal system is that it is the antithesis of stories like these. To cite the common interpretation of the work of the great sociologist Max Weber, a core function of law is to grant the state a monopoly on legitimate violence. We vest the state with the ability to coerce and punish precisely so we don't do it to each other; and whatever violence the state does in the process of coercing and punishing us is constituted and constrained by law—in the form of generalizable rules that have reasons as their justification.

With regard to race, our most famous charter of law is the Fourteenth Amendment of the United States Constitution, in particular its Citizenship, Due Process, and Equal Protection clauses, which brought many, although not all, previously excluded racial groups within the bounds of law and disciplined the violence that might be applied to them. On this account, the world of racial violence that has now come into view is contrary to how law should be functioning.

As we will see, in practice the Fourteenth Amendment as a charter protecting against racial violence has an uneven history. It protects far less than we might imagine. But perhaps it's still true that the law *should* be protecting us, particularly outsiders, from both public and private violence, rather than doing the opposite. If that's the case, advocates for racial justice should focus on doing the necessary political, legal, and organizing work to make the legal system take on the task that it should be performing.

But there's a second view of the relationship between law and racial violence that might explain recent developments. And to encapsulate that second view, we can turn to the work of the legal scholar Paul Butler. Butler, in his 2017 book entitled *Chokehold: Policing Black Men*—which itself is part of the post-Ferguson literature on racial violence—focuses on policing and racial violence. Butler argues that the well-known instances of police violence against black men are not the exception or in any way aberrational but in fact are the way the system is supposed to work. "The work of the police is to preserve law and order," Butler argues, "including the racial order." "Throughout the existence of America," from slavery to Jim Crow to the civil rights movement to today, Butler asserts, "there have always been legal ways to keep black people down." In Butler's account, the violence that the law does, or does not fail to prevent, is simply a manifestation of that larger racial order and the social need to define certain groups of people as being at the core of the American project and others as outsiders.

Thus we have two views of the relationship between law and racial violence: one account where law is the means of disciplining racial violence and another where violence is just a tool that the legal system employs to maintain the existing racial order. In our post-Ferguson world, many of those who are working for racial justice are more sympathetic to the second view than the first.

But there is a more complex view of this question, and of the task of reckoning with the long history of racial violence. For that view we might turn to the work of the late legal scholar Robert Cover and his famous essay, "Violence and the Word," originally published in 1986, around the time of its author's untimely death. Cover's text is famous for its evocative and disturbing first line. "Legal interpretation," Cover wrote, "takes place in a field of pain and death." Pain and death—and violence—Cover argued, are not antithetical to how law works, but rather are at its core.

Cover was a law professor at Yale, as well as a person with his own set of experiences with pain and violence. Like a number of white progressive scholars of his generation, Cover had gone South during the civil rights era, and that experience was a turning point in his life. He spent weeks in jail in Georgia while working for the Student Nonviolent Coordinating Committee, where he went on a hunger strike and suffered beatings at the hands of other prisoners. He returned to Georgia during law school to work with the African American civil rights lawyer C.B. King, and on one occasion Cover and his black lawyer associates narrowly escaped serious harm after being pursued by a carload of armed white men.

Cover was also deeply affected by the Vietnam war and by what he viewed as judicial rulings that legitimated a violent and immoral war. Out of that experience, he wrote a book about nineteenth-century anti-slavery judges and their struggles with law and morality. Cover also wrote about outsider traditions in American life—traditions that he derived from Jewish law and the experiences of African Americans and Mormon dissenters. He was critical of the cultural violence with which the law sometimes suppressed those traditions.

So what did Cover mean when he said that the core narrative of law was "pain and death?" Cover focused on criminal law—although he admitted that his idea might apply to other areas of law as well—and argued that when judges interpret law, "somebody loses his freedom, his property, his children, even his life." Of course, we can offer reasons that seem to justify these losses, but our reasons are simply what Cover called "justifications for violence which has already occurred or which is about to occur."

When the legal system is done with its work, as Cover argued, it "frequently leave[s] behind victims whose lives have been torn apart by these organized, social practices of violence." These victims can never fully understand the violence being done to them; they can only feel the fear and pain that is being imposed. In Cover's estimation, what law does to those upon whom it visits its violence is to silence them and inflict upon them a form of suffering and pain that is literally impossible to describe.

On its surface, Cover's account appears to echo our now-familiar critiques of racial violence in the criminal justice system. Cover's tale of losing one's freedom, one's property, one's children or one's life seems recognizable to us, as does his story of ordinary people's lives being torn apart by the pain that the legal system visits upon them. Recent scholarship, for instance, has documented the massive spillover effects of the types of violent encounters with law that Cover invoked in his essay. Mass incarceration, for instance, produces devastation for families as well as entire neighborhoods and communities through both its direct and indirect effects on those who are connected to the imprisoned. According to one study in the *Du Bois Review*, for instance, 44 percent of black women have a family member in prison, as do one quarter of all women in the United States.

While empirical research is now documenting the effects of law's violence, Cover was interested in a somewhat different and in many ways more intractable problem. He described and analyzed the question of law's violent interactions with the lives of ordinary people as a moral question. Cover argued that as long as we have a legal system that declares winners and losers, a system that punishes and delivers pain of some sort, we have a system that is based on violence, as well as the moral problem of how to justify that violence. What law does so often, he argued, is to deflect these moral questions and to turn them into something else, something that makes the system more palatable to the purveyors of law's violence.

From our perspective, decades after Cover wrote this in the mid-1980s, it's apparent that there are silences in his famous narrative of the violence of the American legal order. First and foremost, the victims of that violence are silent. Indeed, for Cover, the horror of law's violence is so acute that those swept up in the legal system simply have no language with which to express their views of it, at least not any language that would be cognizable within the legal order. Indeed, Cover likened these victims of state-sponsored violence to Christian or Jewish martyrs. "Martyrs insist in the face of overwhelming force that if there is to be continuing life, it will not be on the terms of the tyrant's law," Cover insisted. Later he wrote: "the miracle of the suffering of the martyrs is their insistence on the law to which they are committed, even in the face of world-destroying pain." If victims speak, according to Cover's account, it is on terms that the mainstream legal order cannot recognize. The larger society simply cannot hear them.

Despite their silence in Cover's account, the victims of law's violence, its racial violence, even unspeakable violence, have begun to speak and be heard. Take, for instance, Albert Woodfox, whose account of his more than forty years in solitary confinement, much of that time in a six-by-nine-foot cell in Louisiana—longer than any other person in American history—was shortlisted for both a National Book Award and a Pulitzer Prize. During his time in prison, Woodfox's supporters dubbed him and two others who spent decades in isolation there the Angola Three.

In theory, solitary confinement is supposed to be temporary—a limited disciplinary measure, unrelated to one's sentence. But Woodfox had been convicted on allegedly manufactured evidence for a crime he probably did not commit: the 1972 murder of a white corrections officer. Local whites seemed to have had it in for him since that moment. His conviction was overturned more than once, but even decades later, local authorities would simply keep re-indicting him for the murder. At his trials, prosecutors openly relied on his black nationalist political beliefs to secure his convictions. For someone who believed in "Black Pantherism," as the prison warden described Woodfox's worldview, "there is no rehabilitation."

Yet Woodfox was able to speak out after his release from prison in 2016, and on terms that the larger society is willing to hear. After difficult-to-imagine experiences with law's violence, he found his voice, as have many other formerly incarcerated persons in recent years. They have spoken about their experiences and have played a significant role in debates on subjects such as felon disfranchisement.

The second great silence in Cover's narrative concerns race, and that silence is more difficult to explain. Cover's essay was all about what law, often the criminal law, does to those on the receiving end of its force. Although he did not foreground questions of race in his famous essay, he must have been thinking of them. His formative experience with law was the violence that had been visited upon him and on black southerners during the Civil Rights Movement. Part of Cover's project was to get us to see law from the perspective of the disempowered, those who are the losers in legal conflicts.

As the legal scholar Patricia J. Williams reminds us in a well-known essay, when law teachers and professors talk about the disempowered, they are nearly always talking about racial minorities, women, and the poor. But for some reason, Cover didn't emphasize the context that both backgrounded and foregrounded his text: the violence that the legal system, most prominently the criminal law but also other parts of the system, visits upon racial minorities.

Despite its two great silences, Cover's account has something to add to our project of grappling with racial violence and the law. Cover framed the question of violence in the law as an intractable one, inextricable from the nature of what we do when we apply its techniques in a way that causes pain and death. He argued that everyone involved in the justice system is implicated in the system of legal violence, and that much of what the system does is to deflect the moral consequences of this fact—that law *is* violence—and to allow those who participate in the system to get on with their lives without directly confronting the moral consequences of their acts.

Cover's core insight—that law is violence—speaks directly to the specific problem of racial violence and its long history in America. And to explain how this is so, one has to start with the experiences of those who are outside of the legal system, outside the commands of law, violent or not. These are the experiences of the truly disempowered—those whose voices, according to Cover, could not be heard amidst the suffering and death that law imposes. It is tempting to imagine that because of the rampant violence that law imposes, it might be better to envision someplace outside the legal system—perhaps to abolish it—particularly in the interest of racial minorities. There is a radical left version of this argument, and a right libertarian version of this argument. Cover's framing of the problem might have something to say to both versions, and to better illustrate this, it is best to start with a historical example.

Frederick Douglass gave a speech, or at least tried to give one, in Harrisburg, Pennsylvania, in 1847. By that time, Douglass was the most famous black man in America: he had escaped from slavery, penned an autobiography recounting his years in bondage, and affiliated himself with the leading American abolitionist, William Lloyd Garrison. Garrison found slavery so morally repugnant that he argued that abolitionists should refuse to have anything to do with the political and legal system that sanctioned it. Indeed, when Douglass spoke in Harrisburg in 1847, alongside Garrison himself, he was supposed to endorse a Garrisonian concept he called disunion. The idea of disunion meant exactly what it seems to mean. True abolitionists, according to the doctrine, should argue for the dissolution of the American nation itself, for it was better to be without the protections of national law than to affiliate oneself with a legal system that was complicit in the violence and death imposed by slavery.

It was one thing for a white abolitionist like Garrison to take such a position, but it was quite another for a black man such as Douglass to do so, as the two of them found out when they spoke before a hostile crowd at Harrisburg's courthouse. On that day, according to David Blight's award-winning biography of Douglass, Garrison spoke for about an hour without incident. But when Douglass rose to speak, it only took a minute or two for the crowd to start throwing rotten eggs, rocks, and brickbats. A rock just missed Douglass's head. The crowd started screaming, "Throw out the n—." Fearing for their safety, Douglass locked arms with a group of black men in attendance and in a scrum they forced their way through the front door.

But Douglass's ordeal wasn't done. His next speaking engagement was in Pittsburgh, and to get there the black abolitionist traveled by stagecoach over the Allegheny mountains, stopping in small towns along the way for food and shelter. During his trip, white Pennsylvanians often denied Douglass both sustenance and lodging, and he suffered what he called "brutal insults and outrages." We do not know the exact circumstances of Douglass's trip, but in theory the law was at least marginally on his side in his attempts to get service during his journey. There were a series of legal precedents that stretched all the way back to England, which required that common callings—in particular establishments that offered food and lodging to travelers along the road—serve the public. But Douglass was a black man, and the protections of Pennsylvania law were not for him. He was not able to get anything to eat for two days. Once he arrived in Pittsburgh and had been fed by local African Americans, he was once again supposed to endorse the principle of disunion and separation from the racist American legal system.

The arc of Douglass's subsequent story is well known. The black abolitionist would eventually break from Garrisonianism and fully affiliate himself with the American legal and constitutional order. He famously read the American Constitution as an anti-slavery document rather than a pro-slavery instrument. Douglass had been a fugitive slave and subject to violent capture and return to bondage at any moment, at least until his supporters had finally purchased his freedom from his former master's family. He had suffered further disappointments, such as the Fugitive Slave Act of 1850, which made African Americans in the purportedly free states subject to kidnapping and enslavement without even a rudimentary legal process. But despite those brutal facts, for Douglass it seemed preferable to be subject to the American legal system, suffused as it was with racial violence, than to stand on the outside. It had become untenable to conclude that the story of the American legal order was an unbroken tale of racial oppression and domination.

Douglass's friend and sometime rival—the black lawyer John Mercer Langston—traveled a somewhat parallel path, although in Langston's case, his starting point was black nationalism rather than Garrisonianism. Langston lived in a state whose legal system was so racist that he had to pretend he was white in order to vote, and to be admitted to the bar. That state was Ohio. Ohio was one of a number of middle western states that had enacted the notorious Black Laws that, among other things excluded its free black population from the voting booth, jury service, testifying against whites, the state militia, and the public schools. Ohio was a haven for African Americans who had escaped from slavery, as readers of the late Toni Morrison's novel, *Beloved*, know well, and white Ohioans did their best to exclude its black population from the protection of law. In 1836, a mob of whites moved into the black section of Cincinnati, for instance, and burned part of it, forcing many of its residents to flee their homes.

Langston was relatively lucky, in that he was the son of a white Virginia slaveowner and a formerly enslaved woman named Lucy Langston. (He also happened to be the great uncle of the poet Langston Hughes.) By the early 1850s, he grew so discouraged with the prospects of getting any protection under the laws of Ohio that for the first half of the decade he flirted with the idea of leaving the United States for a place like Haiti, where black people could set up their own republic and be governed by their own non-racist laws. But he had an epiphany in 1854, in the middle of his studies for the bar. At a black emigration conference in Cleveland, he declared publicly that America's Constitution and its Declaration of Independence were "for freedom," and he told his black listeners that he intended to "work out my destiny in Lorain County, Ohio." Two weeks later he would be admitted to the bar—although he had to ask the court to admit him as a white man.

Still, even as a practicing lawyer, violence always lurked around the corner for someone like him. When he came to court, Langston never knew whether he would have to back up his words with his fists. On one occasion, he was hauled before a grand jury after getting into a fistfight with his opposing counsel. Fortunately for him, the jury refused to indict him, and Langston eventually rose to the presidency of the National Equal Rights League, the first national African American civil rights organization.

In a speech before the Equal Rights League convention in Syracuse, New York, Langston demanded the protections of law:

[the Negro] demands absolute legal equality . . . the rights to bring a suit . . . to be a witness . . . to make contracts . . . to acquire, hold and transmit property—to be liable to none other than the common and usual punishment . . . trial by a jury of his peers . . . [and] the free and untrammeled use of the ballot.

Both Langston and Douglas would eventually get their wish—not only the abolition of slavery, but a charter of freedom and citizenship, bringing African Americans fully into the ambit of American law in the form of the Fourteenth Amendment. The conventional story of the origins of the amendment traces its history back to the Black Codes, the post-emancipation southern laws that tried to reduce freed slaves to a condition as close to slavery as possible.

But for many Americans, the Fourteenth Amendment was a response to racial violence. Violent acts perpetuated against African Americans were a significant impetus behind the choice of Congress to draft the Amendment, and of Americans to ratify it. A sobering sample of the violent imagery that surrounded the adoption of the Fourteenth Amendment and its aftermath can be gleaned from Henry Louis Gates Jr.'s *Stony the Road: Reconstruction, White Supremacy, and the Rise of Jim Crow*—yet another entry in the post-Ferguson catalog of writing that has framed racial violence as a core theme of American history.

One marker of the Fourteenth Amendment's violent origins was the Memphis Riot of 1866, which began just as Congress began to consider the provision that would become the Amendment's Section 1. The Memphis Riot involved a confrontation between African Americans and police officers, which would be a recurring theme in the subsequent history of the Amendment. Specifically, it began with a confrontation between demobilized black Union troops and local police officers in the context of repeated complaints about police brutality. Mobs of local whites, about a quarter of whom were local police officers and firefighters, enraged at the sight of black troops, proceeded to murder local African Americans. Forty-six local black citizens lost their lives, and the mob burned eighty-nine of their homes.

Two months later there was the New Orleans Massacre of 1866, where a white supremacist mob attacked a political gathering where black residents met in support of a state constitutional convention called to enfranchise black Louisianans. The mob killed more than thirty-four of them. The 1865–66 period had been marked by great violence, out of which the first Ku Klux Klan would emerge, eventually spreading what the historian Eric Foner has called a "reign of terror" into almost every Southern state. This was a violent struggle taking place against the backdrop of local legal institutions that were complicit in that violence or failed to protect African Americans from it. That was the context in which the Fourteenth Amendment was framed and ratified.

Before and after the ratification of the Fourteenth Amendment, African Americans petitioned Congress, the Freedmen's Bureau, and other parts of government, for assistance in being free from racial violence. They desperately and genuinely wanted the protection of law, and believed that being inside the system, imperfect as it was, was preferable to the alternative. One of the first things they did in the postwar South, as shown in Kidada Williams's *They Left Great Marks on Me*, was to create networks that passed their stories of violence on to one another until they could reach some official with the legal power to do something about it.

Starting in 1865, many thousands of African Americans, across the South, made complaints and swore out affidavits to the Freedmen's Bureau and to the U.S. Army, concerning the violence that was being done to them as part and parcel of daily life. In 1871 and 1872, when Congress convened the Joint Select Committee on "the Affairs in the Late Insurrectionary States," African Americans from North Carolina, South Carolina, Alabama, Mississippi, and Florida, lined up to tell the story of Ku Klux Klan murders, school and home burnings, whippings, and other violence. Those petitions and complaints helped write the Fourteenth Amendment and the Civil Rights Act of 1866 into the constitutional order, and also pushed Congress to write several more statutes around 1870. These were the Enforcement Act of 1870, the Ku Klux Klan Act of 1870, and the Ku Klux Klan Act of 1871, each one progressively more sweeping in its attempt to bring the rampant racial violence inside the legal order.

African Americans asked, again and again, to be free of racial violence and petitioned and advocated for some legal response to it. These efforts produced much disappointment and frustration but also garnered some hard-won victories. In our own more pessimistic times, it's sometimes asserted that freedom and citizenship for African Americans was simply the substitution of one form of violent racial control for another. To be sure, postwar black Americans often experienced one heartbreaking disappointment after another. But they had also known firsthand what it meant to be without the protections of law, and they kept petitioning.

Postwar African Americans endured many reversals in their campaign of complaint, petition, and advocacy. They found that the judges and federal officials who interpreted and administered the laws that purported to guaranty their safety were often engaged in a process of apology, deflecting the great moral questions raised by the violence being done against them. Here we should recall that Cover emphasized that legal decisionmakers often deflect the moral questions that surround the violence that law imposes or authorizes, and transform those moral questions into different types of questions—a process that makes the system more palatable to the purveyors of that violence.

From the first moment that the post-emancipation civil rights laws and constitutional amendments began to be debated in Congress, Americans grappled with intertwined questions of law and morality. The civil rights laws and the Fourteenth and Fifteenth Amendments threatened to work a fundamental alteration in the constitutional structure of American government. For the first time, these laws and constitutional provisions potentially brought a number of fundamental citizenship rights under the direct protection of the national government, whereas traditionally state and local governments had retained primary responsibility for protecting the basic rights of citizens. The great legal question of the age involved federalism—how much of the basic structure of citizenship had been federalized. But driving that legal question was the stark moral question of the relationship between law and violence. Enlightenment political thinkers had justified law and government as an alternative to violence. African American petitioning had sought to make the case again and again for protection against violence as a fundamental right of citizens. Protection from assaults, murders, and mayhem was supposed to be one of the principal duties of any legitimate legal system, and that system had abjectly failed in its duty with regard to its new black citizens.

Violence had played a key role in bringing about the post–Civil War civil rights laws and constitutional amendments, and it was widely understood that without substantial federal protection, black citizens, particularly in the states where they had recently gained their freedom, would have little protection from continued racial assaults. The moral and legal questions were intertwined, although the Supreme Court would quickly begin deflecting the great moral question of the age, and would go out of its way to permit that violence to continue.

This was evident by the time the Supreme Court had finished deciding the first major case in which the Court had to confront the question of federal and state responsibility for basic citizenship rights in the aftermath of the Civil War. That case was not the famous *Slaughterhouse* decision—the opinion that constitutional law casebooks traditionally use to begin their discussions of citizenship in the post-emancipation period. Rather, it is an often-overlooked case decided the year before: *Blyew v. United States*. The facts were horrific.

In the spring of 1868, the Ku Klux Klan had gone on a killing spree in Kentucky, murdering former black union soldiers, assassinating a United States Marshal, and driving many black families to escape across the Ohio River. The violence only increased across the Southern states that fall, as white supremacists tried to suppress black voting in the coming elections. In August, two white men, after attending a Democratic Party rally, entered the home of a black family, the Fosters, and hacked most of them to death with an ax. The family's sixteen-year-old son, Richard, survived the attack briefly and was able to get to a neighbor's house, where he signed a written statement before dying. The ten-year-old daughter, Laura, survived by hiding, while the six-year-old daughter, Amelia, was scarred for life. Laura testified at the subsequent trial, and, with the help of Richard's statement, the two men were tried in federal court under the authority of the Civil Rights Act of 1866 and were initially sentenced to death.

One might ask, why weren't they tried in state court? The reason was that this was a case, like the Memphis riot, where state authorities were complicit in the violence or were unwilling or unable to prosecute it. In addition, Kentucky still held on to the pre–Civil War rule that blacks could not testify against whites in court, and the only witness statements were from the surviving children.

Even so, additional questions present themselves. Weren't these two men essentially convicted of murder, which is a state law crime? How could they be tried under the Civil Rights Act of 1866, which modern lawyers know as a statute that protects contract and property rights and allows certain state officials to be sued? It turns out that the statute—which Congress passed in response to racial violence—was a quite complex legal enactment. In addition to protecting common law rights, the Civil Rights Act was also an attempt to protect African Americans from *state violence*, either through neglect or direct participation of state actors in violent acts.

To see how that is so, we have to turn to the text of the Act, which provides:

Sec. 1 . . . "citizens . . . shall have the same right . . . to full and equal benefit of all laws and proceedings *for the security of person and property*, as is enjoyed by white citizens"

Sec. 3 . . . the district courts of the United States . . . shall have . . . cognizance . . . of all causes, civil and criminal, *affecting persons who are denied or cannot enforce . . . any of the rights secured to them by the first section of this act*"

Thus if citizens are denied certain rights under state law, or cannot vindicate those rights in state courts, including those involving the security of
persons or property, federal court jurisdiction can be invoked to vindicate
these rights. Thus, Kentucky federal prosecutors reasoned that the Fosters' killers could be tried in federal court, given that no state prosecution
was possible.

When *Blyew v. United States* came before the Supreme Court, the
stakes of the decision were quite large. By then, a number of African
Americans, like the surviving members of the Foster family, had invoked
federal jurisdiction in order to bring cases of state violence into federal
court. Congress had responded and had passed several more statutes
under its Fourteenth Amendment power—the Enforcement Act, and the
Ku Klux Klan Acts of 1870 and 1871. And federal district attorneys had
begun to bring cases in federal court invoking the new statutes to prosecute state violence, as the legal scholar Robert Kaczorowski has shown.
The more this kind of violence was cognizable in the federal courts, the
more courts were going to have to confront the moral obligation of governments, both state and federal, to protect against it.

The decision in *Blyew* was the Supreme Court's first opportunity to
confront the legal and moral questions presented by the burgeoning racial
violence. The justices quickly made their position clear. A five-to-two majority signaled that new civil rights laws were going to be of limited use in
prosecuting state violence. Specifically, the Court ruled that because the
statutory language contains the phrase "affecting persons," there must be
some "affect[ed] person" who is denied rights that are protected by the
Civil Rights Act, in order to invoke federal jurisdiction. The various members
of the Foster family might seem like prime examples of such "affect[ed]
persons," given that most of them had been murdered and the killers could
not be brought to justice in state courts because of Kentucky's ban on black
testimony against whites.

According to the majority, however, this seemingly straightforward interpretation of the statute's meaning and purpose was incorrect. The majority conceded that the state laws of Kentucky did deny the right to testify

in court to the two black witnesses, ten-year-old Laura and the murdered son Richard, who had managed to sign a statement before his death. But the justices concluded that they weren't "affect[ed] persons" since they were mere witnesses. The case, according to the Court, did not primarily involve them. The case certainly did involve the murdered members of the family who were not witnesses, principally the grandmother, Lucy Armstrong. But, reasoned the justices, they had been murdered and thus could not appear in court, so these family members hadn't been denied any rights under the act, such as the right to testify under state law. Thus, the murdered family members also were not "affect[ed] persons."

This was not the only, or even the most obviously egregious, interpretation of the statutory language, as the legal scholar Robert Goldstein has observed. The dissent's author, Joseph Bradley, pointed out that this reasoning seemed to "put a premium on murder." Bradley objected that the majority "took a view of the law too narrow, too technical and too forgetful of the liberal objects it had in view." Murders, violence, and mayhem—and the inability of black Southerners to protect their basic rights in state courts—had been the impetus for the writing of those statutory words, and Americans of that time were well aware of that context.

The inability of state law to protect the Fosters from being murdered, as the Court framed the issue, merely raised a narrow legal issue of statutory interpretation, in the context of background principles of federalism. But it is also clear the majority was going out of its way to deny access to federal law to victims of the racial violence that had engulfed the Southern states. It was a simple act of interpretation but, as Cover argued so long ago, behind that seemingly technical legal ruling was a decision by legal interpreters to authorize violence, to destroy lives and livelihoods, and to hide the stark moral stakes of what they were doing.

One could tell the story of the end of Reconstruction, the transition to Jim Crow, the beginnings of the Civil Rights Movement, and the history of the Fourteenth Amendment entirely through well-known episodes like these. In so many of these cases and controversies, a similar logic was at work. Again and again, advocates for racial equality ran up against the question of whether the Fourteenth Amendment would provide a backstop to victims of localized state violence—either through active participation of the state or through neglect. It was generally understood that the way the system worked—*indeed the way the system had always worked*—was that without some backstop, such violence would continue without remedy.

Still, African Americans kept asking for a legal remedy, asking for law to protect them against state violence, and out of those claims would emerge the modern Civil Rights Movement. For instance, the National Association for the Advancement of Colored People was founded in response to yet another instance of racial violence—the Springfield Riot of 1908—where reports of assaults by black men on white women caused a mob to ransack the black neighborhoods in the city most identified with Abraham Lincoln. In its early years, the main civil rights priority of the NAACP was not school desegregation but passing an anti-lynching law to federalize cases of violence against African Americans where state actors were complicit in the violence, or declined to protect against it.

A growing network of African Americans pushed the civil rights organization to prioritize lynching and the failure of state law to protect its black citizens from violence. In its early years, the NAACP's core leadership consisted mostly of a group of well-meaning white reformers in New York, alongside a few leading African Americans such as the anti-lynching crusader Ida B. Wells-Barnett and the scholar and activist W.E.B. Du Bois. In the historiography of the NAACP's anti-lynching crusade, the organization's knowledge that an act of racial violence has occurred in some far-off place in Mississippi, or Oklahoma, or Indiana is sometimes taken for granted. But that knowledge was hard-bought. African Americans around the country petitioned the NAACP. They wrote it letters, identifying cases of violence and asking the organization to send someone in to seek some legal recompense. When officials in its national office learned of an incident of racial violence, they relied on this network of correspondents for information in coordinating its response. For instance, in December 1913, after the lynching of Frank and Ernest Williams for their alleged involvement in a murder of a white man in Caddo Parish, Louisiana, provoked inquiries from the national office, a local resident took the time to write back, appraise them of the situation, and ask that "If the Association would spend a few dollars in this vicinity [to collect] evidence sufficient to arrest and convict, it would go far in diminishing these crimes." The organization responded by writing to a loyal member in New Orleans, asking advice about the lynching and its course of action. Indeed, the NAACP's anti-lynching crusade was built out of the patient and persistent efforts of African Americans across the country to set up networks that reported local racial violence and demanded that the organization make some legal response, as the historian Kidada Williams has demonstrated.

Even the organization's most famous achievement, the Supreme Court victory in *Brown v. Board of Education*, was given a crucial push forward by its crusade against racial violence, as federal Judge Richard Gergel has demonstrated in a well-researched book on the 1946 blinding of an army veteran named Isaac Woodard at the hands of a Southern sheriff. Indeed, Judge Gergel is someone who has intimate experience with the persistence of racial violence in recent years. He is the judge who presided over the trial of the white supremacist who massacred nine African Americans at Emanuel AME Church, after which Judge Gergel sentenced the killer to death.

Shortly after his 1946 discharge, Isaac Woodard was beaten senseless and permanently blinded by a South Carolina sheriff for the offense of failing to call a white bus driver "sir." The NAACP used the horrific nature of that incident to convince President Harry Truman to embark on his unprecedented campaign of support for civil rights for African Americans. That famous incident of racial violence was also a defining event in the life of the blueblood Southern federal judge, J. Waties Waring, who presided over the unsuccessful prosecution of the sheriff who had blinded Woodard. Until the mid-1940s, Judge Waring had lived his life among Charleston's white elite, never publicly questioning racial segregation or the violence that accompanied it. But after Woodard's trial he became a changed man. Waring evolved into an outspoken advocate for black equality, issuing a series of pro–civil rights rulings in cases involving peonage, voting rights, and school desegregation, including in the South Carolina case that would become part of the *Brown v. Board of Education* decision. In fact, it was Waring who convinced an initially reluctant Thurgood Marshall to use the South Carolina case to launch an all-out attack on school segregation rather than simply asking for equal resources for segregated schools. It was racial violence and the campaign to discipline it, in part, that produced *Brown v. Board of Education*.

Through much of the long history of struggles for racial justice, legal decisionmakers have often furthered racial violence or at least been complicit in its perpetuation. Yet, there is also a long history of African Americans petitioning to be brought inside the legal system, despite the violence that it perpetuates and allows. There is a long history, as well, of legal decisionmakers reinterpreting that violence, engaging in acts of legal interpretation that deflect the moral questions it raises and converting them into technical questions of law. Judge Waring tried to buck the trend. The Charleston federal judge wrote an opinion in the South Carolina school desegregation case that, unlike the Supreme Court's later opinion in *Brown*, forthrightly called segregation a manifestation of white supremacy. For his candor, he was eventually run out of his native state, spending the rest of his life in exile in New York. His story is hardly one of triumph.

This brings us back to the question with which we began: How should we think about the continued attention to racial violence in recent years, and what should law do about it? How should we act in our everyday lives? One theme that emerges from this history is one of apology and deflection. Again and again, legal decisionmakers and interpreters have failed to acknowledge this history, or the true stakes behind their decisions. It's as if the truth is too horrifying to acknowledge. Years after the shooting in Ferguson, Missouri, that set in motion our current spate of racial reckoning, perhaps we should return to the work of Claudia Rankine, who reminds us of the work that we do every day to ignore the racial violence all around us, the work of political leaders to justify it, and the work that we must do to confront that violence and to bring the moral questions that it raises to the forefront.

Tributes to Derrick Bell from
the Bell Lecturers

Sherrilyn Ifill on the Importance
of the Derrick Bell Lecture

Derrick Bell was an unusual man—an extraordinary lawyer, scholar, and teacher. We all know this, but often, when even extraordinary people leave us, no matter how much we love them or admire them, we lose sight of them. They move slowly to that other shore called memory. They lose their potency and power.

But Derrick Bell is still with us because of his extraordinary spirit, because of the force, truth, imagination, and brilliance of his scholarship, because of the example he set of uncompromising conviction, because he was strong and still gentle, and a great intellect, and a man of faith, because he was serious about justice but wore it lightly, and made us smile. And Derrick lives because of his wife, Janet Bell, who organized this lecture series and works so hard to keep the spirit of Derrick and the example of his leadership alive.

This lecture calls upon those of us who are activist scholars to remain true to the standards set by Derrick, one of uncompromising truth-telling, meticulous research, clear vision. We need to support the intellectual development and scholarship of our study of race. It's a complicated subject. We very often face a Supreme Court that treats race very simplistically. But those of us who engage with this issue know that it takes an understanding of history and psychology and social science and demography and economics and labor patterns, and every discipline you can imagine.

This lecture plays a vital role in that project, not only because it keeps Derrick's memory alive, but because it pays him forward by providing a platform for serious, honest, scholarly engagement on one of the most important, most potent, and most vexing issues in our country since its very beginning.

John Sexton, Former Dean of New York University School of Law and Host of the Inaugural Derrick Bell Lectures

When I arrived at Harvard Law School in 1975, I already had spent almost two decades in teaching, and I thought I was reasonably good at it. Then in my third year of law school, both my wife and I were drawn to Derrick Bell's course, and I encountered one of those spectacular teachers who helped you—wherever it was you came from—you just learned to view things very differently. Derrick, for all of us who've had him as a guide through learning, is a person who would stretch you to see things as you hadn't seen them before. And that certainly is what he's done through his books, where he's created a whole new way of doing legal scholarship. No one ever conceived of the foreword to the Supreme Court issue of the *Harvard Law Review* quite the way Derrick did in the manuscript that I remember he sent me with much delight, knowing that it was provocative not only in its ideas but also in its genre, and giggling all the while about that.

I became the dean of New York University School of Law in 1988, and at that time our faculty identified five people in legal academe that we hoped someday to attract, and that was when Derrick and I began our conversations about his coming to NYU. We talked and lived and counseled each other through the turmoil and struggle that Derrick had with Harvard, and finally, in 1992, my heart leapt when he made the decision to come and join us.

Derrick understands me when I say that institutions, like human beings, are victims of original sin. He's always demanded higher performance from the institutions that he's joined, so we set upon a formula when he came to NYU—by analogy, I hope, to a great manager of the Brooklyn Dodgers, Walter Alston, who you might remember managed the Dodgers for nineteen years on nineteen one-year contracts. Derrick was not hopeful that in NYU he had found an institution that wasn't suffering from original sin, and he announced to his students the first day at the school that he certainly hadn't discovered a dean who was not a victim of original sin. He said I had many, many imperfections known to him, and the institution was seriously flawed. That was the positive part of his talk. But his hope, I believe, and I know mine, is that he won't have to accept responsibility for institutional sins, he'll just be our guest forever, as the Walter Alston of legal education.

For me, it's impossible to think of Derrick and not think of liturgy. There's a way in which Derrick's life was sacramental, in the sense that sacrament is designed to cause the best to shine through, whether one wants to associate that with a theophany or simply with the transparency of the essential goodness of humankind at its best.

Derrick pushed me in 1979, when everybody thought the world was going to end after the *Bakke* decision, to write a piece for the *Harvard Education Review*, saying that, "after Bakke, the world is not over." I also remember how, on New Year's Day of 1980, in an otherwise dark Supreme Court of the United States, as Warren Burger interviewed me, Burger said, "What would your mentor Derrick Bell think of your clerking for me?" And I said, "Mr. Chief Justice, Derrick thinks it's a good thing for people who have different viewpoints to be in discourse with each other. And he might think that I could learn from you, because, you're right, I don't agree with you on most things."

Then, of course, I remember the wonderful memory of Derrick's wedding to Janet; he saw Janet as utter perfection, even as she tormented him by never allowing him to think that he was perfect. One night, Derrick and Janet, and my wife Lisa and I, were sitting in that front corner booth in Valerie, and Derrick and I were in one of our classic arguments about the ways to make the law school better. And Janet looked at him and said,

"Derrick, shut up." I've never seen anyone treat Derrick that way, let alone seen him actually shut up. And she said, "Tell John he's right." And Derrick looked at me and said, "You're right." Then of course there was a beat, and he said, "But you can do better."

And that is the kind of memory we have to have of Derrick Bell, because he will remind us of the goodness that he modeled, and of the goodness that could be us if we behave at our best. But even when we get to that point, he'll be there to say, "You can still do better."

Charles Ogletree

When I received tenure at Harvard Law School, the accolades from public television were one nice thing, and the news articles were another. But what really made me feel that I had arrived as a practitioner and an activist and a scholar happened at a dinner in honor of Judge Robert Carter. I was lamenting the Democratic Party and the failure of integration and affirmation action, and Judge Carter in his old, crusty way said, "Ogletree, you're beginning to sound just like Derrick Bell." And I know he meant it as a criticism, but it was the highest honor I could ever imagine.

Oscar Chase

Derrick Bell's work spans a universe that includes the classic text on race, racism, and American law, which is a great teaching text. It's not too much to say that Derrick has taken legal writing to the realm of poetry, for which all of his readers are very, very grateful. But some people may not know that Derrick is also a marvelous and very valued teacher. Sometimes, we encounter the scenario or the example of the great man or woman who is a great scholar, but who seldom has time for the work of the students who are just coming along. And that is exactly the opposite of our colleague, Professor Bell. I know firsthand, from working with him and talking to students, what a devoted professor he is. And the amount of time that he spends critiquing, teaching individual student work is absolutely an example to all of us.

Charles Lawrence

I don't really have sufficient eloquence to express what Derrick has meant to me. It was Derrick who first told me that I should be a law teacher when I had never thought about that at all; he's been a pathfinder and a barrier breaker for all of us, an advocate and a source of inspiration. But for me and for so many others, he's been so much more, a teacher extraordinaire, a friend, a loving brother.

Patricia J. Williams

I would not be here without Derrick Bell. Derrick does not remember that he actually met me when I was nineteen years old and dating one of his students. Derrick inspired me to go to law school. Derrick inspired my then boyfriend to stay in law school. When I got to law school, Derrick gave me a role model to continue on what, at that time, was a tough road: I entered law school when Harvard had only 8 percent women, all told, with nine of us black women out of a class of five hundred.

Derrick encouraged me to stay in law when I was looking for jobs upon graduation from law school because, frankly, the day I graduated I clicked my heels on the top doorstep and vowed I would never darken the doorstep of any law school again. Derrick kept me in the profession of law, and then Derrick pushed me back into law schools when I had decided I was a little burned out from trial work, and he encouraged me to go into teaching.

Teaching has given me the forum in which to write, and I have been grateful repeatedly to Derrick's good grace. Derrick was also one of the few professors who supported his women law students, and this is remarkable. Derrick treated us as colleagues, not as collector's items. Derrick was an inspiration to an entire generation of women and black women, minorities, who went into law teaching because of his encouragement, because of his respect, because of his inspiration that we had something to contribute.

Emma Coleman Jordan

Derrick Bell is a legend. Some legends are deservedly so, and some are not. Derrick is deservedly a legend because I can't think of a single law professor, and especially an African American law professor today, who has not benefited from his generosity and kindness.

When we think of scholars, we think of people who are in the stacks, in the books, and in their heads. But in addition to being in the stacks, in the books, and in his head, Derrick Bell has been opening his heart to the people coming after him.

I was a brown-skinned Doogie Howser law professor at the beginning of my career. And, you know, when you go to the annual meeting of the AALS, you have your badge on and you're just so proud, you're just walking around and just bouncing around: "I'm a professor!"

I was twenty-seven years old—could have been a student. Derrick had not seen me before, and he came up to me and asked me my name and where I was teaching. And he said, "Come with me." And he led me into one of those sumptuous private receptions for the authors of casebooks. It was an inner sanctum and only the elite people had been invited, but he sneaked me in and there I was.

Later, in 1991, Derrick was in Washington, DC, to give a talk, and he was staying on the third floor of my house, which I run like a civil rights hotel for anybody who comes through and needs a space to stay. I got up in the morning, got the coffee started, and fixed some croissants for him. And he asks me, "Where are you going today?" And I said, "Well, I'm going down to Capitol Hill. Anita Hill needs some support for her testimony in the Clarence Thomas confirmation hearings."

And I said, "Derrick, come along." And Derrick kind of hunched up his shoulders, he said, "I know you got it covered." (Laughing.) So, I said, "That's a statement of faith in me and I'm absolutely delighted to have that." So I went with Derrick's blessing.

And when I was a White House Fellow in the Justice Department, working as a special assistant to William French Smith, the attorney general of the United States, who had been appointed by Ronald Reagan, there was all of this discussion about who was going to be the assistant attorney general for civil rights in the Reagan administration. I preserved every ounce of confidentiality in that office, much to my peptic distress. On one occasion, however, I did call Derrick. And I said, "They are proposing this person. What should I do?" Derrick's response to me—at the time I didn't understand it, but he knew better than I—was, "Well, what's the problem?" I said, "They're going to nominate this terrible person. He has such a horrible background." Derrick said, "Child [laughing], that's a good thing." He said, "Let them pick that person, he'll raise more money for the NAACP than I could."

So, I've learned my lessons from Derrick Bell.

Annette Gordon-Reed

I did not have the privilege of having Derrick as a professor. He came back to Harvard a couple of years after my husband and I were classmates at Harvard Law School. But we knew about him because my husband's sister and brother-in-law were at the law school when Derrick was a professor there. And they talked about him quite a bit—he meant a great deal to them and to the other black students who were at Harvard during that time period. He was legendary the way they discussed him.

When I was an associate at Cahill Gordon and realizing that that's not really what I wanted to do with my life, I was writing short stories and sending them to *The New Yorker* and getting rejection slips, and writing a book about W.E.B. Du Bois that's probably sitting in my closet somewhere right now. And the first time I was actually published was when I did a review of Derrick Bell's *And We Are Not Saved* for *In These Times* (the nice radical newspaper that was the only place that would publish me).

And that gave me an idea: Derrick Bell was a good role model for me. I left the firm and I did a stint in a city agency for a time, and then I became a professor, and I was doing something else I didn't really want to do, which was writing law review articles. And after toiling on one for the longest amount of time, I realized I wanted to do something different. I actually wanted to write the thing that I wanted to write. And I remembered *And We Are Not Saved*—here was a law professor who did something out of the ordinary.

He did writing in a way that you wouldn't typically think that a law professor was supposed to do. So he came back into my life in that way again, as an inspiration for somebody who could do something different. And I'd had in my mind that I wanted to write an op-ed piece about the controversy over whether or not Thomas Jefferson and Sally Hemings had had a long-term liaison. And I started an op-ed piece that got longer and longer and longer, and decided I'll do a book. Certainly Derrick Bell was an example of someone who broke the mold and did things that he thought were important and things that he thought would make a contribution to the world, not in the traditional sort of way that you think law professors are supposed to do them.

William Carter Jr.

I had the opportunity early on in my deanship at the University of Pittsburgh School of Law to meet one of our distinguished alumni who was in Professor Bell's class, Governor Richard Thornburgh—of a very different political persuasion. We got on the subject of Professor Bell, and the first words he said were, "Boy, that was a good man. That was a good man."

And even though they found themselves as law students on quite different sides of the issues of the day, he noted that even in law school, Bell was deeply, deeply respected for his intellect, for his compassion, and for his fierce commitment. And he has that kind of effect and impact on everyone I've encountered who is fortunate enough to know him.

It would not be an exaggeration to say that I would not be standing here were it not for the work of Professor Bell. Of course it's due to his trailblazing and pioneering work for social justice that paved the way for people like me to assume positions like this. It's also due, of course, to his path-breaking in the academy—his willingness to put himself out there as an intellectual leader on issues that mattered so much to so many of us in the room, and to liberate us and give us the permission to speak truth to power in the way that he did.

But I also mean this in a very specific way. I was born a working-class kid in the blue-collar town of Cleveland, Ohio, in the 1970s. I did not have many of the advantages that most of my peers now in the academy had. And while I can't say I grew up poor—that would be an exaggeration—I did grow up broke. And I faced all of the challenges that go along with being a working-class kid in the 1970s in a city like Cleveland, not one of the most racially progressive places in the country, at least not at that time. I didn't have access to the kind of social networks and social capital that can protect you at least to some extent from the slings and arrows that come your way as a young person of color in this country.

And I found myself, like so many other people, confused, and angry, passionate but not knowing what to do. I was lucky enough to be one of the very few people in my family who went to college, let alone law school. And I had a sociology professor who turned me on to this thing called Critical Race Theory in his class. And he said, "You know, you should really engage some of this. It sounds like the directions you want to go in are aligned with this school of thought. Why don't you read some of the work of Professor Bell?"

At that time in my life I hadn't been exposed to the law very much, but I was interested in these issues. I don't remember what I said in response to that, as a young man in his twenties, but I'm sure it was rather haughty and pompous, something like "You know, I will only engage this literature if it helps me tear down the oligarchical oppression that is keeping my people shackled. Power to the people!"

I remember what he said, like a good teacher, who is helping a person grow and develop. He said, "I can hear and respect that. Now just go read it."

So I did and I was hooked. I was hooked. I remember this very well: I was at my sister's house, my second summer home from college, and I pulled down *And We Are Not Saved* from her bookshelf, and I literally, and this is no exaggeration, stayed up all night reading that book front to back. The ability of Derrick Bell's work to both wake up and affirm the things that you have been feeling—to give you a language to express all of those things that he expressed so eloquently, and tools like the law and a commitment to social justice that can speak to the issues that you want to address—was an incredibly powerful experience, and led directly to my decision to go to law school. So I am being sincere when I say were it not for his impact and his legacy, I would not be where I am today. Even those who didn't know him personally have benefited from Derrick Bell's legacy.

Stephen Bright

I've admired Derrick Bell since the day that I read *Faces at the Bottom of the Well*. Derrick Bell didn't just talk the talk. Derrick Bell didn't just sign a petition. He didn't just write a letter to the editor. He didn't just give a speech somewhere and say what people ought to be doing. He said, "If you don't change the hiring policy, I'm outta here! I don't care if this is Harvard Law School! I'm outta here!" And out he went. A lot of people wouldn't do that. I admire that, because we have to stand up in this time today. We have to stand up! For poor people. For people accused of crimes. For people who are homeless. For people who are in all kinds of dire straits. And it's not good enough to just talk about it. Like Derrick Bell, we have to do something about it.

Sherrilyn Ifill

Derrick Bell was a mentor to me. He convinced me that I could get a fellowship at the MacDowell Colony to finish my book. He said, "You can do it. Apply." And I thought, "That's crazy! There's no way they'll accept me." But I did it, and I was accepted, and I did some of my best writing there.

Derrick was always a great sounding board. But he was never congratulatory about anything I did; no, he was always pushing me to the next level. And that's really true and honest mentorship.

The place where I have worshiped for the last fifteen years in Baltimore is a church called Mount Calvary AME Church. The pastor of that church is a woman named Dr. Ann Lightner-Fuller, and she often tells a story about how she got her college degree. She was a secretary at Harvard. And the person she worked for was a lovely man—by now you can probably guess that it was Derrick Bell—who told her that he was going to fire her if she did not apply to college. She had a young son. She wasn't college educated but wanted to be.

And he took her to the admissions office at Boston College, which is where she wanted to attend, and he had her pick up the application and fill out the application. And she attended Boston College, and you just heard me describe her as Rev. Dr. Ann Lightner-Fuller. She later received her doctorate and has been listed as one of the fifteen greatest women preachers by *Ebony* magazine. When she told the story the first few years I was at the church, she never mentioned the name of the person. And then one year, she just said that it was Derrick Bell.

I share that story with you because I just believe we will never know how many people's lives Derrick Bell impacted. It's not just the people that we meet at Harvard and the people we meet at NYU; it's people all over this country.

Acknowledgments

Janet Dewart Bell

The Bell Lecture series began in a conversation with my dear friend, the late Paulette Jones (PJ) Robinson. She not-so-casually asked me what I was going to do to celebrate my husband's sixty-fifth birthday. I clumsily responded, "Oh probably fix his favorite meal." Relentless, she said that was not good enough. After a bit, we decided that yes, a lecture series was more befitting. It was then just a couple months before Derrick's birthday. There was little time to go through a more formal process at NYU, where he was teaching, so I reached out to the Schomburg Center for Research in Black Culture, part of the New York Public Library, and arranged an event there.

The hard part was convincing Derrick that people would actually attend a lecture. Remember, at that time, lectures, particularly on subjects as challenging as race, were not in demand. Undaunted, I enlisted the support of Derrick's mentor, the Honorable Robert L. Carter—who argued the first *Brown v. Board of Education* case at the Supreme Court—to convince my dear husband to go along with this then wild idea. John Sexton, the NYU Law School dean and Derrick's former student at Harvard Law School, joined in, and we became the first Bell Lecture committee.

Now, for a lecturer. There was only one first choice, and that was Charles Ogletree, a stellar law professor, critical race theorist, and also

Derrick's student at Harvard. Charles graciously said yes—with the support of his wife and life partner, Pamela Ogletree.

To raise the necessary funds to pay for this event (lecturers are not paid as per NYU's policy), I reached out to more friends, who, like me, sometimes walk on faith and not by sight. Some would say that this was a crazy notion, but others would in hindsight realize that it was indeed a Derrick Bell curve. See what needs to be done and then get it done. We formed the Friends of Derrick Bell and the Geneva Crenshaw Society, the latter named after the fictional heroine of Derrick's books.

Responding to that first appeal—without question and without any expectation of reward—were Valerie Cavanaugh and William Kerstetter, who guaranteed the seed money. Joining were Dr. Kitty M. Steel and Lewis Steel, Alice Young, Lisa Marie Boykin, Mark Munger, and many others who donated enough for us to host the first event at the Schomburg.

In attendance were legal and cultural luminaries, including John Sexton and Gloria Steinem. Lisa Jones contributed a video. The evening was a success! Derrick's other mentor, Judge Constance Baker Motley, could not attend in person, but sent greetings and did come to subsequent lectures.

John Sexton, ever the visionary and a steadfast friend of Derrick's, offered to arrange for the lecture series to be housed at NYU, where it has remained and is a key Law School event. We thank the subsequent deans, Ricky Revesz and Trevor Morrison, for their continued support. I would also like to thank Anthony Thompson, the founding faculty director, and Vincent M. Southerland, the founding executive director of New York University School of Law's Center for Race, Inequality, and the Law, which is where the Bell Lecture is housed. I am very pleased to be co-editor of this book with Vincent, a skilled civil and human rights attorney, a committed social justice advocate, and a most gracious collaborator.

Special thanks goes to Randy Hertz, Vice Dean. When Derrick died, Randy, who had always attended the lectures, became the faculty liaison for the series and has been the shoulder on which I lean over the years. Students love him for his brilliance, humility, and humanity—and so do I.

Why a lecture series? First of all for the students. The Bell philosophy has always been "students first." We wanted to present the best thinkers on race in the country—established and emerging—with intentional diversity. We also wanted to bring together the students with a broader community— legal, social justice, and political. We felt strongly that NYU was more than a vibrant intellectual institution, one that took seriously its motto "a private university in the public interest."

These lectures stand the test of time.

The lecturers are now seen as the prophets they have always been. To honor Derrick and in his memory, my heartfelt thanks, respect, and appreciation to each of them.

While the Bell Lectures stand on their own, this book, however, is the result of the vision of Diane Wachtell of The New Press. She has a publisher's zeal for a good story and a social justice advocate's heart and commitment to tackling tough issues in order to move society forward. She recognized the need for a book to gather the lectures in one place and, with tenacity and care, brought it into being in record time to celebrate the twenty-fifth anniversary of the Bell Lecture series! The title is from her vision of the impact of the lecture series here. Thanks, too, to Kameel Mir, Emily Albarillo, and the entire staff at The New Press, a publishing house, which is also a welcoming *home* for progressive voices.

In the spirit of Derrick Bell, the lectures are not just great speeches, they represent serious scholarship about race, provocative ideas, compelling arguments, foundations for dialogue, and ideas for sustainable change. Thanks to the choir of the First Presbyterian Church Brooklyn, every Bell program also incorporates the music Derrick loved.

With a twenty-five-year run, there are a lot of people to thank, in addition to those already acknowledged. I apologize in advance for any I may have missed.

First of all, the Bell family. Bell sons Derrick Bell III, Douglass DuBois Bell, and Carter Robeson Bell, along with Derrick's sisters Janet A. Bell and Constance Andrea Bell. Derrick's late parents provided inspiration and support. Derrick has dedicated much of his work to his mother Ada

Elizabeth Childress Bell. His father, Derrick A. Bell Sr., provided more than financial support for their family of four children, all of whom finished college—a remarkable achievement then and now, especially for a working-class family. His parents provided guidance on how to survive and thrive as full human beings while fighting racism and white supremacy. Their lessons ring true, especially during these times.

My beautiful, brilliant, and fierce late mother Willie Mae Neal, born in rural Arkansas, self educated, and a lifelong freedom fighter, gave me wings.

We remember Derrick's first wife, who died before Derrick and I met. Jewel Hairston Bell set the standard for leading with love, vision, and fierce loyalty. She was stellar in every way. She helped define the person we know as Derrick Bell. I will always be grateful for her and lift up her memory.

Thanks to Bell adopted daughters: Lisa Marie Boykin (NYU Law '95); Lisa Jones; and Linda Singer. And to cultural son Camilo Romero (NYU Law '12), the Law Association of Color (LACA) Alumni and its president Rafiq Kalam Id-Din (NYU Law '00) for continuing major support, and to other alumni and law students who give generously.

Other more recent major supporters include Theodore V. (Ted) Wells and Nina M. Wells and Gerald T. Hathaway and Kate Hathaway.

Kelley Spencer, Associate Director of Alumni Relations, has been the engine who has kept the lecture running beautifully for many years. The original coordinator was Bobbie Glover.

I must acknowledge Derrick's teaching fellows and assistants for being literally the best in class. Their support of this series has been extraordinary, as is the dedication of those students in his last class in the fall of 2011. When Derrick died, they bravely persisted and embraced me and the Bell family even in their own time of need.

Finally, my kitchen cabinet. My late brother Dr. William V. McCoy; my loyal and brilliant niece Professor Theresa M. Davis; Lindbergh Porter, Letty Cottin Pogrebin and Bertrand B. Pogrebin, and Arthur Lee Butler; and sister friends Dr. Naomi Nightingale, Catherine Chadwick,

Joyce S. Johnson, and Dr. Camilla Grace Fusae Ka'iuhono'onālani Wengler Vignoe. They are there in the light of day and in the midnight hour when they are needed the most.

Vincent M. Southerland

A book like this would not be possible without the dedication and commitment of a number of people. I would like to thank each of the Derrick Bell Lecturers, for their brilliance, thoughtfulness, and tremendous work, all of which is an extension of Professor Bell's legacy. Their profound contributions to this volume and their collective efforts to advance racial justice serve as a reminder of how far America has come, how far it still has to go, and the responsibility we all have to bend the arc of the moral universe toward justice, day by day and bit by bit. I would also like to thank my co-editor, Janet Dewart Bell, who established the Derrick Bell Lecture on Race in American Society at New York University School of Law as a gift to Professor Bell. Her perseverance and all around excellence drove this project every step of the way.

I would like to thank my colleagues at the Center on Race, Inequality, and the Law. The Center's founding faculty director, Professor Anthony Thompson, has been a source of inspiration, guidance, and mentorship for legions. I count myself lucky to be among them. The Center's faculty director, Professor Deborah Archer, has provided unwavering support and excellent leadership while driving the Center's work forward. The Center's administrator, Danisha Edwards, worked steadfastly to gather the raw materials for this book, as did the Center's undergraduate student assistants Gabrielle Buchanan and Isha Mazumdar. Their collective support and friendship have been invaluable.

I would also like to acknowledge the strong support of New York University School of Law, including Dean Trevor Morrison, and his predecessors, Dean Richard Revesz and Dean John Sexton; Professor Kim Taylor-Thompson, Professor Paulette Caldwell, and Vice Dean Randy Hertz; Associate Director of Alumni Relations Kelley Spencer and all of her colleagues at NYU Law's Office of Development & Alumni Relations, who worked tirelessly to ensure that the events that serve as the occasion for these lectures are not only flawlessly executed, but special occasions for all in attendance; and the Law Alumni of Color Association for their unyielding support of the Derrick Bell Lecture series.

Thanks are due to countless others over the years, far too numerous to mention, who have supported the lecture in every way imaginable. Professor Bell's former students, mentees, colleagues, and generations of others have, through their efforts, ensured that his work and words will live on, shaping our world for the better. An unquantifiable debt of gratitude is also owed to those who have battled racism through the decades, in ways large and small, and who inspire us all to continue those battles today.

Thanks to Diane Wachtell, Kameel Mir, and Emily Albarillo at The New Press for their incredible efforts in turning the vision of this book into a reality. Diane's encouragement and steady leadership led to the publication of these lectures.

I would like to thank my mother, Gilda Southerland, my father, Duke Southerland, and my brother, Chad Southerland, for making me all that I am. Finally, I would like to thank my wife, Ndidi Oriji, who once served as a teaching assistant to Professor Bell and later introduced me to him. There are no words that could adequately convey the depth of support, care, and love she has shown me over the years. And last, but certainly not least, I would like to thank my daughter, Lekwachi Sojourner Oriji Southerland, for allowing me to be hopeful about all that the future holds.

Permissions

"Justice Undone: Color Blindness After Civil Rights," by Ian Haney López, was previously published as "Intentional Blindness" in the *New York University Law Review* 87, no. 6 (2012).

"Badges and Incidents: Lingering Vestiges of Slavery and the Thirteenth Amendment," by William Carter, was previously published as "The Thirteenth Amendment and Constitutional Change" in the *New York University Review of Law & Social Change* 38, no. 4 (2014).

About the Editors

Janet Dewart Bell is a social justice activist with a doctorate in leadership and change from Antioch University. She founded the Derrick Bell Lecture on Race in American Society series at the New York University School of Law and is the author of *Lighting the Fires of Freedom: African American Women in the Civil Rights Movement* (The New Press). She is the founder and president of LEAD InterGenerational Solutions, Inc. An award-winning television and radio producer, she lives in New York City.

Vincent M. Southerland is the executive director of the Center on Race, Inequality, and the Law at New York University School of Law. He has served as a federal public defender with the Federal Defenders of New York, a senior counsel at the NAACP Legal Defense and Educational Fund, Inc., a state public defender at The Bronx Defenders, an E. Barrett Prettyman Fellow at Georgetown University Law Center, and a law clerk to two federal judges, the Honorable Louis H. Pollak and the Honorable Theodore A. McKee. He lives with his wife and daughter in the Bedford-Stuyvesant neighborhood of Brooklyn, New York City.